The Practices of Global Ethics

The Practices of Global Ethics

Historical Backgrounds, Current Issues and Future Prospects

Frederick Bird, Sumner B. Twiss,
Kusumita P. Pedersen, Clark A. Miller,
and Bruce Grelle

EDINBURGH
University Press

Edinburgh University Press is one of the leading university presses in the UK. We publish academic books and journals in our selected subject areas across the humanities and social sciences, combining cutting-edge scholarship with high editorial and production values to produce academic works of lasting importance. For more information visit our website: www.edinburghuniversitypress.com

Edinburgh University Press Ltd
The Tun – Holyrood Road
12 (2f) Jackson's Entry
Edinburgh EH8 8PJ

Typeset in 10.5/12 Sabon by
Servis Filmsetting Ltd, Stockport, Cheshire,
Printed and bound in the United States of America

A CIP record for this book is available from the British Library

ISBN 978 1 4744 0704 5 (hardback)
ISBN 978 1 4744 0705 2 (paperback)
ISBN 978 1 4744 0706 9 (webready PDF)
ISBN 978 1 4744 0707 6 (epub)

Contents

Preface

When the co-authors first met to discuss writing this book, we thought we would be writing a book about globalization and the *pursuit* of global ethics. We were committed to adopting a broad and historically informed view of globalization, viewing it both in terms of processes reaching back over the past half millennium that have recently gained greater momentum as well as in terms of new ways of viewing the world as a common global ethical space. We were also committed to looking at ethics as social practices. Initially we focused on various efforts to establish relevant systems of global ethics. But over time our focus began to shift. We became much more aware and appreciative of the range of existing authoritative statements of global ethics, such as the Universal Declaration of Human Rights and subsequent UN covenants enacted with respect to specific areas of concern, the Geneva Conventions, and the Declaration of the Rio Conference on the Environment and Development. In addition, we became increasingly aware and appreciative of the hundreds if not thousands of organizations – intergovernmental, civic, business, and religious – that were working to foster global collaborations to address global ethical issues. As our understanding regarding the practices of global ethics deepened, we saw that we did not need to pursue the articulation of a global ethic as yet not fully realized or acknowledged. Rather, by means of this book we could call attention to, share our appreciation for, and offer a reflective analysis of the many practices of global ethics that have emerged and gained authority and influence in the years since the Second World War.

As we worked on this book, two contrasting sentiments moved us. On the one hand, many aspects of the world today aroused, worried, and upset us: threats such as possible pandemics, climate change, and increasing resort to terrorist tactics; the failure of our economies to find full employment for so many; the increasing inequality between and among people and nations; and widespread feelings of political dispiritedness. On the other hand, numerous examples of global cooperation to address these imperatives gave us hope. Compared to the situation prior to the Second World War, much has been and is being done. We also recognized that, when we link these contrasting sentiments – profound alarm and the commitment to hope – it describes in a meaningful way the current practices of global ethics.

The subtitle of this book refers to the past, the present, and the future. It is a book written at a particular moment in time – 2015 – and attempts to examine the practices of global ethics with a lively sense of historical developments and possibilities.

This is a co-authored book. All of the authors have read, commented on, and contributed to all of the chapters. Still each of us has accepted primary responsibility for the writing of particular chapters. Sumner Twiss assumed the major responsibility for Chapters 1, 3, and 5. Kusumita Pedersen took the lead in drafting Chapters 2, 9, and 10. Clark Miller assumed the major responsibility for Chapter 4, while Bruce Grelle took responsibility for writing Chapter 11. Frederick Bird organized the meetings among the co-authors and assumed the major responsibility for writing the Introduction and Conclusion as well as Chapters 6, 7, and 8. He also edited the book as a whole.

In Chapter 11 we use the term 'public' to refer to state schools because this is the term used in most countries and it is the term used in the documents and initiatives we review in this chapter. We recognize that the term 'public school' has a different meaning in the United Kingdom (UK) and in school systems influenced by the UK. We explain our usage at the beginning of Chapter 11.

Several of the chapters of this book are based in large part on essays that have or will be presented at special conferences or published by other publishers. These include considerable parts of Chapters 1, 3, 5, 10 and 11. Material previously presented or published has been revised and rewritten for this book.

Frederick Bird, Sumner B. Twiss, Kusumita P. Pedersen,
Clark A. Miller, and Bruce Grelle
January 2015

Abbreviations

AAR	American Academy of Religion
AIDS	acquired immune deficiency syndrome
CBD	The Convention on Biological Diversity
CERES	Coalition for Environmentally Responsible Economies
CFC	chlorofluorocarbon
CIA	Central Intelligence Agency
CoE	Council of Europe
CRT	Caux Round TAble
CSE	Centre for Science and the Environment
DHDR	Declaration of Human Duties and Responsibilities
DTGE	Declaration towards a Global Ethic
ERB	Education and Religions and Beliefs
ERC	Ethics and Religious Culture
EU	European Union
FKUB	Forum Kerukunan Umat Beragama (Inter-Religious Harmony Forum)
GATT	General Agreement Tariffs and Trade
GCM	general circulation model
GRI	Global Reporting Initiative
HIV	human immunodeficiency virus
IARF	International Association for Religious Freedom
ICC	International Criminal Court
ICCPR	International Covenant on Civil and Political Rights
ICESCR	International Covenant on Economic, Social and Cultural Rights
ICNY	Interfaith Center of New York
IEA	Interfaith Encounter Association
IFAPA	Inter-Faith Action for Peace in Africa
IFC	International Finance Corporation
IGO	international governmental organization
IGY	International Geophysical Year
ILO	International Labour Organization

IMF	International Monetary Fund
IPCC	Intergovernmental Panel on Climate Change
IRA	Irish Republican Army
IUCN	International Union for the Conservation of Nature
MDGs	Millennium Development Goals
NAFTA	North American Free Trade Agreement
NATO	North Atlantic Treaty Organization
NCCJ	National Conference for Community and Justice
NGO	non-governmental organization
ODIHR	Office for Democratic Institutions and Human Rights
OECD	Organization for Economic Cooperation and Development
OSCE	Organization for Security and Cooperation in Europe
PCID	Pontifical Council for Interreligious Dialogue
PRS	Poverty Reduction Strategy
REDCo	Religion in Education: A Contribution to Dialogue or a Factor of Conflict in Transforming Societies of European Countries
SAI	Social Accountability International
UDHR	Universal Declaration of Human Rights
UN	United Nations
UNCED	United Nations Conference on Environment and Development
UNCTAD	United Nations Conference on Trade and Development
UNDP	United Nations Development Programme
UNEP	United Nations Environment Programme
UNESCO	United Nations Educational, Scientific, and Cultural Organization
URI	United Religions Initiative
WCED	World Commission on Environment and Development
WHO	World Health Organization
WMO	World Meteorological Organization
WRI	World Resources Institute
WSF	World Social Forum
WSSD	World Summit on Sustainable Development
WTO	World Trade Organization
WWF	World Wildlife Fund

Introduction: The Practices of Global Ethics

What are the practices of global ethics?

This book examines the diverse expressions of the practices of global ethics developed especially in the years since the Second World War. It focuses on documents such as the Universal Declaration of Human Rights (UDHR) (1948), the Geneva Conventions (1949), the Declaration towards a Global Ethic (DTGE) (1993), and the Earth Charter (2000), as well as efforts to set and maintain global normative standards by groups such as the Intergovernmental Panel on Climate Change (IPCC), the Global Compact, the International Atomic Energy Agency, the Parliament of the World's Religions, and the International Committee of the Red Cross. The book argues that the practices of global ethics are especially characterized by the commitment of people from different political, religious, and ethical backgrounds to collaborate together to develop and to hold people accountable to act in keeping with common normative standards as a way of addressing a wide range of boundary-crossing global ethical issues. The book seeks to appreciate the work of the thousands of organizations and the hundreds of thousands of people who have engaged in the practices of global ethics, moved by diverse concerns and interests but with a common sense of fiduciary responsibility to address the global challenges confronting humanity. Fostering reciprocating dialogue, respectful of cultural differences, and committed to care for the Earth and its inhabitants, those involved in the practices of global ethics have called attention to and helped to address a wide range of global crises.

In this book we reach a number of conclusions about the practices of global ethics. First, the practices of global ethics are especially embodied in all those normatively informed communicative activities by which humans from diverse backgrounds have collaborated with each other to shape and evaluate human conduct with respect to global issues. They are paradigmatically expressed through actions rather than statements. Second, the collaborative actions undertaken by these diverse groups – from civil society organizations such as Oxfam and Greepeace, private-sector initiatives such as the Equator Principles or Business Association for Sustainability, interfaith activities associated with Religions for Peace or Religion United, to public organizations such as the International Development Agency or the World Health Organization – have been truly impressive. These actions demonstrate that international relations are not just guided by political realism and economic calculations. They are also influenced in major ways by the values and norms championed by those practising global ethics. Third, the practices of global ethics are appropriately evaluated not by the extent to which humans have in fact realized the ideal visions associated with various expressions of global ethics but by the degree to which humans increasingly over time pay serious attention to global crises and work collaboratively to address these issues. The practices of global ethics are works in progress. Accordingly, it is fitting to begin this book by looking at the state of the world during the early decades of the twenty-first century as envisioned by those engaged in the practices of global ethics.

Current state of the world

We are living at a critical juncture in the history of human life on Earth. Our lives are more interconnected than at any other point in history and we face a diverse array of truly troubling global crises.

As we think seriously about prospects for human life on Earth over the next several hundred years if not much longer, we can easily see that we face a number of very disturbing realities. In relation to the Earth and its resources, we humans have clearly been living beyond our means with several really dire consequences.[1] As a result of human activity, the overall temperature of the Earth's climate is steadily rising. We have seriously depleted the Earth's fish stocks. We have put at risk billions of people who lack ready access to clean potable water by steadily depleting ground water reserves. We have contaminated significant portions of global coastal waters by excessive use of fertilizers. We face serious food crises as the overall levels of food production decline owing to diverse factors. While the Earth seems to possess vast reserves of minerals, gasses, and oil, many of these resources face depletion over the next century and/or will become extravagantly expensive.[2] At the same time, human activity has subjected an alarming number of species to threats of extinction and in many cases to extinction itself. Humans face a wide range of additional troubling threats, such as the real possibility that some new strain of disease will turn into a pandemic or that some rogue group or state will gain the capacity to build nuclear weapons and the determination to use them. In spite of tremendous worldwide economic expansion in the post-Second World War years, more than two and half billion people live in poverty with an average per capita income of less than $2.25 per day. More than a billion people live in urban slums that continue to grow. Many of these people experience extreme hunger and low life expectancy. If we have been unable to do a better job of reducing poverty over the past couple of generations, then it seems unlikely we will make greater progress in the decades ahead as overall prices for energy are predicted to rise (even accounting for near-term gluts in some fossil-fuel markets) and as population pressures intensify the struggles over access to land, jobs, food, and healthcare. Difficult and challenging times seem to lie ahead.

This dim view is reinforced as we consider a number of prevailing economic, social, and political characteristics of our times. For example, economic inequality seems to be on the rise in many parts of the world, exacerbating tensions between those very well off and those very poor. Many countries have found it difficult to emerge successfully from the 2007–8 financial crises. Unemployment and underemployment rates remain very high in many areas from North Africa and southern Europe to the Middle East and the Americas. Some underemployed young people find themselves attracted by radical religious and political movements. Internationally, terrorist organizations continue to spread. Religious and ethnic tensions continue to aggravate social conflicts in South Asia, diverse parts of Africa, the Middle East, and parts of the Americas. More people live in refugee camps than in any previous time in human history. What is especially troubling are the difficulties that international governmental organizations have in finding solutions to these problems. We witness distressing human rights violations in the Middle East, Central Africa, North Korea, and many other places and seem unable to find the effective ways to intervene.[3]

Correspondingly, many people have begun to view the world in apocalyptic terms. These visions are quite varied. They include images of the doom of the West and the revival of a new Caliphate, the descent of the industrial nations into a new dark age, and the possibility of a nuclear holocaust. Others envision cataclysmic changes unleashed by a warming environment and the intensification of social conflicts as both energy and food resources become scarcer. A number of articulate observers have called for humans to establish local and comparatively small self-sustaining communities, withdrawing active concern for the problems of the global society.[4]

Yet, despite the prevailing mood that humanity confronts diverse, seemingly unsolvable global challenges, a remarkable array of people from all over the planet continue to work together with others from other places who hold beliefs different from theirs to address global issues through the creation of global normative standards, collaborative actions, and institutions. In this book, we review their efforts, which we describe broadly as the practices of global ethics. Taken as a whole, the individuals and groups involved in these practices operate with neither utopian nor apocalyptic assumptions. In practical terms, they simply want to foster global cooperation in order to explore ways of managing global ethical crises. They acknowledge their ideological, religious, and philosophical differences but seek grounds both from within their own traditions and on the basis of their shared determination to make a difference.

General features

The practices of global ethics have greatly expanded since the Second World War. We can now easily point to numerous examples of people from diverse constituencies working together to create and put into practice common normative standards and effective institutions as means for addressing significant global concerns. Before we describe more fully what we mean by the practices of global ethics, it will be useful to refer to a number of well-known examples.

Probably the best-known and perhaps most influential example of the practices of global ethics is the UDHR and the international covenants as well as the national codes and charters enacted and ratified to embed this declaration as a compelling social reality. In this case the practice of global ethics refers not only to these written statements but also to the committees, legislatures, courts, and agencies that have developed, interpreted, and implemented these statements. As a social practice, this declaration has also been supported and reinforced by countless civil society organizations that have advocated, protested, and demonstrated on its behalf. The revised Geneva Conventions (1949) provide another often-cited example, which as a social practice involves not only these documents and the committees that drafted them but also the International Committee of the Red Cross, which acts to implement some of their basic precepts, as well as diverse officials and citizens in national armed forces and civil society that monitor military conduct in the light of these conventions. As a further example of global ethics in practice, we refer to the international conventions enacted at global environmental conferences in Stockholm in 1972 and Rio de Janeiro in 1992 as well as all those public, private, and civil agencies working to honour and support these conventions.

Another expression of the practices of global ethics are those specially constituted, international commissions organized to analyse concrete global issues, to develop fitting normative ways of thinking about these issues, and to foster ongoing collaborations to address them. These include the Commission on International Development (1969), chaired by former Canadian Prime Minister Lester Pearson, the Independent Commission on International Development (1980), chaired by former German Prime Minister Willy Brandt, and the World Commission on Environment and Development (WCED) (1987), chaired by former Norwegian Prime Minister Gro Harlem Brundtland. Other examples of these international commissions include one focusing on norms for the construction of large dams (1999), another assessing the war in Kosovo (2000), and another seeking to develop common norms with respect to Intervention and State Sovereignty (2001).[5]

A number of international organizations have also engaged in practising global ethics as they have sought to establish and enforce authoritative norms with respect to particular global problem areas. These include organizations like the World Health Organization (WHO), which sets normative standards with respect to the ways countries and health officials identify, monitor, and respond to infectious diseases, as well as the International Atomic Energy Agency, which has sought to set and enforce norms with respect to the safe and legitimate uses of material involved in nuclear energy production. Many other international organizations that variously have endeavoured to identify, mobilize support for, and hold others accountable to worldwide norms include the Intergovernmental Panel on Climate Change, the International Union for Conservation of Nature (IUCN), and the General Agreement on Tariffs and Trade (GATT), which later evolved into the World Trade Organization (WTO). The International Law Commission has played an important and often overlooked role especially as it has developed procedural norms, based on received customs, with respect to the character of treaties, the rights and duties of states, and state responsibilities.[6]

A host of international civil society organizations has been engaged worldwide in championing and seeking to further cooperation with others in enforcing particular sets of norms related to specific sets of global problems. These include groups such as Transparency International, working to limit corruption by business and governmental officials; Amnesty International and Human Rights Watch, which have worked to protect human rights; the UN Global Compact, an association of businesses initially sponsored by the Secretary General of the United Nations, which has acted to promote responsible and sustainable business practices; and the International Organization for Standardization, which has developed normative frameworks with respect not only to safety but also to environmentally and socially responsible business practices.[7] It is also worth calling attention to a couple of international movements, which organized relatively successfully to address particular global problems – in particular, the International Campaign to Ban Landmines, and the Jubilee Campaign, which mobilized public pressure on governments to help highly indebted developing countries, either by cancelling debts altogether or by helping countries to manage them. Also, we should call attention to those groups that have been working since 1987 to establish an international convention against ecoside – the deliberate destruction of environments in peacetime or during wars.

In this volume we direct special attention to the role of global interfaith movements in fostering diverse forms of cooperation among otherwise competing religious traditions and in identifying and supporting certain shared ethical affirmations. As one expression of the interfaith movements, during the second Parliament of World's Religions meeting in Chicago in 1993 (a first parliament had been held there 100 years earlier), an Assembly of Religious Leaders adopted a 'Declaration toward a Global Ethic', announcing that it was time now to affirm certain common normative principles, which the document referred to as 'irrevocable demands'.

A special form of global ethics in practice has been embodied in all those individuals, whether acting through centres, associations, or collegial debates, who have sought to identify and defend universally valid ethical principles in the languages of philosophy and/or political theory. Notable examples of this way of engaging in global ethics include the international network of people and institutions fostered and supported by Globethics.net located in Geneva, the Centre for Ethics and Value Inquiry at Ghent University in Belgium, the Dialogue Institute organized by Leonard Swidler at Temple University in the United States and the Global Ethic Foundation in Tubingen, Germany, organized by Hans Küng. Other noteworthy examples of this philosophical approach to practising global ethics can be found in the writings of Amartya Sen and Martha Nussbaum, as well as in the efforts of the World Institute for Development Economics Research in Finland and the United Nations Development Programme to identify common human capabilities and then use these as normative standards to promote and gauge human development.[8]

We could easily point to numerous other expressions of global ethics in practice, such as forums like the InterAction Council, a group of thirty or so former heads of state, which since 1983 has met annually as a body of elder statesmen to consider and propose fitting and ethically responsible ways of addressing targeted global problems, such as the small arms trade or the volatility of global financial markets. Since 1997 this group has championed a Universal Declaration of Human Responsibilities, which it helped to draft.

All these varied examples share a number of features in common. In each case people from diverse constituencies – identified by differences in political allegiance, religious affiliation, economic status, and/or moral traditions – have created forums for conversing about and acting on one or more global issues. In each case efforts have been made to gain cooperation to the widest extent possible, attempting not to overcome diversity but to build on it. In practice, this has meant communicating with and gaining cooperation from individuals, groups, organizations, and governments with quite different priorities and agendas. Common goals or points of reference have served to facilitate the negotiation of terms for cooperation and subsequent collaborations. Common normative statements have helped deepen understanding among people of different worldviews, values, and priorities.

In all these examples, expressions of global ethics were formulated as a way of addressing boundary-crossing global issues. Some issues have been fairly focused, such as protecting and caring for the wounded in times of war or limiting the sales of arms. Others have had a grander focus, such as a desire by the framers of the UDHR to find ways of reducing the risk that the world might again experience the suffering associated with Fascism and the Second World War. In various ways people have engaged in practising global ethics to reduce poverty, protect endangered species, reduce the threat posed by the existence of nuclear weapons, and more effectively manage the threats associated with epidemics. They have engaged in global ethics to foster more open and reciprocating conversations between heretofore suspicious adherents of different religious traditions.

As various groups have engaged in the practices of global ethics, they have worked to bring into being, establish parameters for, and create much more widely embraced shared commitments to new objects of moral considerations. These include obvious ones, such as the inherent dignity and basic rights of all persons and the intrinsic value of the Earth, all of its inhabitants, and its atmosphere as common home for all, as well as less obvious ones, such as respect for the diversity of cultures and religions, the intrinsic value of restraint in armed conflict, and the intrinsic value of reciprocating dialogues as a means of addressing conflicts.

Characteristically, global ethics in practice assumes a public and often a political form. As they have written their declarations, prepared their reports, and issued their recommendations, those involved have sought to gain public endorsement and/or ratification by relevant governments and organizations. For example, the framers of the Geneva Conventions, the UDHR, the Rio Declaration on Climate Control, and the UN Convention banning landmines all sought official governmental support for their normative statements. International Commissions are typically addressed not only to the general public but also to national governments. Those who argued that it was best to view and evaluate processes of development in terms of the access and acquisition of human capabilities in turn worked to institutionalize these notions in an annual Human Development Index sponsored by the United Nations. As they have attempted to monitor and manage endangered species and infectious diseases, groups such as the Conservation Breeding Specialty Group of the IUCN and the WHO have worked to gain the cooperation of relevant agencies, bureaus, professional associations, community groups, and governments. While seeking to foster greater mutual understanding, interfaith meetings also seek to influence recognized authorities within their own religious communities as well as those in public bodies who hold positions of influence affecting these religions and/or the issues at stake.

It may well be asked whether it makes sense to refer to all these diverse activities as expressions of ethics. To what extent and in what ways, for example, are activities as different as those represented by international commissions on development or global governance, by advocacy groups such as Transparency International and Oxfam, by international agencies such as the WHO and UNESCO, the Parliament of the World's Religions, and groups like the InterAction Council all involved in the practice of global ethics? We answer this question in two complementary ways.

One, we observe how the people involved in all these activities are engaged both in seeking to establish compelling normative standards and in articulating justifying rationales in support of these standards. Thus, they act like advocates of any other kind of ethics – whether personal or social, political or religious. They seek to set forth and communicate both normative expectations – variously associated with ends, ways of acting, and the dispositions – as well as discourse that justifies these standards on the basis of authority, beneficial outcomes, and/or ontological or anthropological assumptions. Although these people may not think of themselves as ethicists like the authors of well-known moral codes or philosophies, nevertheless, they, like other ethicists, work to articulate and effectively justify particular normative standards. Thus, while these various conferences, councils, organizations, and movements may be involved in political action, social advocacy, and economic deliberations, they are also involved as ethicists in so far as they are also defining and defending normative expectations.

Two, by thinking about ethics as a social practice, we recognize that this practice involves not only discursive statements about how people ought to act and why but also organizational forms. Broadly, in relation to any societal expression of ethics, these organizational forms work to socialize, educate, and motivate people to act in keeping with normative expectations; to observe conduct and hold people accountable for their behaviour; and to offer authoritative interpretations and resolve disputes with respect to these standards. There are organizational aspects for all ethics – whether these are associated with cultural mores, professional codes, organizational credos, or philosophical principles – in so far as these expressions of ethics have become socially compelling practices. Therefore, it is not surprising that all of the expressions of global ethics, cited above, possess organizational forms.[9]

The ethical character of these varied examples of global ethics in practice is evident in their strong sense of fiduciary responsibility. As they have worked to craft and implement these varied expressions of global ethics, those involved have expressed a strong sense of responsibility for finding feasible ways of addressing the global issues in their focus. Whether or not as observers we think their responses are as effective as alternatives we might propose, those involved have acted not just to describe and interpret the world or identify compelling moral truths: they have acted to address these problems in ways that change the world.[10]

Most of those involved in practising global ethics begin by recognizing the world as it is: a place that has experienced and will likely continue to experience conflicts and wars; a place that has been ravaged by disease, hunger, and drought; a small planet with extensive, often newly discovered, but still limited resources; a world inhabited by people with diverse languages, diverse and often competing faiths, and varied and often antagonistic political and economic philosophies. While acknowledging the world as it is and has been, those practising global ethics then in their diverse ways assume responsibility to work collaboratively to explore ways to manage these problems as best they can.

We can illustrate this mindset with several examples. For example, the preamble to the UDHR indicates that this declaration was drafted as a response to recent acts of barbarism during the period of the world wars that 'outraged the conscience of mankind'. Therefore, it was necessary, the declaration affirms, 'to promote the development of friendly relations between nations' and demand greater respect for the 'inherent dignity ... of all members of the human family ...'. To cite a further example, the 1995 report of the Commission on Global Governance, entitled 'Our Global Neighborhood', begins with a sober recognition of how the world has changed in the fifty years since the end of the Second World War and the founding of the United Nations. After calling attention to worries about the arms trade, the rise in civil conflict, the persistence of global poverty, and threats to the environment, the report sets forth recommendations for promoting security, managing economic interdependence, reforming the United Nations, promoting global civil society, and strengthening the rule of law. To refer to a further example, the 1993 declaration of the Parliament of the World's Religions, entitled 'Declaration toward a Global Ethic', vividly illustrates this fiduciary mindset. The declaration begins by announcing 'we all have a responsibility for a better global order'; and 'our different religious and cultural traditions must not prevent our common involvement in opposing all forms of inhumanity'. The normative recommendations proposed by the declaration are viewed as a means of addressing a wide range of current social problems from drug trafficking and violence, hunger and unemployment, poverty wages and corruption, widespread deceit and swindling, to abuses in families and sexual relations. In all these examples, the proposed normative standards are championed as responsible ways of addressing serious, not easily solved, public problems. As they prepared these various normative statements, the authors and subsequent defenders of these documents were not, to paraphrase a famous essay by Max Weber, merely expressing highly regarded ethical convictions in the face of a world that often behaved quite differently. Rather they were seeking responsibly and realistically to engage this otherwise indifferent world and to align political and organizational support behind their various normative visions.[11]

The diverse expressions of global ethics vary, often markedly, in their scope. With respect to the scope of their concerns, some practices of global ethics are especially delimited, focusing, for example, on norms related to the treatment of prisoners of war, fitting forms of religious education, trade in endangered species, or standards for good sportsmanship in international competitions. Other practices of global ethics, such those associated with general statements regarding human rights or environmental responsibilities, include a much wider range of concerns.

These diverse expressions of global ethics clearly differ as well in their authority. Statements of global ethics possess more or less authority to the degree that people worldwide generally, and people in positions of relevant authority especially, defer to these standards and refer to them as they make their own decisions. Some expressions of global ethics, like the human rights conventions, have come to possess both broad and deep authority. They are widely cited and regarded as having more compelling claims than alternative expressions of global ethics. Other expressions, such as the recommendations of many international commissions, are viewed as possessing much less authority. They are typically regarded as standards and arguments that need to be seriously considered in forthcoming deliberations rather than as obligatory norms.

Before the Second World War, the authority possessed by existing expressions of global ethics, such as the earlier versions of the Geneva Conventions, the emerging law of the seas, and working standards championed by the International Labour Organization (ILO), were neither widely acknowledged nor deeply respected when viewed from a global perspective. The authority they possessed was modest, although not insignificant. However, since the Second World War, the establishment of the United Nations, and the steady expansion in global commerce and communication, varied expressions of global ethics – from standards with respect to human rights to standards regarding sustainable uses of natural resources – have steadily gained in the deference they elicit with regard to both numbers involved and the depth of corresponding commitment. Over time various contemporary expressions of global ethics have gained authority as they have been cited by courts, invoked by policymakers, supported by civil society groups, referred to by businesses, and defended in written accounts.

Those involved in the practices of global ethics employ several typical strategies to enhance the authority of the standards with which they are concerned. One, they seek to gain wide-based support and endorsement for these standards from representatives of relevant constituencies, such as national governments, varied civil society associations, and different faith communities. Two, they often seek to strengthen their normative claims by invoking relevant empirical evidence and scientific studies. Scientific evidence has been variously marshalled to defend global norms with respect to climate change, the spread of disease, the protection of endangered species, uses of nuclear material, collateral damage in armed conflicts, and the impact of trade subsidies. Three, over time particular expressions of global ethics have gained greater authority as they have been invoked to resolve debates, cited as precedents, and utilized to formulate policies. They lose authority in so far as they ignored.

The practices of global ethics and the processes of globalization

The practices of global ethics have emerged both as responses to and as by-products of the processes of globalization. Different people attach different meanings to the term 'globalization'. Thomas Friedman's views, first articulated in his book *The Lexus and the Olive Tree: Understanding Globalization* and later in *The World is Flat*, sum up what many think about globalization. Accordingly, globalization is associated with the commercial, financial, and communications processes that are strengthening economic interconnections among people worldwide. It is a world where the borders between nations seem increasingly unimportant, where far-flung people know more and more about one other, and where businesses increasingly operate globally. Often this understanding of the processes of globalization has become associated and intertwined with a particular economic philosophy that calls for increased government deregulation of economic affairs, more free trade, more privatization, and reduced taxes. Both these processes and this philosophy have been championed and celebrated as the expression and product of the 'Washington Consensus' and neo-liberalism.[12]

When people discuss and analyse globalization, they often have this economic view of globalization in mind. For its critics, this view of globalization has come to be associated with a world dominated by large and powerful international business and financial organizations. This 'globalized' world, accordingly, is one in which inequality between the very wealthy and the rest has been steadily increasing since the end of the 1970s, where the overall ecological system of the Earth is endangered by increasing carbon emissions, where humans are steadily using up many limited natural resources, where population increases aggravate problems of poverty, and where in many areas political processes have increasingly come under the influence of powerful business and financial interests.[13]

We have adopted a broader, more historically informed, and more neutral view of globalization in this book. Viewed historically, globalization processes have increased the possibility that peoples from scattered areas of the Earth will interact and collaborate with each other. These processes have also produced developments that make the need for these practices more pressing. Broadly understood, globalization refers to two interrelated processes. By means of the first process the peoples of the world have in fact become more interconnected. The second process involves a change in consciousness as humans increasingly understand themselves as being interrelated with other peoples and with the Earth itself as a shared ethical space.

Humans have become more interconnected, especially over the course of the past couple of centuries, as a result of a number of quite different developments. For example, although there were earlier eras of long-distance commerce, worldwide commerce expanded markedly during the latter part of the nineteenth century and the early twentieth century, and then even more markedly during the post-Second World War years. As a result of interrelated developments in communications technology, including the laying of intercontinental cables more than a century ago and the recent expansion of electronic media, humans from diverse parts of the world interact and communicate with each other more frequently, more quickly, and with regard to a wider range of interests than ever before. Increasing numbers of businesses have become transnational enterprises.

However, economic globalism represents only one of many forces promoting both increased global interconnections and the rise of global consciousness. The global expansion of a number of faiths such as Islam, Buddhism, Hinduism, and Christianity has brought people from distant parts of the world into closer connection and identification. These faiths have thus been fostering a form of global interconnection over the course of many centuries. In a related way, globalization has also been occasioned by the migration of peoples, especially during the past century and a half.

In decisive but ultimately partial and particularistic ways, global interconnections have been established as the by-product of the imperial expansion of European countries and the United States since the sixteenth century. During these years, until at least the middle of the twentieth century, Russia, the United Kingdom, France, Italy, Germany, Portugal, Spain, Netherlands, Denmark, Spain, and the United States established colonies, expanded their spheres of influence, and took possession of lands all over the world. Thousands of different indigenous peoples as well as long-established nations were incorporated within these expanding empires, sometimes as direct colonies, sometimes as well-defended trading ports, and sometimes as sites for military outposts. In the process the languages associated with these imperial powers as well as with the particular expressions of the missionary religions became more dominant, often gaining decisive footholds in parts of Asia, Africa, the Americas, and Oceania. During the same period several versions of the dominant political and economic ideologies originating in these industrializing countries of the North Atlantic – classical liberalism, socialism, and more recently neo-liberalism – have spread and in varying degrees shaped public discourse around the world.[14]

Nonetheless, several factors since the Second World War have in marked ways altered these processes of globalization. One of these has been the creation of a large number of global institutions, such as the United Nations, the WHO, the Food and Agriculture Organization, UNESCO, the World Bank, the International Monetary Fund (IMF), the WTO, and the IUCN. All these organizations, formed by representatives from national governments and other relevant constituencies, operate to foster worldwide cooperation with respect to issues under their mandates. In the process these institutions both helped to bring into being something like a global public domain and helped to create and steward international law. In particular these institutions have greatly influenced the degree to which people think globally about a wide range of issues.[15]

Another factor that has decisively altered the processes and character of globalization has been the end of the era of colonization. The process of decolonization began in the nineteenth century with the decline of the Spanish and Mughal empires and the collapse of the Ottoman and Austro-Hungarian empires at the end of the First World War. This process became more extensive and more dramatic in the decades after the Second World War as more than 100 new nations gained independence, as most of the colonial empires of France, the United Kingdom, Portugal, Netherlands, Italy, Germany, and Belgium came to an end. Finally, in 1990 the Soviet empire collapsed. To be sure, using their economic, political, and military power, several superpowers, such as the United States, Russia, China, France, and the United Kingdom, still exercise some forms of imperial influence, not only with respect to nations these powers formerly held as colonies but also more generally. However, the character of the relationship among the nations of the world has shifted. Instead of a world constituted by a fairly small number of large empires, a larger number of smaller states, and thousands of self-governing indigenous peoples, the world has largely become a society of nations.[16] At the same time several regional groupings of nations, such as the European Union (EU), the Southeast Asia Treaty Organization, and the Arab League, have formed to foster greater economic, military, and political collaboration within particular areas. Even though many new nations remain politically and economically weak, the people of the Earth are now grouped into more than 190 nations, all of which enjoy at least minimal recognition as nations, and in which these people are nominally viewed as citizens. As citizens of particular states, we also recognize others, especially in areas of distress and conflict, as citizens whose basic rights as humans ought to be protected by their own governments, and, failing that, protected by the not easily defined larger reality we variously refer to as the inter*national* community or the community of *nations*.

As increasing numbers of people from diverse countries and cultures interact, the notion of a global civil society has emerged. While it remains somewhat amorphous, it nevertheless represents an increasing number of cosmopolitan people who have become familiar with people from others parts of the world, who often interact with them, work with them, and in the process learn from them. Global civil society is likely to continue to grow in numbers and importance as the by-product of increased global tourism and travel, the steady increase in the number of transnational business enterprises, and the expanding universe of international non-government organizations (NGOs) involved in offering aid and engaged social action.[17]

Steadily during the past several decades the processes of globalization have also been shaped by the ways ever larger numbers of people, organizations, and governments have come to acknowledge their joint responsibility for carefully managing the Earth and its resources. The increasing concern to protect and assume responsibility for the Earth's biosphere began in the nineteenth century with the conservation movements in various countries and has continued to expand since then. The wide range of conservation, ecological, and environmental groups, which assume both local and international forms, especially represents this concern. This concern is embedded as well in diverse and widespread public and business actions to reduce pollution, foster sustainable practices, recycle and reuse products and materials, and consume endangered resources more responsibly. Although these environmental initiatives have been far from successful, they have had measurable impacts. More conservation laws have been enacted. More businesses are trying to use resources more sustainably. Moreover, these initiatives have modified how many people view their relationship to the Earth and its finite resources, endangered climate, and vulnerable ecosystems. One often assumed or overlooked aspect of globalization processes is the way people worldwide have come to think of themselves at least in part as interrelated inhabitants of a common Earth-grounded commonwealth of life.[18]

Viewed as a whole, as a result of these diverse processes of globalization, humans are not only more interrelated worldwide but also related in many different ways. The processes of globalization have been multidimensional. Through international commerce, growing numbers exchange goods and services. Increasing numbers communicate worldwide. Many are related through faith and others have become interconnected through migration and tourism. Many are at least nominally connected through the increasingly dense webs of international politics and global civil society associations.

The processes of globalization have proceeded in relation to quite different agendas and goals. While the imperial expansions clearly increased the interactions among peoples, the processes of decolonization have not reduced those connections. Rather, in interesting ways these latter processes have both redefined those relationships, giving greater political and civic status to formerly subjected peoples, and increased contacts through expanded trade, migration, and civil society endeavours. Each of these different processes of globalization has unfolded in relation to particular constellations of values and norms – associated, for example, with free trade, the interests and visions of particular faiths, the self-assertion of particular media, and the mandates of particular political associations, including the United Nations. While serving the common good of the particular global communities with which they are identified, such as the United Nations, international commercial enterprises, specific world faiths, the world conservation movement, global civil society, and/or the global human rights movement, those exercising governing authority in these communities also tend to seek and protect the good of their own strata. None operate purely as impartial observers or invisible hands, inherently seeking the whole global good at particular moments in time.

In several different ways the practices of global ethics have arisen as responses to these processes of globalization. One, in an important way the processes of globalization have made it possible for people from different parts of the world to engage in the practice of global ethics. By developing connections between distant peoples, globalization processes have developed organizational and communicative links by which individuals from diverse political and religious communities can engage in debates, consultations, and negotiations to develop and defend shared moral visions. Two, at the same time, a number of the distinct practices of global ethics have arisen to respond to crises occasioned by some of the processes of globalization, especially those associated with industrial and commercial expansion and particular expressions of imperial ambitions. In different ways, conservation movements and human rights organizations often see themselves as addressing the negative consequences associated with particular expressions of globalization. However, three, in decisive ways the varied practices of global ethics in turn have helped to shape the character and meaning of these processes of globalization. They have functioned to remind the contemporary world that we share a joint responsibility for taking care of our small planet and its inhabitants.

Our approach to global ethics

The approach to global ethics we have adopted in this book both differs from and overlaps with alternative ways of thinking about global ethics. In the following paragraphs we will more fully describe our approach by comparing it with those adopted by others. To begin with our understanding of the practices of global ethics follows from our understanding of ethics as a social practice. We view the social practices of ethics broadly as those discursively informed activities by which people seek to guide and evaluate behaviours in relation to normative expectations. Accordingly, people engage in the practice of ethics as they organize, develop, and maintain institutions, protest, craft codes, instruct others, and act in other comparable ways in so far as they deliberately and expressively do so by invoking beliefs about what they regard as good, right, obligatory, or otherwise morally valued. The practice of ethics is inherently a social and communicative activity. Correspondingly, we regard ethics as a practical calling for all humans, not just for philosophers, professionals, or experts. The discursive and behavioural aspects of ethics as a social practice are dialectically related; they can be distinguished but not separated; each shapes the other. Ethics as a practice is not the application of discursive statements. Rather it involves at once communicative and social efforts to articulate normative ideas and to guide and evaluate behaviours. The social practice of ethics remains a dialectic reality both because discursive expressions never fully articulate what is involved as people act and because the corresponding behaviours never fully reflect normative expressions.

It is important to add that the practice of ethics is also a rational activity in several decisive ways. When people communicate normative expectations, they do so to persuade others how they should act. They seek voluntary and intentional responses from others. Correspondingly, they provide reasons for directions and judgements and attempt to communicate in ways that are intelligible to others. Additionally, their communications are more likely to become credible and compelling to the degree that arguments they make are coherent and provide verifiable evidence to support their reasons and claims. Ethical discourse thus gains in authority, especially when communicating with others from different and diverse cultural, political, and moral backgrounds, to the degree it is reasonable, intelligible, coherent, empirically verifiable, and, therefore, rational in these several ways. The multiple expressions of the practice of global ethics reviewed in this book have gained in authority as they correspond to these characteristics.

Several authors, including, for example, Mervyn Frost in a book called *Global Ethic* and Nigel Dower in a book entitled *World Ethics*, depict global ethics as a normative approach to thinking about, arguing for, and evaluating international relations. From a somewhat similar perspective, others associate global ethics with efforts to foster global justice as well as a more humane and ecologically responsible world. For some, global ethics has been especially interrelated with efforts to examine, appreciate, and critique the processes of globalization from an ethical perspective.[19] Many others associate global ethics with efforts to arrive at an inclusive moral position. A global ethic then becomes a statement of norms that all humans, in spite of their differences, can respect and should comply with.[20] Finally, many use the term global ethics to refer to the processes of adapting and transforming existing ethics for a globalized world. Correspondingly, we can point to efforts to recast national and commercial expressions of business ethics so that they address a world of transnational business activity and acknowledge the accountabilities of businesses with respect to ecological systems in which we all live. We can also refer to efforts fostered by interfaith encounters to encourage more open and mutually appreciative relations among world religions.[21] All these approaches to global ethics share in common a commitment to formulate moral visions that are truly inclusive and do not thereby camouflage particular interests in universalistic rhetoric.

The approach we have adopted in this book differs from these alternatives in several ways. By viewing global ethics as a set of practices, we recognize global ethics not only as a project that people are seeking to realize now and in the future but also as a set of activities in which people have been engaged for quite some time. As we have set out in the examples already cited, over time there have been many expressions of global ethics in practice. Also, we focus not only on written normative statements and supporting arguments but also on the diverse communicative activities and corresponding organizational forms that have been undertaken and developed to articulate, defend, and institutionalize these norms. In particular, we have emphasized the way in which practising global ethics is inherently collaborative. The heart of this practice is not found in efforts by thinkers to identify moral universals, whether these are associated with natural law, human rights, or global justice, but is rather embodied in the collaborative efforts of people from diverse constituencies seeking to articulate and champion normative statements as viable responses to current global issues. One might make the case that, by viewing global ethics as a set of practices, we have adopted a historical and sociological perspective that is largely descriptive. To a degree this is true, because in our accounts we have largely attempted to depict representative expressions of global ethics in practice as these have developed over time. However, in at least three very important ways, our approach has also been normative.

For example, one, we believe it is important to appreciate the moral value of the diverse expressions of global ethics that have already been developed. It is possible that some of those currently engaged in trying to craft or defend particular expression of global ethics think of themselves as inventing something comparatively new. We argue, contrariwise, that the practice of global ethics began long ago, certainly by the late nineteenth century, as representatives of different nations met to develop authoritative transnational standards with regard to concerns such as the freedom of the seas, the humane treatment of prisoners, and the end of trade in slaves. It may also at times prove useful to identify expressions of global ethics that are ranked as having greater authority or as being more fundamental and foundational. The judgements of international courts, the proclamations of the international bodies, and reasoned arguments of those involved have and will affect this process. However, we see no need for establishing any kind of necessary hierarchy. These varied expressions of global ethics address differing even though sometimes overlapping problems. They serve varied but often complementary purposes. Even as we seek to clarify the relationships between these varied expressions of global ethics, we think it is important also to appreciate the collaborative efforts to create and gain support for them. As we seek to craft more inclusive and more compelling global standards, we can learn much from reflecting on the diverse actions taken by those who have variously engaged in the practices of global ethics through civil society associations, intergovernmental organizations, international commissions, and globally oriented institutes.

Two, our focus on the practice of global ethics presupposes a prior assumption that regards reciprocating dialogue or conversation as an integral part of this practice.[22] It is by means of open, honest, reasonable, and reciprocating communications between people of different moral, religious, political, legal, and economic persuasions that the practices of global ethics take place. For these communications to occur fruitfully, those involved must at a minimum be able and ready to voice the concerns embedded in their diverse cultures and concerns and to listen attentively enough to others so that they can understand why the others say what say. For these dialogues or conversations to proceed in ways that lead to mutually accepted agreements, it is necessary that those involved follow widely held norms regarding civil communications. Thus, those participating should take turns, respond reciprocally to what others present – thereby avoiding bypassing monologues – communicate intelligibly providing reasons for their positions, and communicate honestly and without deception or intentional evasion.[23] The deliberations leading to normative agreements may require much time, useful pauses, and occasional demonstrations of power so that positions are taken seriously by others, and, almost inevitably, may involve some forms of compromise. In the end, the social practice of global ethics clearly favours agreements reached as a result of discourse and negotiations, however difficult and aggravated corresponding interactions have been, over regimes unilaterally imposed by force.

Three, from our perspective practising global ethics especially embodies an ethic of responsibility. To be sure, particular written expressions of global ethics are set forth quite differently as universal principles, utilitarian frameworks, value statements, and legal codes. However, as we have already indicated, a common feature of these diverse practices of global ethics is the way each expresses a lively sense of fiduciary responsibility with respect to targeted global issues. Thus, each clearly acknowledges the crisis the Earth and its inhabitants will face with respect to certain problems – from the practice of genocide to the use of banned weapons, from endangered forests and species to widespread corruption – unless humans find ways of responsibly addressing these issues. Moreover, beyond a sense of crisis, those engaged in these practices embody a commitment to assume responsibility and thereby to take steps to exercise care with respect to those people and environments affected. In spite of expressed alarm with respect to various threats and outrages, overall, the proponents of global ethics are deeply moved by hope.

Typical expressions of global ethics in practice

This book is divided into three parts. In Part I, we look at characteristic efforts to articulate and gain support for encompassing, universal statements of global ethics. Each of the declarations and charters reviewed is addressed in principle to all humans. Each provides a fundamental framework for analysing and finding appropriate responses to one or more of a wide range of ethical issues, especially those facing humans in the contemporary world. Each seeks to provide a basic ground for thinking about diverse moral concerns, for exercising appropriate judgements, and for mobilizing fitting responses.

In Chapter 1 we analyse some of the basic features of the UDHR and how over time, in response to the continuing processes of globalization, the authority and significance of this document have expanded as various groups have sought to elaborate its basic normative assumptions in other codes, covenants, and declarations. In particular the legally binding International Covenant on Civil and Political Rights (ICCPR) and the International Covenant on Economic, Social and Cultural Rights (ICESCR), initially adopted by the General Assembly of the United Nations in 1966, have been ratified by large numbers of countries. We briefly review efforts to elaborate and extend these normative principles with respect to humanitarian interventions, transnational businesses, indigenous peoples, women's rights, and the right to a healthy environment. In the chapter we also discuss how this declaration has gained authority as people have explored and expanded the ways to justify its normative claims in diverse ways.

In Chapter 2 we analyse the long processes beginning in the 1980s that led to adoption of the Earth Charter in 2000. Rather than being a statement of potentially legally binding rights, the Earth Charter functions as an aspirational expression of the kind of global community that the charter challenges humans everywhere to work at bringing into being. Recognizing that we are living at an especially critical period of the Earth's history, the charter calls on humans to act responsibly to respect and care for the Earth's larger community of life, to foster social and ecological justice, and to work for democracy, non-violence, and peace. Without any formal political or legal status, this civic statement has attracted attention both because of the large number of people and groups that participated in the consultations that led to its formulation and because of its attempt to articulate a holistic, Earth-centred global ethic.

Chapter 3 looks at three declarations, all of which pointedly identify basic human responsibilities, regarded in these documents as complements to fundamental human rights and duties. The first of these, Declaration toward a Global Ethic, was written largely by one man, the Christian theologian Hans Küng, in preparation for, and subsequently endorsed by, the 1993 meeting of the Parliament of the World's Religions. It identifies four sets of basic principles, referred to as 'irrevocable directives', that it claims are in keeping with the core teachings of all religions. These directives, articulated as commitments to non-violence and respect for life, human solidarity and just economic order, tolerance and a life of truthfulness, and equal rights and partnership between men and women, are set forth as ways of addressing current global crises. The second document, A Universal Declaration of Human Responsibilities, was developed in 1997 by an ongoing group of formers heads of state, the InterAction Council. Largely a recasting of the Parliament of the World's Religion's declaration, this document was consciously designed as a complement to the UDHR. The third document, The Declaration of Human Duties and Responsibilities (DHDR), was published in 1998 under the auspices of the United Nations Educational, Scientific, and Cultural Organization (UNESCO), after a series of consultations, congresses, and drafting sessions involving internationally respected jurists, academics, statesmen, and other professionals from all over the world. The document identifies those moral duties and legal responsibilities that are called for in order to protect basic human rights in an increasingly complex, globalized, economically unbalanced, and ecologically precarious world.

In Part II we examine concrete examples of the practices of global ethics with respect to a range of global ethical issues, and to the efforts of groups and people from different moral, political, religious, and philosophical backgrounds to work to address these concerns. People with quite different types of expertise – as natural scientists, social scientists, business executives, international lawyers, military officials, civil society leaders, international bureaucrats, as well as philosophers – have variously drafted standards, developed organizations, and monitored activities as they have engaged in practising global ethics. In Part II, we review the practices of global ethics with respect to global environmental concerns, genocide, the uses of lethal force, global poverty, and the practices of international businesses. If we had time and space we might well have examined the global ethics in practice with respect to a number of other concerns, such as health standards and responses to disease, the status of women, international financial regulations, the status and care of refugees, immigration issues, as well as global trade. We hope that the following chapters provide a fairly representative description of a much wider field of activity. On a day-to-day basis, tens of thousands of people have been devoting their energy, imaginations, and time to practising global ethics in all its forms. Without their efforts, we would be living in a quite different and less hospitable world.

In Chapter 4 we review the development of global environmental ethics since the Second World War. We begin the chapter by looking at the emergence of a widely shared mindset that views the Earth as a whole that is put at risk by human activity and therefore needs protection by and from humans. We trace a number of important developments, such as the creation of the World Meteorological Organization in 1951, the UN Conference on the Human Environment in Stockholm in 1972, the Montreal Protocol on Substances that Deplete the Ozone Layer in 1987, the creation of the IPCC in 1988, the statements on climate change and biodiversity at the UN Earth Summit in Rio in 1992, and the Millennium Ecosystem Assessment report in 2005. Overall, we document what we regard as an increasingly broadly shared commitment to shared stewardship with respect to the Earth and its well-being.

Chapter 5 focuses on concerted international efforts to find more effective ways to reduce the risk that some people will become the targets of genocide. The chapter examines public and private responses to the genocides perpetrated in Nazi Germany, Bosnia, and Rwanda. Because acts of genocide are so morally outrageous, we have adopted a more active voice in this chapter. After examining evidence and arguments regarding these three instances of genocide, we set forth our own position both about how to respond to actual genocides and about actions that we think should be taken to deter future genocides. Moreover, owing to the fact that the role(s) of religion in both the perpetration and prevention of genocide have been significantly downplayed or overlooked in the critical literature, this chapter focuses special attention on the interaction between religion and politics regarding the ethics of genocide.

In Chapter 6 we look at efforts since the mid-nineteenth century to create effective standards with respect to how and when lethal forces are employed, focusing primarily on the period since Second World War. We analyse the increasingly broad normative acceptance of standards designed to restrict armed attacks on wounded soldiers, prisoners, and unarmed civilians; to restrict or prohibit the use of particular kinds of arms, such as nuclear bombs and chemical weapons; and to call for the proportionate use of arms both in relation to specific military objectives and in response to harm already suffered. These kinds of norms, many of which were set forth in the Geneva Conventions, have been codified in international law, particular treaties, and even military handbooks. We analyse as well another set of standards regarding the resort to lethal force, which have also been widely and internationally accepted, although less legally codified. These include principles regarding when the resort to lethal force is justified, the ways military practices should be subordinated to political purposes, and when and how it becomes acceptable to use lethal force by third parties to intervene in intra-state conflicts. Overall, this emerging ethic, which calls for greater restraint in the uses of lethal force, has gained in authority and has been partially reinforced by deployment of international peacekeeping forces, largely under the aegis of the United Nations. We observe that this emerging global ethic with respect to lethal force is sometimes confused with varied expressions of ethics, championed by diverse groups, sometimes using similar language, which call for righteous and often unrestrained uses of lethal force in relation to particular causes from fighting evil empires to championing religious crusades. We end the chapter calling attention to recent morally intense global debates with respect both to uses of non-lethal chemical weapons and to the use of targeted assassinations.

In Chapter 7 we review the practices of global ethics with respect to global poverty. We begin by describing in general terms how communities and later countries variously responded to poverty as local and national concerns during pre-industrial and then industrializing times. We focus on the ways poverty came to be viewed as a global problem during and after the Second World War. We analyse how the practices of global ethics with respect to poverty have in these years assumed three broad strategies. One, a humanitarian approach has been expressed through aid and relief programmes, the development of refugee services, and diverse initiatives to provide food and health assistance. A second approach has sought various ways to foster economic development in developing countries. Various tactics have been initiated from state aid to debt relief, from efforts to reform business practices to initiatives to restructure budgetary processes in developing states by means of poverty reduction strategy policies. We look at the role played by organizations such as the UN Conference on Trade and Development and the UN Development Programme as well as the UN Millennium Development Goals (MDGs) to foster effective developmental policies. A third approach, associated with various civil society associations and the World Social Forum, has especially called attention to the ways existing patterns of injustice seem to occasion and reinforce global poverty. We note that, while critics have emerged to challenge all these approaches to global poverty, nonetheless it is possible to discern a number of shared normative assumptions about the importance of recognizing and acting constructively to address poverty as a shared global concern.

In Chapter 8 we examine the efforts, especially since 1980, to establish global standards regarding the practices of international businesses. A number of international business associations have been established to promote specific standards and monitor the practices of businesses with respect to these standards. We review the actions undertaken by the Caux Round Table (CRT), Social Accountability International (SAI), the Global Reporting Initiative (GRI), and the UN Global Compact. We also look at the impact of the World Bank's Performance Standards on Environmental and Social Sustainability and the UN Human Rights Council's Guiding Principles on Business and Human Rights. We argue that these several initiatives embody a number of important internationally recognized normative assumptions regarding business practices, which are as follows: businesses are socially and environmentally accountable; businesses are accountable to all their stakeholders; and businesses should operate transparently and be governed responsibly. We observe that the associations named along with many industry associations and government review boards are increasingly auditing businesses with respect to these standards. We note both, one, that many businesses adopt these standards as a means of managing their risks and reputation and, two, that this emerging global business ethic still fails to address a number of notable ethical issues, including serious long-term environmental concerns and the extent to which many businesses in practice tend to adhere to an alternative, neo-liberal economic ethic.

The five chapters in Part II describe and assess the practices of global ethics with respect to a representative sample of global issues. We have not, however, directly examined the practices of global ethics with respect to global governance, although this is a very important area of concern. In practice, a range of normative assumptions seem to have gained acceptance about how authoritative decisions regarding global matters ought to be made. For example, most people and countries accept as legitimate the guidance offered by scientists at the WHO about monitoring and controlling the spread of diseases. Similarly, most people and countries defer to the counsel and direction of the International Atomic Energy Agency. With some exceptions, in practice people and countries have respected the rulings of various tribunals regarding the violations of the Geneva Conventions and international humanitarian law. However, it is not now possible to identify clear, widely accepted normative standards about how global decision-making in general ought to be undertaken. For many, this question remains highly politicized. Nonetheless, several underlying normative assumptions continue to retain widely acknowledged authority: namely, one, as humans, we must respect our differences; two, the Earth and its inhabitants are at risk for diverse reasons; and, three, we are each and all responsible for taking care of the Earth and its inhabitants.

In Part III we explore the relationship between faith communities and emerging practices of global ethics from several perspectives. Chapter 9 reviews the development of interreligious organizations and activities from the 1893 meeting of the World's Parliament of Religions until the present. Although inherently global in their aims and perspectives, interreligious movements characteristically have been expressed more through local and regional associations, ceremonies, institutes, and projects than at international gatherings. Through these varied activities interreligious movement have sought to promote greater understanding and appreciation among the followers of diverse religions as well as greater collaboration in addressing global social and environmental concerns. In this chapter we examine several expressions of interreligious movements and the significance of these activities for the practice of global ethics.

Chapters 10 and 11 focus on particular issues that have arisen as varied religious communities have sought to work out their relationships towards each other in what might be described as civic institutions in an emerging global polity. In Chapter 10 we review contemporary efforts to think about and develop patterns of action that both guarantee religious freedom and allow for proselytizing. These issues emerge because many religious groups, such as the missionary religions of Buddhism, Christianity, and Islam, have actively sought to gain increasing numbers of new adherents. In this chapter we look at initiatives that seek to defend the rights of humans to communicate their basic convictions, their rights to religious freedom, as well as their rights to be protected from misleading and manipulative communications. In Chapter 11 we examine contemporary efforts to develop common standards for education about diverse religions in public school systems. For centuries religions have played and continue to play a large role in human communities generally and with respect to ethics in particular. Because accounts of the religions of other people have often assumed biased and stereotypical forms, it has become especially important to provide public accounts that fairly represent diverse religions as multidimensional social realities. In this chapter we review current collaborative initiatives to craft normative guidelines regarding public instruction with respect to the beliefs and practices of diverse religious communities.

Religions play an important and decisive role with respect to the practices of global ethics for at least three reasons. One, religions continue to constitute one of the primary expressions and sources of the 'thick' ethics by which many people live.[24] Religious symbols, rites, and associations often function as the motivational context and grounds for how and why people act morally. Since a large proportion of humans draw upon religious thought, feelings, and communities to make up their minds, it becomes important for those seeking to foster the practice of global ethics to find ways of connecting with these religious roots.

Two, religious diversity has become especially important for the practices of global ethics precisely because unresolved differences between religions have often served to occasion, reinforce, or justify major conflicts between nations as well as between groups within nations. This fact points to the corresponding importance of the efforts by interreligious movements to foster greater appreciation and understanding between different religious communities. In the process, while they may be operating in the background, interreligious movements have functioned to open up space for collaborative initiatives by people from diverse cultural and national backgrounds, often associated with particular religious traditions, to promote the practising of global ethics with respect to specific global environmental and social concerns.

Three, interreligious movements have especially championed a dialogical approach to the practice of global ethics that at once recognizes and respects diversity while exploring relevant ways for collaborating together in spite of these differences. This dialogical approach, characterized by civil, open-ended, reciprocating conversations, seeks to achieve workable agreements rather than unanimity, negotiated understandings rather than universal laws. Each of the chapters in Part III provides examples of this dialogical approach to global ethics in practice.

Global ethics, history, and hope

In the Conclusion we look at the overall significance of the diverse examples of the practices of global ethics. We note the ways in which these practices have taken seriously the wide range of transborder global issues facing the world today, from ecological crises to the threats of pandemic disease, from economic crises to the threats from insurgents using terrorist tactics, from questionable business practices to human rights abuses. We call attention to the several ways in which the practices of global ethics have made noticeable differences: they have been embedded in various global institutions such as International Committee of the Red Cross, international humanitarian laws, the MDGs, the Equator Principles, the IUCN, diverse human rights charters, and many other organizations, treaties, and associations. While many people continue to act on the basis of narrow economic self-interests, nationalistic concerns, loyalties to particular religious and ethnic traditions, and their own visions of righteous causes, at the same time a growing number of global political and civil organizations along with millions of people associated with these organizations have been working to realize their commitments to creating and sustaining global normative standards. While not dramatically changing the course of history, they have acted to make the world a more habitable place.

Those involved in practising global ethics have not attempted to overcome or supersede the diverse existing moral cultures expressed in and through religious faiths, philosophical traditions, economic theories, political doctrines, and legal systems. Rather, they have sought to work with people committed to these moral cultures to craft global normative standards they all can embrace as practical ways of addressing serious global issues.

Over time these diverse examples of the practices of global ethics have created a number of new global normative standards. In this sense, these standards are products of history. Correspondingly, we ask to what extent these standards should be regarded as having only relative validity. In spite of their historically contingent character, we argue that many of these standards have gained considerable authority and something like objective validity for three reasons. Much like global social contracts, they have gained in authority and validity to the degree that they have been endorsed and ratified by national governments, civil society associations, and faith communities. They have gained in authority and validity as well, because most of these standards are based on and seek to realize particular intrinsic goods – basic values associated with human dignity, respect for diverse human cultures, and care for the Earth and its biosphere. In this manner the practice of global ethics functions much like traditional natural law traditions by seeking to identify universally valid normative standards designed to realize and protect basic moral goods. Finally, these standards have gained in authority and validity to the extent that they have in fact functioned in a pragmatic fashion to resolve conflicts, arouse concern about emerging ecological dangers, mobilize support for disasters, restrain the exercise of violence, and to address other similar outcomes.

Finally, we end by calling attention to the ways those engaged in the practices of global ethics remain hopeful in spite of their aroused concerns regarding the crises the Earth and its inhabitants are facing. Although it assumes many forms, this hope springs not from an easy optimism but from diverse sources, including a commitment to make a difference.

Notes

1. Millennium Ecosystem Assessment, *Living beyond our Means.*
2. Rubin, *The End of Growth.*
3. Berman, *Radical, Religious and Violent; The Economist,* 'The Unquenchable Fire'; Davis, *Planet of Slums.*
4. MacIntyre, *After Virtue,* ch. 18; Jacobs, *Dark Age Ahead;* Korten, *When Corporations Rule the World,* 22–4 and Epilogue.
5. Thakur et al., *International Commissions and the Power of Ideas.*
6. Miller, 'Democratization, International Knowledge Institutions, and Global Governance'; Miller, 'Epistemic Constitutionalism in International Governance'.

7. Power, *Like Water on a Stone*; McIntosch et al., *Learning to Talk*.

8. See also report of Group i from the 2009 Nairobi Conference: 'Defining Global Ethics', in Cisneros and Premawardhana (eds), *Sharing Values*, 375–84; Sen, *Development as Freedom*; Nussbaum, *Women and Human Development*; Nussbaum, *Creating Capabilities*.

9. See Kurasawa, *The Work of Global Justice*, who views the efforts to establish global justice as a multidimensional set of social practices: witnessing, forgiving, offering foresight, providing aid, and fostering solidarity.

10. We are here paraphrasing parts of Karl Marx's last thesis on Feuerbach: 'The philosophers have only interpreted the world in various ways; the point is to change it' (*Karl Marx: Selected Writings*, 158).

11. Universal Declaration of Human Rights, found in Sullivan and Kymlicka (eds), *The Globalization of Ethics*, 213–18; Commission on Global Governance, *Our Global Neighbourhood*; Parliament of the World's Religions, 'Declaration toward a Global Ethic', found in Sullivan and Kymlicka (eds), *The Globalization of Ethics*, 236–46; Weber, 'Politics as Vocation'.

12. Friedman, *The Lexus and the Olive Tree*; Friedman, *The World is Flat*; Saul, *The Collapse of Globalism*.

13. See Peters, *In Search of the Good Life*; Brown, *Ethics, Economics and International Relations*.

14. Coates, *A Global History of Indigenous Peoples*; Johnson, *The Sorrows of Empire*; Ferguson, *Empire: How Britain Made the Modern World*.

15. Kennedy, *The Parliament of Man*; Thakur, *The United Nations, Peace and Security*; Ruggie, 'Reconstituting the Global Public Domain'; Alvarez, *International Organizations as Law-Makers*.

16. On the status and character of this society of nations, see Bull, *The Anarchical Society*.

17. Keck and Sikkink, *Activists beyond Borders*.

18. This phrase is used in the Earth Charter.

19. Dower, *World Ethics*; Frost, *Global Ethics*; see also Pogge, *World Poverty and Human Rights*; Coney, *Justice beyond Borders*; Nielsen, *Globalization and Justice*.

20. See Outka and Reeder (eds), *Prospects for a Common Morality*, chs 1, 2; Cisneros and Premawardhana (eds), *Sharing Values*; Küng, *A Global Ethic for Global Politics and Economics*.

21. Sullivan and Kymlicka (eds), *The Globalization of Ethics*.

22. On the importance of dialogue for global ethics, see Parekh, 'Principles of Global Ethics'; Verlinden, 'Global Ethics as Dialogism'.

23. These basic guidelines are spelled out more fully in the chapter on 'Good Conversation' in Bird, *The Muted Conscience*, ch. 7.
24. See Walzer, *Ethics Thick and Thin*.

PART I

Developing Common Grounds

1 Human Rights and Globalization

Introduction and background

This chapter discusses the practices of global ethics with respect to human rights, including the interaction between processes of globalization, on the one hand, and the international human rights movement, on the other.[1] To tackle such a large topic, it is useful to begin with the basics, starting with the nature and function of human rights in the modern era.

There are two firmly accepted types of human rights norms identified in international declarations, conventions, and treaties – civil-political and socio-economic – both of which represent potential claims of individual persons against their respective governments. Civil-political rights include two subtypes: norms regarding physical and civil security (for example, prohibitions of torture, slavery, arbitrary arrest; guarantees of legal personhood, equality before the law, due process) and norms regarding civil and political empowerment (for example, freedoms of thought, assembly, voluntary association; guarantees of effective political participation in one's society). Socio-economic rights also include two subtypes: norms regarding the provision of conditions and goods meeting basic personal and social needs (and for meeting basic economic needs (for example, work and fair wages, adequate living standard, a social security net). There is also a third class of human rights now acknowledged in international agreements but less settled and more contested than the preceding types. We label these 'collective-developmental rights' of peoples and groups held not only against their respective states but also in some sense the entire world community, and they appear to include at least three subtypes: the self-determination of whole peoples (for example, to their political status and economic, social, and cultural development); the security claims of all peoples to conditions such as peace and a decent environment; and certain special protections and guarantees for ethnic and religious minorities (for example, to the integrity of their cultures, languages, and religions).

Taken as a whole, human rights represent a modern social practice at the international level that functions to regulate diverse social and political systems in a manner that encourages them to advance conditions and goods perceived to be crucial for personal and communal flourishing.[2] Beyond requiring states to adopt legislative, economic, and political measures to guarantee the priority interests represented by human rights, the international covenants say very little about the precise mechanisms of guarantee that should be developed. This implies that the regulative function of human rights can be accomplished in diverse ways appropriate to different economic, political, and legal systems. The incorporation of the language and concepts of human rights into national constitutions and bills of rights, combined with judicial enforcement procedures, is one such way – and probably the most effective – but one could imagine others as well, just as one can conceive of different forms of democracy.

In addition to human rights, our other term of art for the present discussion is globalization. The meaning of globalization is very contested territory, with historians, economists, and political and cultural theorists all having enlightening characterizations of this complex phenomenon. Rather than entering into this debate – or cacophony – we will simply stipulate that we are using the term as described in detail in the Introduction to this book. In connection with globalization, human rights scholars and advocates alike often deploy a heuristic developed by Richard Falk over a decade ago: globalization-from-above versus globalization-from-below.[3] The first refers to economic and political activities (including collaboration) among big powers on the world stage such as state actors and financial and corporate agents, and the second refers to social, political, and cultural activities of and among local, national, and international agencies (for example, non-governmental organizations, UN organs, grass-roots groups) all interested in advancing the quality of civil societies across the world, perhaps even forming a global civil society. Human rights and their development are relevant to both of these perspectives or levels of globalization.

It is important to realize that the modern practice of human rights has been subject to progressive development. Human rights negotiation and agreement at the international level encompass a wide variety of developments and activities. Included here, for example, are successive international human rights declarations, treaties, conventions, and covenants promulgated and adopted since the Second World War; investigations, reports, and diplomatic mediations of international human rights commissions; judicial findings, rulings, and precedents of international human rights tribunals and courts; and comparable regional human rights charters, commissions, and juridical mechanisms in Europe, the Americas, and Africa. Such ongoing development and activities, considered collectively, represent a historically grounded pragmatic process of interpretation and expansion of human rights in the world community – a progressive, practical, and public consensus about shared human rights norms that is continually evolving. Much of this evolution is responsive to world-historical crises, ranging from the Second World War genocide and atrocity, through post-war Third World struggles for liberation from colonial domination and repression, to more recent cases of ethnic conflict leading to genocide (or ethnic cleansing) and the struggles by vulnerable populations for the recognition of their human rights. Indeed, some are now suggesting that the international human rights community may be facing its biggest crisis and challenge precisely in relation to the recent expressions of economic globalization and their effects. Whatever one might think of this somewhat alarmist characterization, there is no gainsaying the fact that recent processes of economic globalization are affecting the practice of human rights in a profound manner.

To see how this is so, we will focus first on developments related to what we shall refer to as the practices of global ethics-from-above perspective, and then turn to those connected with practices of global ethics-from-below. Obviously, there will be overlaps and interactions between the two levels, as world events are not so neat and tidy as to divide easily into analytically separable categories. Also, for the purposes of this discussion, we are selecting only illustrative developments, and are making no effort to be exhaustive.

Global ethics and human rights-from-above

The two large developments that we will now discuss with respect to the practice of global ethics-from-above are the emergence of humanitarian intervention (and certain related phenomena), on the one hand, and transnational business (and related factors), on the other. These topics are more fully discussed in Chapters 6 and 8 of this book.

Humanitarian intervention

At the outset of the modern human rights movement (roughly mid-twentieth century), the goal of its declarations and conventions was to rein in abuses of state power by granting protections to individual citizens against their respective governments. At this time, the reality of world politics was premised on a strong presumption of state sovereignty over internal domestic policies and practices, which, in turn, presented the problem of how to control the exercise of that sovereignty without radically changing this presumption. The answer adopted was to develop a 'compact' among states agreeing to hold themselves accountable for the provision and protection of the human rights of their respective citizens. And, within the terms of this compact, even with the presumption of state sovereignty, states were envisioned as being able to bring other compacting states to the bar of justice, so to speak, when and if it became apparent that they were breaking the compact by violating the human rights of their citizens in an egregious manner. This had the result of making the presumption of state sovereignty porous (at least in principle) to external critique and possible international intervention and account-ability in situations of massive non-compliance with the compact. So, a conceptual basis was laid for the subsequent development of interventionist strategies in later years. But, in fact, owing largely to the cold war, the bipolar stand-off of the superpowers (US and USSR) and their aligned blocs had a severe restraining effect on the political feasibility and wisdom of humanitarian intervention, which, if undertaken by either side, might have led to another world war or even a nuclear holocaust. How has this situation changed in more recent years, and how might this change relate to globalization?

We hypothesize that the recent processes of economic globaliza-tion played a significant role in the break-up of the Soviet Union (and its bloc), whose 'command economy' was simply outstripped by global capitalism and then imploded, leading to significant political disruption and change. At the same time, we also hypothesize that global communications and media had much to do with the increas-ing restiveness of the populations of Eastern Europe when they were confronted with images of wealth and social achievement by the democratic countries of Western Europe and North America, leading them to put pressure on their own governments for economic and political reform. In addition to these effects of economic and com-municative globalization, it seems to us that it is also true that such globalization processes make ever more apparent to an interdepend-ent world population that, when massive human rights violations do take place in domestic contexts, they have considerable negative effects on international peace, security, and prosperity. Continuing massive human rights violations have driven home to the world that internal domestic abuses of such magnitude are of interna-tional concern and that domestic jurisdictions are limited by human rights norms. In effect, a 'liberal' conception of state sovereignty

– where states are explicitly constrained by international human rights conventions and customary international law – has definitively supplanted the 'classical' conception – which had insisted on non-intervention except in cases of aggression across borders threatening international peace and security.[4] Thus is further groundwork laid for the development of humanitarian intervention beyond the seed initially planted at mid-century.

Humanitarian intervention divides into two types: non-military (for example, diplomacy, withdrawal of aid, and use of economic and trade sanctions) and military (that is, the use of coercive force to rescue and protect the innocent in another country). The first type has a somewhat longer history of use. The paradigm case, of course, is South Africa, where systematic pressures brought by states – in addition to other agents such as corporations responsive to socially conscious shareholders – helped to end apartheid. This situation and action led to the adoption of an international convention against the crime of apartheid, which is now classified as a crime against humanity. The second type of intervention has a much briefer history – beginning in the early 1990s and up to the present (for example, Somalia, Kosovo, Mali, and, arguably, Iraq) – compelling attention to a set of issues not envisaged or discussed at mid-century. Examples of these issues include: What are the exact grounds justifying military humanitarian intervention? Who is the competent authority for undertaking such intervention – for example, the United Nations only, or regional coalitions of states also? What is the international legal basis for intervention? This is not the place to debate and settle such controverted matters, but we do believe it is fair to say that, owing to effects of the globalization processes described above, a new international human rights phenomenon has emerged in the form of humanitarian intervention along with a developing consensus on criteria and rules for such intervention, for example: prior ineffectiveness of diplomatic and other non-military methods; likelihood of success and net benefit for the victims; proportionate and discriminate use of force; preferable prior authorization by the United Nations; compliance with the laws of war and the Geneva Conventions; and clear and reasonable planning for the post-intervention period, including instituting the rule of law, transitioning to democracy of some form, and normalizing social and economic relations.[5]

A correlated development – which is also due in large part to the same changes in superpower balance and globalization – is the emergence of legal accountability for the perpetrators of human rights atrocities, including heads of state. The changes here involve the establishment of ad hoc international criminal tribunals, the development of universal jurisdiction in prosecuting agents of crimes against humanity (any and all countries have jurisdiction over them), and the recent establishment of the permanent International Criminal Court (ICC), all of which indicate the emergence and strengthening of a 'global conscience' of sorts for bringing violators to the bar of justice. This was, of course, first done in the Nuremberg and Tokyo trials at the end of the Second World War, an experiment in international criminal justice whose development was inhibited by the cold war and has now been given new life by the processes of globalization.[6]

Transnational business

One novelty spawned by the practices of global ethics-from-above takes the form of a new class of actors on the international human rights scene probably not envisaged at mid-century. Here we are referring to how the processes of economic globalization in particular have brought into being transnational financial institutions and corporations whose economic power exceeds that of many states. The picture of the roles of these actors vis-à-vis human rights is ambiguous at best, for they can be seen simultaneously as both violators and promoters of human rights. Let us take each of these 'faces' in turn.

If we set aside the question of any nefarious intentions of these institutions and corporations, the manifest fact is that many of their policies have resulted in rather large and systematic violations of human rights, especially socio-economic rights. For example, beginning in the 1980s the World Bank and the International Monetary Fund (IMF) attached conditions to the loans they granted to developing countries, which required these governments to reduce public spending in a number of areas and to devote significant portions of public budgets to paying the interest on these loans during periods of economic slowdown. These structural adjustment policies resulted in higher unemployment rates and the redeployment of resources away from social programmes, all of which clearly worked to the detriment of the socio-economic rights of many, while at the same time fattening the purses of a number of political and corporate leaders. Furthermore, the cost-minimization policies of certain transnational corporations (they shall remain nameless) – with their underlying threat of withdrawal of capital and production facilities from non-compliant states – have tended to result in, for example, low wages, skirting of worker safety regulations, worker abuse in the form of child labour, and the encouragement of lax (or no) regulation of health-threatening environmental pollution, again clearly disadvantaging the socio-economic welfare of many in underdeveloped countries. The upshot is that economic globalization processes have encouraged the emergence of a new kind of human rights abuser largely beyond the control of international human rights conventions and mechanisms that are directed largely to state actors.

The other face of this new class of actors is more positive and should not be overlooked. One can begin by considering the fact that recently transnational financial institutions of the sort mentioned above are making their decision-making processes more transparent and responsive to the genuine and complex needs of underdeveloped nations and modifying their structural adjustment policies to take into account their socio-economic impact on vulnerable populations. This is well illustrated by initiatives, further discussed in Chapter 8, such as the Extractive Industries Transparency Initiative and the World Bank's performance standards for international businesses. In addition, these policies are also being modified in such a way as to encourage more democratic and political involvement of affected citizens in developing countries. Second, one can cite certain treaties among states regarding the regulation of transnational corporate activity, although these are still largely restricted to the developed 'core' states of America, Europe, and East Asia. Third, one might also cite various examples of an emerging global business ethic, also further discussed in Chapter 8, which attempts to address not only issues of corporate corruption and bribery in transnational business but also issues of gender discrimination, worker safety, and human health.[7] Fourth, and perhaps more important, are the market-building strategies of some transnational corporations involving long-term capital and human investment in Third World countries. Such strategies include, for example, increasingly higher wages for workers, provision of high-quality working environments, and progressive worker training, all of which arguably enhance the human rights of workers directly and which may also result indirectly in a more hospitable human rights ethos in the host countries.

In the latter regard, one must take into account the optimistic view – supported by some data – that transnational corporate investment in developing countries not only provides new employment opportunities but also helps give rise to a middle class and civil society desirous of human rights.[8] In addition, the corporate need for consistency in business practices helps to promote the development of the rule of law, which has a 'spill-over' effect on citizens who appreciate the connection between human rights and legal guarantees for their protection. It is further hypothesized that these effects, in turn, have a strong tendency to lead to citizen demands for a more liberal political sphere in the form of civil-political empowerments.

Finally, owing in part to the influence of the practices of global ethics-from-below, there are recent important developments in the management of transnational corporations that have a bearing on the promotion of human rights norms. These developments range across, for example, legal rulings about the liability of managers for the malfeasance of subordinates, advocacy pressures on corporations to make ethics a higher priority, the adoption by corporations of internal codes of conduct and values/mission codes, and the rise of corporate 'social audits' of management policies and practices.[9] All these developments pointedly raise the issue of corporate responsibility for protecting human rights. A few transnational corporations committed to market-building rather than cost-minimization strategies (for example, Motorola, Levi-Strauss) now explicitly recognize that they have responsibilities, for example, to avoid worker abuse, to monitor the practices of their business partners and subcontractors (and to intervene when necessary), to educate their employees and partners about applicable human rights norms, and to cooperate with other corporations and transnational agencies in setting and enforcing higher labour standards.[10] While certainly prompted in part by outside advocacy groups, these developments also represent an acknowledgement by large transnational businesses that with power comes responsibility, especially when that power is a result of an implicit contract with states that, in return for economic benefits, corporations have a duty to operate in a socially responsible manner in host countries.

Global ethics and human rights-from-below

Turning to our other globalization perspective – the practices of global ethics-from-below – we can discern the emergence of another type of actor on the international scene – this time one who unambiguously intends to promote human rights. The processes of globalization associated particularly with communication and information technologies are helping to birth the development and collaboration of more grass-roots social movements – some of which we have already alluded to – locally, regionally, and internationally: for example, environmentalists, consumer movements, labour movements, anti-sweatshop campaigns, and Third World debt-relief campaigns, just to mention a few.[11] These movements appear to be gaining increased power – social, political, and even economic – to demand more humane policies and practices from, for example, states and transnational corporations, that is, policies and practices protective of human rights.

In 1987, Richard Falk identified at least five types of social movements that are by all accounts becoming ever more evident: (1) resistance movements for the causes of ecology, environmental protection, peace, and disarmament; (2) international tribunals conducting inquiries and issuing opinions about cases of state oppression (for example, China's oppression of Tibet); (3) movements of nongovernmental organizations (NGOs) to pressure states to punish perpetrators of egregious human rights violations and to recover the property of victims wrongfully appropriated; (4) consumer-based movements to hold governments and corporations accountable for technological disasters and other practices adversely affecting human welfare; and (5) counter-conferences held in tandem with official state and international conferences, challenging the latter's representational legitimacy by evoking more relevant grass-roots agendas.[12] The three illustrative cases of such movements that we would like to discuss in a bit more detail are those concerned, respectively, with the rights of indigenous peoples, the rights of women, and the emergence of a right to a healthy environment. These cases, discussed further in Chapters 4 and 7, show how globalization is giving rise to the recognition of new human rights or at least new human rights emphases.

Human rights of indigenous peoples

It is well known that at the outset of the modern human rights movement human rights were quite self-consciously conceived as representing the priority interests of individual persons and that the international community at that time was wary of ascribing rights to entire groups (for example, ethnic and religious minorities) for fear that such group rights might encourage inter-group conflict as well as (and more dangerously) conflict between states and those groups that might reside within their borders. In the latter case, the memory of the Third Reich's persecution of Jews and other minorities loomed large. So the framers of the Universal Declaration of Human Rights (UDHR) in 1948 followed the course of emphasizing the rights of individuals and deliberately avoided identifying group rights as another possible type of human right.[13]

Subsequently, however, following the demise of colonialism in the 1950s and 1960s, the issue of the rights of peoples, minorities, and related communities re-emerged, specifically in the form of the identification of the right of a people to determine its own polity and political future and to pursue its own path to economic, social, and cultural development. This right of self-determination of all peoples is specified in the initial articles of both of the international covenants, which at long last legally implemented the norms of the UDHR, with this one new addition.[14] The right of self-determination eventually led to the articulation of a right to development in a 1986 declaration that mandates that the right to development of peoples includes 'full sovereignty over all their natural wealth and resources'.[15] Thus was born the concept of a collective (rather than individual) human right. In order to appreciate the challenge that these rights to self-determination and development pose to the international community, and also to appreciate how the processes of globalization play a role, it will help to focus on one significant and poignant example of their application to a certain class of people – namely, the indigenous peoples of the world and their own efforts to bring into force an official declaration regarding their collective rights.

Indigenous peoples are those communities, groups, or nations often referred to as tribal peoples or First Peoples who inhabited (and are still inhabiting) lands colonized by others. Their worldviews and practices connect them socially, economically, and spiritually to certain natural environments crucial to their identity and survival as distinct peoples and cultures. Although found in diverse areas of the world, these peoples have been subjected to a similar history of oppression, involving, for example, military conquest bordering on genocide, dispossession from and exploitation of their lands, forced relocation, deprivation of their traditional means of subsistence and livelihood, removal of their children and denial of traditional cultural education, interference with their religious practices, active discrimination from the dominant surrounding society, and marginalization in political processes bearing on their well-being.

This history, then, is a shared history of systematic destruction and oppression of these peoples – their traditions, cultures, and very identities as tightly bonded communities with long-standing and deep ties to ancestral lands and customs – that can be summed up in a word: ethnocide. Following this history, more recently the processes of globalization-from-above – involving the collaboration, whether intentional or not, of state actors and agents of capital formation (as identified earlier) – have instituted policies and practices that have so accelerated the destruction of these peoples, their environments, their economies, and their cultures that many of these peoples have been brought to the brink of annihilation. Third World states in particular have been lured by the prospect of trickle-down effects of capital investment and production by transnational corporations in their societies into closing their eyes to, or even colluding in, the oppression, environmental destruction, and near-total marginalization of these peoples from the sources of their existence.

At the same time, however, processes of globalization-from-below – including advances in communication, information, and travel technologies and NGOs assisted by these technologies – have made it possible for these peoples to come together to share and diagnose their similar plight and to develop strategies of resistance. One such strategy, over two decades in the making, eventually led to the adoption by the United Nations of the Declaration on the Rights of Indigenous Peoples (2007) in which these peoples articulate in a unified voice the claim that they have collective human interests and rights in preserving their respective ethnic and cultural identities, their ancestral territories (or what remains of them), and their continuation as distinctive communities with their own unique social institutions and practices, including language, education, economy, governance, and cultural and religious expression.[16]

The articles of this declaration address almost point by point the oppressive techniques and conditions imposed on them by others. Many of the rights claimed are collective rather than individual, for example: collective right to self-determination; collective right to maintain their own distinct political, social, and cultural characteristics as well as legal systems; full guarantee against genocide and ethnocide, including prohibitions of removal of their children, dispossession of their lands, and any form of population transfer; collective right to practise and revitalize their cultural traditions and to practise their spiritual traditions and have access in privacy to their religious sites; collective right to establish and control their educational systems; collective right to participate in decision-making in the dominant society in all matters affecting their lives and destinies; and collective right to restitution of their lands and natural resources where possible and to fair compensation where not.

What is particularly interesting about the declaration and its claims is that there is a concentrated effort to coordinate collective rights with individual human rights in two prominent ways. First, the language of collective rights is often correlated with the language of individual rights as in the formulation 'individual and collective right to x' – for example, the individual and collective right to maintain and develop a distinct identity, and the individual and collective right not to be subjected to ethnocide and cultural genocide. And, second, parts of the declaration quite explicitly guarantee all individual human rights in international law as well as introducing special systematic guarantees for gender equality, economic non-discrimination, and the special protection of certain vulnerable groups within their societies (for example, elders, women, children, and the disabled). Taken together, these two features suggest that the declaration construes collective rights of the group as the intersection of shared individual interests that are being asserted against those outside the group who would deny or otherwise interfere with those shared interests.[17] That is to say, the collective rights function rather like long-term class-action claims by its members against those who might deny or devalue the individual rights of these people. At the same time, the declaration appears to eschew the conception of the group as an independent rights-holder having a moral standing independent of its members in such a manner that it could assert its rights against the interests of individual members – this is the import of assuring all individual human rights in international law.

In sum, we believe that this declaration addresses problems made exigent by processes of globalization-from-above and that such address (or redress) represents the empowerment made possible by processes of globalization-from-below. In this way, globalization has brought into significant view a new historical moment in the development of human rights: the opportunity to acknowledge needed collective human rights in addition to individual ones. And, somewhat ironically, the world's most oppressed peoples and traditions have led the way in showing the world how it is possible to integrate group rights with individual rights.

Women's human rights

At the beginning of the modern human rights movement, the UN Charter laid special emphasis on the importance of the principle of non-discrimination, which was subsequently codified in the UDHR's Article 2, mandating that all persons are entitled to all human rights 'without distinction of any kind', including race, sex, religion, political opinion, national and social origin, among others. Although a number of delegates argued for giving more explicit attention to issues of gender discrimination beyond simply the statement of Article 2, the framers of the declaration declined to identify and address the particular vulnerabilities of women in traditional and modern societies as a special group.[18] This approach was, of course, entirely consistent with their general strategy of emphasizing individual human rights, while avoiding the singling-out of particular groups or classes of people for special protection and treatment. As we have seen, however, this strategy left various groups (such as minorities and indigenous peoples) vulnerable to systematic abuse by others, and this is no less true for other vulnerable classes of people (for example, women the world over).

Since the period of the UDHR, and especially most recently, empirical studies have shown that there is considerable justification for more focused concern about the human rights of women.[19] It is clear, for example, that, particularly in the underdeveloped and developing countries of the world, women suffer disproportionately from hunger, malnutrition, and lack of access to healthcare; they are subjected to domestic violence, rape during peacetime and war, and sexual abuse and harassment outside the home; they are often denied opportunities to work outside the home and, when not, suffer from unequal pay and other discriminatory treatment; in many cases there are substantial barriers to political participation in their societies, including home confinement, illiteracy, curtailed educational opportunities, and bans on public protest; and they often suffer from unequal treatment before the law, including inequality in making contracts, unequal treatment in courts, unequal power to hold and administer property, and unequal treatment in matters of divorce and inheritance.[20] Increasing awareness of these problems, as well as the fact of their ineffectual redress, led to women's liberation movements across the world, which in turn focused attention on the need to empower women's agency in all areas of social, political, economic, and cultural life. In the late 1960s, through the 1970s and 1980s, and continuing to the present day, these movements have increasingly coordinated their efforts, assisted by global information, communication, and transport technologies – globalization-from-below – to liberate women from the oppressive conditions and practices of the sort just mentioned. Three illustrative developments or achievements are worthy of note.

First, in 1979, these movements, through political pressure, virtually compelled the UN to adopt a convention on eliminating all forms of discrimination against women.[21] Although this convention is somewhat analogous to the indigenous peoples' declaration in being designed to enpower the agency of the oppressed so that they themselves can address their problems in a manner best suited to their social and cultural locations, there are important differences as well. One big difference stands out. The women's convention specifically advances a set of women-specific individual human rights and protections – not collective rights – explicitly redressing problems of gender discrimination in the areas of law, political participation, education, employment, healthcare, and other spheres of economic, social, and cultural life. The reason for the emphasis on individual rights should be evident: women are everywhere in the world and do not in themselves constitute a distinctive people, community, and culture integrally tied to a specific bioregion in the way that indigenous peoples are. So, the strategy of specifying and enhancing their individual human rights makes more sense.

Second, in 1995, the power of coordinated women's human rights movements – both local and otherwise – was dramatically and symbolically demonstrated at the Beijing Conference on Women's Rights. There, women's NGOs launched a counter-conference of sorts outside the official UN conference, but in tandem with it, to initiate cross-cultural dialogue about local interpretations of women's rights and to share ideas and collective experience of practical strategies for their implementation and enhancement. It could be argued that the women's movements came of age in coordinating and empowering themselves for the advancement of their human rights.[22]

Third, during the 2000s, this international women's human rights movement has been initiating local mutual assistance women's NGOs in the areas of education, vocational training, financial support and lending for community projects, and legal and social reform. Examples of these NGOs in the South Asian subcontinent include the Annapurna Mahila Mandel Project, the Bangladesh Rural Advancement Committee, and the Self-Employed Women's Organization.[23] Through such projects – and they are emerging all over the underdeveloped and developing world – we can vividly see the practical strategies and effects of globalization-from-below.

It might be a fitting conclusion to this section on women's human rights to mention special efforts to combat the growing phenomenon of human trafficking with respect to women. Human trafficking in general refers to the recruitment, transportation, and obtaining of persons for labour or other services, through the use of force, fraud, or coercion for the purposes of subjection to involuntary servitude, peonage, and debt bondage.[24] It is, in brief, a modern form of slavery, with all the benefits of 'ownership' to the perpetrators without the 'legality' (referring to past forms of slavery where one person could legally own another). While all types of persons are trafficked – men, women, and children – women in particular are an especially large part of the trafficking trade – principally for the purposes of prostitution and cheap labour. In trafficking, women are lured, duped, and transported by traffickers – which could be a criminal syndicate, family 'business', or some other sort of 'business' enterprise – from an origin country (usually in the Third World) to a destination country (usually in the First World) and then either sold to another or exploited by the trafficker himself (in a continuing exploitative relationship) in the destination country. Immediately, we can see the processes of globalization-from-above at work in helping both to create and to sustain the problem, in at least two respects. First, the reason why these women are vulnerable is due to the conditions of poverty, unemployment, and low wages in their origin countries, which are more often than not exacerbated by the structural adjustment policies of transnational financial institutions and the social effects of exploitative practices of many transnational corporations. Second, the trafficking itself makes parasitical use of relatively sophisticated communication and transport technologies developed by big business. Furthermore, it must be pointed out that the part of the trafficking industry that is sexually exploitative is fuelled by the 'sex tourism' business, which itself employs global technologies of transport, information, and communication.

While it is obviously the case that human trafficking is a significant human rights abuse and is explicitly condemned by the convention of women's human rights, the redress by the international community has come in the form of international conventions and protocols addressing transnational crimes, which include drug and other forms of smuggling as well as human trafficking. Specifically, there is now a UN Protocol to Prevent, Suppress and Punish Trafficking in Persons, Especially Women and Children, which requires signatory states to criminalize human trafficking in their countries (whether they are origin or destination countries). But, since the protocol is only an effort to address the 'criminal' aspect of trafficking – and not part of the human rights regime – it simply calls upon those states to *consider* implementing measures to provide for the physical, psychological, and social recovery of the victims, which means that such redress is not mandatory. Thus, the agents of the practice of global ethics-from-below are left with much work to do in this regard.

Right to a healthy environment

With respect to health and the environment, we encounter a development made possible by two different sets of agents – namely, the UN (and its organs) and the environmental movement (local, regional, and international). There appears to have been a fruitful dialectical interaction between these two types of agents, which has simultaneously moved human rights to recognizing the significance of environmental protection and opened up the environmental movement(s) to greater appreciation of human rights generally.

The right to health as initially framed in the UDHR's Article 25 mandates a standard of living adequate for the health and well-being of self and family, including adequate medical care, necessary social services, and a social security net in the event of unemployment, sickness, or disability. While this might seem to be an inauspicious beginning for linking the right to health to environmental protection, it should be observed that the international public health community (in loose connection with the UN) has always defined human health much more broadly than the standard biomedical model of health, which defines it as the absence of physiological disease. In 1947, for example, the World Health Organization (WHO) defined health as 'a state of complete physical, mental, and social well-being and not merely the absence of infirmity'.[25] In

1966, the International Covenant on Economic, Social, and Cultural Rights (ICESCR) refined the UDHR's Article 25 – reflecting in part the influence of Third World developing countries and their past exploitation by imperial powers – mandated the right of everyone to 'the enjoyment of the highest attainable standard of physical and mental health' and imposed specific obligations on all states (singly and in concert) to help reduce stillborn rates and infant mortality, to improve 'all aspects of environmental and industrial hygiene', and to prevent, treat, and control 'epidemic, endemic, and occupational and other diseases'. This refinement brings to the surface a human rights concern with the quality of the environment.

This environmental concern was ramified considerably by a revised 1984 WHO definition of health, which, under the influence of the growing environmental movement, defined health as 'the extent to which an individual or group is able to develop aspirations and satisfy basic needs', including the ability 'to change or cope with' their natural and social environments.[26] The international public health community has since come to emphasize the underlying conditions that establish the basis for realizing physical, mental, and social well-being, including 'peace, shelter, education, food, income, a stable eco-system, sustainable natural resources, social justice and equity', the lack of which heightens the vulnerability of individuals and groups to a wide range of impairments.[27] Building on the ICESCR Article 12's identification of states' obligations to improve all aspects of environmental and industrial hygiene, various human rights commissions and even the case law of the European Court of Human Rights have interpreted these obligations as recognizing 'the right to a healthy environment', mandating, for example, removing causes of ill health such as pollution and exposure to radioactive substances, as well as others steps to prevent industrial accidents and to protect the environment.[28]

Not insignificantly, international environmental law – a separate regime that emerged from the political pressures of environmental movements as well as from the increasing concern by states that environmental problems are transnational in cause, effect, and scope – has recently converged with human rights law to advance explicitly the human right to a healthy environment, in addition to encouraging a more global approach to the environment requiring action at all levels and by all countries to mitigate problems of 'common concern' to all humanity. Such problems as depletion of the ozone layer, the greenhouse effect, marine pollution, and acid rain – all of which have negative effects on human health, whether directly or indirectly – are trans-boundary phenomena calling for concerted and coordinated actions by all who are (or will be) affected. This convergent development in refining the right to health to extend to a right to a healthy environment was not envisaged mid-century, and its recognition was clearly made possible by agencies of globalization-from-below.

What is interesting and significant about these illustrative social movements is that they have had considerable success, at least as measured by their concerns becoming more mainstream and instantiated in the international community. We have just seen how environmental protection has been incorporated into human rights law. We now have officially recognized international criminal tribunals as well as a developing consensus on criteria and rules for humanitarian intervention. Transnational corporations are now attending to human rights issues. Women's human rights issues are high on the agenda of various NGOs. The rights of indigenous peoples are being actively debated and collective human rights appears to be becoming an accepted new category. Capitalizing on this apparent success, some activists have suggested that the clear potential exists to coordinate many of these movements more systematically in advancing strategies to compel, for example, the adoption of minimum human rights 'floors' or standards in all international trade agreements and lending policies, transnational corporate policies and practices, and state regulatory policies.

Global ethics and the justification of human rights

The justification of human rights seems like a theoretical topic but it has a very practical dimension as well. This practical aspect can be seen in the fact that cultural critics of human rights in various regions of the world – for example, East Asia, the Middle East, Africa, and even the Americas – frequently charge that the human rights advanced by the international community represent nothing more than an attempt by the West to impose its version of moral and political liberalism upon societies, cultures, and traditions that see the moral world quite differently as informed by their own unique philosophies and religions. We believe that such charges are simply wrong-headed, even when they are sincerely made. Sometimes, to be sure, these charges are put forward by state actors interested only in throwing up a smoke screen around their violations of their own citizens' human rights. But sometimes these charges are made also by well-intentioned representatives of cultural, moral, and religious traditions concerned about the possibly deleterious effects of liberalism and capitalism – perceived aspects of globalization-from-above – on their own socio-moral visions and behavioural codes.

The development of the UDHR went through a year-and-a-half-long

process involving delegates from no fewer than fifty-six countries representing quite diverse cultural, moral, political, philosophical, and
religious traditions, ranging across systems and traditions such as, for
example, forms of Western liberalism (from Europe and America),
socialism (from Soviet Russia and the Eastern bloc), Christianity
(Catholic, Protestant, and Orthodox), Hinduism, Buddhism, Islam
(conservative and progressive forms), and Confucianism, among
others. There were in fact some delegations (from both South
America and Europe) that wanted to build into the UDHR explicit
justificatory appeals to certain of these systems. Prominent here
were efforts to invoke theistic concepts (for example, God as the
ultimate source of human rights) and even Thomistic versions of
natural law. In the actual debates of the Third Committee, which
was responsible for producing the final draft of the UDHR, these
efforts were vigorously discussed and thoroughly aired with a somewhat complicated outcome. On the one hand, the delegates viewed
themselves as reaching a pragmatic agreement on a set of essential
human rights norms, eschewing the use of contestable metaphysical
and theological language and appeals (thus, no mention of 'God' or
'natural law'), in order to make the UDHR acceptable in principle
to all the world's cultural and philosophical systems and traditions.
On the other hand, a careful reading of the UDHR reveals elements
of a 'spare' natural law appeal as well as references to some form of
moral intuitionism.

In the first case – pragmatic agreement – one can discern the following possible approaches to human rights justification: either a
simple pragmatic agreement on norms being deemed sufficient in
itself with no further concern for justification, or a pragmatic agreement that permits all the world's cultures and traditions to develop
their own justifications of those norms as appropriate to their worldviews and cultural and moral idioms. In the second case, we find in
the UDHR some rather explicit language (especially in Article 1 and
the 'Preamble') that propounds an inherence view of human rights –
that they inhere in people as such simply by virtue of being human
– and an epistemic claim – that reason and conscience are the means
by which we come to know of people's human rights. The 'inherence
doctrine' seems to imply the claim that human beings share significant
common characteristics in virtue of which some conditions and practices are bad for every human being and some other conditions and
practices are good for every human being, with the whole point of the
declaration being to identify these shared harms and goods and proclaim them to the world. These project a minimal vision of the human
good that amounts to a very spare natural law position, shorn of religious implications, claiming that we share a common human nature

that makes these protections and conditions good for us all. By the same token, in speaking of reason and conscience, and most particularly making appeals to 'the conscience of humanity', the declaration also forwards the view that all normal human beings (of mature age, sufficient comprehension, and the like) can have unaided access to (or intuit) the basic moral truths represented by human rights.[29]

The upshot of the UDHR's seemingly alternative approaches to the justification of human rights is that it laid the seeds for subsequent alternative developments, which have been spurred by processes of globalization. It is a fact that globalization has enhanced cross-cultural contact, awareness, and exchanges among worldviews, moral and political systems, and religious traditions, involving diverse patterns of reasoning and justification. It is also a fact that these processes have affected the international human rights community's awareness and explicit acknowledgement – emergent in the early 1980s and continuing to the present – that human rights norms and their recognition are contextually imbedded, interpreted, and justified in culturally diverse ways. Such acknowledgement can be seen in UN conferences about human rights, the rise of governmentally sponsored human rights dialogues, and the emergence of non-governmental cross-cultural and cross-traditional dialogues about the interpretation and justification of human rights norms.[30] All this activity, in turn, has resulted in the explicit awareness and acknowledgement by the human rights movement itself that there are different approaches to the issue of justification. Four approaches appear particularly important.

Pragmatic consensus

To begin with, it must be said that there are many human rights scholars and advocates who regard the pragmatic international consensus on human rights as a largely self-sufficient and legally binding compact among states needing no further justification. Even though this consensus is progressively evolving in terms of refining previously identified norms and identifying new ones (as illustrated earlier), these scholars and advocates regard this evolving consensus exclusively as a pragmatic process of negotiation and attainment of new practical developments. This is not to say, however, that the view of what this pragmatic consensus means at a deeper level has gone unchanged since the time of the UDHR. Quite the contrary, since some scholars and advocates have offered meta-reasons (for want of a better term) for accepting the self-sufficiency of the pragmatic consensus. Two such lines of reasoning appear dominant in this approach.[31]

One line of reasoning stems from the postmodern position that is sceptical of any attempt to ground human rights norms in essentialist understandings of human nature. This position regards all such appeals as philosophically troublesome because they are no more than quasi-mythical creations of outmoded currents of thought driven by anxieties over possible nihilist or relativist implications of our lacking absolute foundations for moral claims. A second line of reasoning, while agreeing with this critique of foundationalist thinking, gives another sort of meta-reason for accepting the self-sufficient consensus, appealing to history and arguing that all essentialist efforts to ground human rights have been shown to be futile in the light of past and continuing human rights atrocities. History, in effect, demonstrates that human rights can have no foundation whatsoever in natural human moral attributes, since these atrocities explode the myth of a supposed natural human pity or solidarity as being either innate or universally distributed. For both of these lines of reasoning, the lesson is the same: all that we have to rely on is our collective desire not to be similarly abused in the future, to which we respond by prudentially creating a pragmatic consensus about human rights and doing all we can to maintain it in the full knowledge that it is unfortunately but unavoidably fragile.

It might be commented here that the bare invocation of a pragmatic consensus has the strength of focusing exclusively on behaviour and avoiding possibly indeterminate philosophical disagreement. By the same token, its weakness is its failure to engage people, communities, and traditions on matters dear to them – their deepest beliefs – that if engaged, rather than dismissed almost out of hand, might result in greater social acceptance of human rights norms in the form of a cultural human rights ethos. Moreover, it is not clear that its eschewal of essentialist or foundational claims of any sort is finally correct (see the next section for contrary views).

Moral intuitionism

Although seemingly similar to the aforementioned pragmatic position, another type of view explicitly embraces and builds on the UDHR's epistemic appeals to reason and conscience.[32] The apparent similarity to the preceding approach is this: human rights norms need no explicit justification in essentialist understandings of human nature or the person. But the similarity ends there, for this view goes on to argue that these norms need no such justification because they identify claims that are logically prior to any theoretical justification whatsoever and can be used to critique the very propriety of trying to provide such justification. It is argued, for example, that, if any moral theory were to sanction the indiscriminate torture of innocent children, then that very fact would demonstrate the bankruptcy of the theory itself. Crucial norms of the human rights variety, then, precede theory, and to use theory to justify these norms is question-begging if not downright absurd. This position goes on to distinguish primary moral intuitions (such as non-torture) from other secondary human rights norms that are an outgrowth of them (for example, norms of physical and civil security), since the latter are necessary to instantiate the former in a more complete protective system. In effect, this approach interprets the pragmatic consensus as epistemically, rather than metaphysically, grounded and then further developed on a rational basis to preserve and expand these intuitions – putting reason in the service of the primary moral intuitions.

Of course, appeals to moral intuition to ground the consensus epistemically will doubtless be unconvincing to those who view any and all intuitions as no more than contingent products of social conditioning. This may be the position's Achilles heel, so to speak, but there is also no gainsaying the fact that virtually all moral systems and traditions rest at some level on appeal to intuition – considered intuitions no doubt, but intuitions nonetheless. Indeed, there are considerable efforts currently underway to resuscitate early twentieth-century positions on moral intuitionism, many of which appear quite promising and easily adaptable to the human rights context.[33] One might also consider as a strength of this position that it coordinates very nicely with the human rights movement's distinction between non-derogative and derogative rights, with the former being construed as foundational intuitions of the human rights system and the latter being construed as fences, so to speak, that preserve and protect the more fundamental rights. This approach, then, may capture the very logic of human rights development.

Overlapping Consensus

Yet another group of human rights scholars and advocates tend to interpret the international consensus as a cross-cultural overlapping agreement on practical norms that is explicitly supported by diverse cultural, moral, religious, or philosophical schemes.[34] This approach builds upon the UDHR's attempt to craft an agreement on human rights norms in such a way as to be acceptable in principle to diverse peoples and traditions, and it views these schemes as alternative and complementary ways of justifying human rights norms, in which peoples and communities are encouraged to develop their own ways of justifying the norms in local cultural idioms. This approach, then, emphasizes and capitalizes on the fact that there are diverse cultural justifications all of which are on par, so to speak, since in our post-modern age we must recognize that no one cultural justification is likely to become dominant or succeed in convincing others outside a given culture that only it is reasonable and true.

This sort of approach is sometimes viewed as an extension of John Rawls's understanding of Western liberal values in a constitutional democracy as an overlapping consensus supported by diverse comprehensive schemes held by its citizens but now applied in an analogous manner to international human rights norms. One recent thinker characterized the logic of this position quite aptly in writing that 'the regime of human rights should rely on many foundational arguments. A human rights regime that welcomes an overlapping consensus is more compatible with moral pluralism . . . the evidence has only increased on the side of the idea that many cultures can converge in support of human rights.'[35] The 'convergence in support' nicely captures the notion that the diverse cultural justifications may function in a complementary manner to provide a coordinated set of foundational arguments, or one large justification with many ancillary supports.

This overlapping consensus approach clearly addresses the weakness of the self-sufficient pragmatic consensus view by encouraging peoples and communities to develop their own ways of justifying human rights, thus helping to ensure social acceptance of and compliance with the norms. It may, however, suffer from some weaknesses of its own. One is its optimism about convergent justifications, for it is possible that, as cultural justifications are shared, their adherents might discern some deep incompatibilities between them. A second is that the fact of mere agreement on reasons does not in itself look like a justification; that is, the fact that we agree on something does not in itself demonstrate why we *ought* to, implying perhaps that some other justificatory argument may be needed. By the same token, however, this approach may respond by pointing out the possibility that, in exploring the deeper reasons for why diverse cultures are able to reach a practical consensus, it might well find a convincing argument or justification acceptable to all, and that therefore its strategy leaves the door open to this possibility in a way that other approaches to human rights justification might not.

Natural law and capabilities

We have already seen that the UDHR itself forwards a spare natural law justification of human rights that is predicated on the notion that certain conditions and practices are harmful for all human beings and other conditions and practices are beneficial for all, in virtue of their common humanity. It does appear that there are many human rights scholars and advocates who accept this line of argument, whether or not they use the language of 'natural law' (many do not because of its traces of religious resonance).[36] In addition, of course, there are many human rights thinkers and advocates who are religious and openly embrace various aspects of the natural tradition in a robust manner. A particularly interesting and increasingly influential approach that does not use such language at all but nonetheless functions like a natural law argument combined with an effort at identifying an overlapping consensus is Martha Nussbaum's capabilities approach, developed in part with Amartya Sen. This approach explicitly attempts to identify a range of 'central elements of truly human functioning that can command a broad cross-cultural consensus' that she suggests permits us to understand why diverse cultures accept human rights.

In effect, Nussbaum's basic capabilities of life, bodily health and integrity, imagination and thought, emotional attachment, affiliation, and control over one's environment, among others, identify shared rationales for cross-cultural agreement on basic human rights norms. At the same time, however, her argument for why these capabilities (and human rights) are important is integrally tied to a vision of truly human functioning applicable to all in virtue of their common humanity. True enough, these capabilities can take different cultural forms, but the fact that they are all necessary and crucial for human functioning is her basic claim, and therefore it certainly counts as a minimal natural law position in defence of human rights. When one realizes this and then reviews the literature pertaining to human rights justification, it appears that there is no human rights scholar or advocate who fails to relate human rights in a significant justificatory manner to the recognition of common causes of human suffering and common capabilities necessary for human agency and well-being. The conclusion that we draw is that the natural law approach to the justification of human rights is not only alive but flourishing.

The weakness of this approach comes principally in the form of its possible association with a dominant religious tradition (Christianity and more specifically Catholicism), which may make it unpalatable to other traditions and communities. By the same token, however, if one pares away this religious association, as the UDHR framers did – with other subsequent human rights advocates following suit – then we discover a strength of this approach in the fact that many traditions and cultures have strands of natural law thinking (or functional analogues to it) internal to them, making it possible for them (and all of us) to identify and work with a very powerful line of justification.

Concluding reflections

In concluding this chapter, we might note how human rights norms have gained considerable authority both in response to cross-boundary global crises and because of the processes of globalization. We have seen how ideas about human rights have become organizationally, institutionally, legally, and socially connected with several important developments concerning, respectively, humanitarian intervention, transnational business, indigenous peoples, women, and environmental health. While we distinguished the diverse theoretical arguments people have made to justify human rights norms, we can also witness, somewhat ironically, that these diverse arguments have in fact worked cumulatively to embed those norms more deeply into local cultures and into common, widely shared assumptions of our age. Since the broader practices of global ethics are significantly influenced by human rights norms, this chapter has attempted to provide some essential groundwork for understanding and appreciating more fully the ethical dimension of this volume's subsequent chapters.

Notes

1. This chapter is a considerably revised, reorganized, and compacted (with the addition of some new material) version of Twiss, 'History, Human Rights, and Globalization'.
2. Some of the observations about human rights in this section are drawn from Twiss, 'Moral Grounds and Plural Cultures'.
3. Falk, 'The Making of Global Citizenship'.
4. See, e.g., Monshipouri and Welch, 'The Search for International Human Rights and Justice'.
5. See, e.g., Lepard, *Rethinking Humanitarian Intervention*.
6. See, e.g., Sands (ed.), *From Nuremberg to The Hague*; and McGoldrick et al. (eds), *The Permanent International Criminal Court*.
7. Green, 'Religions and the Ethics of International Business'.
8. Howard-Hassmann, 'The Second Great Transformation'.
9. Zipkin, 'Getting Religion on Corporate Ethics'.
10. Santoro, *Profits and Principles*, see especially pp. 114–58.
11. On communication and information technology, see, e.g., Metzl, 'Information Technology and Human Rights'.
12. Falk, 'The Global Promise of Social Movements'.
13. The text of the UDHR can be found in Brownlie and Goodwin-Gill (eds), *Basic Documents on Human Rights*, pp. 23–8.

14. 'International covenants' refer to the ICCPR and ICESCR, the texts of which can also be found in Brownlie and Goodwin-Gill (eds), *Basic Documents on Human Rights*, pp. 348–57.

15. The text of the Declaration on the Right of Development can be found in Brownlie and Goodwin-Gill (eds), *Basic Documents on Human Rights*, pp. 83–7.

16. UN Declaration on the Rights of Indigenous Peoples (2007), available at <http://www.un.org/esa/socdev/unpfii/documents/DRIPS_en.pdf> (last accessed 23 January 2015).

17. See Jones, 'Human Rights, Group Rights, and Peoples' Rights', as well as Kingsbury, 'Reconciling Five Competing Conceptual Structures of Indigenous Peoples' Claims in International and Comparative Law'.

18. See Glendon, *A World Made New*.

19. See, e.g., Sen, *Development as Freedom*.

20. Nussbaum, 'Religion and Women's Human Rights'.

21. The text of the Convention on the Elimination of All Forms of Discrimination against Women can be found in Brownlie and Goodwin-Gill (eds), *Basic Documents on Human Rights*, pp. 388–99.

22. See Korey, 'Human Rights NGOs', and Bazilli, 'Reflections of a Global Women's Activist'. It is important to note that, while NGO conferences are now a standard feature of all UN international conferences, they still become 'counter-conferences' of sorts because NGO voices are somewhat marginalized by UN member states and are often shunted aside (even to different locations) by the governments of the countries hosting the international conferences.

23. See Nussbaum, *Women and Human Development*.

24. See Human Trafficking Project, *Florida Responds to Human Trafficking*, and Coonan, 'Human Rights in the Sunshine State'. The law has, in fact, been passed by the Florida legislature in spring 2006. We are also indebted to Monica Esquibel's BA Honors Thesis on 'Human Trafficking: A Violation of Human Rights, a Universal Issue'.

25. Cited in Mann et al. (eds), *Health and Human Rights*, p. 8.

26. Ibid. p. 8.

27. 1986 *Ottawa Charter for Health Promotion*, cited in Mann, *Health and Human Rights*, p.17.

28. Cançado Trindade, 'Environmental Protection and the Absence of Restrictions on Human Rights'. See also Murphy, *The United States and the Rule of Law in International Affairs*, ch. 9, and Shelton, 'Environmental Rights'.

29. See Morsink, *The Universal Declaration of Human Rights*, pp. 280–301.

30. For further insight on such dialogues, see Twiss, 'Comparative Ethics and Intercultural Human Rights Dialogues'.
31. Examples include Rorty, 'Human Rights, Rationality, and Sentimentality', among many of his other essays, and Ignatieff, *Human Rights as Politics and Idolatry*.
32. Examples here include Morsink, *The Universal Declaration of Human Rights*, and Little, 'The Nature and Basis of Human Rights'.
33. Particularly suggestive here are Thomson, *The Realm of Rights*, and Audi, *Moral Knowledge and Ethical Character*.
34. Examples here include Taylor, 'A World Consensus on Human Rights?', and Gutman, 'Introduction'. See also Reeder, 'Foundations without Foundationalism'.
35. Gutman, 'Introduction'.
36. For examples, see Perry, 'Are Human Rights Universal?', and his *The Idea of Human Rights*, as well as Nussbaum, *Women and Human Development*, and her 'Capabilities and Human Rights'.

2 The Earth Charter

A global ethic is one that seeks to be authoritative for a global community. Universal in intent, it sets forth the obligations of 'global citizenship'.[1] It is not a consensus in the minimal sense of a pragmatic compact based on mutual self-interest, but rather an aspirational agreement on 'what is best in us' and what we must do and become to achieve a life together for the common good. J. Ronald Engel says: 'The Earth Charter may be viewed as a culminating product of repeated attempts since the founding of the United Nations in 1945 to rewrite the global social compact on more covenantal lines'.[2] A statement of a global ethic such as the 1948 Universal Declaration of Human Rights (UDHR) or the Declaration towards a Global Ethic adopted by the 1993 centenary Parliament of the World's Religions can be said to have two phases of affirmation. The first affirms that a global community of some sort, such as 'we the peoples of the United Nations' or 'women and men who have embraced the precepts and practices of the world's religions', already agrees on the moral norms that have now been clarified and rearticulated. The second phase promotes the statement so it is known and accepted and its functioning as normative can be strengthened and expanded. Thus a global ethic is the expression of an emerging global community and at the same time aspires further to establish this community – it is both *of* global community and *for* it.

Seen in this light, the Earth Charter is an important achievement not only because of its content but also because of the process that created it. It articulates an ethics intended to expedite the formation of 'a sustainable global society founded on respect for nature, universal human rights, economic justice and a culture of peace' ('Preamble'). In its drafting, the Earth Charter built on and synthesized other statements already accepted at the international and national levels. It also drew from philosophy, religious and cultural traditions, legal scholarship, civil society groups of all kinds, and the findings of science. In addition to its extensive research, the drafting process conducted what has been called 'the most participatory consultation of any document in history'[3] before finalizing a text in 2000. The Earth Charter is not an intergovernmental instrument but a civil society document or people's treaty seeking to attain the status of a 'soft law' declaration like that of the UDHR which it emulates. Its political future cannot be predicted, but with wide and growing endorsement and increasing use in education and by non-governmental organizations (NGOs) and community groups, the Earth Charter has already been having a significant impact. In this chapter, we trace the history of the proposal for a universal declaration on the environment, from its roots in the post-Second World War environmental movement through the international documents that are the Earth Charter's direct predecessors. We describe the creation and promotion of the Earth Charter before considering its ethical content. The narrative of its genesis casts light on the ways a global ethic is conceived as normative, as is also true of the UDHR.[4]

Historical background

In the first half of the twentieth century, the environmental movement focused mainly on two areas of concern, generally stated: land and wildlife conservation and management of natural resources. After the Second World War and the founding of the United Nations in 1945, environmental consciousness increased and changed as new issues began to impact on public awareness. One set of issues concerned various new kinds of toxic pollution, including radioactive fallout from nuclear testing, acid rain, marine pollution, and pesticides and their effect on human health as well as on the natural world. Rachel Carson's *Silent Spring*, published in 1962, is now seen as emblematic of a change in attitudes towards the environment. The oil crisis of 1973 dramatized the potential effects of scarcity of critical resources. Scientific knowledge of the effects of new substances and technologies grew at the same time that new substances and technologies continued to be developed and used. Understanding increased that human practices can have consequences that are unforeseen and unpredictable as well as far-reaching and long-lasting. It became apparent that environmental damage, exemplified by toxic pollution, is not local or national, but regional in scope. Concern also began to arise about whether continued economic growth and rapid population increase might exceed the Earth's carrying capacity.[5] The complex and systemic character of environmental issues began to be better appreciated, and environmental consciousness started to open to a planetary horizon, as the concept of 'the biosphere' came to prominence.[6]

In 1972, the UN Conference on the Human Environment was convened in Stockholm with the slogan 'Only One Earth'. One hundred and fourteen governments were represented and there was a dynamic gathering of NGOs. The Stockholm Conference was a milestone, as it formally placed environmental concerns on the global international agenda and called for cooperation on these concerns by all countries belonging to the United Nations. As Lynton Caldwell notes: 'The concept of the collective responsibility of nations for the quality and protection of the Earth as whole did not gain political recognition until the years immediately preceding the Stockholm Conference.'[7] Among the immediate outcomes of the Stockholm Conference was the creation of the United Nations Environment Programme (UNEP), which has played an important informational and catalytic role.

How did the Stockholm Conference envision environmental problems? In its title, 'human environment' refers not only to non-human nature but also to the whole environment of human beings, artificial as well as natural. Its declaration states that 'both aspects of man's environment, the natural and the man-made, are essential to his well-being and to the enjoyment of human rights – even the right to life itself' (Proclamation 1), thus making explicit its continuity with human rights documents. It refers throughout to the need to protect 'resources' yet affirms that 'states have ... the sovereign right to exploit their own resources' consistent with no harm to the resources of other states. The declaration is human-centred or 'anthropocentric'; while it warns of a crisis, it defines this crisis in terms of harm to human beings. The principle of intergenerational equity is already firmly in place, with several mentions of 'future generations' or 'posterity', but there is no mention of 'respect for Nature' or the intrinsic value of non-human life.

The central tension at the Stockholm Conference was one that is no less critical today and is now prominent in discussions of climate change – the tension between environmental concerns and the imperative of 'development' to reduce poverty. Many countries feared that environmental regulations would hamper their efforts to develop economically through restrictions on trade, requirements for less polluting technology, limits on the use of resources, and other measures that would be imposed on them by the already developed countries, whose concerns for the environment could be seen as an elitist luxury. As Jim MacNeill observes:

When the notion of reconciling environment and development was first put forward at the United Nations Conference on the Human Environment in Stockholm in 1972, it was considered revolutionary. Indeed, the conference was barely able to contain the fears and suspicions of most developing and some developed countries that concern for the world's environment threatened their development prospects. Their watchword, taken from the experience of the rich countries in the 1950s and 1960s, was 'development now and environment later, when we think we can afford it'.[8]

Efforts had been made in preparation for Stockholm to convince developing countries that harm to the environment would in fact affect their development negatively, while their environmental problems could be helped by development itself. (For example, poverty may impel people to destroy forests or wildlife in order to survive, or worsen the problems of urbanization.) These concerns are reflected in the Stockholm Declaration, and persist more than four decades later, as the reconciliation of environmental protection with development is a goal still far from attainment.

In May 1982, ten years after the Stockholm Conference, a meeting of 105 governments in Nairobi assessed environmental progress since Stockholm. It issued a statement that reaffirms the 'integrated approach' to environment and development, analyses specific aspects of problems, and calls for action. The Nairobi Declaration does not state any general ethical principles, except to affirm that the Stockholm principles are 'as valid today as they were in 1972' and are 'a basic code of environmental conduct for the years to come' (para. 1). In contrast, in October of the same year the UN General Assembly adopted the World Charter for Nature, with 111 countries in favour, 18 abstentions, and only the United States against. It is possible to dismiss the World Charter as a political exercise intended to embarrass the United States, as it is not legally binding,[9] but its importance as a document of global ethics is clear, especially given its endorsement. The idea for the World Charter for Nature had been put forward at a meeting of the International Union for the Conservation of Nature (IUCN), the world's leading environmental network, which assisted in the drafting.[10]

The difference of the World Charter for Nature from the Stockholm Declaration in tone and vision is noticeable. The first words of its opening section on 'Principles' are 'nature shall be respected and its essential processes shall not be impaired'. The first three of the five Principles make no mention of humans, but call for the preservation of life forms, their habitats, and ecosystems in 'all areas of earth'. Principle Four states that ecosystems and organisms used by man 'shall be managed to achieve and maintain optimum sustainable productivity, but not in such a way as to endanger the integrity of those *other ecosystems or species with which they coexist*' (emphasis added). The World Charter's second section, on 'Functions', enumerates thirteen points emphasizing restraint, renewability, and regeneration, all aspects of sustainability. After the third section, on 'Implementation', the World Charter closes by saying, *inter alia*, that 'mankind is part of nature and life depends on the uninterrupted functioning of natural systems', 'civilization is rooted in nature, which has shaped human culture and influenced all artistic and scientific achievement', and, most strikingly, 'every form of life is unique, warranting respect regardless of its worth to man, and, to accord other organisms such recognition, man must be guided by a moral code of action'. *Earth Ethics* comments that the World Charter for Nature is in fact a

> landmark document in the development of a global environmental ethic. It is the first intergovernmental declaration to affirm respect for nature as the foundation principle of environmental protection . . . However, it does not articulate fully the links between environmental degradation and issues such as poverty and equitable human development and was drafted before the concept of sustainable development was formulated.[11]

In 1983, responding to growing recognition that the environmental crisis was deepening, the UN General Assembly adopted a resolution creating a World Commission on Environment and Development (WCED). Gro Harlem Brundtland of Norway was asked by Secretary General Javier Perez de Cuellar to serve as chair. The commission released its final report, *Our Common Future* (often called the Brundtland Report), in spring 1987. It was this report that gave a central role in environmental debates and policy to the concept of 'sustainable development'.

In its closing pages, *Our Common Future* calls for a universal declaration on environmental principles and sustainable development to serve as the basis for a legally binding convention. It says:

> Building on the 1972 Stockholm Declaration, the 1982 Nairobi Declaration, and many existing international conventions and General Assembly resolutions, there is now a need to consolidate and extend relevant legal principles to guide state behaviour in the transition to sustainable development.[12]

It is this as yet unwritten document that would come to be called an Earth Charter.

The UN General Assembly in the autumn of 1989 called for a second global conference on the environment, its themes and content largely influenced by *Our Common Future*. The United Nations Conference on Environment and Development (UNCED), also called the Earth Summit, met in June 1992 in Rio de Janeiro, attended by representatives of more than 170 countries and 7,000 NGOs.[13] Canadian Maurice Strong was the Secretary General, as he had been at Stockholm twenty years earlier. To adopt an Earth Charter in accord with the recommendation of the Brundtland Commission was one of the stated goals of the Earth Summit in its planning stages. The Earth Charter was to be a declaration strongly ethical in character that would also lay the foundation for legally binding treaties in the foreseeable future. In the previous two decades, the world's countries had adopted over seventy declarations, charters, and treaties concerning cooperation on environment and development. The late 1980s and early 1990s leading up to the Earth Summit were a time of great ferment among civil society groups concerning the environmental crisis and its moral, religious, and spiritual dimensions. In 1978, Thomas Berry's seminal essay 'The New Story' had been published and James Lovelock's *Gaia: A New Look at Life on Earth* came out the following year. In 1986, the Worldwide Fund for Nature, then called the World Wildlife Fund (WWF), held its twenty-fifth anniversary convocation in Assisi with an interfaith dialogue component that issued the Assisi Declarations by five religious traditions.[14] The Global Forum on Environment and Development held in Moscow in January 1990 was attended by over 1,000 participants who included religious leaders from around the world, members of the world's parliaments, scientists, and artists. NGOs including religious groups began to create statements on the environment and many wrote their own 'Earth Charters' from various perspectives. Hoping to contribute to the Earth Summit process, they 'drafted and circulated at least two hundred of their own declarations and people's treaties that address issues of environment, development and social justice'.[15]

An Earth Charter was drafted during the four intergovernmental Preparatory Committees, which developed the documents to be considered for approval by governments at the Earth Summit. Discussions were contentious. An intervention circulated by Daniel Martin during the final Preparatory Committee said:

> There is concern about a growing division between the Earth Charter perspectives of the industrialized nations and the developing countries: one group emphasizing apparently narrow environmental issues, the other concerned about more immediate issues of poverty and development.

There is also a growing fear that agreement will not be reached or that the Earth Charter will be so diluted as to be ineffectual.[16]

Negotiations between governments failed to reach an agreement on a draft of an Earth Charter, and the Earth Charter was removed from the agenda of the Earth Summit so that no draft of it was introduced, discussed, or voted upon at the summit in Rio.[17]

The Earth Summit did, however, bring forth the Rio Declaration, a plan of action entitled Agenda 21, two treaties (on climate change and biodiversity), and a statement on forest principles. The Rio Declaration is a terse statement of twenty-seven principles intended to be 'a blueprint for sustainable development'. It focuses on the obligations of states and equity between states, especially between developed and developing countries, as well as between peoples and social groups. In its brief 'Preamble' the document reaffirms the Stockholm Declaration (with no reference to the World Charter for Nature) and, after calling for 'a new global partnership', uses the phrase 'Recognizing the integral and interdependent nature of the Earth, our home'.[18] Principle 1 reads: 'Human beings are at the centre of concerns for sustainable development. They are entitled to a healthy and productive life in harmony with nature'. This is the extent of references to 'Earth' or 'nature'. The document reiterates the language of the 1986 Declaration on the Right to Development, saying: 'The human person is the central subject of development' (Article 2). The Rio Declaration then reaffirms the sovereign right of states to exploit their own resources, the right to development and the principle of intergenerational equity, and the need to consider the roles and welfare of women, youth, indigenous people (without the s for 'peoples'),[19] and 'people under oppression, domination and oppression'.

The Rio Declaration was not the fulfillment of the WCED's recommendation that a new universal charter be created, nor did it meet the expectations of concerned people in general for a coherent and developed ethical statement. It has little ethical content and is not regarded as inspiring, while many if not most of the NGO 'Earth Charters' begin with a ringing and even poetic announcement of the crisis now facing humanity, and speak of the urgent need for a change of heart, a new vision, and a change of course for civilization. In 1992, this meant for many, as it still does, extending moral duty not only to humans but to the non-human world or 'Nature', recognizing kinship with 'the Earth community' or 'the community of life' – phrases that became familiar and charged with value. But, while these themes had been touched upon in the World Charter for Nature, no such language is found in the Rio Declaration. It and Agenda 21 are entirely human-centred, looking upon nature as having only instrumental value for human welfare.[20]

Creating an Earth Charter

Following the Earth Summit, there was widespread discontent among civil society groups at the failure of the Earth Charter effort. Governments, however, showed no interest immediately post-Rio in restarting the process. Leadership in doing so was provided by Maurice Strong, who had founded the Earth Council to promote the implementation of Agenda 21, and Mikhail Gorbachev, who after the dissolution of the Soviet Union had become the founding president of a new international environmental organization, Green Cross International. In 1994, Strong and Gorbachev came to an agreement to work together on a new Earth Charter Initiative (ECI).[21] Their agreement was facilitated by Jim MacNeill, the former Secretary General of the WCED and principal author of *Our Common Future*, and Ruud Lubbers, Prime Minister of the Netherlands. The project was housed at the headquarters of the Earth Council in Cost Rica. Collaboration with the IUCN was established and an extensive research process was carried out in 1995 and 1996. A global consultation process was begun with a conference at the Hague in spring 1995, and a study of more than fifty international law instruments was prepared by Steven Rockefeller and circulated to all those participating in the consultation process.[22] The Earth Charter process was from the very beginning intended to be inclusive and civil society based, resulting in 'a people's Earth Charter' that could stand on its own even though it would also seek government approval. Adoption by the UN General Assembly was at first aimed for in the year 2000.

In 1997, an independent Earth Charter Commission was formed of eminent persons from all regions. Steven Rockefeller was asked to head an international drafting committee and the work of writing the Earth Charter began. The overall nature of the document was the first matter that had to be decided. The account given by *Earth Ethics* casts light on the undertaking of a 'global ethic'.

> It was established that the Charter should be: a declaration of fundamental ethical principles for environmental conservation and sustainable development; composed of principles of enduring significance that are widely shared by people of all races, cultures, religions, and ideological traditions; relatively brief and concise; a document with a holistic perspective and an ethical and spiritual vision; composed in language that is inspiring, clear and uniquely valid and meaningful in all languages; a

declaration that adds significant new dimensions of values to what has already been articulated in relevant documents.[23]

The first drafting meeting was held in January 1997 and produced ten versions of a Working Draft. Another ten were written during the 'Rio + 5' Forum convened by the Earth Council in Rio de Janeiro in March 1997 to assess progress on Agenda 21. 'During the six days of the Rio + 5 Forum', Steven Rockefeller recollects,

> the drafting committee issued a new text every day and conducted an open dialogue with anyone at the Forum who wished to become involved. The Earth Charter Commission met during the final two days of the Forum. The final text of the first draft – the Benchmark Draft – was finished at 4:30 a.m. on the final day of the Forum and was presented to the media by the Commission shortly thereafter.[24]

The *Earth Times* reported that the issue of the Earth Charter had 'dominated' the conference, adding: 'Delegates at the forum representing indigenous groups had been enthusiastic in their support of the Charter but many delegates and observers at the Forum [said] it is too "nature-centered" and ignores mainstream Judeao-Christian–Muslim values.'[25] Indeed, the first words of the draft are not only 'Earth is our home and home to all living things', but also 'Earth itself is alive', and in Principle 9 there is a reference to 'Mother Earth'. There followed an intensive series of conferences and meetings throughout the world for the next two years. Earth Charter National Committees began to be set up. Two years after Rio + 5 an international drafting meeting was held to bring the Earth Charter closer to its final form and Benchmark Draft II was released. Meetings and consultations, including multi-stakeholder forums, national and regional meetings, and a review by lawyers from the IUCN, all continued. Input from over 5,000 people and hundreds of organizations and groups was ultimately received. A final review was conducted by the Earth Charter Commission at the headquarters in Paris of the United Nations Organization for Education, Science, and Culture (UNESCO) in March of 2000 and the final version of the Earth Charter was published on 24 March. The commission reserved the right to make changes if there were compelling reasons to do so.

Finalization of the text of the Earth Charter and a launch ceremony at the Hague in June 2000 was followed by an endorsement campaign. Efforts began to gain some degree of recognition by governments taking part in the World Summit on Sustainable Development (WSSD) in Johannesburg in 2002.[26] As a result of ongoing advocacy by members of the Earth Charter Commission and others, the Johannesburg Declaration included wording almost identical to the opening paragraph of the Earth Charter. It reads:

> From this continent, the cradle of humanity, we declare, through the Plan of Implementation of the World Summit on Sustainable Development and the present Declaration, *our responsibility to one another, to the greater community of life and to our children.* (para. 6, emphasis added)

As well, in spite of resistance to talk of 'ethics' in the prevailing emphasis by governments on implementation of Agenda 21, the Plan of Implementation states: 'We acknowledge the importance of ethics for sustainable development.' At Johannesburg, the ECI also established partnerships on education with the governments of Costa Rica, Honduras, Mexico, Niger, UNESCO, and thirteen NGOs.

The ECI has since developed an array of programs supported by an ever-growing network coordinated by its secretariat at the UN-mandated University for Peace in Costa Rica. [27] Over 4,000 international, national and local organizations and institutions in all sectors, representing many millions of people, have endorsed the Earth Charter, as have thousands of individuals. A wide variety of workshops, courses, conferences, dialogues, exhibits, online programs and arts activities promote the Earth Charter's global ethics of sustainability. The ECI has made a major commitment to 'education for sustainable development' at all levels and in diverse settings, collaborating with UNESCO in the context of the UN Decade for Education for Sustainable Development (2005–15). It has developed *EC-Assess: The Earth Charter Ethics-Based Assessment Tool* for use in civil society, business, and government;[28] one of the tool's applications has been to the 'post-2015 development agenda' of the United Nations, referred to as the Sustainable Development Goals (succeeding the Millennium Development Goals (MDGs), which had a target date of 2015).

Advocates of the Earth Charter are increasingly aware that implementation of its ethics with 'strong sustainability' is likely to require extensive, even radical, transformation of the world's legal and economic systems along with cultural change.[29] Nonetheless, hope has not been abandoned that in the fullness of time the charter will be adopted by the UN General Assembly.[30] The plan is that, as recognition, formal endorsements, and implementation by local and even national governments accumulate, pressure will mount on the governments of member states, the only entities that can propose and vote on a resolution in the General Assembly. This civil society strategy had been quite consciously adopted by Maurice Strong and Mikhail Gorbachev as they started the Earth Charter project. It had worked in other cases, such as the 1979 Convention on the Elimination of all Forms of Discrimination against Women; this decision signals confidence in the growing importance of non-state actors in global governance.

Ethics of the Earth Charter

From its beginnings, the idea of the Earth Charter was that it would be an ethical statement comprehensive and compelling enough to provide guiding norms for solving the global environmental crisis in all its complexity and profundity. It would need to embrace human rights, equitable and sustainable development, and the well-being of the non-human natural world, and to do all this in a way that would unite people rather than dividing them. It would build on but go beyond earlier declarations and treaties, be universal in reflecting shared values, and also 'inspiring'. In addition, it would be able to serve as a basis for law. This was indeed a challenging task, as it would be necessary to judge which 'fundamental' and shared ethical principles should be included, as well as which principles from existing international law should be chosen and how these should be worded, and also whether new principles should be defined. Still early in the process, in his essay 'The Emerging World Ethic and the Earth Charter Project', Steven Rockefeller asked:

> What fundamental principles regarding the nature of the universe and life on Earth should be affirmed? Should the language of the sacred, which has not been used in international legal documents, be employed in the Earth Charter? If so, how? Should the Earth Charter give expression to certain attitudes such as thanksgiving, wonder, humility, reverence for life?

Finally, how should all of this content be organized?[31]

The structure of the final version of the Earth Charter reflects an agreement between those who felt that the text should be a short poetic document, and those who insisted that it mention their particular urgent concerns in specific ways. Steven Rockefeller explains that, while some wanted a text with eight or ten principles, 'the drafting committee soon discovered that many other groups – particularly those in the developing world where people were struggling on the front lines of social change – urgently needed a more substantial document'.[32] In a consultation process that attempted to be as inclusive as possible, an enormous exercise in comparative ethics, there was much debate and disagreement. Certain parameters were maintained. Rockefeller describes the process:

> There *were* times when it took as much as two years to find acceptable language. And there were times when we had to abandon certain ideas simply because disagreements persisted and there was not a consensus. In most cases, however, we were able to find common ground.[33]

Two interesting examples of results of the consultation process are given here. First, the decision was made not to use the phrase 'intrinsic value' because it is problematic for Buddhists, but to keep the phrase 'every form of life has value regardless of its worth to human beings' (Principle 1.a).[34] Second, it was decided not to use the word 'compassion' in the section dealing with humane treatment of animals (Principle 15), although it is used in Principle 2, because of objections by people from indigenous, especially Arctic, hunting cultures. Instead, the wording 'respect and consideration' for all living beings was accepted.[35] A very important rule in consultation and drafting was that of building on previous agreements, so that 'the Commission and drafting committee were clear with all who participated in the consultation process that the Earth Charter could not retreat from any principle that had been established in international law and United Nations summit meetings', Rockefeller recalls.[36]

The final result is a layered document with a 'Preamble' in five parts, the 'Introduction' beginning: 'We stand at a critical moment in Earth's history', followed by 'Earth, Our Home', 'The Global Situation', 'The Challenges Ahead', and 'Universal Responsibility', followed by sixteen main principles, and a conclusion, 'The Way Forward'. The sixteen main principles are divided into four parts, and the four principles in the first part are intended to be broad and general enough to serve as a summary of the ethics of the whole Earth Charter. The sixteen main principles each have below them two to six additional 'principles', sixty-one in all, which are often more in the nature of prescriptions or requirements for action that would realize in practice the more general principle. The decision had initially been made to state the principles as imperatives, following the Tokyo Declaration of the WCED,[37] but the principles can also be read as affirmations of commitment, vows, or promises. J. Ronald Engel, a core member of the international drafting committee, points out that these 'pledges' are open-ended and have a transcendent reference, since 'they lead at every point to our need to reach out to more than we can ever experience, do or know'.[38] The 'Preamble' ends: 'We affirm in hope the following interdependent principles for a sustainable way of life as the common standard by which the conduct of all individuals, organizations, businesses, governments, and transnational institutions is to be guided and assessed' ('Preamble', para. 5), so that all these entities are identified as moral agents held accountable by this global ethic.

Abelardo Brenes, also a member of the drafting committee, convincingly argues that responsibility is the core moral principle of the Earth Charter,[39] and suggests that the first four principles – to respect, care, build, and secure – converge in the norm of responsibility. While rights language is not absent from the Earth Charter, responsibility is primary. Responsibility presupposes consciousness both of interdependence and of a critical situation that calls for action; it also presupposes the freedom to act. Thus the Earth Charter in its 'Preamble' uses language of awareness and awakening – 'recognize' or 'realize' – and also offers a worldview, a picture of what it is that we must recognize. 'To move forward we must recognize that in the midst of a magnificent diversity of cultures and life forms, we are one human family and one Earth community with a common destiny' ('Preamble', para. 1); 'Humanity is part of an evolving universe. Earth, our home, is alive with a unique community of life' ('Preamble', para. 2). We are responsible because we are free; thus the Earth Charter declares: 'The choice is ours, form a global partnership to care for Earth and one another, or risk the destruction of ourselves and the diversity of life. Fundamental changes are needed in our values, institutions and ways of living' ('Preamble', para. 4). Responsibility is 'universal but differentiated' (a concept defined in earlier international documents) in the sense that the responsibility one has depends in kind and degree on the freedom and capacity of the agent; Principle 2.b states: 'Affirm that with increased freedom, knowledge and power comes increased responsibility to protect the common good.'[40] Acceptance of responsibility arises from the understanding that people and all forms of life are not separate but interdependent. While there is a prudential aspect to seeing the interdependence of things – namely, that, if others do not survive or flourish, neither will I – this does not exclude acceptance of responsibility for others as well as oneself in the spirit of the common good, knowing that we are part of one another in 'the Earth community'. The fifth and final paragraph of the 'Preamble' is entitled 'Universal Responsibility', a phrase often used by the Dalai Lama and adopted by the research and consultation of the Earth Charter process. 'Universal' here has a double sense: all of us are responsible, and it is for all others that each of us is responsible. Embrace of responsibility in the Earth Community leads at once to the basic norms of 'respect' and 'care'.

Engel situates the Earth Charter within the history of debates on the nature of democracy and takes the centrality of the norm of responsibility as showing that 'its grounding premise is the democratic faith that human beings have the rational and moral capacity to govern themselves for the common good of all under the uncertain evolutionary and historical circumstances of life on this planet'.[41] He notes that, in articulating its vision of this 'democratic faith', the Earth Charter

> strongly affirms twentieth century doctrines of human rights. It retrieves strands within the democratic tradition that have been muted in recent years, in particular, our common humanity, the embeddedness of the human community within the order of nature, and the dependence of politics and ethics upon a substantive ontology or conception of the good.[42]

Thus the Earth Charter affirms human dignity as well as the value of all life forms. It calls for equity in sharing the benefits of development at the same time that it critiques the idea of development as growth by saying: 'We must realize that when basic needs are met, human development is primarily about being more, not having more' ('Preamble', para. 4). It finds the causes of the present crisis in failure to establish peace and justice in human communities, as it also squarely blames 'dominant patterns of production and consumption' and 'unprecedented rise in human population' for 'environmental devastation, the depletion of resources, and a massive extinction of species' ('Preamble', para. 3) along with the undermining of communities and threats to security.

The Earth Charter overall adopts an 'eco-justice' ethical approach, a term first developed in Christian theology for an ethical perspective that holds together concerns for justice in human societies, for the welfare of future generations, and for the flourishing of all life and ecosystems.[43] An eco-justice approach views these concerns as indivisible; care for God's creation must be care for all of it in its wholeness. It has long been generally recognized (not only in churches and other religious contexts) that, when there is pollution, other damage to the natural world, or breakdown of ecosystems, the impact on humans will be worst on those already marginalized and disadvantaged. Thus social justice concerns for the welfare of human beings are inextricably bound up with concerns for the non-human 'environment'.[44]

Beyond this immediate and pressing pragmatic reality, there is a deeper and more ontological one. As Larry Rasmussen puts it: 'Nature is not what is around us or where we live but the reason we are alive at all; nature is the reason each and every society and culture that ever existed did so.'[45] As he emphasizes, the reality of the interconnectedness and interdependence not just of all life, but of all that exists, is not only delivered to us by deep feelings or even 'spiritual experience', but is also the testimony of natural science.[46] Therefore, any ethics that separates out the human from the rest of the natural world rests on an empirical falsehood, as well as being at odds with much of the core teachings of the world's religious traditions.[47]

> We will not understand where we are, how we got here, where we might go, and how we might get there so as to live sustainably [Rasmussen says], until our analysis reads history and nature *as one piece*, until we read eco- and social location together. Clarity about sustainability and sustainable development means clarity about nature-in-culture and culture-in-nature on their long journey *together*.[48]

The cosmos is a unity and, on Earth, everything that has evolved has co-evolved. The flourishing of each part interdepends on the well-being of the other parts and of the whole; it is a community held together by the ongoing relationships of its members. The moral is the ecological. This vision is the basis of the ethics of the Earth Charter and is expressed in its repeated use of the phrases 'Earth community' and 'the community of life'.

The Earth Charter, while not theistic, is a 'religious' document in a number of its utterances. It makes clear and powerful references not only to Earth but also, as just mentioned, to the cosmic context: 'Humanity is part of a vast evolving universe' ('Preamble', para. 2). The words 'spiritual' and 'spirituality' are used in several places, and it is stated that 'The protection of Earth's vitality, diversity and beauty is a sacred trust' ('Preamble', para. 2). The Earth Charter evokes emotions that can surely be called 'religious' when it says: 'The spirit of human solidarity and kinship with all life is strengthened when we live with reverence for the mystery of being, gratitude for the gift of life, and humility regarding the human place in nature' ('Preamble', para. 5); or: 'Recognize that peace is the wholeness created by right relationships with oneself, other persons, other cultures, other life, Earth and the larger whole of which all are a part' (Principle 16.f).

The Earth Charter is strongly biocentric in its consistent references to 'the community of life' and to 'the Earth community', 'kinship with all life', 'the larger living world', and 'other life'. It goes beyond the language of the 'value' of life as such to call for the attitudes and practices that arise from valuing of non-human life: respect and care (Principles 1 and 2). While the oneness of humanity, human dignity, and the universality of human rights are affirmed, these are placed within a vaster context. The Earth Charter as a global ethics statement seeking to be normative for a 'global community' clearly proposes expanding the understanding of moral community beyond the global in the sense of 'the human family' to the global in the sense of 'the Earth community' of all life.[49] This biocentrism is perhaps its greatest innovation as a document seeking to be recognized by governments, and still may prove to be an obstacle to its wider acceptance. The commitment of those involved in the consensus-building consultation process nevertheless to preserve this language did not grow only from a conviction of its truth. It came also from the perception that, without such a radical change in shared moral vision, the energy and will to deal adequately with the worsening global environmental crisis surely cannot be mustered in time. The wording of the Earth Charter itself makes this abundantly clear. Its closing section declares: '

> As never before in history, common destiny beckons us to seek a new beginning . . . This requires a change of mind and heart. It requires a new sense of global interdependence and universal responsibility . . . Let ours be a time remembered for the awakening of a new reverence for life. ('The Way Forward', paras 1, 2, 5)

The Earth Charter going forward

Concerning the political future of the Earth Charter, Klaus Bosselman and Prue Taylor suggest several scenarios. They note that a number of international institutions, including UNESCO and the IUCN, have already adopted it as an ethical guide for policy. While a 'decisive step towards soft law recognition' would be recognition by a vote of the UN General Assembly, even without this, another pathway would be

> continued promotion of the Earth Charter within countries and among international organizations . . . up to the point where the Earth Charter reaches a certain omnipresence. This process could lead to its gradual transformation from soft law into a hard law instrument, in much the same way as nascent principles of law gradually gain recognition and status as binding 'customary' international law.[50]

Another scenario for the UN system, different from the 'recognition' just mentioned of the document 'as is' by the General Assembly, would be conversion of the Earth Charter into a UN Draft Earth Charter, which would then be subject to negotiation and revision by member countries before a vote of approval. This process includes the risk of extensive alteration of the existing document. Bosselman and Taylor go on to say:

> However, the most promising path of all is to insist on the Earth Charter's validity as a novel instrument of global law. Never before have so many people, in so many different countries, representing so many countries and religions, reached a consensus on a central theme of humanity. To some extent, the Earth Charter can be celebrated as a global civil society's first and foremost founding document.[51]

This comment locates the Earth Charter at the forefront of an important development in global governance, the greatly increased influence of NGOs or civil society, here used loosely to mean voluntary associations that are neither governmental nor organized for commercial purposes.[52] It is significant that the 1992 Earth Summit is considered to have been a turning point in the role of civil society organizations in relation to the United Nations. NGO participation is now not only sought for implementation of agreements made at international conferences and monitoring compliance; also, according to Michael G. Schecter, 'it is not contestable or indeed hard to demonstrate that NGOs have come to be accepted as integral actors at world conferences, at least in the post-Rio era'.[53] One reason for the growing influence of civil society organizations is increase in their sheer numbers; another is the expertise they amass as groups devoted to particular issues. Governments may not have equivalent information and, if they do, may refuse to share it. The United Nations may have readier access to better information on many issues by dealing directly with NGOs, as well as relying on their extensive networks for implementation of its programmes, as UN authorities often repeat. As this trend of the increased importance of civil society continues, it bodes well for the recognition of the Earth Charter as a soft-law document, as well as as a tool for education and transformation of cultural values. As the Earth Charter is embraced more and more by civil society, acknowledgement and appreciation of it can continue to widen towards the 'omnipresence' spoken of by Bosselman and Taylor.

The Earth Charter was created at the late-twentieth-century confluence of two great streams of ethical concern: concern for universal human rights and concern for the non-human natural world. It aims to epitomize the union of these two ethical concerns in a statement of a new 'Earth ethics' in the hope and determination that this ethics of 'the Earth community' will be the main current of both morality and law in the future. The process by which the Earth Charter has been drafted and endorsed has probably been more broad-based and inclusive, or more 'global' in actuality, than the process of any other global ethics document. In its thoroughgoing commitment to the value of non-human life and the ecological integrity of Earth itself, it is also more fully 'global' in moral scope than any earlier document aspiring to international legal status and acceptance by all the world's peoples. The Earth Charter self-consciously situates itself within the global ethics movement, and without question can be seen within this movement as a landmark and a major achievement. It is too soon to say whether it will succeed, together with other statements of a global ethic, in offering 'a basic vision of shared values to provide an ethical foundation for an emerging world community' ('Universal Responsibility').

Notes

1. Dower, *An Introduction to Global Citizenship*, ch. 2.
2. Engel, 'The Earth Charter as a New Covenant for Democracy', p. 41.
3. Hassan, 'Earth Charter', p. 29.
4. See Glendon, *A World Made New*, for a detailed account of the drafting of the UDHR.
5. See Meadows et al., *The Limits to Growth*.
6. This historical narrative draws on the first two chapters of Caldwell, *International Environmental Policy: Emergence and Dimensions*, as well as the reflections of Callicott, 'Toward a Global Environmental Ethic'.
7. Caldwell, *International Environmental Policy: Emergence and Dimensions*, p. 55.
8. MacNeill et al., *Beyond Interdependence*, p. 30.
9. Caldwell, *International Environmental Policy: Emergence and Dimensions*, pp. 90–3.
10. Founded in 1948, the IUCN is, according to its website, 'the world's oldest and largest environmental network, with more than 1,200 government and NGO Members and almost 11,000 volunteer experts in some 160 countries', as well as six commissions, available at <http://www.iucn.org> (last accessed 15 January 2015).
11. *Earth Ethics*, 'History of the Earth Charter', p. 16.
12. World Commission on Environment and Development, *Our Common Future*, p. 332.
13. Schecter, *United Nations-Sponsored World Conferences*, p. 197.
14. See Worldwide Fund for Nature, *The Assisi Declarations*.
15. *Earth Ethics*, 'History of the Earth Charter', p. 16.
16. Martin, 'An Intervention on the Earth Charter', p. 1.

17. Vilela and Corcoran, 'Building Consensus on Shared Values', p. 18.
18. United Nations Department of Publication Information, *Agenda 21*, p. 5.
19. The use of the final *s* in 'Indigenous Peoples' is considered to be of great political importance as 'peoples' are comparable to 'nations', while the generic 'people' is similar to 'populations', a quantitative term which has no connotations of the distinct cultural and historical identities of 'peoples' or of their sovereignty as 'nations'. See Ewen (ed.), *Voice of Indigenous Peoples*, p. 22.
20. See Brown (ed.), *The Ethical Dimensions of the United Nations Program on Environment and Development, Agenda 21*.
21. In what follows we rely on Vilela and Corcoran, 'Building Consensus on Shared Values', and *Earth Ethics*, 'History of the Earth Charter'.
22. Rockefeller, *Principles of Environmental Conservation and Sustainable Development*.
23. *Earth Ethics*, 'History of the Earth Charter', p. 17.
24. Sides, 'Ethics and the Earth Charter', p. 8; see Earth Charter Commission, 'The Earth Charter, Benchmark Draft I'.
25. Freeman and Yoon, 'How Important is an "Earth Charter"?', pp. 1, 7.
26. The following account is based on Earth Charter Steering Committee and International Secretariat, 'The Earth Charter at the Johannesburg Summit'.
27. Detailed information on all aspects of the ECI and its work can be found at <http://www.earthcharterinaction.org> (last accessed 15 January 2015).
28. See AtKisson et al., *EC-Assess*.
29. See Westra and Vilela, *The Earth Charter, Ecological Integrity and Social Movements*.
30. See the statements by Mikhail Gorbachev and Parvez Hassan in Corcoran et al. (eds), *The Earth Charter in Action*, pp. 9–10, 29–31; on its website the ECI includes 'recognition and endorsement' by the United Nations as one of its five main goals; available at <http://www.earthcharterinaction.org/content/pages/Strategy.html> (last accessed 15 January 2015).
31. Rockefeller, 'Global Ethics, International Law, and the Earth Charter', p. 2.
32. Sides, 'Ethics and the Earth Charter', p. 7.
33. Ibid. p. 8.
34. Rockefeller and Bernstein, *Earth Charter Commentary*, p. 12; see also King, 'What is of Value? A Buddhist Response to the Earth Charter'.
35. Vilela and Corcoran, 'Building Consensus on Shared Values', p. 19.
36. Sides, 'Ethics and the Earth Charter', p. 8.

37. World Commission on Environment and Development, *Our Common Future*, pp. 363–6.
38. Engel, 'The Earth Charter as a New Covenant for Democracy', p. 49.
39. Brenes, 'The Earth Charter Principles' and 'Universal and Differentiated Responsibility'.
40. Brenes, 'Universal and Differentiated Responsibility', p. 35.
41. Engel, 'The Earth Charter as a New Covenant for Democracy', p. 39.
42. Ibid. p. 39.
43. For a history, see Bakkan et al., *Ecology, Justice and Christian Faith*.
44. See, e.g., Aaron Sachs, *Eco-Justice*.
45. Rasmussen, *Earth Community, Earth Ethics*, p. 9.
46. See Rasmussen, *Earth-Honoring Faith*, chs 1, 2.
47. For an overview, see Pedersen, 'Environmental Ethics in Interreligious Perspective'.
48. Rasmussen, *Earth Community, Earth Ethics*, p. 51.
49. See Pedersen, 'Inclusion and Exclusion'.
50. Bosselman and Taylor, 'The Significance of the Earth Charter in International Law', p. 172.
51. Ibid. p. 172.
52. The term 'civil society' is not uncontested, and has many senses, as does 'NGO'. This is because of the great diversity of organizations, which may be local, national, international, massively funded or poor, providing services or devoted to issue advocacy, groups of professionals or ordinary citizens, affiliated to the United Nations or not, and so forth. See Schechter, *United Nations-Sponsored World Conferences*, p. 184 and note 1.
53. Schecter, *United Nations-Sponsored World Conferences*, p. 189; see ch. 8 for an overview.

3 Three Visionary Declarations

Introduction

Since the early 1990s, various agencies, organizations, and groups have been discussing the framing and adoption of a global ethic appropriate to the twenty-first century.[1] Much of this discussion revolves around the leitmotif of moving beyond, while not leaving behind, human rights and embracing some sort of declaration that articulates human responsibilities for peoples' welfare, the quality of the natural environment, and the good of future generations. This reorientation of emphasis – from rights to responsibilities – appears to be the result of a number of factors, foremost among which are the pressures of globalization (economic, political, and cultural) and a concomitant appreciation for transboundary problems whose solution appears to require international cooperation and coordination on a hitherto unprecedented scale. These problems range across, for example, poverty, environmental pollution, genocide and refugee flows, regional political destabilization, destruction of animal and plant species, economic inequity among states, oppression of vulnerable populations, and many others, all of which appear to call for an intellectually and motivationally compelling practical global moral vision. The reorientation is also shaped by the confluence of ethical categories from diverse moral, philosophical, and religious traditions that tend to focus on communities and their common good, in contrast with, for example, Western neo-liberal individualism. The wager of the aforementioned agencies and organizations pursuing this vision is that the language of global ethics and responsibility best matches up with the problems needing redress.

Both secular and religious organizations have made this wager and, in so doing, have articulated and published declarations on global ethics and responsibilities. Although these declarations may differ in inspirational sources – some religious, others not – they are all specifically intended to be inclusive and to resonate with both secular and religious communities and peoples. Indeed, all that is meant here by using the terms 'religious' and 'secular' is simply to draw attention to differences in inspirational sources and argument strategies. 'Secular', in particular, is not being used here to connote hostility to religion, nor is the use of the term intended to imply some sort of subtle supplanting of religions and their place in the world – for example, a secularization thesis, whether of a sociological or Marxist–ideological variety. Similarly, to draw attention to 'religious' aspects of certain declarations is not meant to assert or otherwise imply that they are somehow more adequate or well grounded than secular ones.

In this chapter we will compare and contrast three illustrative declarations of global ethics and responsibility, with the aim of clarifying their background histories, goals, argument styles, and proposed norms. We will also attempt to characterize their respective strengths and weaknesses, and conclude by offering a few observations about how these declarations could learn from each other in articulating a global moral vision. The illustrative declarations are Declaration towards a Global Ethic (DTGE) (1993; Parliament of the World's Religions), A Universal Declaration of Human Responsibilities (1997; the InterAction Council), and Declaration of Human Duties and Responsibilities (DHDR) (1999 and reissued 2002; Valencia Third Millennium Foundation and the United Nations Educational, Scientific, and Cultural Organization (UNESCO)).[2]

Declarations like these are moral expressions of goodwill issued to the world by communities and agencies in response to urgent situations where there are evident violations of, or threats to, the well-being of persons and collectivities. They aim to provide frameworks and norms for redressing or mitigating such violations and threats and to inspire and motivate appropriate concerted practical action. Some declarations result in legal codification in specially adopted and ratified conventions and treaties. Also certain norms within declarations can attain the status of international law through more informal means: for example, use and citation in legal cases, general acceptance by jurists and legal scholars, and implicit acceptance and thus recognition by the widespread practices of states and state authorities. The three declarations to which we will now turn have not gained formal legal status by means of treaties or conventions, though some of the norms involved have.

Declaration toward a Global Ethic

History

The Declaration toward a Global Ethic (DTGE) has as its original and full title 'Towards a Global Ethic: An Initial Declaration' and was adopted by the Assembly of Religious and Spiritual Leaders at the 1993 Parliament of the World's Religions, held in Chicago (151 signatories, representing 33 religious traditions and subtraditions).[3] While its 'Introduction' was produced by an editorial committee of the leadership council for the parliament, its 'Principles of a Global Ethic' was initially authored by Hans Küng, a German Catholic theologian who was commissioned by the council to draft the declaration. Subsequent to his initial draft (1992), the Principles were circulated for comment among a large international consultative network of scholars and leaders in various fields. Comparison of Küng's initial draft with the declaration finally adopted does reveal some editorial changes in language and paragraphing, but it is also utterly clear that the declaration bears Küng's signature hand. After its adoption by the 1993 parliament, the DTGE has been continuously available over the Internet (on countless sites), has garnered additional endorsement by individuals and groups, and has been used as the orienting framework for yet further focused application in such areas as international economics and business. In addition, the declaration has been explicitly used by other interfaith organizations and projects in designing and guiding their own work – for example, the World Congress of Faiths, the Peace Council, the United Religions Initiative (URI), and the World Council of Churches – as well as the politically oriented InterAction Council. And, most prominently, extensions and applications of the DTGE have been pursued by the Parliament of the World's Religions itself at its other meetings (for example, Cape Town in 1999; Barcelona in 2004; Melbourne in 2009). Available over the Internet is a dazzling display of references to, and commentaries on, the declaration.

Content

Although the DTGE has its own internal structure – including introductory sections, a 'Fundamental Demand', 'Four Irrevocable Directives', and a concluding section on 'Transformation of Consciousness' – we will use our own analytical structure in order to highlight, characterize, and clarify its implicit arguments. The DTGE articulates a normative foundation for its ethic; this foundation is further informed by a set of distinctively religious insights, images, and concepts; and both of these (foundation and images) are used to project a global moral vision, consisting of both expanded (globalized) practical norms and a set of transformative virtues for being a responsible citizen of the contemporary world.

The foundation may at first blush appear quite simple, since the declaration begins with the assertion that 'there is already a consensus among the religions which can be the basis for a global ethic – a minimal fundamental consensus concerning binding values, irrevocable standards, and fundamental moral attitudes'. Yet the foundation may be more complex than that, since the consensus in question is subsequently characterized in different ways, ranging across, for example: (1) recollection of the 1948 Universal Declaration of Human Rights (UDHR)[4] ('what it formally proclaimed on the level of rights we wish to confirm and deepen from the perspective of an ethic: the full realization of the intrinsic dignity of the human person'); (2) invocation of the 'fundamental demand . . . that every human being must be treated humanely' (as an end); (3) appealing to 'reason and conscience' to support the claim that 'every human being is obliged . . . to do good and avoid evil'; and (4) appealing to

> the principle . . . What you do not wish done to yourself, do not do to others. Or in positive terms: What you wish done to yourself, do to others. This should be the irrevocable unconditional norm for all areas of life . . . [and] . . . implies four broad, ancient guidelines for human behavior [non-maleficence, justice, truth-telling, and sexual propriety] . . .

These formulations, while admirable, are not obviously equivalent, though some may be derived from the others. Thus in (1) we have an appeal to a relatively modern consensus about basic human rights; in (2) a Kantian-like appeal to human beings as always to be treated as ends, never as means only; in (3) an appeal to a Thomist-like first principle of natural law – to do good and avoid evil; and in (4) an invocation of both the positive and negative versions of the Golden Rule. And we also must contend with the additional oddity that all of these appeals might well be interpreted as empirical claims to one or another consensus among religions *about* norms, rather than those norms themselves being proffered as the declaration's own normative argument in its own right.

Applying the well-known principle of interpretative charity to the formulations, we propose the following clarifying commentary on the declaration's normative foundation. First, since a good bulk of the formulations is normative in terms of their content, we interpret the empirical claims about there being some sort of normative moral consensus among religions to be primarily motivational and informative; that is, these claims are intended to remind the readers of the declaration about the normative content of religious traditions, rather than providing an explicit empirical (and therefore contingent) basis for accepting the norms at issue. Second, it seems to us charitable to interpret the normative appeal to the Golden Rule as a specification of what reason and conscience enjoin when speaking of doing good and avoiding evil; that is, the Golden Rule specifies how to go about determining what is good and what is evil. Third, although the text does not explicitly say this, the Golden Rule as a principle of reciprocity clearly involves the idea of taking up empathetically the standpoint of the other in one's own conscientious decision-making. Moreover, fourth, sustained application of the Golden Rule appears to entail respecting others as ends (just as the primary agent regards him- or herself), never as a means only. Fifth, the meaning of treating all (including oneself) as ends is further specified in recognizing and respecting all human beings' fundamental claims to freedom, security, and minimal material conditions necessary for leading a human life worthy of the appellation (that is to say, basic human rights); alternatively, these claims can be characterized as 'ancient' norms of non-maleficence, social justice, truth-telling, and non-exploitation. Finally, how all of this is known epistemically involves the use of reason and conscience together, with 'reason' surely involving reciprocal thinking and 'conscience' being understood in its etymological sense as a knowing and feeling with others (a basic sense of moral awareness and sympathy).

Taken together, these elements and their interconnection appear to articulate a firm and coherent normative moral basis for the declaration. And, as an empirical matter, it seems quite apt for the declaration to claim that this normative foundation is not alien to many – if not all – religious traditions. Indeed, arguably, most moral traditions and systems – religious or otherwise – would accept this normative foundation, which brings us to the question: what exactly, if anything, is distinctively religious about the DTGE? The answer, we believe, lies not in the foundation itself, but rather in a set of religious insights, concepts, and images that surround the foundation and its extension into a global moral vision. Here are some concrete examples of religious concepts and imagery:

[The ethic] does supply the moral foundation for a better individual and global order: A vision which can lead men and women away from despair, and society away from chaos.

As religious and spiritual persons we base our lives on an Ultimate Reality, and draw spiritual power and hope therefrom, in trust, in prayer or meditation, or word, or silence.

A vision rests on hopes, goals, ideals, standards . . . it is the communities of faith who bear a responsibility to demonstrate that such hopes, ideals, and standards can be guarded, grounded, and lived.

Action in favor of rights and freedoms presumes a consciousness of responsibility and duty, and . . . therefore both the minds and hearts of women and men must be addressed.

Religions . . . can provide what obviously cannot be attained by economic plans, political programs, or legal regulations alone: A change in the inner orientation, the whole mentality, the 'hearts' of people, and a conversion from a false path to a new orientation for life.

The spiritual powers of the religions can offer a fundamental sense of trust, a ground of meaning, ultimate standards, and a spiritual home.

Now, these images and their linguistic formulation can obviously be interpreted in various ways – even in non-religious ways – but taken together as a set they appear to represent reasonably distinctive religious ideas: order versus chaos, hope versus despair, conversion of the heart, bearing witness to the efficacy of ideals and standards, a fundamental basic trust in the world's meaning, and the idea of being at home in the universe. These are not just Christian or even more broadly theistic notions. Religions serve the classic sociological function of bringing or maintaining social order against chaos. Religions also psychologically bring and sustain hope in the face of despair and suffering. All salvation and enlightenment religions speak of a reorientation of heart and mind (or even heart–mind) away from egoism to other-regard in some form. All religions in some sense witness, demonstrate, and/or exemplify normative ideals and standards. And all religions serve in some way to interpret the meaning of life in order to encourage their adherents to be at home, or in attunement with, the cosmos – whether, for example, because of providential concern, insight into natural cycles, or enlightenment about an implicit moral dimension of reality.

Whether or not the declaration proposes a deeper sort of grounding or justification of its moral basis in an 'Ultimate Reality' is difficult to determine. If such a referential grounding were to be intended, it would seem that this 'Ultimate Reality' is sufficiently open-textured to accommodate various religious conceptions of some sort of authoritative source, whether personal or non-personal, beyond, underlying, or deeply implicit in ordinary reality. By the same token, however, the declaration seems to restrict itself to claiming only that some idea of 'Ultimate Reality', however specified, functions as a source from which religious people draw spiritual power and hope – which is more in the nature of a psychological–functional claim rather than explicit additional justification for the moral foundation.[5]

However this particular issue is resolved, it is utterly clear that the declaration's religious insights motivate and inform its task of developing a global moral vision. This vision articulates both expanded practical norms and internal attitudinal (or character) features necessary for the consistent application of the norms. The practical norms are derived from the 'ancient guidelines' of various religious traditions, and the needed attitudes or character traits are articulated in the form of virtues typically advanced by religious traditions. Let us examine each of these two broad aspects of the declaration's moral vision, beginning with its expanded practical norms.

We have already made the point that the declaration claims that the Golden Rule implies concrete standards in the form of 'four broad ancient guidelines for human behavior'. What it does further is to interpret each of these guidelines more expansively in contemporary global terms. Thus, the guideline or principle of non-maleficence (put negatively) or respect for life (put positively) is interpreted to imply (1) the human rights 'to life, safety, and free development of personality, thereby proscribing torture, ethnic cleansing, and genocide as well as prescribing non-violent conflict-resolution', and (2) an obligation to protect other species, integral ecosystems, and the biosphere as a whole for the benefit of present and future generations. Similarly, the guideline of not stealing (put negatively) or fair dealing (put positively) is interpreted to imply (1) the use of private property is subject to the concomitant obligation to serve the common good, and (2) obligations to work to end poverty and to build a just economic global order. The guideline on non-deception (put negatively) or being truthful (put positively) is interpreted to imply (1) special obligations for selected professions (for example, mass media, artists, scientists, politicians, statesmen) to be truthful, and (2) the rights of all to have accurate information (and, in the case of children, the proper education) sufficient to make informed decisions bearing on the quality of their lives. And the final guideline mentioned – no sexual immorality (put negatively) or injunction to mutual respect (put positively) – is interpreted to imply (1) proscription of sexual exploitation and gender discrimination, and (2) positive obligations to develop loving and supportive relationships within marriage, the nuclear family, the extended family (including care for the elderly), and the family of humankind as a whole.

The derivation of these proscriptions, obligations, and rights from the Golden Rule may not be immediately evident, but who among us would want to be on the receiving end of, for example, torture and genocide, a despoiled environment, living in poverty amid wealth, deception and lies about factors bearing on our well-being, sexual exploitation, denial of intimate relationships, or social discrimination? The rhetorical force of this question appears to indicate that appeal to the Golden Rule is not terribly far-fetched, subject to a caveat we will discuss shortly. In fact, when treated unjustly, most of us at one point or another are likely to say 'put yourself in my shoes', attempting thereby to invoke both reciprocity and empathy.

The attitudinal, character, or virtue features associated with the declaration's global moral vision may be a bit more elusive than its practical norms, so it may be helpful to highlight some pertinent passages bearing on the matter. Before we do so, however, it seems wise to reiterate what we said earlier – namely, that the declaration takes the position that moral action 'presumes a consciousness of responsibility and duty and that therefore both the minds and hearts of women and men must be addressed', and further that 'a global ethic' must include 'personal attitudes', 'a transformation in individual and collective consciousness', and 'a conversion of the heart'. Now for some passages:

> Every form of egoism should be rejected: All selfishness, whether individual or collective, whether in the form of class thinking, racism, nationalism, or sexism. We condemn these because they prevent humans from being authentically human.

> To be authentically human in the spirit of our great religious and ethical traditions means that in public as well as in private life we must be concerned for others and ready to help. We must never be ruthless and brutal. Every people ... must show tolerance and respect ... for every other.

> We must develop a spirit of compassion with those who suffer ... We must cultivate mutual respect and consideration ... We must value a sense of moderation and modesty instead of unquenchable greed ... In greed humans lose their 'souls', their freedom, their composure, their inner peace, and thus that which makes them human.

> When they stir up prejudice, hatred, and enmity towards those of different belief ... they deserve the condemnation of humankind ... Let no one be deceived: There is no global justice without truthfulness and humaneness ... We must cultivate truthfulness ... and incorruptible sincerity ... We must remain constant and trustworthy.

> To be authentically human ... we need mutual respect, partnership, and understanding ... We need mutual concern, tolerance, readiness for reconciliation, and love ... Only what has already been experienced in personal and familial relationships can be practiced on the level of nations and religions.

In many areas of life a new consciousness of ethical responsibility has already arisen.

Passages such as these – and more could be cited – clearly identify a set of virtues that define the sort of character or moral agent who can be counted on to implement the declaration's practical norms: concern for others, compassion, mutual respect, humaneness, sincerity, trustworthiness, temperance and moderation, openness to reconciliation, and a strong and constant sense of responsibility for the welfare of peoples, the planet, and future generations. Traits such as these are not usually singled out and discussed in most international declarations and conventions, and their presence in this one appears in large part to be due to the fact that many religions (though there may be exceptions) conceptualize the moral life less in terms of legalistic regulations and more in terms of character formation.

Critical assessment

Now that we have a reasonably comprehensive view of the declaration's content, we are in a position to consider certain criticisms that have been made of it. Awareness of these criticisms has the virtue of clarifying the declaration yet further. One set of criticisms often made is that the declaration is too minimalist, by which is meant: (1) its norms, even when taken together, do not constitute a full-bodied or thick ethic adequate for living a flourishing moral life; that is, the declaration lacks a comprehensive worldview and theory of the good; (2) what norms are offered constitute a bare minimum needed for human and planetary survival; and (3) its norms lack specificity and constitute only vague moral platitudes. A second set of criticisms revolves around the theme of ethnocentric bias, by which is meant: (1) the declaration makes too much use of recognizably Western moral categories such as 'rights' language that are alien to, and resisted by, many of the world's cultures and traditions; (2) its religious concepts and imagery are theistically oriented and thus inapt for encapsulating the thought and orientation of non-Abrahamic traditions; and (3) some of the norms identified in the declaration, such as gender equality, are distinctively liberal and/or feminist in content and thus inappropriate for that part of the world that does not accept them.

Some of these criticisms have merit, others do not. It is certainly the case that the declaration is by no means a thick ethic with a full theory of the good, nor is it intended to be. It is intended principally to provide a skeletal framework of an ethic that can be used by the world's peoples to help address cooperatively certain transboundary issues that bear on their and future generations' survival. At the same time, while the declaration lacks a comprehensive worldview, it surely does identify various common goods, restraints, and virtues needed for such survival over the long term. While certain of its norms may lack specificity, this feature seems largely inherent to framing a general ethic that, of course, needs additional specification when it comes to concrete application, but the declaration leaves, while also calling for, this hard work to the world's peoples and communities in taking up the problems needing redress.

With respect to the criticisms of the declaration's ethnocentricity, it must first be pointed out that the language of 'human rights' – whatever its original conceptual origins – is now used by much of the world, and, further, that oppressed peoples have no difficulty in either understanding or using it. Indeed, this has been true throughout the history and progressive development of the modern human rights movement. Regarding the religious concepts and images deployed by the declaration, we have already seen that many if not all of these are shared by the world's religious traditions, not just by the Abrahamic faiths. While the phrase 'Ultimate Reality' does appear to have a transcendental tone, we have also seen that it is sufficiently open-textured to encompass radically immanent conceptions of life-guiding normative authority. It is true that some of the norms identified in the declaration – such as gender equality – might be unacceptable to some 'fundamentalist' strands within some religious traditions, but the declaration rightly contends, in our view, that sexual and other forms of discriminatory treatment are flatly ruled out by the Golden Rule and the declaration's affiliated norms. This is where the declaration takes a justified stand. Any ethic worth its salt is expected to prescribe right conduct, and not just to acquiesce to an illegitimate status quo.

Thus far, we have been responding from the declaration's own viewpoint to criticisms made by others, but we would be remiss if we failed to point out that there may be philosophical problems with the declaration's primary emphasis on the Golden Rule and then its aim to seek to derive other norms from it. For example, if one considers the Golden Rule from the standpoint of the agent – whereby I (as agent) should treat others the way that I would want to be treated by them – we encounter the Nazi problem. To wit: a consistent (and, of course, perverse) Nazi agent could say that I (as agent) believe in eliminating Jews, and if I were a Jew then I would still want to be treated this way. On the other hand, if one considers the Golden Rule from the standpoint of the recipient – whereby one is to do unto others as they would want one to do – then one would appear to be held hostage to the desires, whatever they might be, of the recipient.

Thus, it appears either that the Golden Rule itself needs to be modified or otherwise supplemented by qualifying it in terms of 'rational' wants or desires on the part of both agent and recipient (the solution of Alan Gewirth), or, perhaps more appropriately, that we need to admit that to be properly employed the Golden Rule presupposes that agents and recipients have a prior understanding of and commitment to moral norms not derived from the Golden Rule itself.[6] This observation suggests that the Golden Rule is not itself a fundamental moral norm, but rather only a secondary guide for properly applying moral norms that precede it.

If this line of criticism is correct, then possibly a better way to (re) construct the declaration's normative basis would be to argue that its ancient guidelines and human rights are really at the heart of the matter. Or, yet another possibility would be to argue that the declaration's fundamental attitudes and virtues are crucially important in characterizing the conscience or heart–mind of those agents and recipients who, so informed, are the only ones that could properly employ the Golden Rule in the first place.

Universal Declaration of Human Responsibilities

History

The DTGE appears to have significantly informed the second declaration that we wish to analyse in this chapter, namely, 'A Universal Declaration of Human Responsibilities', issued by the InterAction Council in 1997. The InterAction Council is comprised mainly of high-level former political leaders from across the world (for example, former prime ministers and presidents), though on particular issues it consults with both academic specialists (from a variety of fields) and religious leaders (of varying faiths). Since the time of its original formation in 1983, this council has issued statements, recommendations, and position papers on global problems, such as assistance to the least developed countries, unemployment, arms control, international debt, global deforestation and other ecological issues, global financial markets, population control, global governance, humanitarian intervention, nuclear disarmament, global energy policy, terrorism, international law, and the like. As far back as 1987, it contemplated initiating a dialogue among political and religious leaders focusing on global ethics and particularly issues regarding peace, development, and the environment, and since that time the council has held no fewer than seven high-level expert group meetings dealing with religion and world politics. Of special interest to us, of course, are those on global ethical standards, which resulted in its declaration on human responsibilities. Hans Küng was one of the religious experts involved in these meetings, and it is clear from the council's official record that it had the Parliament of the World's Religions DTGE in mind when it issued its own 1997 declaration.

Content

The InterAction declaration in fact shares much of the moral content of the DTGE, but shorn of religious rhetoric, concepts, and images, as well as explicit discourse about 'transformation of consciousness'. The declaration itself is preceded by an 'Introductory Comment', whose italicized subtitle is the claim, 'It is time to talk about human responsibilities', and whose content purports to 'complement . . . and strengthen' the 1948 UDHR by 'bring[ing] freedom and responsibility into balance and . . . promot[ing] a move from the freedom of indifference to the freedom of involvement'. Indeed, it takes the position 'that the exclusive insistence on [human] rights can lead to endless dispute and conflict'. The declaration itself reiterates this contention in its 'Preamble': 'whereas the exclusive insistence on rights can result in conflict, division, and endless dispute, and the neglect of human responsibilities can lead to lawlessness and chaos . . .'. And the 'Introductory Comment' makes the further claim that the subsequent declaration is 'also a means of reconciling ideologies, beliefs and political views that were deemed antagonistic in the past'.

Following its 'Preamble', the declaration presents nineteen articles, divided into 'Fundamental Principles' (for example, humane treatment, promoting good and avoiding evil, and the negative form of the Golden Rule); 'Non-Violence and Respect for Life' (for example, respect for human life, non-violent dispute settlement, and protection of animals and the natural environment); 'Justice and Solidarity' (fair treatment, poverty reduction, property use in accord with justice); 'Truthfulness and Tolerance' (for example, speaking and acting truthfully, especially applicable to the media and various professions); 'Mutual Respect and Partnership' (for example, proscription of sexual exploitation and the injunction of love in marriage and family); and 'Conclusion' (for example, mandating consistency with the 1948 UDHR). Much of this content should be familiar, since these articles largely reiterate the DTGE's normative moral basis and expanded practical norms, but there are differences, which are primarily signalled in the accompanying report of the declaration's drafting group. For example, that report claims that the 1948 UDHR was drafted instead of a Universal Declaration of Human Duties, and that this choice 'undoubtedly reflects the philosophical and cultural background of [that] document's drafters who, as is known, represented the Western powers who emerged victorious from the Second World War'. The report goes on to intimate that human rights are largely a matter of 'unrestricted freedom . . . as dangerous as imposed social responsibility', allowing for 'extreme economic freedom and capitalist greed' that result in 'great social injustices'. The report also makes it clear – as does the DTGE – that globalization has resulted in transboundary problems the solution to which requires a new sort of global ethic and set of ethical standards, on pain of 'humankind . . . revert[ing] to survival of the fittest', with a subsequent intriguing reference to Mahatma Gandhi's 'seven social sins'. The report concludes that 'Bearing in mind the Golden Rule, the Universal Declaration of Human Rights provides an ideal start-ing point from which to consider some of the main obligations which are a necessary complement to those rights', for example: rights and correlative obligations to life, liberty, security, political participation, work, freedom of thought/conscience/religion, education, and use/restoration of the Earth and its natural resources.

Although its 'Introductory Comment' claims that the declara-tion 'builds on the wisdom of religious leaders and sages down the ages', the principles appear to be a religiously sanitized version of the DTGE. Moreover, in spite of the fact that the drafting group report explicitly mentions the DTGE, the InterAction declaration itself makes no reference to it. Nonetheless, it is fairly evident that the declaration articles largely track the norms articulated by the prior DTGE. It may be that the InterAction Council thought that its version would be more acceptable to a broader audience if it avoided the use of religious concepts and images. Whether or not this speculation is the reason for the apparent sanitization, it appears that accompanying the loss of such concepts and images there is also a de-emphasis on the moral virtues aspect of the DTGE's global moral vision. Furthermore, by so strongly contrasting human responsibili-ties with human rights, the declaration also appears to say less about human rights *per se* than the DTGE.

Critical assessment

After the InterAction declaration had been issued, it became the object of intense criticism, so much so that the council itself held a meeting and published what amounts to an attempted rebuttal of that criticism under the title 'Dissemination of the Universal Declaration of Human Responsibilities' (1998). The criticisms were wide-ranging and often political in character. Many government representatives took the view that 'the promotion of the Responsibilities will weaken the issue of human rights' and further that some 'Asian governments may readily embrace the concept of human responsibilities as a substitute for the advancement of human rights'. Many human rights activists, including the UN High Commissioner for Human Rights, took the position that 'the introduction of another declaration may be a distraction' from more needed progress in human rights and further that Universal Declaration of Human Responsibilities overlooks the fact that the 1948 UDHR 'is designed as a bulwark against excessive use of power and authority by governments and other established authority'. The Western press media attacked the declaration as watering down 'freedom of the press' and encouraging interference by government authorities.

The council's response to all this controversy principally came in the form of simply reiterating over and over again that the declaration was intended 'to strengthen the concept of human rights through a broader acceptance of the concept of responsibilities that goes with rights' at the level of individual and collective moral conscience and ethical behaviour. It also responded to the media's criticism by saying it meant only to encourage the press to develop its own professional code of ethics, rather than invoking the spectre of government censorship or control. And the council took the interesting tack of suggesting that, in issuing its declaration, it was largely concerned with encouraging attitudinal moral changes and people's ethical impulses. The difficulty with the council's rebuttals is the fact that they do not entirely square with the original tone and claims made by the declaration's own 'Introductory Comment' and accompanying report; for example: (1) the claim that the 1948 UDHR is no more than a biased Western construct (a false assertion); (2) the clear implication that human rights are simply an expression of neo-liberal economic thought (another false claim); and (3) its overall focus on moral obligations rather than attitudes, virtues, and character traits. In sum, rather than being holistic in its thinking and expression, the council's declaration appeared divisive and combative from its very inception, and knowledgeable people reading it noticed and took strong exception.

Declaration of Human Duties and Responsibilities

History

The other global ethics declaration that we want to discuss is manifestly not the product of a religiously oriented group or organization. The drafting and publication of the Declaration of Human

Duties and Responsibilities (DHDR) were sponsored by UNESCO in concert with the Valencia Third Millennium Foundation. UNESCO has a long history of sponsoring philosophical discussions of human rights and related concerns, even dating back to the time of its original formation when in 1948 it sponsored a symposium on the philosophical bases of human rights. In more recent years UNESCO has launched a Universal Ethics Project whose work is described fairly fully by Yersu Kim in a 1999 UNESCO interim report entitled 'A Common Framework for the Ethics of the 21st Century'.[7] This report even discusses, though briefly, the DTGE, the InterAction Council declaration (which simply mimics the DTGE), and even the DHDR itself, which we are about to examine. The process leading to the DHDR involved over sixty participants (representing thirty-four countries from all parts of the world) who contributed in one way or another to its drafting and an even larger number who participated in debates and congresses about the subject matter. The drafting committee itself was chaired by Richard Goldstone, a noted international jurist, and the numerous participants taken as a group were significantly international, intercultural, interprofessional, and interdisciplinary. There were a few participants from the interfaith community (for example, Rushworth Kidder, Institute for Global Ethics), but they did not constitute a major force. (Interestingly, Hans Küng was not involved.) The language and argument strategies of the DHDR are different from the other declarations we have discussed. And, interestingly again, it is much more comprehensive than the other declarations – at least in terms of overall length and scale of detail.

Content

The DHDR is best approached with an analytical framework similar to the one we used with respect to the DTGE, but with one big difference: the DHDR lacks any religious concepts or imagery. We divide its argument structure into (1) normative moral foundation, (2) explicitly identified world developments calling for the language of duty and responsibility, and (3) a global moral vision marked by expanded conceptual normative categories and expanded practical norms.

As stated in the declaration's 'Preamble', its principal normative basis is the set of all those human rights enunciated in the UDHR, the international covenants, and other international human rights instruments. Given the fact that since 1948 the UDHR has been codified in legal conventions, with some of its norms also arguably acquiring the status of customary international law, it may appear, then, that the

DHDR's normative basis is legal rather than moral. But this interpretation would overlook the fact that the UDHR – and, by implication, the successive instruments – ground human rights, dignity, and equality in a fundamental moral appeal to reason and conscience. This appeal, in turn, has been interpreted in a variety of ways within the international human rights community – for example, as a minimal natural law position (for example, Michael Perry, many natural lawyers), as a Kantian-like claim that all persons as ends have intrinsic value (for example, Gewirth), as an invocation of moral intuition (for example, Johannes Morsink), as the product of an overlapping cross-cultural consensus (for example, Amy Gutman), or even some combination of these.[8]

These observations suggest that the deep normative basis of the declaration may not be all that divergent from the one employed by the DTGE, but with this difference: in the DHDR human rights constitute the decidedly primary category, from which human duties and responsibilities are then secondarily derived. As the DHDR puts it, 'duties and responsibilities [are] implicit in those [human] rights'. This mode of derivation or implication is mentioned a number of times in the declaration itself, and in Goldstone's own introduction to the declaration, he avers:

> The notion of duties and responsibilities is implicit in any human right. It is the purpose of the Declaration ... to emphasize this relationship between rights, duties, and responsibilities and in this way to further the realization of human rights.

From the declaration's own perspective, this implication or relationship was clearly made in the 1948 UDHR's Article 29, which states in part: 'Everyone has duties to the community in which alone the free and full development of his personality is possible'. As the DHDR states:

> Article 29 of the UDHR recognizes that individuals have duties and responsibilities towards their communities, and therefore emphasiz[es] ... that the assumption of the duties and responsibilities implicit in human rights and fundamental freedoms rests upon us all.

At this point it would be fair to ask why exactly does this declaration take human rights as the primary category from which duties, obligations, and responsibilities are derived. There are at least two sets of reasons to account for this feature – one moral and the other pragmatic – now reflecting a bit more on the original UDHR and its form of moral argument or appeal, as well as real-world considerations operative at that time. We begin with the moral point. Although, as we have already indicated, the framers of the UDHR formally invoked reason and conscience as the way to discern what they regarded as the moral truths of declaration – embodied in human rights language – they appear to have regarded these truths as the result of epistemic intuitions systematically measured or tested against the backdrop of the atrocities perpetrated by the Third Reich in 'outraging the conscience' of humankind (a formulation also consistently invoked in subsequent instruments).[9] The framers then used their reason (ordinary practical reason) to build a bulwark of crucial legal protections, civic empowerments, and basic social and economic goods needed to avoid such atrocities in the future. In this regard, it is an interesting exercise to read autobiographical accounts of Nazi victims in the light of the human rights identified by the UDHR, in order to see that all of the latter were systematically subverted and violated by the Nazi regime. Moreover, from the viewpoint of the UDHR framers, the moral truths embodied within human rights hold, regardless of whether or not we can readily identify all those who have the responsibility to guarantee their satisfaction. Pragmatically speaking, at the time that the UDHR was formulated, time was running out for meeting a deadline for General Assembly action, the framers were also cognizant that there could be myriad responsible agents – ranging across, for example, parents, families, community leaders, state authorities, international organizations, and so forth – and, further, they explicitly envisioned that appropriate duty-bearers would be identified in subsequent human rights declarations and conventions, which brings us back to the DHDR.

Unlike the DTGE, the DHDR is not apparently informed or guided by any specifically religious insights or concepts, but it nevertheless makes clear that it is significantly informed by new developments in the world that, in turn, mandate conceptual advances in how human rights and responsibilities are properly framed. The new developments – at least since the time of the UDHR – include the complexification of agency in the global community (for example, beyond states and individual persons – international and regional government organizations, non-government organizations, citizen associations, and transnational corporations), the recognizable need for a healthy and stable natural environment, the emergence of the notion of sustainable development, the need for worldwide cooperation in addressing transboundary problems, the need to respect diversity among peoples, and the need to protect especially vulnerable populations and groups (for example, indigenous peoples, women, children, the elderly, and the disabled). According to the declaration, these developments call for progressive changes in how rights, duties, their protection, and advancement are properly conceived. Thus, one broad aspect of the declaration's global moral vision involves making these conceptual changes explicit. There are at least five changes to consider.

The first one involves clarifying the types of bearers of duties and responsibilities, which appear to go well beyond the aforementioned 'communitarian' Article 29 of the UDHR. The phase 'duties and responsibilities' is not a redundancy, for the declaration's first article explicitly, and stipulatively, defines 'duty' as a moral obligation and 'responsibility' as a moral obligation that is *also* legally binding under international law. Moreover, the second article explicitly identifies different types of duty- and responsibility-bearers within the international community. For example, states – including their governments, legislatures, and judicial institutions – have a duty (moral) and a responsibility (legal) to ensure respect for, enforce, and proactively promote human rights in all circumstances, whereas international governmental organizations (IGOs), non-governmental organizations (NGOs), private and public corporations, individuals, and communities have mainly duties (moral) to promote awareness of and respect for human rights, to monitor compliance by states, and to use advocacy to help enforce such compliance.

A second conceptual change involves the highlighting of the idea of temporality and the fact that duties and responsibilities – for example, those regarding hunger, disease, and environmental protection – are owed not only to present but also to future generations. Thus, from the declaration's point of view, globalization has led to and mandates an expanded moral vision, both spatially and temporally. Yet a third conceptual change stems from the fact that obligations – whether moral, legal, or both – are held by all and that therefore all collectively have a stake in appropriate decision-making about their interpretation and application. Therefrom is born the explicit affirmation of participatory decision-making and governance at all levels of society and meaningful involvement of all parties (or their representatives) in public affairs bearing on the commonweal. A fourth conceptual moral change stems from the wealth versus poverty disparity in the world, and the declaration's explicit proposal that economically more endowed states have a moral duty to contribute to the economic and social development of lesser endowed states. This claim appears to be at the heart of the declaration's subsequent vision for promoting an equitable international order. And a fifth and final conceptual change is the declaration's explicit embrace of group rights, beyond the human rights of individual persons. Thus, for example, its section on the rights of minorities (national, ethnic, religious, and linguistic) and the rights of indigenous peoples details collective duties and responsibilities owed to these groups and peoples – respecting, protecting, and promoting their identities, means of livelihood, and communally autonomous decision-making. The nefarious effects of economic globalization have rendered the continuing existence of indigenous peoples particularly precarious.

The other broad aspect of the declaration's global moral vision involves its expansive practical norms – in the form of coordinated rights, on the one hand, and duties and responsibilities, on the other. It is simply not possible here to discuss all the declaration's projected duties and responsibilities, since not only does the declaration have no fewer than forty-one articles, but also each of these has carefully detailed and numbered subsections. Suffice it to say that these duties and responsibilities cover, for example, survival of present and future generations, collective security and peace, disarmament, humanitarian assistance and intervention, environmental protection and stability, equitable economic order, technological development and implementation, transnational corporate activities, control and punishment of international crime, participatory governance, information and communication technology, physical and personal integrity and security, human trafficking, prevention and punishment of war crimes, equal treatment and non-discrimination, protection of vulnerable populations and groups, material goods needed for a decent quality of life, basic personal and social freedoms, and provision of effective remedies. The level of detail with respect to these duties and responsibilities is extraordinary, making this declaration the most comprehensive and sophisticated of any so far produced on this matter.

Critical assessment

Part of the reason accounting for this declaration's relative comprehensiveness is that it adapts many of its articles from the pithy components of previously adopted human rights declarations and conventions – for example, those regarding the protection of vulnerable groups and classes of people; those proscribing slavery and similar modern practices, torture and inhumane treatment, and discrimination on racial or religious grounds; and those promoting various social and political freedoms, disarmament, environmental protection, and the prosecution of international crimes. But this is not to say that the declaration fails to break new ground. For example, with respect to preventing gross human rights violations, the declaration in no less than three articles speaks of the duty and responsibility of states – preferably under the aegis of the Security

Council but open to other regional and subregional entities as well (if the Security Council fails to act) – to assist, interdict, and rescue citizens from the grossly abusive actions of their governments – similar to the emerging Responsibility to Protect doctrine.[10] For another example, the declaration is quite clear about all states having the duty and responsibility to promote an equitable international order, singling out for special mention the obligations of the economically more endowed states and international financial development organizations to overcome extreme poverty and to promote economic policies explicitly aimed at advancing social justice. For yet another example, the declaration explicitly address the duties and responsibilities of public- and private-sector corporations to contribute to the just development of host communities, to respect and enforce human rights and universally accepted labour standards, and to monitor the activities of subcontractors, suppliers, and other contributors so as to ensure their compliance with such rights and standards as well. And, for a final example, not only does the declaration articulate that states have a duty and responsibility to provide for effective remedies for all human rights violations but it also proposes that state and competent intergovernmental organizations have a duty to establish tripartite councils comprised of state, civil society, and private-sector representatives tasked with monitoring and ensuring compliance with all the duties and responsibilities set forth in the declaration.

Aside from the lack of religious inspiration, the other large difference between the DHDR and the DTGE is this: though the former clearly projects an extensive sphere of responsibility, it nowhere explicitly discusses anything like a transformation of consciousness or a set of particularly appropriate attitudes, virtues, or character traits. As if aware of this lacuna, in his introduction accompanying the DHDR (but not an official part of it), Goldstone writes: 'Notwithstanding the specific focus chosen by the high-level group [of drafters], participants recognized that there are and continue to be personal responsibilities of individual members of the human community that transcend and complement the scope of our endeavor'. This statement is followed by the identification of such 'personal responsibilities' as mutual cooperation, care, solidarity, self-respect, mutual respect, being just, tolerance, honesty, and sincerity. These 'personal responsibilities' that 'transcend and complement' the declaration are arguably similar to the moral attitudes and virtues of the DTGE's moral vision. It is also perhaps arguable that such virtues or traits are presupposed by the DHDR or in some manner implicit in what it does say about all individuals, peoples, and communities being duty-bearers, along with other agents in the global community.

Conclusion

What are the relative strengths and weaknesses of the three declarations that we have examined, and what conclusions might we draw from these comparisons for the adequate formulation of a global ethic? The principal strengths of the DTGE appear to be these: (1) its normative foundation – however complex the elements – is more fully stated and straightforwardly worked out than is that of the other declarations; and (2) its global ethic makes a clear effort to address the transformation of moral agency, certainly more so than the other declarations. The principal weakness of the DTGE comes in the form of a lack of scope and detail in its expanded practical moral norms, which appear woefully short of the achievement of the DHDR. By the same token, of course, this feature is a dominant strength of the DHDR, in comparison with the other declarations, while its principal weakness is the evident lack of attention – within the declaration itself – to a transformed moral agency. An additional strength of the DHDR is the way that it shows precisely how developments in the contemporary global setting require important refinements in our conceptualizations of duty-bearers, the temporal scope of obligations, participatory decision-making, and the relative weight of obligations between the greater and lesser endowed states in the world.[11]

Can or should more be said? We believe so, since, in the light of our earlier criticism of the DTGE's invocation of and reliance on the Golden Rule, its normative basis may be somewhat suspect. If it is true that to be properly employed the Golden Rule presupposes other more primary norms – whether in the form of ancient guidelines, basic human rights, virtues associated with conscience, or some combination of these – then how are we to construe these and their source and grounding? We have a suggestion that is inspired by Jacques Maritain's introduction to a 1948 UNESCO symposium on various cultural, philosophical, and religious understandings of human rights. Maritain wrote:

> Because . . . the goal of UNESCO is a practical goal, agreement between minds can be reached spontaneously, not on the basis of common speculative ideas, but on common practical ideas . . . upon the affirmation of a single body of beliefs for guidance in action . . . [a] body of common practical convictions . . . Is there anything surprising in systems antagonistic in theory converging in their practical conclusions? It is the usual picture which the history of moral philosophy presents us. The phenomenon proves simply that [such] systems . . . are the products of reflection by the intellect on ethical concepts which precede and govern them, and which

of themselves display . . . a highly complex geology of the mind where the natural operations of spontaneous reason, pre-scientific and pre-philo-sophic, is at every stage conditioned by the acquisitions, the constraints, the structure and evolution of the social group. Thus, if I may be allowed the metaphor, there is a kind of plant-like formation and growth of moral knowledge and feeling, in itself independent of philosophic systems and the rational justifications they propound . . . What is chiefly important for the moral progress of humanity is the apprehension by experience which occurs apart from systems and on a different logical basis – assisted by such systems when they awaken the conscience to knowledge of itself, hampered by them when they dim the apperceptions of spontaneous reason . . . If thereafter we adopt a practical viewpoint . . . we have before us an entirely different picture . . . then the operative factors are less the schools of philosophy . . . than currents of thought . . . where the principal part has been played by the lessons of experience and history and by a kind of practical apprehension.[12]

Maritain's formulation here – while not justificatory in any obvious sense – speaks of the growth of moral knowledge and feeling as informed by historical and social experience accumulating over time – indeed centuries – passed down to us in the way that we are conditioned and shaped by our social and cultural circumstances. The resulting practical apprehension, then, is one that has been shaped and tutored by history, social experience, and tradition. This sort of practical apprehension is in reflective equilibrium – to borrow a notion from John Rawls – with other facts, beliefs, and commitments forged over time. We believe that Maritain is ascribing this type of practical apprehension to cultures and traditions across the world, suggesting that they have yielded convergent practical convictions that have been tested, shaped, retested, and reshaped, culminating in a practical moral wisdom recognizable across cultural differences – that is, a set of convictions that are stable, indeed unshakeable, because they are in an even wider reflective equilibrium with shared facts, beliefs, and commonalities. When we reflect on the views of great representatives of these traditions – paradigmatic characters, sages, and normative teachings recognized as such by their traditions – there does seem to us to be a convergence of practical moral wisdom that was codified – or, to use Maritain's word, 'crystallized' – in the UDHR.

We would observe that Maritain's ideas of practical apprehension, convergent practical convictions, and a practical moral wisdom tested, shaped, retested, and reshaped in the evolution of the social group and by lessons of history can apply well beyond the UDHR and be framed alternatively as ancient guidelines, basic human rights and responsibilities, or conscientious virtues of competent moral agents, all suitably updated for the contemporary and increasingly complex world in which we now live.

A generation from now how will we assess the historical significance of these visionary declarations? In Chapter 1 we reviewed the considerable historical impact that the UDHR has had in the two generations since its adoption. Over time that declaration has gained in authority and in influence. It has become a public global document that has resulted in changes in both international and national law; it is widely invoked and supported by activities of hundreds of civil society organizations. We doubt that the declarations discussed in this chapter will gain corresponding authority and have similar impact. To be sure, they all represent expressions of moral concern regarding the responsibilities of humans with respect to the cross-boundary crises now facing the Earth and its inhabitants. In a way, each is addressed to particular constituencies, however broad these may be. In practice, the DTGE is addressed to the diverse communities of religious people. In terms of the way it is drafted, the DHDR is especially addressed to those who are philosophically and legally informed. Again because of how it was written and how it has been advocated, the InterAction Council's declaration has failed to gain wide support. Still, these declarations have served as a means of engaging large numbers of people in discussions of how humans from diverse moral and cultural traditions can and ought to act collaboratively and individually to protect basic rights and to work to address current and impending transboundary global crises. These declarations represent an expression of the wider set of activities that constitute the developing practices of global ethics. These declarations came into being because of the prior actions of those already engaged in the practices of global ethics. In turn, these visionary declarations have also served as a means to call others to become involved in these practices.

Notes

1. Much of what is written in this chapter was initially presented by Sumner Twiss at a plenary address at Indiana University, 2012.
2. These declarations are readily available over the web. See, e.g., <http://www.parliamentofreligions.org/_includes/FCKcontent/File/TowardsAGlobalEthic.pdf>; <http://interactioncouncil.org/univer sal-declaration-human-responsibilities>; <http://globalization.icaap. org/content/v2.2/declare.html> (last accessed 27 January 2015).
3. By our count.

4. The UDHR is available at <http://www.un.org/en/documents/udhr/> (last accessed 27 January 2015).
5. Here we differ from Grace Kao's interpretation of the DTGE as offering an explicitly religious justification; see her *Grounding Human Rights in a Pluralist World*, ch. 2.
6. See, e.g., Gewirth, 'The Golden Rule Rationalized', reprinted in his *Human Rights: Essays on Justification and Applications*. Similar problems were noted with respect to R. M. Hare's universalizability principle dating back to the 1960s. For another more recent and positive approach to the Golden Rule, see Enderle, 'Ethics and Personhood'; Enderle, however, does not address the objections noted above.
7. Available from the UNESCO website at <http://unesdoc.unesco.org/images/0011/001176/117622eo.pdf> (last accessed 27 January 2015).
8. We mention these names only to intimate the broad range of figures who have concerned themselves with this justificatory issue. For further discussion of this matter, see Chapter 1 of this book, especially the section on the justification of human rights and the practice of global ethics.
9. Here we are taking as evidence much more than the UDHR's 'Preamble' and Article 1, but in addition the entire debating record (in excess of 700 pages) of the Third Committee, which then referred the UDHR draft for action by the UN General Assembly.
10. R2P is shorthand for 'Responsibility to Protect'; for more on this doctrine, see Chapter 6 of this book. See also Twiss and Chan, 'Classical Confucianism, Punitive Expeditions, and Humanitarian Intervention'.
11. For the purposes of full disclosure, Twiss has gone on record as arguing that the human rights movement in all its progressive complexity constitutes the pivotal foundation for a practicable global ethics now and for the foreseeable future. See Twiss, 'Global Ethics and Human Rights'.
12. Maritain, 'Introduction'.

PART II
Addressing Global Ethical Issues

4 Practising Global Environmental Ethics

Introduction

Our aim in this book is to describe the practices of global ethics. To this point, we have examined the work of developing, drafting, and negotiating statements of global ethical principles. The work of evolving and codifying principles is central to global ethical practice and its most visible form. It represents only the tip of the iceberg, however. Ethical ideas are created, shaped, articulated, and put to work in global affairs and activities that extend far beyond the work described thus far. This rich array of activities enlivens the practice of global ethics and makes it real for many of the world's peoples as they seek to advance and implement a normative basis for human life on Earth.

We begin to explore a broader and more distributed practice of global ethics in global environmental governance. As described in Chapter 2, the Earth Charter is a core statement of global ethics, whose evolution and significance are properly understood as the products of broader patterns of activity in international environmental law. Over several decades, countries have signed hundreds of environmental treaties, including a few that stand among the most important treaties governing human affairs. These treaties contain statements of ethical principle that stand on their own merit and are embedded in the practices of treaty implementation and compliance. They include environmental treaties (for example, the Convention on International Trade in Endangered Species and the UN Framework Convention on Climate Change) and a range of related legal agreements (for example, the Limited Test Ban Treaty in 1963 and the sanitary and phytosanitary standards set by the World Trade Organization (WTO)). Beyond treaties, global environmental governance encompasses the work of international agencies, from the World Meteorological Organization (WMO), the World Bank, and the International Energy Agency to the recently established

International Renewable Energy Agency, as well as less formal diplomatic efforts, such as the Solar Radiation Management Governance Initiative, a multi-stakeholder body examining the deliberate geoengineering of the Earth's climate system.

This chapter considers several domains of ethical practice in global governance. It looks first at the work of scientists who have transformed human understanding of the environment from a concern for localities into a global ethical imperative. That the planet should have a place in global ethics, epitomized by the Earth Charter, derives in large part from the efforts of scientists to describe, analyse, and represent to publics a suite of global-scale processes and systems at risk from human activities: the biosphere, ozone layer, and climate, among others. Their actions have established new objects of analysis, deliberation, and negotiation, altering the terrain and foundations of proper ethical reasoning about the environment. This work reflects the ethical responsibilities of scientists to understand, assess, and publicize common risks facing humanity. Perhaps most importantly, it weaves together facts and values in new stories and narratives that establish a basis not only for holding states and societies to account for taking actions to address those risks but also simply for talking and reasoning together, ethically and factually, about what it means for humanity collectively to inhabit a shared planet at this particular moment in history.

Second, the chapter examines the practices of legal, diplomatic, governmental, and advocacy communities working to define and implement ethical principles for the global environment. The practices of global ethics take shape not only in treaty negotiations but also in the new organizations and institutions, forms of civil society association and activity, and work programmes created by treaties, all of which further develop, evolve, negotiate, and put into effect both substantive ethical principles (for example, standards of global protection, fair sharing of risk burdens, and payment by polluters) and principles of ethical governance (for example, whose voices must be heard, how to hold accountable those who violate global rules, and who has rights to appeal global decisions).

Third, the chapter analyses ethical work by people across the globe to interpret, specify, apply, and implement global ethical principles in day-to-day life. Individuals, organizations, and communities all contribute to a common purpose: to transform the socio-technological systems at the root of modern economies in order to reduce global environmental risks and enhance sustainable development. These systems bind the organization of human affairs to technological capacities for transforming the Earth into material and biological resources for human enterprise. They are thus responsible for much of what is unsustainable about present modes of human living. Transforming these systems into more sustainable forms is both an ethical imperative and a challenge. The lives and livelihoods of everyone are bound up in their organization and operation, governance, and distributions of power and wealth. Changing them will require fundamental changes to human societies with deep implications for justice and ethics. How these implications are understood, analysed, and incorporated into the design and reconstruction of socio-technological systems is thus a crucial facet of global ethical practice.

The chapter also includes two interludes that examine key ethical debates in global environmental governance. The first examines divergent framings of global environmental ethics and policy: a duty of care framing, focused on promoting ethical human behaviour vis-à-vis the environment; a crisis framing that portrays risks as dire and demanding of an ethics of survival that prioritizes protecting civilization over other considerations; and a governance framing that emphasizes the integration of environmental issues into a larger suite of global governance challenges. The choice of framing impacts how one understands and weighs global ethical obligations. The second interlude examines ethical dilemmas embedded in choices of policy approach: whether to adopt unicentric or polycentric approaches; whether to prevent change, adapt to it, or engineer systems to meet human needs; and how to respond to relocalization initiatives that threaten to undermine support for global projects.

Altogether, the chapter highlights the critical importance of a broad approach to the practice of global ethics. The practice of global ethics is widely distributed in human affairs, anywhere that individuals, groups, organizations, and communities grapple with key questions about the human future: what kind of a world should we inhabit; what challenges should rise to the level of global concern; what ethical ideas and principles should guide human responses; and how ethical ideas and principles should be applied, concretely, to the governance and management of the socio-technological systems that dominate human and environmental affairs. This includes the rigorous philosophical construction of global ethical standards, the working-out of what normative frameworks humanity can agree on to guide global affairs, and the pragmatic work necessary to debate the meaning of those frameworks, their application in specific contexts, and the consequences of failures to comply with their requirements.

The practice of global ethics is thus fully integrated into the practice and work of all domains of global activity, including science, politics, and business. Acknowledging this work as an exercise in the practice of ethics gives it an arguably novel tenor. Too often, its practitioners view this work either as political, charting the waters of the possible rather than the desirable, or as technical, working out the details necessitated by reality. Neither is the case. Every aspect of global governance entails the subtle, nuanced enmeshing of ethical values and principles with science, technology, business, law, policy, and politics. Only by admitting that ethics is inextricable in human affairs and by excavating the implications of this insight will we find ways to understand and enhance the practice of global ethics and create a more just future for humanity.

The ethics of planetary imagination

The 1948 Universal Declaration of Human Rights (UDHR) served as the foundational act of a new form of post-war ethics by establishing human rights as an essential category of ethical imagination, analysis, and concern. The parallel invention of planet Earth as an object of ethical imagination, analysis, and concern constitutes the second great post-war ethical transformation.[1] The history of global environmental ethics, as illustrated in Chapter 2, centres on the Earth as a common home for humanity. The 1972 Stockholm Conference on the Human Environment adopted the slogan 'Only One Earth'.[2] *Our Common Future*, the 1987 report of the World Commission on Environment and Development (WCED), opens: 'In the middle of the twentieth century, we saw our planet from space for the first time.'[3] In 1992, world leaders chose the Earth Summit as the venue to sign the UN Framework Convention on Climate Change, the UN Convention on Biological Diversity (CBD), and Agenda 21.

How did the Earth acquire its standing as a central object of ethical concern? The answer lies largely in the work of science. Scientific studies of global processes at risk from human activities predated both the rise of the discourse of economic globalization and the ability to photograph the Earth from space. As Sheila Jasanoff has observed, images of the Earth helped usher in an era of global environmental consciousness, because people were already prepared to understand the Earth as a global environmental object.[4] The work of creating that perspective – of making it possible to see the Earth as an ecological whole, as a suite of interconnected systems at risk from human activities, and thus as an object of global ethical concern – was conducted by scientists in the two decades following the Second World War.

Globalizing nature and its ethics

Starting around 1950, scientists began to fashion several ideas essential to the subsequent evolution of discussions of global environmental ethics. These ideas principally take the form of and give shape to a new global ontology of nature: the biosphere, the ozone layer, the climate system, and the Earth's biological diversity. This work began with efforts to track the movement of radioactive materials from nuclear explosions through the air, water, and natural ecosystems and to exploit that movement as a tool for studying environmental processes. This work transformed the study of ecology[5] and established new fields of research, such as atmospheric chemistry, that would later become essential components of global environmental science.

Building on these innovations, scientists developed new conceptual frameworks, models, and tools for understanding the atmosphere. Atmospheric chemistry provided the basis for understanding the chemical composition of the atmosphere, how that composition changed, and how it impacted on other phenomena, such as how the atmosphere absorbed solar radiation and converted it to heat. Networks of data collection sites provided real-time information on weather patterns. And the rapidly evolving capabilities of electronic computers provided the tools for modelling atmospheric dynamics. By the 1960s, scientists had linked these developments together to create the first general circulation models (GCMs) of the atmosphere. These models predicted the dynamics of the atmosphere on a global basis, establishing the foundation for the idea of the Earth's climate system as a single, planetary-scale ontological framework.[6] GCMs modelled the atmosphere as a global system based on the physical principles of fluid dynamics and the energy input of the sun, with the goal of improving weather forecasting. Scientists also established the first evidence of rising concentrations of carbon dioxide in the atmosphere, a key finding that would further propel the significance of the new field of atmospheric chemistry and help establish how humans were putting the planet at risk through greenhouse gas emissions and climate change.[7] A little over a decade later, atmospheric chemists identified another planetary system at risk, the ozone layer, thanks to the actions of another minor chemical constituent being added to the atmosphere by industrial processes: chlorine.[8]

Following their physical science colleagues, biologists also began to study biological and ecological processes on global scales. Their early efforts included a focus on net primary productivity: the capacity of the Earth's ecosystems to convert sunlight into biological activity. Capitalizing on this work were a cadre of innovative ecologists, like

G. Evelyn Hutchinson, who had trained in the study of lake ecology but whose post-war work explored the interactions of biological and physical systems to create biogeochemical cycles in key minerals such as nitrogen and carbon. This work became, for Hutchinson, the foundation of a new science of biology on global scales. In 1970, Hutchinson and several colleagues published this work in a now famous series of essays titled 'The Biosphere' in the popular journal *Scientific American*. Hutchinson's cover article introduced and described in detail the planetary systems that underlay the functioning and sustenance of the biosphere.[9]

This work was not merely scientific, as in narrowly technical and objective analyses. These scientists clearly understood themselves, as David Takacs has so eloquently described, as engaged in self-conscious attempts at moral reimagination: efforts to 'change the terrain' of people's mental maps, 'reasoning that if you were to conceive of nature differently, you would view and value it differently'.[10] The atomic bomb ushered the scientific community into a role of responsibility in world affairs. The subsequent return of many of the atomic scientists to their home academic institutions guaranteed that their engagement in geopolitics would spill over into university life rather than remaining isolated in the narrow confines of the new nuclear weapons laboratories taking shape at Los Alamos, Livermore, and Oak Ridge. The atomic physicists were grappling with critical questions of the science, ethics, and politics of human survival,[11] and it is not entirely surprising that those concerns drew their colleagues in other fields into similar questions about their own domains of specialization.[12]

Scientists were integral to the burgeoning environmental movement, whose first Earth Day celebration, in 1970, coincided with the publication of 'The Biosphere'.[13] Yet, the environmental movement's slogan, 'Think globally; act locally', suggested a core tension between most people's primary concerns – local environmental problems, such as clean air and clean water – and the emerging concerns of early Earth systems scientists. Published in the context of the run-up to the 1972 UN Conference on the Human Environment in Stockholm, 'The Biosphere' put global environmental risks squarely in the scientific, policy, and public imagination: 'the earth's thin film of living matter is sustained by grand-cycles of energy and chemical elements. All of these cycles are presently affected by the activities of man.'[14] In an understated, scientific, yet compelling narrative, Hutchinson fired the opening shot of an effort by biologists to transform the politics of the environment from a local to a global affair. Since the late nineteenth century, conservation policies have focused on either individual spaces or individual species. With the rise of systems ecology, however, biologists began after the Second World War to frame life in different terms, picturing complex webs of interactions among both living and non-living systems, all across the Earth. The concept of the biosphere was their first major effort to depict all life on the planet, as a single entity of analysis, at risk from human behaviour, and hence an object of global ethical concern.

Others followed Hutchinson's lead. Paul Crutzen, who along with Mario Molina and Sherwood Roland identified the threat posed to the ozone layer by chlorofluorocarbons (CFCs), published his research not only in specialized atmospheric chemistry journals but also in *Ambio*,[15] a widely read environmental journal established by the Swedish Royal Academy of Sciences in conjunction with the 1972 UN Conference on Environment and Development (UNCED) in Stockholm. The article's abstract makes clear the ethical implications of Crutzen's scientific findings using language with clear moral resonance: 'The ozone layer in the atmosphere protects life on Earth from a deadly overdose of ultraviolet radiation from the sun.'[16] The article goes on to document human activities that would significantly reduce the ozone layer's protective effects: nuclear war, supersonic transport aircraft, global air pollution from automobiles, and use of Freon.

These ideas are part of a larger transformation of scientific thought focused on planetary history and formation (for example, the theory of tectonic plates and the geographic evolution and migration of species). Yet, their significance derives at least as much from their importance as objects of normative concern as from their depiction of nature's operations on global scales. This scientific work fashioned not only the idea that the Earth's physical and ecological systems are global in scope but also the idea that these systems are at risk from human activity and thus of significance in human moral reasoning and public affairs.[17]

Organizing science for social responsibility

To imagine the Earth as more than an empty space that humans inhabit – as a suite of interconnected systems that function as an ontological whole – and to convey that imaginary[18] to people around the planet is not only a profoundly ethical act, as a number of environmental philosophers have observed,[19] but also an act of significant social and organizational transformation. Scientists had to reorganize their work to make it possible to analyse, assess, and model global phenomena and to portray the results as the objective work of a global scientific community, transcending the geopolitics of the post-war era.[20] Alongside their conceptual and communicative work, therefore, scientists put extensive efforts into the international organization of the scientific community for social responsibility.

The earliest such organizations took shape as diplomats and government agencies were beginning to frame the agenda for establishing a new post-war international order.[21] In 1946, for example, medical scientists established the World Health Organization (WHO), and, in 1947, their colleagues in the atmospheric sciences negotiated the treaty to establish the World Meteorological Organization (WMO). Numerous other organizations followed, in fields from civil aviation to nuclear energy, ultimately comprising close to twenty organizations that became known as the UN Specialized Agencies. In each case, the goal was to deploy science and expertise in the service of confronting common challenges facing humanity and to build institutions to advance the scientific work necessary to achieve that success.

Needing to justify itself on both scientific and geopolitical grounds, the WMO launched a programme to build a global weather monitoring system, known, by 1961, as the World Weather Watch. Underlying this effort were multiple initiatives to expand the capacity of weather services worldwide to work together to create and analyse data on the Earth's atmosphere. One programme standardized weather instruments and observational protocols around the globe. Another fashioned a global telecommunications network to collect data from the world's weather stations, synthesize it, and retransmit the results back to national weather services. Still other programmes helped countries to expand their national networks of weather stations and to extend networks of weather stations into remote regions of the globe where national weather data collection efforts did not reach.

As a result of this work, long before satellites would ever duplicate its capabilities, the WMO produced a global data set on the current state of the atmosphere – temperature, pressure, humidity, rainfall, cloud cover, and more – every three hours and shipped its data to scientists worldwide. For the first time in the history of the planet, scientists could do more than imagine global ecological processes, they could study them – and they did. In 1957–8, the International Geophysical Year (IGY) transformed what had been a periodic, long-term effort to understand the Earth's polar regions into a global scientific effort oriented towards the study of systematic geophysical processes that encompassed the world. The WMO was front and centre in this effort, helping to support the atmospheric sciences in their research efforts and to shape the global vision of the programme as a whole.[22] The data produced by the IGY and the World Weather Watch was integral to every aspect of the evolution of climate science, from the discovery of rising carbon dioxide levels in the atmosphere to the successful development of GCMs.[23]

Following the highly acclaimed success of the IGY, biologists also persuaded their funding agencies to support a decade-long organizational effort through the 1960s.[24] The International Biological Programme helped create the scientific foundations for not only the calculation of net primary productivity described above, as well as Hutchinson's 1970 portrayal of the biosphere, but also for a growing array of scientific efforts to measure and model the biosphere's contents and dynamics. Models of the global carbon exchange between the Earth's atmosphere and vegetation, for example, later fed into the design of integrated GCMs that could model the partitioning of carbon emissions into the atmosphere, ocean, and terrestrial ecosystems. Building models of carbon exchange demanded, in turn, global estimates of carbon loss and uptake from the destruction and regrowth of forests worldwide. Other biologists estimated the total number of species on the planet. Brought together in the early 1980s, forest loss statistics and species counts helped put the destruction of tropical forests in the public imagination in the form of a new global ecological catastrophe: the loss of biological diversity.[25]

In all these organizations, scientists understood themselves to be engaged in ethical as much as technical work. In 1947 US Assistant Secretary of State Garrison Norton highlighted this fact in his welcoming address to the world's chief weather scientists negotiating the World Meteorological Convention.[26] Scientists' work, in Norton's eyes, was ethical in at least two ways. First, weather scientists transcended politics with a 'global outlook' and an 'appreciation of international cooperation' essential to any hope the world had to secure peace during an era of profound international conflict. Second, their collective work in securing and sharing improved weather data contributed instrumentally to solving key international problems, in this case, for example, by improving weather forecasts that could help 'agriculture, commerce, industry, and transportation' in a world dealing with the severe hardships brought on by the prior years of war and violence.

More recently, scientists have begun to organize international assessments to synthesize scientific research and put it to work in the development of global environmental policy. The exemplar of this work is the Intergovernmental Panel on Climate Change (IPCC). Every five to seven years, the IPCC organizes thousands of scientists worldwide to review the scientific literature on climate change, synthesize it, and present it to decision-makers. Over the past quarter century, the IPCC has emerged as the most authoritative global voice on climate change and a powerful illustration of scientists' global organization for social responsibility.[27] The IPCC has also become a model for political action in the field of biological diversity, where scientists have recently organized the Intergovernmental Platform on Biodiversity and Ecosystem Services as an equivalent for the biodiversity regime.[28]

In summary, the science of global environmental change has evolved at the pace and scale it has because individual scientists, the communities of global environmental researchers, and the institutions that fund science have all understood themselves to have an ethical obligation to pursue, support, and communicate research addressing concerns potentially impacting on all of humanity.[29] That this normative concern evolved out of an earlier variant of normative commitment, in which scientists pursued wartime research in service of their nations' fights against one another, is one of the ironies of the twentieth century.[30] In many respects, however, it was precisely the experience of devoting their talents to weapons of mass destruction that led scientists to work together after the war in the search for global peace and prosperity.[31] Such weapons posed, after all, the first global environmental risks.[32]

Interlude: Framing global ethics

As we pass the mid-point of the second decade of the twenty-first century, the global environment has evolved, alongside trade and security, into one of the most central, important, and controversial domains of global affairs.[33] Throughout this period, critical ethical questions have confronted participants in global environmental debates: How should global environmental problems be framed? How should responsibility be allocated for global environmental risks and responses? How should the costs of solutions be distributed? And who should have a voice in resolving these questions?

From the responses to these questions, three broad ethical framings have emerged.[34] We label these a *duty of care* frame, a *crisis ethics* frame, and a *global governance* frame. Each represents a different framing of global environmental risk, policy responses, and the ethical values that underlie them. Over time, the relative weight and significance of each of these approaches waxes and wanes in global affairs as proponents argue back and forth about the ethics of global environmental policy.

The *duty of care* framing concerns our duties to protect the environment (whether on its own terms, to prevent harms to humans, or for future generations) and operates on the basis of relatively simple scientific narratives of global environmental risk, causality, and ethics. Borrowed from a prior generation of local environmental science, policy, and ethics, the duty of care focuses on the proximate causes of environmental problems. Proximate causes are those causes that are most closely associated in time and space with environmental impact. For example, if a pollutant is causing a problem, and if a polluter can be identified who is responsible for emitting that pollutant into the air or water, then that polluter has an ethical obligation to clean up his or her act and, via the polluter-pays principle, to pay for that clean-up. More distant causal factors – for example, the role of markets in driving down prices, which results in wastes being discarded as cheaply as possible, or the role of customers in purchasing the polluter's products – are typically given less weight in this framing.

More generally, this perspective lies at the heart of risk assessment and risk management approaches, perhaps most emblematically articulated for the global environment by William Clark in his 1989 article 'Managing Planet Earth'.[35] The duty of care narrative – which posits simple facts and values – suggests that global environmental risks are well-defined problems that can be relatively easily understood and solved, if only individuals, organizations, or countries will act ethically: halt the emission of pollutants into the atmosphere or ocean, stop the dumping of waste from rich countries into poorer neighbours, and resist the encroachment of humans into biodiversity-rich areas like tropical rainforests.

The relative simplicity of the duty of care approach has tended to make it attractive in global environmental policy. Major treaties have often drawn their logic from the duty of care ethic. The 1985 Vienna Convention for the Protection of the Ozone Layer and 1987 Montreal Protocol on Substances that Deplete the Ozone Layer largely follow this logic. Both start from the proposition that human activities damage the environment by emitting pollutants and ban the use of those pollutants. The treaties expect those who emit ozone-depleting pollutants to find alternative technologies to use instead. In global politics, this framing is often further simplified by the assumption that countries are the only relevant agents. The complexities of implementing effective and just bans on ozone-depleting substances are thus left as problems for domestic law. The only major exception to this logic in the case of ozone depletion was the creation of the Montreal Protocol Fund to compensate developing countries for the costs of finding alternative technologies, so as to speed implementation of the treaty and reduce its impacts on poorer countries.

Similarly, early proposals to address climate change followed a duty of care logic, including proposals tabled in Toronto in the late 1980s for a 20 per cent reduction of greenhouse gas emissions, as well as the final negotiated text of the 1992 UN Framework Convention on Climate Change, which called for a voluntary commitment on the part of wealthy countries to reduce emissions to 1990 levels over the period of a decade.

Climate negotiators almost immediately encountered complexities, however. In 1991, as part of the run-up to the Earth Summit, the World Resources Institute (WRI) published an accounting framework that assigned responsibility for climate change proportionally to countries based on their annual emissions of greenhouse gases.[36] WRI's report was quickly embroiled in a firestorm of controversy, led by an Indian non-governmental organization (NGO), the Centre for Science and the Environment (CSE). The CSE's response, *Global Warming in an Unequal World*, lambasted the WRI for assuming that moral responsibility for climate change could be assigned solely on the basis of counting up a country's emissions.[37] Such an approach, the CSE argued, made several ethical mistakes. One mistake was to assume that the only relevant moral significance of an act was its impact on the environment. By contrast, the CSE insisted, the moral significance of any human act can also be assessed based on its purpose. Thus, the CSE pointed out, some emissions are necessary for poor peoples to feed themselves, while others derive from luxury behaviours. The latter, the CSE argued, should receive initial attention from a climate change treaty, while the former should be exempted.

Another mistake, the CSE suggested, was to ignore the historical responsibility of wealthy countries, who had been adding carbon dioxide to the atmosphere since the nineteenth century and thus were proportionally more responsible for climate change than the WRI's annual emissions accounting determined. The CSE also argued that the WRI's approach misallocated the world's greenhouse gas emissions sinks. The ocean, especially, the CSE observed, absorbed a significant amount of the world's carbon dioxide emissions each year. The WRI, the CSE suggested, had tacitly allocated those sinks proportionally to each country's emissions, thus granting the lion's share to countries that already emitted the most greenhouse gases. The CSE suggested, instead, that it would be fairer to allocate these sinks on a per capita basis, as the ocean was a shared resource for all humanity, thus offsetting emissions from poor countries. The CSE thus suggested that moral and legal responsibility for climate change was complex and would take considerable and careful working out among the world's nations.

In making these claims, the CSE sought to shift the ethical narrative and calculus of climate change from a duty of care framework to a more explicitly *global governance* framework. In this framing, a central task of global negotiators is not simply to identify and solve problems but rather to hear, adjudicate, and balance a wide variety of competing moral and ethical claims about how the Earth and the problems of the global environment should be governed. A second task is to establish fair institutional procedures for accomplishing the first task. In making this argument, the CSE built on a history of debates, discussed in Chapter 2, about the relationship between environment and development in global environmental policy. These debates highlighted that inequality among countries significantly complicated the question of how to assign responsibility for action in protecting the global environment and led, ultimately, to the Earth Charter placing 'social and economic justice' on a par with 'ecological integrity' and 'respect and care for the community of life' as key principles. In turn, the CSE took the argument one step further: it is not enough to articulate general principles. Principles must be translated and applied in particular contexts of action. How to apply principles like social justice to global environmental treaties must be worked out in the details and implementation of legal, scientific, and administrative rules and actions. Ethical practice, in other words, demands careful attentiveness to the day-to-day decisions and practices of global governance.

Poor countries also learned the lesson of the necessity of paying careful attention to the details of global environmental science and politics from their experience with the Montreal Protocol Fund. The fund was established when India, China, and a few other countries objected at the last minute to a deal reducing ozone-depleting chemicals that had largely been negotiated between the USA, Japan, and Europe. The deal went forward, with rich countries agreeing to provide compensation via the fund to poor countries to mitigate the impacts of the deal on their rapidly growing refrigeration industries. The fund was initially estimated at about $10 billion, but specific accounting rules for disbursing funds tied compensation strictly to the actual costs of transition from old to new technologies, limiting the fund's disbursements. In the end, in a major political disappointment, poor countries received only a small fraction of what they had expected from the fund.[38] That result, along with a broad recognition in the mid-1990s that funds for environmental aid were, in many cases, simply displacing other kinds of development aid, introduced a serious complication into a wide variety of efforts to use monetary transfers to encourage poor countries to undertake action on behalf of the global environment.[39]

As we describe more extensively in the next two sections, the global governance framing has emerged as the most important ethical framing in international environmental politics. The divide between rich and poor countries has persisted as a major thorn in the negotiation of global environmental agreements, fostering disagreements about both policies and the values that should guide them. At the same time, other factors have also contributed to the evolution towards an ethics of global governance. The highest-profile global environmental issues such as climate change and biodiversity conservation cut across both major industrial sectors (agriculture and energy) and core economic policy domains (land use, forests, transportation, electricity, taxes, and finance). Consequently, the diversity of organizations and communities with a stake in global environmental policies has proliferated enormously, while the diversity of economic interests has fractured countries into dozens of networked political alliances and voting blocs. A growing blurring of the boundaries between domestic and international policymaking has also encouraged a variety of groups, from environmental organizations to business trade lobbies, to become active participants in global environmental debates. As a consequence, meetings of the major global environmental treaties and the now decadal UN conferences on environment and development (Rio 1992, Johannesburg 2002, Rio 2012) have become enormous social forums, with tens of thousands of individuals and organizations converging on host cities both to advance a variety of social and environmental agendas and to lobby global policymakers. Finally, indigenous groups have also begun to wield growing influence in global environmental governance, asserting claims to specialized knowledge and rights in many of the world's most important environmental areas, including the Arctic and tropical forests.

The evolving complexity of global environmental governance has, perhaps inevitably, slowed progress toward major global policies that would transform human interactions with our planetary environment. Governing large nations is hard enough, after all, even for strong states, and international institutions remain extraordinarily weak by comparison. Consequently, some groups have come to fear that the world will not adequately address global risks and so have adopted a more radical *crisis framing* to global environmental ethics. The crisis framing offers, at its most vivid, an apocalyptic view that portrays global environmental risks not merely as serious challenges for humanity but as existential threats to modern societies. In the field of biodiversity, these risks include the possibility, for example, that pollinators may die out or some other critical ecosystem service will collapse and threaten the viability of agricultural systems. In climate change, advocates of a crisis framing point to the possibility of a rapid melting of the West Antarctic ice sheet or other abrupt climate catastrophe that would likewise put at risk major human populations.

Like the global governance framing, crisis ethics perspectives have been integral to global environmental debates from the beginning. Garrett Hardin's 1974 essay 'Lifeboat Ethics' was one of the earliest and most influential statements of an ethics of planetary survival, suggesting that global environmental ethics should be driven not by the general ethical principles and practices that govern day-to-day life but rather by an alternative ethics that recognizes the possibility of existential threats and acts, as necessary, to prevent those threats from becoming reality.[40] Hardin argued specifically against efforts to provide food to poor populations facing starvation and hunger, contrary to our conventional moral judgement to help neighbours in times of trouble, intimating that such actions would only worsen the long-term food and environmental crisis facing the world. Others followed Hardin's lead. Environmental groups such as Greenpeace and Friends of the Earth, for example, have justified disruptive and even, on occasion, violent actions on the basis of claims that a conventional ethics of non-violence was inadequate to address such global existential threats as nuclear weapons, environmental degradation, or genetic engineering.

More recently, crisis ethics has re-emerged with respect to both biodiversity loss and climate change. In biodiversity conservation, since 2000, major conservation organizations have drawn on crisis ethics to challenge the traditional sovereignty of nations. These organizations have used their financial leverage (some have larger budgets than small countries), as well as that of the World Bank, to coerce countries into protecting biodiversity rich areas of the planet. On occasion, they have also deployed their own paramilitary organizations to carry out protection. More recently, advocates of geoengineering have offered a crisis ethics logic, arguing that the repeated failure of global policymakers to address the looming threat of climate change, alongside a rising risk of abrupt climate catastrophe, justify radical actions to engineer the Earth's climate system. Whether the world agrees or not, they suggest, and whether or not the application of geoengineering may be highly disruptive in other ways, they argue for developing and deploying technological solutions to fix the Earth's climate system.[41]

By the second decade of the twentieth century, the planet has arguably come to occupy its most significant place in humanity's ethical imagination ever. Despite the rise of terrorism and financial crises as major global concerns, for example, neither has displaced climate change from local, national, or global policy agendas. Yet, competing ethical frames combined with the depth of changes demanded in the organization of human affairs have prevented climate change from receiving the same mobilization of resources and action as these other more immediate and visible security threats. Does this mean that the practice of global environmental ethics has failed? Far from it. As we describe in the rest of this chapter, the work of global environmental ethics remains active and alive in a wide range of settings, from global environmental institutions to efforts across the planet to transform the world's socio-technological systems in ways that will make them more sustainable.

The ethical practices of global environmental governance

The practices of global ethics occur across multiple layers of ethical work. We have already described several of these layers: the formulation of global ethical principles, the identification and delineation of the proper objects of ethical imagination and analysis, and the articulation and deliberation of broad ethical framings. Two layers remain for discussion. The first is the work of interpreting, deliberating, adapting, and putting to work values and ethical principles in the development of global environmental institutions, policies, and standards. The second is the comparable work within efforts to find solutions to global environmental risks. We address the first in this section and the second in the following one.

The significance of these forms of global ethical practice cannot be overemphasized. If global ethics is to have any meaning whatsoever, it can happen only because people and institutions transform abstract moral principles and statements into functioning patterns of human behaviour at all levels of society from the individual to the planet. The transformation of ethics from principles to practices involves the translation and specification of ethical principles, applying them to specific contexts. In this, ethical practice parallels the role of courts in applying law to individual cases, in the process determining what the law means in practice. This transformation also entails the creation of institutions that enable the performance of governance: the writing and binding of new global ethical principles and the administration of global ethical rules and procedures. The practice of global environmental governance is thus virtually indistinguishable from the practice of global environmental ethics. This is not to trivialize the practice of global ethics but to recognize its pervasiveness. The practice of global ethics is enmeshed in virtually every aspect of global environmental governance. Hence, to practise global ethics successfully entails attending carefully to ethics throughout the rules and institutions of global environmental governance.

The past half-century has witnessed an explosion of these forms of global ethical practice: the establishment of major *new interna-*

tional environmental organizations; the negotiation of dozens of *major environmental treaties*; numerous *permanent negotiating and deliberation forums*, each with its own modest bureaucratic support, subsidiary bodies, and work programmes; and hundreds of *minor environmental agreements*.[42] Collectively, this work has transformed the practice of global ethics into a daily business for tens of thousands of individuals around the world working in foreign ministries, state agencies, international organizations, NGOs, research facilities, industry lobby groups, international law offices, and many, many more.

This activity is replete with ethical significance. Taken as a whole, even considering only the major environmental treaties, these activities represent a massive effort to identify, articulate, deliberate, and codify an enormous array of global ethical principles and to interpret and apply their meanings to specific cases and decisions, reconciling and balancing their relative significance where appropriate. While it would be a gross overstatement to suggest that ethics, alone, formed the basis of global environmental governance, we can say two things. First, normative commitments are pervasive in global environmental governance, not least in the arguments made by participants in these forums in support of or against any given proposition. Second, and just as significant, the upshot of these negotiations determines just which ethical standards the world is willing to put into practice on a global basis.

This work can be differentiated into a range of distinct domains of ethical work that have evolved broadly across global environmental governance. In doing so, we will use the UN Framework Convention on Climate Change as an illustrative case, but the domains have clearly evolved similarly across many if not all of the major environmental arenas. These domains include what might be termed the objectives and principles of global environmental ethics, standards of practice, regimes of accountability, and norms of participation. Others may want to expand this list. We use it only to exemplify the general idea of global ethical practice.

Perhaps the most important domain of global ethical work has focused on *normative standards for humanity*. The Framework Convention articulates in Article 2 that its objective is 'to achieve . . . stabilization of greenhouse gas concentrations in the atmosphere at a level that would prevent dangerous anthropogenic interference with the climate system'.[43] This objective constitutes an important ethical principle for the globe, establishing a limit beyond which humans should not interfere with the dynamics of the Earth's climate. It is illustrative, however, that this statement, which is relatively powerful as an ethical limit and represents a major agreement among countries, does not stand on its own. Left unspecified is precisely what level of greenhouse gas concentrations is to be considered dangerous. While this was, on the part of negotiators, at least partially a nod to scientific uncertainty, it also left vague the precise meaning of dangerous. Danger, after all, is both socially and materially relative. What is dangerous to a child may not be dangerous to an adult. Likewise, what one person views as dangerous another may view as an exciting pastime.

Over time, therefore, a significant strand of ethical work on climate change has been to pursue analysis, deliberation, and negotiation to determine whether countries could agree on a more precise articulation of Article 2. The IPCC, while always acknowledging that the ultimate decision of what counts as dangerous is fundamentally political and ethical, has undertaken significant work designed to clarify scientific factors that could feed into that decision. This work has been presented in synthesis and technical reports, as well as in IPCC assessments. In turn, IPCC reports have become fodder for diplomatic negotiations within the regime, illustrating the dynamic interactivity between the scientific and political communities common to the practice of global ethics in the environmental arena.[44]

Following the IPCC's discussion of Article 2 in its 1995 report, for example, the European Union (EU) established in 1996 a long-term target of minimizing global average temperature increase to two degrees Centigrade.[45] This target quickly became an informally agreed-upon target, although it was never formally adopted as an official standard, and subsequent scientific work has shown that even this amount of climate change will have significant consequences for people and ecosystems. Scientists quickly began to use the two-degree target, in turn, as the basis for studies of the impacts of two, four, and six degrees of warming and the reductions in future greenhouse gas emissions necessary to achieve these targets.[46] Building on this work, the G8 hosted a scientific conference in 2005 on the topic of 'Avoiding Dangerous Climate Change',[47] which was followed up in 2009 by a second conference titled '4 Degrees and Beyond'[48] to explore the implications of failing to achieve a low warming target. In 2011, the US National Research Council released its own reports: *Climate Stabilization Targets*[49] and *Warming World: Impacts by Degree*.[50]

In addition to establishing normative global standards, international environmental law also sets *standards of practice* for countries. For the Framework Convention, the primary standard established was for wealthy countries to reduce their greenhouse gas emissions to 1990 levels. While this was a voluntary commitment, it set an important benchmark that has influenced national policy in numerous contexts. In fact, both the EU and the USA continue to benchmark their emissions inventories to 1990. As of 2015, the EU is well below this level, while the USA is close to achieving it. In 2012 US emissions were below 1994 levels. Japan had also achieved reductions to 1990 levels in 2010, before the closure of their nuclear reactors after the Fukushima disaster revived their dependence on coal-fired power plants for the time being.[51]

Closely linked to standards of practice for countries are *accountability regimes* specifying who is to be held accountable for what actions. Adding to their efforts to insert new objects of ethical concern into the human imagination and to organize themselves to pursue global social responsibility, scientists have also played a central role in fashioning the frameworks of accountability and associated rituals of audit and verification[52] through which ethical and political responsibility for global environmental risks gets parsed. Scientists have undertaken an enormous number of studies to document and assess all the major forms of atmospheric emissions that contribute to climate change and their distribution across forms of activity, industries, and countries. This is ethical work because, as Sheila Jasanoff has observed, regulatory science is inevitably a hybrid construction of facts and values.[53] Accountability frameworks and verification rituals not only document the causes of environmental risks; they embed that documentation in narratives that establish and distribute moral responsibility for risks.[54] Indeed, in many cases, the facts themselves cannot be established independently of the considerations of responsibility embedded in accountability practices.

Building on this scientific work, the Framework Convention spells out not only that countries must reduce their national greenhouse gas emissions but also that countries must develop and publish periodic reports detailing their greenhouse gas emissions in the form of emissions inventories. The text requires that countries:

> Develop, periodically update, publish and make available to the Conference of the Parties, in accordance with Article 12, national inventories of anthropogenic emissions by sources and removals by sinks of all greenhouse gases not controlled by the Montreal Protocol, using comparable methodologies to be agreed upon by the Conference of the Parties.[55]

Embedded in this short text are a remarkable number of normative commitments regarding accountability under the Framework Convention. First, countries are to be held accountable. They must develop and publish their own inventories for assessing treaty performance. They are to include both emissions and sinks, but only anthropogenic not natural sources or sinks, and they are not to include those gases already controlled by the ozone treaties. And they are to use comparable methods.

Developing standard inventory methods has been, in turn, a lengthy exercise in international scientific and political collaboration. Work began even before the Framework Convention had been negotiated, under the auspices of the Organization for Economic Cooperation and Development (OECD). The IPCC later took over this work and published standard methods for measuring national inventories.[56] These methods embody the normative commitments expressed in the treaty text, as well as additional values interwoven with the relevant science. They thus represent another domain of ethical work involving both scientists and, on occasion, political delegates to the Framework Convention.

As one illustration, the designation that countries will compile national inventories of emissions does not sufficiently specify which emissions should be included in which countries' inventories. The generally accepted definition has been to use national boundaries to define responsibility for emissions, but this has left open cases in which emissions occur in international domains (air, oceans, space) or when emissions or their precursors (for example, fuel) are traded or carried across national borders. This definition has never formally been specified, to our knowledge, by the Framework Convention parties, leaving open the possibility for other definitions, such as emissions that are the direct responsibility of the state (for example, from military operations) or result from consumption by a nation's citizens of products produced in other countries. The latter, for example, would significantly alter the moral implications of China's rapid increase in emissions in recent years, as most of those derive from industrial activity that ultimately produces products for export. The former raises the interesting question, for example, of whether emissions from US army operations in Iraq or naval operations in international waters are counted in the US inventory. One presumes they are, despite the precise locations at which the emission occurred, but it does matter, as the US military is the largest purchaser of energy in the world. Insisting on a single, strict definition of national responsibility, whatever that definition, would require widespread adjustments to the methods. Part of the ethical work necessary, therefore, in global environmental governance, is to determine when accountability regimes provide information that is good enough.

Finally, *norms of participation* are an increasingly important arena of significant ethical innovation in global environmental governance. Historically, international law has been a matter for diplomatic engagement among states. Moreover, diplomacy as practised by the state has most frequently occurred among relatively small numbers of countries, and most treaties have only a handful of signatories. The major exception to this rule, aside from the significant environmental treaties, is the United Nations itself, which now has universal membership among states. Indeed, recognition as a UN member is generally taken as the de facto test of membership in the community of sovereign states. Despite the success of the United Nations (and worldwide UN membership was achieved only slowly), most major international treaties after the Second World War neither pursued nor achieved universal membership of states.

With the rise of global environmental governance, however, two significant normative shifts have occurred in international law. First, all of the major international environmental treaties now have nearly universal membership, with the climate, ozone, biodiversity, and desertification treaties having 195+ members each. This signifies the extent to which these institutions are now seen as essential sites of global deliberation. Even in the one significant case of non-membership, the USA and the Convention on Biological Diversity (CBD) (it is the only state not a member as of 2015), the USA routinely attends every meeting. Strikingly, many of the UN Specialized Agencies, including the International Monetary Fund (IMF) and World Bank, have membership only in the 180s, while the WTO includes only 159 members. At the same time, as discussed briefly earlier in the chapter, participants in global environmental treaty processes have insisted on expanding membership beyond states. Thus, international organizations, environmental groups, business groups, and indigenous peoples now both attend and participate as non-voting members in treaty meetings and have formal representation and are allowed to provide input into diplomatic negotiations.

The ethics of global environmental solutions

Thus far, this chapter has emphasized the practice of ethics in global environmental science and governance. We now turn to another arena that is also highly significant: the range of sites within which people are reconfiguring the socio-technological systems at the heart of modern societies as a consequence of the imagination of global environmental risks. The Earth as an object of ethical imagination infects not only global environmental governance but also numerous sites in which people are rearranging their lived realities in order to accommodate concerns about new risks such as climate change and biodiversity loss. As a consequence, some of the most significant aspects of modern social, economic, and political orders – from land tenure to energy production and consumption – are being completely rearranged around new ideas of the environment and its ethical claims on human affairs. Here, we briefly discuss some of the ethical challenges entailed in these reconfigurations, using energy-systems change as an illustration. Land-use changes entail similar challenges but are not discussed for the sake of brevity.

The ethical dimensions of energy transitions contemplated in response to climate change fall along three axes: the intercalibration of global and local ethical commitments; the redistribution of benefits, costs, and risks; and the allocation of power and voice within decision-making processes.[57] The introduction of the Earth as an element of ethical imagination fundamentally alters the ethical calculus surrounding energy policy, but not in a way that simply dismisses other facets of energy ethics,[58] thus demanding that energy policy find ways *to calibrate new global ethical requirements to reduce carbon emissions with local ethical commitments* already in play. In some cases, local and global ethics may line up easily. Coal-fired power plants, mines, and petrochemical facilities have a long history of contributing to local pollution problems and a variety of concerns about environmental injustice. Reducing our long-term use of coal and oil will inevitably reduce those insults. In other cases, local and global ethics may turn out to be at odds. In the United States, for example, in 2015, renewable energy is still more expensive in most circumstances than electricity generated from coal and natural gas, although the relative price is decreasing rapidly. As a result, investments in renewable energy are raising electricity prices, including for poor communities that struggle to pay their energy bills. At the same time, while wealthy homeowners are increasingly taking advantage of solar energy to reduce their energy bills through rooftop installations, this path is either more costly or cost-prohibitive for poor homeowners and, for those who rent, often unavailable.[59]

As these examples suggest, a second central challenge in the face of energy transitions is the *redistribution of benefits, costs, and risks* associated with the introduction of new energy systems and the phasing-out of old ones. Energy systems are often portrayed as merely technologies, but they are, in fact, extensive socio-technological systems that link far-flung parts of the world in drilling, shipping, transport, and refining operations with a wide variety of human forms of activity that consume energy.[60] Changing the technological hearts of these systems inevitably involves changing human values, behaviours, relationships, and institutions, not to mention the distribution of wealth and power, locally and globally. This fact is central to the extraordinary opposition to climate policies that has arisen in global and national governance, but this is only the tip of the iceberg in terms of the redistributional consequences of energy system change that must be assessed as part of a broadly conceived ethics of the global environment.[61]

Some of this redistribution is simple geography. Many areas that are energy rich in the current energy system will not be so in the future. The Gulf Coast of the United States, for example, is neither terribly sunny nor does it have much wind. Key countries rich in fossil fuels, including Canada and Russia, are likewise not endowed with significant sunlight. The desert US Southwest, on the other hand, which has few fossil fuel resources, has enormous solar opportunities, as does the Sahara, which has long been viewed as a wasteland. Jobs, economic development, and inexpensive energy will thus flow across the landscape as part of an energy transition. So, too, will other challenges. For example, the surge of oil and gas drilling in North Dakota in the 2000s has had major economic and social consequences. As of March 2014, the state had the lowest unemployment rate in the United States, at 2.6 per cent, although this may change rapidly if the drop in oil prices of late 2014 persists. Demographically, the state has the most skewed gender balance, not including Alaska, with 48 per cent women to 52 per cent men, and the state is one of the few in the United States whose population is growing younger, thanks to immigration of young men to work in the shale fields. At the same time, the state is experiencing one of the worst social crises it has ever faced, as it struggles to contend with a massive boom in new labour in a region with relatively low capacity to absorb new people into its social and physical infrastructure.[62] In many parts of the world, popular opposition to the environmental and social consequences of hydraulic fracturing is creating unrest around the prospects of new drilling for natural gas.

Redistribution can also occur in more subtle ways. The rapid rise of distributed solar energy poses serious challenges for electric utilities.[63] Rooftop solar systems on residences and businesses remove load from the electrical grid, thus reducing revenues for utilities, impacting their business model, and putting at risk their financial viability. In turn, groups dependent on utilities experience higher risks. These include low-income communities who cannot afford to 'go solar', as well as businesses that rely on the grid for manufacturing and industrial power and that cannot use solar to meet their needs. These groups face higher costs (as the costs of maintaining the grid infrastructure are spread across fewer customers), as well as potential disruption of service if the utility itself is threatened. Another group is utility investors, who, for example, in the United States, are primarily retirees, for whom utility stocks have been a major source of stable income.

Finally, *procedural justice* concerns also arise in the context of energy transitions. Historically, energy policy in the early twentieth century was a subject for broad democratic engagement. Over time, however, energy policy has narrowed to a technocratic speciality, dominated by energy experts, as a stable energy system has reduced broad public involvement. In the context of large-scale energy transitions, however, the deep social and ethical issues at stake suggest the need to redemocratize energy decisions through new partnerships between communities and the energy sector to envision sustainable futures around novel energy systems. Unfortunately, this reopening of energy policy to a broader array of interests and groups does not seem to be happening, leading to a surge of political protests around virtually all forms of energy technologies.[64] Oil, coal, natural gas, wind, solar – all are generating intense political interest from publics seeking a voice in what may be the most socially, economically, and politically influential choices of the next fifty years.

Interlude: Comparative globalisms and ethical dilemmas

In many respects, the early 1990s was the high-water mark of environmental globalism. Three major treaties were negotiated between 1990 and 1994, on climate change, biodiversity loss, and desertification. These treaties codified in international law the Earth-at-risk model of environmentalism based in a duty of care framing. No longer were environmental challenges viewed as fundamentally local; they truly encompassed the planet. One could be forgiven for all but taking for granted that the environment simply was a unitary global whole. The biosphere, the ozone layer, the climate system, Earth systems science – all pointed towards the idea not only that the environment could be analysed and managed on global scales but also that more localized views simply no longer made sense.

It was probably inevitable that the world would come down from this high. Global risks to the environment remain central features of scientific and public imagination. Indeed, the concept of risks embedded in global systems and processes has proliferated since the early 1990s, becoming common in discussions of national security, health, and finance.[65] Nor has the ethical imperative to cooperate globally to address these challenges diminished. Following in the wake of the global financial market collapse of 2008, for example, major world leaders called widely for the strengthening of global regulatory institutions to manage planetary financial markets. Yet, the ethics and politics of environmental globalism are far more complex and contested today than they seemed in 1990.

Today's complexities arise not only from diverse framings of global ethics, as already discussed, but also from what one might term contested or comparative globalisms. Put simply, as the imagined state of the world has shifted away from states confronting one another, with the primary risk being war, towards states now collectively confronting a range of global risks, the challenge has become to understand what it means to live in a global world, what kind of future to build for that world, and how best to govern the world so as to achieve that ideal. On these questions, deep divisions remain around the world.

Unicentric or polycentric?

One of the central questions of the twenty-first century will be the form of sociopolitical organization that evolves at the global scale around emergent ethical imperatives. In this, the experience of both the United States, at the turn of the twentieth century, and Europe, in the early twenty-first century, are illuminative. As described by historian Samuel Hays, the United States in the Progressive Era could be understood as a struggle between the forces of centralization and a wide variety of local oppositions. Centralization won, and, during the first six decades of the twentieth century, the United States experienced a series of waves of growth in the federal state. By the time the Environmental Protection Agency was established in 1970, the idea that the federal government was the supreme regulatory authority in the country was well established. Several decades of 'small government' conservatism have eroded that project to some degree, but the recent passage of Obamacare demonstrates the continued imaginative and political power of a strong state setting equal conditions for all of its citizens.

Europe emerged as a centralizing political entity in the late twentieth century, amid struggles to unite a fractious continent. Those struggles continue, but the reality of Europe – a single market, a single currency, and a supranational suite of political institutions – has defied a number of predictions of its imminent demise, demonstrating the resilience of the European commitment to working together to confront the challenges of today's world. Despite Europe's resilience, however, as we will describe in greater detail in the next section, the European continent is not exempt from the resurgence of locality now taking place around the globe. In 1999, Scotland, for three centuries an integral part of the United Kingdom, re-established an independent parliament and, in 2014, voted on independence. Several other European provinces are poised to make similar demands. The tug of war between centralizing and decentralizing forces continues apace. Yet, in both the United States and Europe, it is notable that governance takes the form of federalist systems, with both central and distributed institutions, in Europe labelled as subsidiarity. And, in both, a variety of overlapping arrangements draw states together in different kinds of economic and political collaboration that shape policymaking at the highest levels of government. Thus, both exhibit both unicentric and polycentric tendencies.

In international politics, the United Nations has exerted a centralizing pull on global governance since its establishment at the close of the Second World War. The UN Specialized Agencies, in particular, have been major forces in the birth and nurturing of a global social imaginary: creating common forums for identifying global problems, conducting global analyses, and forging global solutions. This pattern seems unlikely to change any time soon. Indeed, over the past two decades, across numerous regimes of global governance, crisis ethics has emerged as a justification for streamlining and empowering global organizations. In areas such as infectious disease, banking regulations, and nuclear arms control, recent events have led countries to upgrade the power and authority of international expert organizations, including the World Health Organization, the International Monetary Fund, and the International Atomic Energy Agency, to combat global threats.[66] These upgrades have been underwritten by the persistence of the view that not only are the risks in question global and demand a global response but that the risks are sufficiently dire to warrant reconfiguration of long-held normative traditions like sovereignty. So long as the tug of the global on the imagination of the world's leaders and peoples remains strong, so will the impulse to search for solutions that encompass the planet in its entirety.

In recent years, however, advocates of a polycentric approach to global governance and global ethics have pushed for an end to the struggle to create global frameworks.[67] The primary driver of this new push for an explicit polycentrism has been the persistent failure of the climate regime to reach a global accord on greenhouse gas emissions reductions. This problem is too hard, the advocates of polycentrism suggest, with too many states, too many divergent interests, and too much need for progress now, not at some nebulous point in the future when agreement might be possible. Instead, they argue, the world should look for smaller alliances of like-minded states that can make progress towards emissions reductions without the need for universal agreement among all parties to the UN Framework Convention.

There is much to like in the polycentric approach. Indeed, global governance has been polycentric from its outset. As important as the United Nations and its Specialized Agencies have been, they have never served as the kind of centralized bureaucracy characteristic of say, the US Presidency or the European Commission. Instead, each agency was the result of a separately negotiated treaty, and, according to international law, each has operated as a sovereign legal entity. The same convention has applied to global environmental governance, with each of the major regimes operating as an independently sovereign treaty organization, alongside other regimes that incorporate environmental dimensions, including the WTO. This has led to forum shopping by countries or advocacy organizations looking for favourable responses to their perspective. For example, much to the annoyance of business interests in the biotechnology sector, the CBD has taken an active role in pushing global biosafety standards. The CBD has also been active in the field of geoengineering, despite the topic's obvious relevance to the climate regime, thanks in part to the latter's reluctance to take it under active discussion. So, even as international institutions and regimes have fostered globalist imaginaries, their disaggregation across distinct but highly overlapping subject domains has created a strong foundation for polycentric governance.

While pragmatically sensible, polycentrism does carry ethical risks. As partial groups of states – or states operating under the partial authority of a particular regime – move forward with their own solutions, they may feel less obligation to attend to the implications of their solutions on other issue domains or in other parts of the world. Parts of the world with large, integrated markets, like Europe, may be powerful enough to assert their regulatory authority to create carbon markets or other rules that companies feel obliged to follow. In other regions, however, companies may feel less obliged to participate. In much the same way, in the United States, California has sufficient market power to force companies to comply with its rules, while other states do not, limiting their power to act on their own or in small groups. Perhaps most disconcerting of all, one of the central benefits of global solutions is the need to negotiate in ways that reduce the impacts on those most harmed by new policies. Much of the incentive for such an approach vanishes in the context of polycentrism. As we suggest below, polycentrism may be acceptable for the cases of greenhouse gas emissions reductions or climate adaptation. Polycentric geoengineering, on the other hand, would probably result in chaos.

A resurgence of localisms?

Polycentrism should not be confused with resurgent localism. Polycentric approaches to global governance acknowledge the importance and significance of global problems but seek, generally for pragmatic reasons, to pursue parallel solutions to those problems across diverse groups or networks in global society. Thus, the idea that a global network of cities might pursue climate policies independently of their national governments is a form of polycentrism. Resurgent localism, on the other hand, derives from a commitment to local communities, local ways of knowing, and local places as the foundation for social, economic, and political order.

The regrowth of a strong Scottish (not to mention Welsh) nationalism offers a prima facie example of localism, despite Scotland's narrow vote not to pursue its political independence from the United Kingdom. Already, Scotland has its own parliament, its own ethnic and national identity, and its own historical imagination. Across Europe, regional groups are surging in power and purpose. Eastern Europe has already witnessed the break-up of both Czechoslovakia and Yugoslavia. Macedonia has split from Greece. And Andorran and Basque nationalists would like to split from Spain, as perhaps would Catalonia. In the former Soviet Union, separatist movements abound. Outside Europe, the Kurdish people are exerting pressure on Turkey, Iran, and Iraq. Across the globe, tribal and indigenous groups are also exerting their strength, insisting on distinct ways of knowing the world, distinct spiritual and ethnic traditions, and distinct political requirements. Tribal groups, especially, have gained new authority throughout the Americas, while the United Nations increasingly recognizes the world's indigenous peoples as a separate and significant category of actors in international affairs.

Perhaps ironically, but certainly causally, divergent localisms have drawn strength and purpose from the rise of globalist and universalist ethical projects. On the one hand, these projects of economic, environmental, and political globalization have galvanized opposition among local groups to the hegemonic narratives of the global. Regional groups in Europe have suffered under the legal regimes of their parent states and the EU, much as indigenous groups have found their land tenure under assault both from large agricultural companies and global environmental advocacy groups. At the same time, the universalist and globalist projects have given local groups tools in their conflicts with national states in the forms of human rights and environmental norms against which to call the state to account to external authorities for its actions. Indeed, by fundamentally altering the geopolitical imagination of the world, either toward the pre-eminence of the individual rights holder or the significance of global systems and process, ethical reimagination has also undermined the sovereign status of the state, thus weakening its grip on the geographic imagination of territory and allowing groups to imagine the patterning of the world's boundaries in alternative terms.

The question at hand is thus not whether to go global or to go local, but rather whether emerging forms of globalizing and relocalizing discourses and institutions are capable of finding strategies to accommodate and promote local diversity within a conversation of the whole. Here, polycentric approaches may have value (with the proviso, above, that they create challenges for ensuring solutions appropriately incorporate a range of distributive and procedural justice considerations), but only if designed appropriately. The Millennium Ecosystem Assessment, for example, conducted a very interesting experiment in what it termed its sub-global assessment working group. The goal of this experiment was not simply to encourage the adoption of ecosystem assessment methods at local or regional scales but also to create dialogue, exchange, and cross-fertilization among assessors from divergent localities, so as to foster 'reasoning together' about global problems – an opportunity for communities that brought different perspectives, frames of reference, and logics of analysis to the study of global problems to engage with one another's forms of rationality.[68]

To mitigate, adapt, or engineer?

Perhaps the most contentious ethical dilemma facing the world today is the question of how to respond to the deep conflict between global environmental and techno-economic imperatives. This challenge is clearest in the case of climate change, where the world now confronts an increasingly stark choice: *mitigate climate change*, requiring the wholesale reconfiguration of the energy system and, potentially, the industrial system with which it is deeply intertwined; *adapt to climate change*, probably requiring the wholesale transformation of human affairs to accommodate not only new climatic risks but the larger ecosystemic transformations that will accompany global warming; or *engineer the climate system* to operate in a regime tolerable to some forms of human affairs and natural ecosystems but requiring constant management of planetary dynamics. Of course, some combination of all three may ultimately be necessary and/or required, pragmatically and ethically.

Ethically, this choice raises profound questions of humanity's obligations both to one another and to natural systems, as well as the ethical capacity of human institutions to reason through the complexities of the choice and arrive at a legitimate decision. On the surface, as a problem in environmental ethics, the choice may seem obvious and straightforward. The Earth Charter as well as numerous global environmental treaties enjoin humanity to act to prevent dangerous climate change, protect the Earth's environment, and avoid actions that will, without a significant reduction of greenhouse gas emissions, produce significant harm for people across the planet. Yet, as a problem in global justice, the question of how to respond appropriately to climate change is inevitably more complex.

One key question about which there is deep and perhaps inevitable scientific uncertainty is how much time is available to transform the world's energy systems. The IPCC has reported that some climate change is already occurring and will continue to occur until we eliminate carbon dioxide emissions. At a minimum, therefore, some adaptation will be required, as well as at least some obligation to address the problems this will create for the world's most vulnerable and least well off. If more severe climate shifts occur as the planet is reducing carbon emissions, calls will also rise for efforts to geoengineer the climate system in order to reduce the worst outcomes – although when to act, on the basis of what criteria, and who decides will be controversial, at best. The ethics of geoengineering will also be complicated by the ability of a number of countries and possibly even business or substate entities to carry out certain forms of geoengineering.

Another key question is the ethics of widespread energy systems change, as we have already discussed. To extend that discussion here, we would simply add that prominent voices have recently argued against strategies that would leave the world with lower levels of energy consumption and high energy costs. This outcome, the authors of a 2014 report from the Breakthrough Institute argue, would severely damage the ability of many of the world's peoples to develop economically – for them, a morally objectionable, indeed repugnant, idea and perhaps in their view ethically impermissible. They call instead for a 'High-Energy Planet' with large quantities of low-cost energy for all.[69] If one accepts this argument, several strategies emerge as possible. One is to aim for rapid advancement in solar and wind energy, along with significant energy storage capabilities, towards low costs, along with the economic and social adaptation required to accommodate both the likely resulting climate change and an energy system that behaves very differently from our current system. Another is to build large numbers of nuclear power plants, which comes with its own political and environmental risks. Last, perhaps, is to commit to geoengineering as a strategy for managing climatic shifts.

Conclusions

In the vast sweep of human history, the twentieth century will stand apart for many reasons. Among them, one of the most notable seems likely to be the birth of a new imaginary of nature, and of human–nature relations. For the first time, in the latter decades of the twentieth century, it became possible to imagine nature as global, as at risk globally from human activities, and as requiring for its protection – and for the ultimate security of humanity – a new transcendent, global ethic of stewardship that renders irrelevant the ravages of war and division in human history. This chapter has offered a brief history of the birth of this imaginative possibility, its embodiment in international law, and the ethical challenges it still poses for humanity a decade and a half into the twenty-first century.

Environmentalism in the twenty-first century is a complex affair. For many, including many environmental scientists and activists in the world's wealthiest countries, environmental globalism remains the primary lens through which to view the world. Planetary risks have grown more serious only in the nearly two decades since the Earth Summit. Yet, the push to impose global regulations to protect the environment must proceed in parallel with serious negotiations over the ethical norms that will govern the world in coming decades. Seemingly, we are further, as of 2015, from accomplishing that task than two decades ago. The retreat of the United States to a position of unilateralism on a wide range of global risks has made the prospect of achieving progress more, not less difficult. Perhaps most discouraging of all is the persistent unwillingness of those who perceive global risks as frighteningly real – whether climate change, terrorism, or avian influenza – to acknowledge that these problems exist alongside a range of other problems, from poverty and under-development to economic exploitation and the very real human consequences of economic globalization.

This refusal to acknowledge the complexities of global ethics and global governance in dealing with global risks results in instrumental strategies that focus on solving the problem of climate change while not admitting that any action taken at the global level will be deeply political, will connect global issues to a wide range of local and regional concerns, and will require careful considerations of justice and equity in a highly unequal world. Put at its most stark, in our view, the problem is not that efforts to achieve a powerful practice of global ethics went too far; they did not go far enough. One can never simply derive a planetary ethics from descriptions of planetary-scale processes and systems. That is the fundamental mistake. Never simply about the future of the planet, global environmental risk must be understood to encompass wide-ranging, complex perspectives on how to shape the future of humanity. Recognition that the Earth is a global system radically alters the grounds and possibilities of human ethics, but it cannot compel a single moral vision of the collective human future. Humanity must still figure out what that global future should be. Today's global environmental politics reflect this profound ethical challenge. What kind of world should we build for those who will live 100 years from now? Whose visions of socio-technological and environmental futures should guide this process? What criteria should we use to make global allocations of environmental benefit, cost, and risk? To see the Earth from space, to know the functioning of Earth systems, is to know the challenges we face as a global society – indeed, it is to require that we envision ourselves as a global society. But the test of forging a practice of global ethics is to work through, with all humanity, the hard ethical questions of what kind of future to build for both humanity and our home planet. In short, we need a yet more robust practice of global ethics.

Notes

1. Miller, 'Globalizing Security'.
2. Ward and Dubos, *Only One Earth*.
3. World Commission on Environment and Development, *Our Common Future*.
4. Jasanoff (ed.), *States of Knowledge*. See also Jasanoff, 'Image and Imagination'.
5. Worster (ed.), *Nature's Economy*.
6. Edwards, *A Vast Machine*.
7. Revelle and Suess, 'Carbon Dioxide Exchange between Atmosphere and Ocean and the Question of an Increase of Atmospheric CO_2 during the Past Decades'.
8. Crutzen, 'Estimates of Possible Future Ozone Reductions from Continued Use of Fluoro-Chloro-Methanes (CF_2Cl_2, $CFCl_3$)'.
9. Hutchinson, 'The Biosphere'.
10. Takacs, *The Idea of Biodiversity*, p. 1.
11. Commoner, *Science and Survival*.
12. Carson, *Silent Spring*.
13. Yearley, *Sociology, Environmentalism, Globalization*.
14. Hutchinson, 'The Biosphere', p. 45.
15. Crutzen, 'Estimates of Possible Variations in Total Ozone due to Natural Causes and Human Activities'.
16. Ibid. p. 201.
17. Schneider, *Laboratory Earth*.

18. We use the term 'imaginary', following Charles Taylor, to mean a constellation of beliefs that coheres and forms the basis for social organization and action. See, e.g., Charles Taylor, *Modern Social Imaginaries*.

19. See, e.g., Caldwell, *International Environmental Policy: Emergence and Dimensions*; Naess, 'The Shallow and the Deep, Long-Range Ecology Movement'; Callicott, 'Non-Anthropocentric Value Theory and Environmental Ethics'; Nash, *The Rights of Nature*; Dryzek, 'Green Reason'; Singer, *One World*.

20. See, e.g., Kwa, 'Local Ecologies and Global Science Discourses and Strategies of the International Geosphere–Biosphere Programme'; Miller, 'Scientific Internationalism in American Foreign Policy'.

21. Miller, 'An Effective Instrument of Peace'.

22. Miller, 'Scientific Internationalism in American Foreign Policy'.

23. Edwards, *A Vast Machine*.

24. Kwa, 'Representations of Nature Mediating between Ecology and Science Policy'.

25. Wilson, *Biodiversity*; Wilson, *The Diversity of Life*. See also Takacs, 'The Idea of Biodiversity'.

26. See Miller, 'Scientific Internationalism in American Foreign Policy' for a full account of Norton's speech.

27. Miller, 'Climate Science and the Making of a Global Political Order'.

28. See, e.g., Loreau et al., 'Diversity without Representation'. For a comparison of the IPCC with the new IPBES, see Beck et al., 'Towards a Reflexive Turn in the Governance of Global Environmental Expertise'.

29. See, e.g., Houghton, *Global Warming*. See also Schneider, *Laboratory Earth*, and Takacs, 'The Idea of Biodiversity'.

30. Dennis, 'Reconstructing Sociotechnical Order'.

31. See Miller, 'An Effective Instrument of Peace'. See also Erickson, 'Mathematical Models, Rational Choice, and the Search for Cold War Culture'.

32. Caldwell, *International Environmental Policy: Emergence and Dimensions*.

33. Miller, 'The Globalization of Human Affairs'.

34. For a discussion of environmental framing, see Miller, 'The Dynamics of Framing Environmental Values and Policy'.

35. Clark, 'Managing Planet Earth'.

36. Hammond et al., 'Calculating National Accountability for Climate Change'.

37. Agarwal and Narain, *Global Warming in an Unequal World*. As a testament to its influence on global environmental thought, *Global Warming in an Unequal World* has been cited 833 times, according

to Google Scholar, compared to 36 for the original publication from WRI.

38. Connolly, 'Increments for the Earth'.

39. Connolly and Keohane, 'Institutions for Environmental Aid'.

40. Hardin, 'Commentary: Living on a Lifeboat'.

41. Keith et al., 'Geoengineering the Climate'; Wigley, 'A Combined Mitigation/Geoengineering Approach to Climate Stabilization'; Crutzen, 'Albedo Enhancement by Stratospheric Sulfur Injections'; Barrett, 'The Incredible Economics of Geoengineering'; Victor et al., 'The Geoengineering Option'.

42. For an excellent review of the first twenty-five years of international environmental law and policy, see Caldwell, *International Environmental Policy: From the Twentieth to the Twenty First Century*.

43. The text of the United Nations Framework Convention on Climate Change can be found at <http://unfccc.int/key_documents/the_con vention/items/2853.php> (last accessed 9 January 2015).

44. Houghton, *Global Warming*.

45. Oberthür and Roche Kelly, 'EU Leadership in International Climate Policy'.

46. See, e.g., Parry et al., 'What is a Dangerous Climate Change?'; Schneider, 'What is "Dangerous" Climate Change?'.

47. A description of the conference can be found at <http://stabilisation. metoffice.com> (last accessed 9 January 2015).

48. A description of the conference can be found at: <http://www.eci. ox.ac.uk/4degrees/> (last accessed 9 January 2015).

49. US National Research Council, *Climate Stabilization Targets*.

50. US National Research Council, *Warming World: Impacts by Degree*.

51. National inventories of emissions can be found at <http://unfccc. int/ghg_data/ghg_data_unfccc/items/4146.php> (last accessed 9 January 2015).

52. Power, *The Audit Society*; Chayes and Chayes, *The New Sovereignty*.

53. Jasanoff, *The Fifth Branch*; Miller, 'Hybrid Management'.

54. Cronon, 'A Place for Stories'.

55. Ibid. p. 41.

56. Indeed, at one point, the IPCC proposed simply to conduct all national inventories for countries to ensure application of standard methodologies, but this was rejected out of hand by nations as a violation of their sovereignty to assess their own behaviours.

57. Miller, 'The Ethics of Energy Transitions'.

58. Mitcham and Rolston, 'Energy Constraints'.

59. Miller et al., 'Socio-Energy Systems Design'.

60. Ibid.

61. Miller, 'The Ethics of Energy Transitions'.
62. Weber et al., 'Rural North Dakota's Oil Boom and its Impact on Social Services'.
63. Graffy and Kihm, 'Does Disruptive Competition Mean a Death Spiral for Electric Utilities?'.
64. Abramsky (ed.), *Sparking a Worldwide Energy Revolution*.
65. Barnett and Duvall (eds), *Power in Global Governance*. See also Miller, 'Globalizing Security'.
66. Ibid.
67. Ostrom, 'Beyond Markets and States'; Keohane and Victor, 'The Regime Complex for Climate Change'.
68. Miller and Erickson, 'The Politics of Bridging Scales and Epistemologies'. See also Jasanoff, 'Harmonization – The Politics of Reasoning Together'.
69. Caine et al., *Our High-Energy Planet*.

5   Religion, Politics, and Genocide

Introduction

This chapter examines the role of religion in three paradigmatic cases of religion and genocide through the lens of a diagnostic schematic of the genocidal process that has been emerging since the 1980s. We will begin by sketching working definitions of the crimes at issue as well as certain social dynamics shared by diverse religions in the contemporary world. Then we will introduce three paradigmatic cases. The bulk of the chapter describes the diagnostic schematic, showing how its various phases are exemplified by the paradigmatic cases. Finally, we will discuss prevention strategies and the possible roles of religion therein. Perforce, given religions' interaction with other spheres of life, religion and politics will be constantly at the forefront of discussion.

Definitions

It is often said that genocide is the 'crime of crimes' in the community of nations, by analogy to murder being the most heinous crime in domestic jurisdictions. Genocide is most certainly a serious assault on humanity considered collectively. Legally speaking, genocide involves acts committed with the intent to destroy, in whole or in part, a national, ethnic, racial, or religious group as such. Genocidal acts include mass murder and causing serious bodily or mental harm to members of the targeted group, deliberately inflicting on the group conditions of life calculated to bring about its destruction, imposing measures intended to prevent births within the group, and forcibly transferring children of the group to another group.[1] It is important to emphasize that in genocide the group as such is the primary target, whereas killing and other abuses are the means used to achieve the intentional destruction of the group. In principle, genocidal activity can be undertaken during times of war and peace, although conditions of war – whether international or civil – are the usual context.

Genocide often shades into what are technically called 'crimes against humanity'. Such crimes constitute a broader range of human rights violations and refer to criminal acts when committed as part of a widespread or systematic attack on any civilian population, with knowledge of the attack but without specific genocidal intent – namely, such acts as murder, extermination, enslavement, forcible population transfer (for example, so-called ethnic cleansing of a territory), torture, rape and sexual slavery, persecution of an identifiable group (short of genocide), disappearances, apartheid, and other inhumane acts of a similar character.[2] Crimes against humanity, like genocide, can be undertaken during times of war (or other conflict) and times of peace.

While the terms 'genocide' and 'crimes against humanity' were developed relatively recently in international criminal law, the phenomena they denote have a long history, since the time that historical records – whether systematic or not – have been kept. Human beings and groups apparently have a proclivity for the destruction and abuse of out-groups ('the other'), and religious ideas, traditions, and people have often been involved, whether in the role of perpetrators, victims, or complicit bystanders or supporters, or in the role of preventers, rescuers, or restorers of peace and justice. That is, when it comes to genocide and crimes against humanity, religions can be Janus-faced: destructive or constructive.

For the purpose of this chapter we identify a religion as a worldview, value system, and way of life oriented around some conception of a special reality, fundamental truth, and normative authority that is construed, alternatively, as transcending, grounding, or deeply implicit in ordinary mundane reality. A religion provides its adherents with existential orientation and meaning – answers to fundamental questions about the world's origins, human destiny, the source and prevalence of suffering and evil, and proper comportment in the world of human relations. In so doing, a religion provides its adherents with a sense of personal and social identity that fosters cohesion, integration, and cooperation among themselves and that distinguishes them – as individuals and a group – from other religious communities and their respective adherents. In this respect, any given religion has both a homogenizing effect within the group – fostering a distinctive identity – and a differentiating effect vis-à-vis other groups. The integrative effects are often quite positive from the perspective of any given religion, and, if it incorporates inclusive ideas of the unity of humankind, compassion towards all – whether in or outside the group – and other similar moral norms and affectivity, such positive effects could extend to the entire world.

By the same token, a religion's differentiating effects can have as a possible consequence the creation of a mentality of 'us' (who have the truth, know the good, and live rightly) versus 'them' (who do not share these characteristics, at least not fully). Herein lies the Janus-faced potential for a religion not only to be life-affirming for all humanity but also, or alternatively, to regard itself as superior to others and to become hostile to out-groups that by their very existence challenge the religion's worldview, values, and way of life. The latter potential derives from the cognitive dissonance and stress produced by others' implicit or explicit challenges to the religion that its members may perceive to be relieved by converting others to that religion, or imposing restrictive and discriminatory social policies on those others, or perhaps resorting to more overt forms of violence against them.

It is also important to observe that religions are often bound up with ethnonational or even 'racial' identity, whereby the latter can become social markers for who really belongs to a given religious group or tradition (or subtradition). And the converse can also happen, whereby, for example, a specific religious identity becomes a marker for who really belongs to the ethnonational community. A couple of examples might help to clarify these general observations. In the Bosnian conflict, for example, Serbian identity was intimately tied to being a member of the Serbian Orthodox Church, making Muslims and Croats (who are largely Roman Catholic) immediately suspect as the 'the other' within the fluctuating and changing national boundaries in the Serbian quest for a Greater Serbia: only Bosnian Serbs, and not Bosnian Muslims or Croats/Catholics, belonged to the aspired-for ethnonational greater Serbian community. To take another example, in Nazi Germany, Jews were excluded from the ethnonational community by virtue of their different ethnic and religious background. In this case, the Nazi ideology of racial and ethnic purity functioned as a radically exclusionary ethnonational religion of sorts oriented to the 'sacrality' and normative authority of Aryan German blood. In this case, ethnonational identity itself became a marker for a political religion of sorts that encouraged the national group to think of itself as a chosen people with superior values, a providential mission, and the perceived right to use the polity to advance that mission aggressively against out-groups – both internally and across international boundaries. These brief examples indicate that complex processes are at work and that religion plays important roles within their dynamics.

Our challenge in this chapter is to clarify, exemplify, and illuminate these processes, including the role of religious thinking and institutions, as best we can within the limited space available to us – to provide a diagnostic schematic of sorts – and then to indicate how religions can also play a positive role in preventing and interdicting genocide and crimes against humanity. Before developing our schematic, it will be helpful to sketch, however briefly, three paradigmatic cases of the role of religion in genocide (and related crimes) that will serve as foci. They are ones that people often think of when contemplating the crimes at issue, and they all involve religious dimensions in one way or another: the Nazi Holocaust of the Jews; the Serbian 'ethnic cleansing' of the Bosnian Muslims; and the Rwandan genocide of the Tutsis by the Hutus.

Paradigmatic cases

In the case of the Holocaust, the Nazi authorities – with the complicity of the broader society – first targeted the Jews for exclusion from the German national community and then targeted all the Jews in Europe for permanent elimination. Against the backdrop of long-standing anti-Semitism – ultimately stemming from earlier Christian anti-Judaism – and new ideas of racial purity for the entire ethnonational German community, the political leaders scapegoated the Jews for losses incurred during the First World War and its aftermath and for various financial crises and political upheavals in the society during the intervening years between the two world wars. In effect, the Nazi authorities defined the Jews as a socially and morally deviant ethnic, racial, and religious group unworthy of being tolerated within the Nazi vision of Germany's historical destiny to become the leader and controller of a new world order. Unlike other 'lesser' races and national groups, which were to be used as ongoing slave labour under the Third Reich, as it gradually assumed control of other European territories and peoples, the Jews were defined as rivals so demonic that they needed to be finally eliminated.

The processes of demonization of the Jews were assisted by German Protestant churches, which, because it would mean eliminating the Jews as dissonant rivals and also because they wanted to share in the Nazi domination of the new world order (or perhaps just continue as a presence in that new order), 'Aryanized' Christian scripture and theology and thus colluded with the Nazi exclusion of the Jews.[3] So too the Catholic hierarchy (within Germany and without) was complicit by means of its deafening silence in failing to condemn Nazi persecution of the Jews – the reason being that it wanted to reach accommodation with the regime in order that the church might continue to exist or be tolerated within the new Germany. The exclusionary actions of the government against the Jews were taken in incremental steps – ranging from civil, occupational, educational, and marital restrictions, to loss of German citizenship, dispossession of property, and forced emigration, and then finally to the radical step of systematic extermination of all European Jews.

Serbian ethnic cleansing of the Bosnian Muslims in the mid-1990s was motivated by the rise of Serbian nationalism after the break-up of the former Yugoslavia. In their rise to power, the Serbian nationalists projected a vision for a Greater Serbia – unifying all Serbs within contiguous national territories and excluding all those of non-Serbian ethnic identity. Within Bosnia itself – even though it was recognized in 1992 by the international community as an independent state with an internally diverse population – the Bosnian Serbs, assisted by the former Yugoslavian army, continued to be inspired by the Greater Serbian vision and attempted to make Bosnia exclusively Serbian, leading to the systematic expulsion of the Bosnian Muslims. Terror tactics were used on the civilian population, amounting to crimes against humanity, and, in the city of Srebrenica, genocide of the Muslims living there. Part of the rationale for these actions involved characterizing the Bosnian Muslims as radically 'other' – ethnically, racially, and religiously – and attempting to trace their presence in the area to the prior history of Ottoman dominance and purported repression of the Serbian Orthodox community. Naturally enough, during this period of Ottoman dominance, portions of the population converted to Islam, a fact that later served as a pretext for the Bosnian Serbs to characterize the Muslims as race and ethnic traitors as well as religious apostates. This 'mythic' historical background was further developed by Serbian nationalist intellectuals in demonizing the Muslim population as inheritors of the Turks, betrayers, and deviants unworthy of being part of an ethnically purified Serbian Bosnia.[4] The Serbian Orthodox Church leadership itself contributed to this demonization by supporting the mythological accounts of betrayal and by sanctifying through sermons and ritual activity the vision and actions of the Bosnian Serbs. Thus, religion played no small role in justifying atrocities against the Bosnian Muslims, which at that time constituted 40 per cent of the Bosnian population.

The Rwandan genocide of the Tutsis was spawned in part by an interethnic classification system initially introduced by Belgian colonial authorities in their effort to manipulate and control the political structure of the society – first giving preference to the Tutsis in subsidiary leadership positions, and then later reversing course prior to Rwandan independence in 1962 and encouraging Hutu political ascendancy (the Hutus comprised a greater part of the population). Catholic and Protestant leaders played no small role in both of these developments, desiring to share power with first the Tutsis and then the Hutus. Beginning with Rwanda's independence from Belgium, the society was riven by interethnic strife, punctuated by atrocities on both sides, which eventually resulted in the emigration of many minority Tutsis into neighbouring countries, especially Uganda. This atrocity-enforced emigration was followed later by emigrant Tutsi military forays back into Rwanda in an effort to regain (and share) power with the Hutu-dominated government.

Not insignificantly, members of the President's group formed an extremist Hutu party that subsequently demonized all Tutsis as inveterate 'cockroaches' who deserved to be stamped out. Although prior to the beginning of the genocide itself, the Hutu President had signed peace accords with the Rwandan Liberation Front (the Tutsis then in exile), his plane was unfortunately shot down, and he was killed, along with the Burundi Hutu President. The Hutu extremist party took this as an urgent signal to begin to kill systematically all Tutsis then in Rwanda (as well as any Hutu sympathizers of the Tutsis). The result is well known: within the space of little over a month, nearly 900,000 Rwandans were massacred by Hutu militia and other ordinary Hutu civilians. When the Tutsis appealed to church leaders to intervene and to provide refuge and sanctuary, their pleas fell on deaf ears.[5] In addition, a number of religious leaders and personnel were subsequently indicted by the International Criminal Tribunal for Rwanda and found guilty of genocide, conspiracy to commit genocide, and other crimes against humanity.

Although none of these cases can be here analysed in full, what has been presented provides a sufficient context for deploying a diagnostic schematic roughly applicable to these and other cases. The schematic is facilitated by the systematic work undertaken by genocide and atrocity scholars, although what is often understated in the latter work is how religious ideas, leaders, and institutions might play a complicit role.

Diagnostic schematic

The diagnostic schematic has four main parts: preconditions, precipitating factors, primary process, and secondary processes. Preconditions refer to the political and sociocultural background of a given society making atrocity possible. Precipitating factors refer to triggering events or crises posed to that society, its leadership, and its citizens that appear to start a causal process leading to atrocity.

Primary processes refer to the decision-making and actions of the society's political leadership involved in the preceding, and secondary processes refer to social psychological dynamics and pressures pertaining to all citizens, but particularly ordinary people in non-elite positions. Although we will present these parts in a sequential manner, it must be emphasized that many of the factors at work in each can also play roles in the other phases, and, further, that different parts of the schematic interact.

Preconditions

The work of a number of political scientists and genocide specialists appears to converge on identifying a set of distinctive preconditions for the occurrence of atrocity. Preconditions are those permissive systemic social, cultural, and political features that appear necessary but not sufficient for the occurrence of such crimes.[6] Much of the analytical study of historical cases of atrocities pivots around the finding that the more unaccountable power a government has, the more it can act arbitrarily according to the desires of the elite in power and the more it can, for example, make war and engage in repression (or worse) against the people under its control.[7] At the extreme of such power, totalitarian systems often engage in such behaviour – consider, for example, Nazi Germany and Soviet Russia.

Thus, the evidence appears to suggest that one significant precondition for crimes against humanity and genocide is an authoritarian political system, which is correlated with, if not defined by, such features as a politically controlled legal system, lack of democratic decision-making, relative isolation of state leadership from civil society, lack of a strong and protective constitution not easily changed by political fiat, a politically controlled state security apparatus, a tendency by the political leadership to use violence in maintaining control over the people, and a tendency to use deviance – or create deviance – by targeting certain groups as enemies of the state. Thus, for example, the Nazi leadership targeted communists, union leaders, and dissident religious groups (for example, Jehovah's Witnesses) – interning them in concentration camps – and even criminalized the Jews as state enemies.

In addition to authoritarianism, there appear to be other preconditions that recur in the bulk of cases. For example, societies that engage in criminal atrocities often do so in the name of a nationalist ideology with strong idealistic elements often religiously tinged – remaking the society or even remaking the world in its own image. The Nazis, for example, wished not only to develop a thousand-year Third Reich purified of its discontents but also to recast the world in terms of master–slave relations – with the Aryans as the master race ruling the world and so-called inferior races as their slave populations. This remaking was perceived by the Nazis as their world-historical destiny. The Hutu extremists had more limited ambitions: to achieve a homogenous Hutu society purged of its rival Tutsi ethnicity, achieving at long last a new 'golden age' of Hutu dominance and purity within Rwanda. And, of course, in the case of Bosnia, we encounter the ideological vision of Bosnia's becoming a part of a Greater Serbia united for the first time and also purged of its impure and deviant ethnicities.

It is important to realize that the leaders of these societies were in their own view possessed of a righteous cause that they saw as good for their societies (or even the whole world). These ideologists seemed to be driven by a religious-like fervour. For example, the Nazi political system modelled itself and its vision on the Christian religion – shifting the focus of normative authority to German blood and soil, producing its own 'sacred' texts (for example, *Mein Kampf* and *The Myth of the Twentieth Century*), swearing loyalty to a prophetic leader who claimed insight into Germany's historical destiny, developing holidays and rituals around 'sacred' times and events associated with the travails in the rise of the Nazi party, and so on.[8] A similar sense of a righteous cause was associated with the vision of Greater Serbia and its embrace of mythic narratives about the travails of Serbs under the Ottoman Empire, conceiving of a new social order without the demonic Muslims, and seeing actions taken against Muslims as righteous even before God.

Rwanda was a bit different in this regard, since the dominant Christian religions in the country included both majority Hutus and minority Tutsis. Here we encounter a clear case of another identifiable precondition – namely, ethnic stratification associated with a history of mutual antagonisms between the two main groups, involving senses of group superiority, devaluation of the other group, and grievances on both sides.[9] Even though this ethnic stratification might originally have been introduced (or at least intensified) by external forces in the form of colonial administrations, the socially constructed ethnicities became 'real' to the people, especially when reinforced and manipulated by the political leadership.

Perhaps the classic case of ethnic stratification and antagonism is anti-Semitism. Historically speaking, within European societies at least, the Jews were regarded as the radical other, as marked by their distinctive ethnic backgrounds, communities, religion, and ritual language and custom. Although, prior to the rise of the Nazis, Jews were granted citizenship, were present in all professions, and often married outside their communities, nonetheless lingering in the background was a history of hostility and periodic episodes of violence expressed towards them by other ethnicities and religious groups in the dominant society.[10] To the rise of nationalism during the nineteenth century and the resurgence of Volk unity in the twentieth, the Nazis added a 'biological' element of racial thinking and 'genetics', making Jewish identity and difference from the dominant population inescapable.

How exactly are we to understand the way in which these three preconditions operate and interact? An initial suggestion comes from criminology in the form of 'routine activities' theory, which holds that crime requires the convergence of a motivated offender (or perpetrator) and a suitable target (or victim) in the absence of a capable guardian (or protector).[11] In essence this theory assumes ordinary motivations on the part of the offender – such as desires for money, status, or power – and it asserts that people simply need an opportunity to commit crime from such motives. The social and political preconditions of, for example, having a weak or politically controlled legal system and no checks or balances on government power create an opportunity for powerful groups to engage in crimes against other groups, precisely because these conditions constitute the absence of a capable guardian. Political leaders under such conditions are free to do whatever they want. At the same time, the other preconditions of a strong idealistic ideology (for example, of remaking the society) and ethnic and/or religious stratification and antagonism help to create a suitable target in the form of a vulnerable group in the society controlled by an unaccountable political elite (that is, without a capable guardian).

By the same token, as we have seen, a religion in such a society can strengthen (that is, worsen) these preconditions in a variety of ways, for example: (1) it can inform and provide a rationale for the idealistic ideology; (2) it can function as an important marker for identifying who or who does not belong to the dominant ethnonational group whose interests are being pursued by the political elite; (3) some forms of ethnonationalism and its ideology can themselves become religious – at least functionally speaking – and take action against a rival religious community and/or ethnicity; and (4) a religion and its representatives within the society can, through their complicit silence, aid and abet the absence of a capable guardian and reinforce the tendency of an authoritarian government to use the tools of force and deviance creation in attaining its goals.

Precipitating factors

In addition to preconditions, social scientists also identify certain difficult social conditions or events as triggering or initiating processes leading to genocide and crimes against humanity. We call these precipitating factors. Preconditions of the sort we have just discussed provide a dispositional – or at least hospitable – social and political context, but the precipitating factors, by contrast, represent crises that, when they occur, immediately put considerable strain on a government and social system. Authoritarian governments of the sort we have characterized tend to respond to these crises by extreme repression and violence, because these are the tools they have at the ready and have used in the past.

Heuristically, we can categorize these precipitating factors, events, and crises into two broad ideal types – external and internal. External crises are represented, for example, by the outbreak of international war or conflict, or, for another example, a global economic meltdown. There is no gainsaying that external crises also produce widespread social disequilibrium internal to societies. Internal precipitating factors range across a spectrum of illustrative examples: outbreak of a civil war, ethnic violence, intense socio-economic problems, ecological disasters, rapid and substantial social changes, and the like, many of which could themselves overlap and interact, having a magnification effect within a given society. And, of course, internal crises could also have grave external effects – for example, refugee flows across national borders, or the sparking of a 'mirroring' civil war or ethnic conflict in neighbouring states.

Our three cases all appear to have been triggered by internal social crises having external effects (and conversely). In the intervening years between the two world wars, Germany was subject to intense social and political instability; and it was hit by an economic depression (worldwide and internally), resulting in massive job loss, which in its turn led to further social upheaval. With the break-up of the former Yugoslavia after the death of Tito, most of the states then emerging were subject to social and political discord; ethnic and religious differences and animosities held in check by Tito's governance emerged; and the economies of those states, drawing upon their own limited resources, broke down. In Rwanda also we encounter intense ethnic rivalry and conflict after independence, a huge downturn in the economy owing to the decline of coffee prices worldwide, exacerbated by government corruption and mismanagement, grave political conflict in revisioning Rwanda, and armed incursions by exiled Tutsis living in neighbouring Uganda.

How are we to understand the nature, operation, and effects of these precipitating factors? Once again, criminology may be helpful, now in the form of what is called 'strain' theory.[12] Strain theories propose socially induced motivations for crimes in addition to the ordinary motivations mentioned earlier. In effect, what happens is this: the precipitating events or crises produce intense strain on the entire society and most particularly in the political leadership, which must somehow alleviate the strain, or otherwise risk outright rebellion and loss of political power. This socially generated pressure initiates – particularly for tenuous authoritarian systems – self-defensive motivations and behaviours on the part of the leaders, involving a distorted perception of the magnitude of the threatening crisis, to which they are inclined to respond with repression and violence.

Primary process

As developed by some genocide scholars – principally sociologists and social psychologists – this process does appear to involve a sequential development, though the length of time involved can vary.[13] Beginning with the intense strain of crisis and the resulting cognitiv distortion of an overwhelming threat, authoritarian political elites often transfer the cause of the threatening crisis to a vulnerable target group that is characterized as the source of the strain. Scapegoating others – say, a particularly despised group – as the source of the strain seemingly makes the crisis more manageable than dealing with the actual cause or causes at work (for example, economic or social). Thus, the reality of what is going on is simplified so that the elite can 'handle' the crisis in ways familiar to it and consonant with its nationalist and/or idealistic ideology. Assisted then by other social and political preconditions – such as ethnic and interreligious animus and tendencies to use violence, repression, and creation of deviance to maintain control – the government further develops and deploys its ideology to designate the scapegoated target as an enemy or obstacle requiring suppression or removal. The government – particularly in the form of its propagandistic intellectuals – creates an ideological springboard for undertaking 'corrective' political actions against the target group.

These adverse actions against the target typically involve a continuum of escalation, ranging from social and economic discrimination based on ethnic/religious/racial identity, to stripping the target group of civil-legal protections, and finally to atrocities of various sorts.[14] In large part, this escalating continuum of destruction functions as a means to gauge the willingness of the dominant population to go along with the actions and to engage its complicit support. Popular support for actions devaluing, dehumanizing, and even demonizing the target group is crucial to the success of the elite's gaining the confidence in resolving the crisis – as it sees it – through adverse action against the scapegoated target. Popular support is also crucial for the elite's justification of its actions – in its own eyes and those of the population at large. Often especially important here is whether or not the religious authorities in the dominant population choose to oppose or at least speak out against the government's actions, since such authorities often define the moral compass of the society at large.[15]

In the case of Nazi Germany, we have already seen the social, political, and economic crises that produced strain within the society, which, in turn, permitted the Nazis' rise to power. We have also seen the cognitive distortion in the political elite in scapegoating the Jews as somehow responsible for the crises, making them a vulnerable target group. Furthermore, we are also aware that the Nazi ideology of racial and ethnic purity and world domination resulted in the Jews being systematically demonized as evil malcontents and a threat to the achievement of the Nazi 'providential' millenarian vision. The escalation of actions against the Jews was taken in an incremental step-wise manner and, when encountering little or no resistance, making the German people complicit in the Nazi crimes, ranging from discrimination to extermination. It is no doubt also the case that, as the Nazi elites eventually encountered external military resistance to their invasions of other countries, the strain of crisis magnified greatly, resulting in ever more significant cognitive distortion and desperation to accomplish at least something projected in their ideology—namely, purifying the world of all Jews. All this was, of course, aided and abetted by religious factors – beyond the Nazis' own political religion – namely, the anti-Semitism of the Christian churches expressed both theologically and in terms of their silent complicity when confronted with Nazi actions against the Jews.

In the case of Bosnia, we have encountered a primary process in some ways similar to and in some ways different from the Nazi case. Here the strain was caused by the political crises stemming from the break-up of the former Yugoslavia and Bosnia's attempt to assert its political independence as a multi-ethnic state and society. For the Serbian elite in Bosnia – already enticed by the political vision of a greater and unified Serbia – this attempt constituted (or promised to constitute) a grave obstacle to Serbian ambitions, involving the cognitive distortion that the source of the threat was directly attributable to the Muslim presence in Bosnia. Channelled by the prior recent resurgence of a national and religious mythology of Slavic Muslims as 'Christ-killers' (!) and ethnonational (and race) traitors, the Bosnian Serb leaders targeted Bosnian Muslims as a deviant ethnicity and religion that had no place in a future Serbian Bosnia as part of a Greater Serbia.[16] Escalating actions were undertaken first to discriminate against and then ethnically to cleanse Bosnia by the use of terror tactics encouraging Muslims' emigration. The ideological justification for the actions taken by the Bosnian Serbs was explicitly supported by the Serbian Orthodox Church leadership – so in this case we encounter not so much deafening silence as rather open collaboration at the intellectual and propagandistic level between political and religious leaders.

We have already mentioned the strain produced by the crises in Rwanda. That the Hutu leaders would blame the minority Tutsi population for all the country's political, social, and economic problems clearly indicates cognitive distortion. The Hutu extremists worked hard at creating the image of the Tutsis as deviant – Tutsi men plotting to take over the government without sharing power, the Tutsis in general as responsible for Rwanda's economic woes, Tutsi women as seductresses out to steal Hutu husbands, Tutsi men as warmongers, and the like, together with the myth that the Tutsis were not only non-indigenous invaders of the region but also the heirs of the biblical figure of Ham. This deviancy – along with suggested steps of ridding Rwanda of all Tutsis and for all time – was systematically propagandized through dedicated media outlets (newspaper and radio station) controlled by the Hutu extremists. Although it is not clear whether the traditional churches in Rwanda participated in the development of extremist Hutu ideology, it is clear that they were in political alliance with the Hutus in an effort to maintain the status quo regarding their power and position in the society. In this respect the traditional churches' actions were in marked contrast with those nontraditional communities informed by liberation theology and ideas of participatory democratic decision-making. These communities did not participate in the genocide other than to become some of its victims.[17]

Secondary processes

Political elites rarely commit genocide or other atrocities with their own hands. They may conceive, plan, and order these crimes, but others do the actual dirty work, so to speak. These others include the military, the police, special militias and squads, and ordinary citizens. So, in addition to the primary process just discussed and exemplified, secondary processes applicable to the lower ranks and ordinary people must be considered. Most of these secondary processes involve social psychological phenomena and mechanisms of group behaviour, hierarchical organization, moral disengagement, bystander behaviour, and so on. There are also processes of simple violence escalation as well as intentional training in dehumanization and abuse that come into play.

Intentional training in dehumanization is undertaken by many societies in the context of military and police training, especially during times of war and internal conflict. Using techniques of systematic indoctrination and propaganda, military trainers, for example, attempt to erode normal feelings of respect and sympathy and otherwise to neutralize soldiers' ordinary moral identities by dehumanizing and even demonizing the enemy (for example, they are 'gooks' or 'vermin', not people like us).[18] Indeed, even without deliberate intentionality, military and police professionalization can easily result in an 'us' versus 'them' mentality, where 'we' as a trained elite are different from and superior to 'them'.

With respect to group behaviour, we encounter the following sorts of phenomena: deindividuation or the submerging of individual identity within the group; a discontinuity effect whereby a group's collective beliefs and behaviour are more extreme than would be the case for individuals apart from the group; communication distortion wherein public group discourse overwhelms and masks individual doubt; diffusion of responsibility within the group affecting the loss of the sense of individual responsibility for the group's actions; and, of course, the group may adopt an ideology and set of values that can result in self-deceptive rationalization of one's behaviour in conformity with the group.[19]

It seems plausible to contend that these kinds of social psychological mechanisms, such as the extreme deferral to authority and appeal of 'groupthink', explain much about the psychology of moral disengagement, which, in turn, permits and encourages people to assist – at varying levels – in the elite's goals and plans.[20] By moral disengagement we refer, for example, to: the cognitive re-construal of one's behaviour (for example, seeing dubious or even heinous actions in a worthy light); the minimization of one's sense of moral responsibility (for example, seeing oneself simply as part of a group or organization and going along with its action); and desensitization to the plight of victims (for example, considering who are other and so less than us, and our enemy to boot).[21]

Also pertinent to the secondary processes is the social psychology of bystander behaviour, which is important because the inaction (or worse – complicity) of bystanders affirms and encourages perpetrators of atrocity: adverse actions against a target group often escalate incrementally because perpetrators (the political leadership) gauge the reaction of the public before proceeding.[22] At a minimum, they seek implicit consent to their actions. Bystander passivity during crisis events is often the first step towards further and more direct complicity in actions taken against a target group. In addition, fear of authorities' reprisals for bystander intervention and of social ostracism from the dominant group in the society may well be at work in helping to explain either bystander passivity or even more complicit behaviour (for example, informing on victims, stealing their property, and even more direct criminal participation in atrocity).

Religions and religious adherents are subject to *all* of the foregoing social psychological mechanisms. Religions are group phenomena and often hierarchically organized; their adherents are subject to group pressures and authority–obedience relations. Moreover, as members of the broader society, religious adherents are also subject to bystander behavioural dynamics in the midst of crisis.

We can illustrate these secondary processes with a few examples, including several references to the role of religion. In the Nazi case, for example, there are book-length studies of the intentional training in dehumanization and the social psychological dynamics of group behaviour and hierarchical organization of the 'ordinary men' associated with mobile killing squads and police battalions[23] as well as studies of the bystander complicity of military chaplains ministering to the spiritual torments of the men doing the killing.[24] There are also suggestive studies of how priests and prelates, in conformity with traditional theology, counselled their congregations about church–state relations and how lay church people should be obedient to the state even in times of troubled conscience.[25] As we mentioned earlier, the German Christian Protestant Church even went so far as to Aryanize scripture and liturgy, thereby, even if only indirectly, providing comfort and support to the Nazi rationale for dehumanizing Jews. The public anti-Semitism of the famous Old Testament scholar Gerhard Kittel is a notorious example of a Protestant intellectual who came close to justifying the Nazi murder of Jews as a necessary pre-emptive strike against a dangerous and perverted people and religion.[26]

In Rwanda, we see virtually all these social psychological dynamics at work – for example, explicit training and arming of Hutu militias; intense ideological propagandizing of the Hutu civilian population through mass media (including directives to kill and reveal identities and addresses of potential victims); peer pressure and group conformity within formal and informal killing squads; explicit efforts – by fear, intimidation, and ideological appeal – to make uninvolved Hutu bystanders complicit in the genocidal action (for example, through informing, refusing sanctuary, stealing property). This genocide generally involved face-to-face personal killing, rape, and mutilation by not only modern armaments but also machetes, homemade axes and maces, and the like. Religious figures were involved as well, particularly those Hutu who identified with the conservative churches. Many priests, pastors, and other religious were complicit in the genocidal activities at one level or another – for example, refusing sanctuary to Tutsi victims, sometimes giving them apparent sanctuary and then contacting Hutu militia about their location, providing lists to the Hutu killers of Tutsi parishioners, proclaiming from the pulpit to Hutu parishioners that they ought to be obedient to the state and its actions, and even in some cases directly killing Tutsis.[27] This is not to deny that there was no religiously motivated resistance to killing, abuse, and scapegoating of the Tutsis – especially by progressive parishes – but it is to say that the Catholic episcopacy and Protestant leaders tended at best to issue only vague pastoral letters and sermons calling for peace and falling short of actually condemning the genocide and that a number of lower-level priests, pastors, nuns, and parishioners were even more directly complicit.

Prevention

All the preceding paints a pretty dismal picture when it comes to genocide and religion. But, as indicated at the outset of this chapter, religion is Janus-faced regarding atrocities. Religions have indeed played more positive roles in genocide prevention and redress. In general terms, thinking realistically about strategies to prevent and interdict genocide and crimes against humanity is difficult, not least because we (humankind) have so little experience in developing and deploying effective procedures. We think it important, therefore, to note that much of what has been written about genocide prevention is tentative and controversial, not to mention unproven. We can, however, try to overcome these deficits by tying proposed prevention and interdiction strategies as closely as possible to the various aspects of the diagnostic schematic already discussed – namely, preconditions, precipitating factors, primary and secondary processes – in an effort to address such crimes at selected points. We also need to discuss the various roles that religious ideas and institutions have played and might play in developing and supporting these strategies.

In order to explore how prevention strategies might actually work, we believe it might help to correlate them with specific features (or phases) of our diagnostic schematic, thus enabling us to see (or at least imagine) what exactly they might interdict. Applying the notion of prevention to different phases of the overall process of genocide production may well require different strategies, which, of course, like the phases themselves, may well interact. In our initial thinking about prevention, therefore, we divide the topic into two broad categories: prevention aimed at preconditions and precipitating factors (before the atrocity processes are seriously underway), and prevention aimed at the primary and secondary processes themselves (as they are taking place). It seems intuitively clear to us that prevention strategies of the first type would be most effective because they aim at removing or mitigating the conditions and factors necessary for genocide and other atrocity even to begin operating. With respect to this type of prevention, four illustrative strategies appear reasonably practicable to us: one, instituting legal accountability for such crimes; two, truth and reconciliation commissions for addressing past group grievances within societies; three, instituting early warning and monitoring systems for identifying societies in trouble combined with preventive diplomacy and humanitarian assistance; and, four, encouraging and supporting active bystandership. We have already discussed the positive role of social movements and humanitarian interventions in Chapter 1. Both of these have and can play a role in prevention. While we will not discuss in detail the positive role of these kinds of actions here – as we will do this in the next two chapters – we will mention them in order to suggest that religions also have positive roles to play in them as well.

Legal accountability

Instituting legal accountability for genocide and crimes against humanity can be done at two levels or in two venues: international and local. The most effective level by far is local legal accountability, since it most directly addresses and involves the population of the society in question, whereas international accountability – on the model of the Nuremberg Military Tribunal for Nazi perpetrators and the ad hoc international criminal tribunals for perpetrators in the former Yugoslavia (for example, Bosnia) and in Rwanda – takes place at some physical and social psychological distance from where such crimes are actually committed. International justice in this regard simply fails to engage the local population in learning about and confronting perpetrator behaviour and in motivating and channelling institutional reform. These shortcomings are now recognized by the international legal community, a fact that helps to account for the preference – built into the treaty establishing the International Criminal Court (ICC) for local legal accountability – with the ICC taking jurisdiction only when societies are unwilling or unable to undertake appropriate legal proceedings. International criminal justice is second best.

Now, how exactly does legal accountability work in genocide

prevention, and why might it be effective, whether locally or internationally? To begin with, naming crimes and tying them to specific events provide a historic opportunity to establish, refine, and enforce criminal justice norms and to renew adherence to them as well as to educate the public about them.[28] As the saga of Raphael Lemkin's successful crusade for naming and defining the crime of genocide teaches us, clearly conceptualized and focused attention on this crime enables people better to understand the pathologies of their social reality.[29] In addition, blaming and punishing individual perpetrators help to inhibit a possible cycle of revenge on the part of victim groups and pave the way for revised normalization of social relations within society. Moreover, punishing the guilty may deter potential perpetrators in the future and assist society in transitioning to the rule of law. Inasmuch as criminal justice proceedings may involve or at least be coordinated with delivering reparations to surviving victims and their families, such reparation also helps to inhibit revenge and refocus attention on needed social reconstruction. In brief, legal accountability works to interdict for the future those preconditions associated with an authoritarian political system lacking checks on its power, and it works for the future to stem the effects of such precipitating factors as unresolved conflict (spiral of revenge) and general social instability and upheaval.

Truth and reconciliation

Truth and reconciliation commissions may have effects similar to those of legal accountability, especially if these commissions operate in tandem with criminal trials, but they have other functions as well.[30] Some of their preventive effects come by way of public acknowledgement of past atrocities, which, in turn, reinforces for the entire society adherence to criminal justice norms, helps to interdict cycles of revenge by victim groups, paves the way for normalization of social, economic, and political relations, and helps to transition a society into becoming a more just one.[31] Beyond what criminal trials can do, however, truth and reconciliation commissions not only establish a narrative of abuse but also project a new vision for the society as a whole based on the full recognition of the panoply of human rights, constitutional reform, and social reconstruction. The operation of these commissions has, historically speaking, been significantly informed by religiously rooted ideas of non-violence, acknowledgement of past 'sins' (personal and structural), and reconciliation between persons and groups, leading in some cases to forgiveness by the victims of the perpetrators. Such ideas and practices derive in large part from religious conceptions of the good modelled on familial and kinship relations, fenced by justice but also committed to norms of active love crucial to closing moral gaps among people individually and collectively. As demonstrated in a number of cases, ranging from South Africa to Latin American countries, religious leaders and institutions are particularly adept in helping to instantiate a social healing process, which, in turn, is informed by religion's positive role as a peacemaker.[32] In addition, many religious traditions in formerly conflict-ridden societies advance such notions as 'solidarity in sin' that form the basis for a reconstituted social psychology supportive of restorative justice well beyond more limited views of retributive justice in the criminal law. Indeed, restorative justice as a practicable and necessary goal is increasingly being acknowledged and embraced by international and global commissions on rebuilding post-conflict societies. This development appears to be a place where religions themselves are influencing transitional moral, political, and legal norms.[33]

Early warning and mitigation

Much creative attention has been focused on developing early warning systems for identifying impending conflicts likely to lead to criminal behaviour, and combining such warnings with preventive diplomacy (regional and international) and humanitarian assistance.[34] While this sort of preventive strategy, well exemplified in the work of the International Crisis Group, takes account of preconditions in the form of risk analysis of remote and intermediate political, ethnic, social, and cultural background conditions, it is especially aimed at the assessment and interdiction of precipitating factors and crisis events likely to trigger or accelerate conflict and associated criminal behaviour. In effect, this assessment involves the development of information networks – employing a combination of field monitoring (where possible) and causal modelling of the matrix of background conditions, intervening processes, and triggers – to warn the international community so that it can take action to help check the escalation of crises into humanitarian disasters, for example, by intensive diplomacy and the provision of targeted humanitarian assistance.

Religious leaders and institutions – particularly those located in conflict-ridden societies – have important roles to play in the further development of such early warning and mitigation systems. Being in responsible positions of moral leadership in their societies and in touch with their populations, such leaders and institutions can function as field agents to convey crucial information about impending conflict and other problems to regional and international organizations. Moreover, as peacemakers they are in a good position to initiate local grass-roots resolution among conflicting sectors of their populations and to try to inhibit criminal activities among those whom they are leading.[35] A good example – though it had an unfortunate outcome – of how the latter is possible is provided by those Rwandan Christians influenced by liberation theology. While advancing ideas and social organizations oriented around the preferential option for the poor, communal solidarity, and the equality of all persons, these religious communities were notably not complicit in the 1994 genocide.[36] However, these liberal communities made themselves into targets of the genocidal action, since they came to be regarded as Tutsi sympathizers and traitors to the Hutu extremist cause. These liberal communities themselves were not directly or even indirectly complicit in the genocide, and that fact stands as a beacon for religion's potential positive role in other future cases that might be more successful. A lamentation is in order here: if more Christian communities had developed the same sort of stance of multi-ethnic unity and solidarity, the genocide might not have taken place or at least been less costly in the loss of human lives.

Social movements

Two additional prevention strategies to which we wish to draw attention address preconditions and precipitating factors in a somewhat longer-term manner, but increasingly people are coming to believe that they are in fact realistic and practical. Here we refer both to social movements for global political reform and to organized efforts to assist societies to transition to more participatory and inclusive political decision-making. Since these two strategies are interrelated, we consider them together in our brief comments here. There are many social movements that simultaneously encourage development that satisfies basic human needs in an efficient, sustainable, and equitable way and also humane governance involving responsiveness to citizens' needs, respect for human rights, non-discrimination, tolerance, and self-governance.[37]

These movements – both international and local – are greatly assisted by the power of the Internet and new media capacities and tools, such as text messaging, video-enabled cell phones, and the like. These media permit the coordination of these movements in advancing further powerful lobbies for minimal human rights clauses in international trade agreements, responsible change in multinational corporate policies and practices that impact on developing countries, effective regulatory policies and practices of states themselves in becoming more open and transparent, citizen-responsive, even to the point of relinquishing power to participatory citizen decision-making.[38] We believe, along with many others, that such movements, collectively considered, will eventually have a beneficial effect in eroding the power and abuse of presently unaccountable authoritarian governments, as well as mitigating crises involving intense socio-economic problems and group conflict that lie behind the processes leading to genocide and other atrocities. In the latter respect, these movements function to reduce the structures, conditions, and situations that generate strain and chronic arousal in both elite political groups and the general population.

We think it goes almost without saying that religious agents and institutions have a positive role to play in such developments, both internationally and locally. International religiously rooted aid societies have long existed, and since the middle of the twentieth century they have been moving to encourage local economic and participatory democratic reform well beyond simply distributing charitable aid and the like. Personnel from religious non-governmental organizations (NGOs) are being trained in practical, real-world skills necessary to effect economic and social reform, and, while unfortunate exceptions may exist, these skills are being used apart from outmoded attempts at proselytism and conversion.[39] Moreover, the range of religious traditions involved extends well beyond the Abrahamic traditions to include, for example, socially activist Buddhist and Hindu NGOs.

Humanitarian intervention

Once the process towards genocide and atrocity has started, it obviously becomes that much more difficult to prevent or interdict. This is true for a whole host of reasons, not least of which is that the political elite has shown its disregard for human rights and the international community (assuming that preventive diplomacy and other means were tried) and is already complicit and bound by its initial abuses as well as cognitive distortion and rationalization. Since, however, we are considering a process that, once triggered, often – though not always – takes time to develop, there is a chance that further efforts at preventive diplomacy and all that this may entail in the form of inducement and threat might work in the earliest stages. But, if they do not, then the only conceivable prevention strategy that has a possibility of success is coercion – humanitarian intervention or the use of military force to protect and rescue a civilian population.[40]

There is no great mystery as to how and why hard humanitarian intervention might work or is intended to work, though logistical difficulties may abound in any particular case. The intervention coerces the perpetrators to stop the abuse (and/or its imminent threat) on threat of death and/or loss of political power, and it involves the rescue of victims in order to prevent further atrocity, thereby directly interdicting primary and secondary causal processes. Following such intervention, of course, it is necessary, morally speaking, for the interveners to take steps to (re)institute the rule of law, to assist the society in transitioning to a more just one, and to assist – materially and otherwise – in helping to rebuild the society and normalize social and economic relations – thereby mitigating preconditions and pre-cipitating factors that might lead to future atrocity.[41]

It might be thought that religion has little or no role to play in humanitarian intervention, but that would be a misperception for a number of reasons. To begin with, modern-day humanitarian inter-vention is an outgrowth from the centuries-long Christian tradition of Just War, which emphasized not only *ius ad bellum* criteria of right intent (to rectify and punish injustice and restore peace and order) and right authority (only a legitimate prince with no other temporal authority superior to him) but also *ius in bello* criteria of discrimina-tion (no targeting of innocent civilians) and, arguably, proportion-ality (regarding collateral damage to civilian life and livelihood). Secondly, it is important to realize that many religious traditions pose analogous conditions for the justification and regulation of the legitimate use of military force. These traditions range from the other Abrahamic ones to those of South and East Asia (for example, Islam, Buddhism, Confucianism).[42] Third, all these traditions maintain a serious interest in updating, nuancing, and adapting their justifica-tions for and limits on the legitimate use of military force in the con-temporary world. This is not to deny that some of these traditions maintain pacifist sub-traditions, but it is to suggest that religious representatives of other sectors of the traditions do countenance, in extreme circumstances, the use of military force. As a consequence, these representatives can in fact play an important role in justifying and regulating humanitarian interventions from their own points of view – both in theory and in application to real-world situations – including response to and rescue of vulnerable populations from massive abuses by government leaders of their own citizens. In this respect, we might think of religious traditions as potential contribu-tors to the development of a different sort of bystandership to atroc-ity than is usually operative: one that is active rather than passive, interventionist rather than permissive, for reasons of humanitarian other-regarding rescue of victim groups.

Active bystandership

The whole notion of activist bystandership introduces a number of other strategies of prevention that could be operative on a variety of levels – international/global, national/local, and personal – involving religions in a constructive manner.[43] At the global level, for example, religions can encourage the international community to speak out and condemn genocide and other atrocities, while at the same time recommending actions that interdict perpetration at various points of the processes we described earlier. This would entail in part helping to deconstruct the shibboleth of appeals to national security, national sovereignty, and the norm of non-intervention and instead emphasize the common responsibility of all for all in line with religious worldviews of a united humanity with shared kinship relations in the broader cosmic scheme. Something similar could be done at the local, more national level – educating citizens into looking beyond national boundaries, maintaining sympathy for all groups, and preparing them for the difficult choices involved in active 'neighbour love' leading to support for humanitarian intervention in extreme cases. On the personal (interpersonal) level, religious leaders could play a significant role in human rights education, including case studies of atrocity, the negative and positive roles that religion can play in them (especially community rescue), and even the social psychological findings regarding primary and secondary processes of genocide.

Addressing secondary processes

The latter point leads into our final set of considerations about prevention strategies aimed at interdicting secondary processes affecting solders, police, and ordinary citizens. Three illustrative strategies come to mind in this regard. The first is revised military and police training that explicitly inculcates respect for all groups and persons encountered by professional forces – through rigorous education in professional codes of conduct enhanced by morally exemplary leadership and anticipatory role-playing in how to respond appropriately to crisis situations. What we are thinking of here goes well beyond simply making these forces aware of, for example, the Geneva Conventions and military and police codes of conduct (which set the standards) to actual practice in interpreting and applying these standards in likely and even atypical situations. A second strategy involves the development for any society as a whole of an ethos of bystander intervention oriented to the protection of the human rights of all citizens.[44] Tactics here could involve the development of more rigorous good Samaritan laws – for example, making it mandatory to report citizen violence against others, with possible legal sanctions for non-reporting, and indemnifying citizens against civil lawsuits if more direct intervention and rescue should go awry. Tactics could also include role-playing bystander reporting and intervention in civics classics at primary and secondary school levels designed to enhance in younger generations a sense of duty to rescue others in dire need and train them in how to make reports to the appropriate authorities and take modest rescue actions short of incurring grave risk to themselves of collateral physical harm.

Yet a third strategy is one that we mentioned earlier with respect to religious educational efforts: providing students at all educational levels with age-appropriate human rights education, focusing on the findings of social psychology about, for example, the negative effects of group behaviour, hierarchical organization, blind obedience to authority, bystander intervention, and the like. Our wager here is that education in these findings – well before and including the college years – will have a self-reflexive effect with the potential to mitigate the influence of secondary processes in ordinary people in their adult lives if they are ever confronted with situations that put others – whether individuals or groups – at risk of being severely abused. The aim here is to inhibit those social influences enabling complicity with moral wrong (or worse).

Concluding comment

It remains to be said that this chapter about religion and genocide quite self-consciously deviates from the more usual discussions that examine the rhetoric and logic of theodicies in confronting moral evil: that is, religious attempts to make sense of why such heinous evil exists and to cope with its effects on reconstructing religious worldviews in the aftermath of atrocity.[45] We are far from denying that such efforts are unimportant or unworthy of examination, but we decided this chapter should be focused – so far as possible – on the practicalities of religion's complicity in genocide and its potential roles in helping to prevent such atrocities in the future.

Notes

1. United Nations, *Convention on the Prevention and Punishment of the Crime of Genocide.*
2. United Nations, *Rome Statute of the International Criminal Court.*
3. Heschel, *The Aryan Jesus.*
4. Sells, *The Bridge Betrayed*; Sells, 'Kosovo Mythology and the Bosnian Genocide'.
5. Longman, 'Christian Churches and Genocide in Rwanda'.

6. Ross, 'Beyond the Conceptualization of Terrorism'.
7. Rummel, *Power Kills*.
8. Vondung, 'National Socialism as a Political Religion'.
9. Fein, 'More Murder in the Middle'.
10. Rubenstein, *After Auschwitz*.
11. Vold et al., *Theoretical Criminology*.
12. Ibid.
13. Staub, *The Roots of Evil*.
14. Ibid.
15. Semelin, *Purify and Destroy*.
16. Sells, *The Bridge Betrayed*.
17. Longman, 'Christian Churches and Genocide in Rwanda'.
18. Glover, *Humanity*.
19. Baumeister, *Evil*.
20. Milgram, *Obedience to Authority*.
21. Bandura, 'Moral Disengagement'.
22. Staub, *The Roots of Evil*; Barnett, *Bystanders*.
23. Browning, *Ordinary Men*.
24. Bergen, 'Between God and Hitler'.
25. Griech-Polelle, 'A Pure Conscience is Good Enough'.
26. Erickson, 'Genocide, Religion, and Gerhard Kittle'.
27. Longman, 'Christian Churches and Genocide in Rwanda'.
28. Mertis, 'Truth in a Box'.
29. Power, *'A Problem from Hell'*; Lemkin, *Axis Rule in Occupied Europe*.
30. Méndez, 'Latin American Experiences of Accountability'.
31. Fletcher and Weinstein, 'Violence and Social Repair'.
32. Amadiume and An-Na'im (eds), *The Politics of Memory*.
33. Bassiouni and Rothenberg (eds), *The Chicago Principles on Post-Conflict Justice*.
34. Gurr, 'Early Warning Systems'.
35. Tannenbaum Center for Interreligious Understanding, *Peacemakers in Action*.
36. Longman, *Christianity and Genocide in Rwanda*.
37. Falk, 'The Global Promise of Social Movements'; Falk, 'The Challenge of Genocide and Genocidal Politics in an Era of Globalisation'.
38. Brecher et al., *Globalization from Below*.
39. Tannenbaum Center for Interreligious Understanding, *Peacemakers in Action*.
40. Nardin, 'The Moral Basis of Humanitarian Intervention'.
41. Bellamy, 'The Responsibility to Protect – Five Years On'.
42. Kelsay, *Arguing the Just War in Islam*; Lo, 'The *Art of War* Corpus and Chinese Just War Ethics Past and Present'.

43. Staub, *The Roots of Evil*.
44. Cohen, *States of Denial*.
45. Brudholm and Cushman (eds), *The Religious in Reponses to Mass Atrocity*.

6 Elements of a Global Ethic with Respect to Armed Conflict

Introduction

Since the mid-nineteenth century, human exercise of lethal force has taken the form of two deadly world wars, numerous civil conflicts, dozens of wars of liberation, diverse insurgencies and various police actions, and assorted terrorist attacks. Weapons have become much more destructive and are often delivered over great distances. During this same time period, a number of initiatives have been undertaken to develop internationally recognized guidelines to restrain the use of lethal force. As these initiatives have made moderate gains in authority and influence, a set of widely acknowledged but thinly spread directives have emerged. From philosophical basis to practical application, the primary concern has been to inflict as little damage as possible: to protect parties not directly involved in conflicts, to limit methods where cruelty outweighs usefulness, to evaluate the necessity for military action according to set standards, and to ensure that interventions stand a reasonable chance of achieving their ends with the resources available.

These directives have been expressed through diverse means, including the Geneva Conventions, broadly described as International Humanitarian Law; comparable standards invoked by various national and international military tribunals; complementary frameworks articulated by specially called international commissions, such as the Independent Commission on Disarmament and Security Issues and the Independent International Commission on Kosovo as well as the revival of Just War discourse, both in religious and secular contexts. In addition, these directives have been incorporated into the work of various institutions and organizations, such as the International Committee of the Red Cross, the International Atomic Energy Agency, the Organization for the Prohibition of Chemical Weapons, the International Law Commission, and the International Criminal Court. Many of these directives have been written into army field manuals (especially those related to the Geneva Conventions) and have had an influence both on military strategy and on public criticism of military practices. The ethic that these directives represent is best characterized as a set of overlapping and interrelated although distinct practices and principles, not fully embodied in any one charter, declaration, convention, or organization. Rather, they are associated with diverse codes, institutions, and patterns of reasoning, which, nonetheless, share a number of fundamental normative assumptions about the legitimate uses of lethal force.

In order to review the salient features of this nascent but still influential global ethic, its current standing and the impacts it has had, and the most important challenges it continues to face, we must begin with a historical review of military and political developments and efforts to identify and gain support for a set of normative directives about the exercise of lethal force. We must examine in particular the initiatives aimed at restraining the use of force, especially with regard to both the use of certain kinds of weapons and respect for wounded and ill soldiers and noncombatants. We must then examine perceptions about the circumstances that justify resorting to lethal force, including the set of discourses that view the exercise of lethal force as an expression of righteous action. We finish with an overall assessment of this emerging global ethic, seeing it both as an expression of humanitarian commitments and as pragmatic means for managing often increasingly destructive military force in a complex, globalized, but vulnerable world.

It may well seem naive and idealistic to attempt to guide and restrict armed conflict by ethical standards. Often, after all, people resort to lethal force precisely because they find they cannot protect their interests by ordinary practices of negotiation, public demonstrations, and politics. The people who have worked to develop the practices that express this modern global ethic well recognize this fact. They have not acted as pacifists. For a variety of reasons, they have worked not to ban war but to limit its horrors.

Historical background

Over the centuries, discourse with respect to the justifiable uses of armed force was articulated by a number of Christian thinkers such as Augustine, Aquinas, and Vitoria, as well as more secular thinkers such as Grotius and Vattel.[1] Their writings and others formed the canon that came to be known as Just War theory, invoking various criteria to determine both (1) whether the use of armed force was justified – the so-called *ad bellum* criteria – and (2) the limits on how this force might be utilized – the *in bello* criteria. These criteria were used to evaluate and criticize the Spanish conquest of the New World; to determine whether, when, and by what means it was justifiable to rebel against tyrannical governments. However, with the beginning of the Napoleonic wars, the development of large citizen armies, and the emergence of political realism, this tradition of discourse, at times reminiscent of traditional chivalric codes, temporarily faded from public attention. When the question of morally justifiable force re-emerged in the mid-nineteenth century, it focused almost exclusively on efforts to reduce needless injury to noncombatants, persons not involved or no longer involved in armed struggles – prisoners, wounded soldiers, and civilians. For example, the Lieber Code, the military code of conduct adopted by the Northern Armies in the American Civil War, was designed to limit those actions, undertaken perhaps out of hatred, revenge, or excessive zeal, that were not militarily necessary and would make subsequent efforts at peace-building much more difficult. In particular because this was a civil conflict, President Lincoln instituted the code so that the Northern Armies would focus on actions that were militarily useful and in so far as possible avoid causing needless injuries to noncombatants that might further aggravate problems of reconciliation at the end of the war. The author of this code, Francis Lieber, drew upon existing customs, laws, and more philosophical treatises to develop a practical set of guidelines.[2]

After viewing a battle in Italy, Henri Dunant, a Swiss businessman, worked not only to develop the International Committee of the Red Cross to provide help to wounded soldiers and prisoners in times of war, but also to enact an international treaty – the Geneva Convention of 1864 – setting forth guidelines to protect unarmed people during armed conflicts. In 1869, another group meeting in St Petersburg attempted to outlaw the use of certain kinds of weapons, like exploding bullets, while later others attempted to ban chemical weapons, in both cases because these weapons caused harm far beyond what seemed to be required by military necessity. These various efforts culminated both in the creation of the International Court of Arbitration in the Hague (1899), established in the hope that countries would settle disputes between themselves by means of discourse and deliberation rather than by weapons, and in the enactment of the Hague Conventions (1907), which set forth detailed guidelines regarding proper treatment of noncombatants.[3]

The Treaty of Versailles that ended the First World War also gave rise to the League of Nations, designed to act both as a forum where countries could voice their concerns and as an agency that might mobilize effective response to armed international threats.

The League's capacities were severely compromised from the outset because a number of countries, like the United States, failed to become members and because it lacked any effective authority to implement its decrees. During the interwar period other conventions, endorsed by many countries, were enacted to ban aggression and the use of chemical weapons. By the late 1930s, war had returned to both Europe and Asia. The Second World War resulted in more than sixty million deaths, including a much larger proportion of civilian deaths than in the First World War. Civilians were starved by blockades, dragged off and deliberately executed in concentration camps, targeted by area bombing campaigns, and collaterally affected by battles between opposing forces.[4]

As a by-product of this war, the allied powers, especially the United Kingdom, France, the United States, the Soviet Union, China and their allies, worked to establish the United Nations, creating a special Security Council in which these five countries as permanent members were given veto powers. These extra powers were extended in order to make sure they did not boycott the organization, as the United States had done with respect to League. The UN charter outlawed the use of lethal force by a nation against any other nation except in situations where a country was defending itself against aggression or when the Security Council itself mandated the use of armed force.[5] The allies also established international military tribunals at Nuremberg in Europe and at Tokyo in Japan to hear cases against military leaders of their enemies, who were indicted by these courts for what the initial charter for these tribunals categorized as crimes against peace, war crimes, and crimes against humanity.

Crimes against peace consisted in the initiation of armed aggression in violation of international law. War crimes referred to the abuse of unarmed persons and deliberate assaults on noncombatants as part of ongoing military activity. War crimes also consisted in plundering public or private property, wanton destruction of cities, and 'devastation not justified by military necessity'. Crimes against humanity included acts of murder, enslavement, and extermination against civilian populations before or during wars.[6]

The international law that these tribunals invoked – as well as the parallel national tribunals that heard many more cases – was not limited to explicit statutory law that the nations involved had actually signed. Rather, the courts adopted a framework that included the Hague Conventions, which the Axis powers had not signed, and other similar conventions, as well as what these courts referred to as customary law – that is, widely held views expressed in documents such as the Lieber Code, various military field guides, and international treaties.[7] In powerful ways these courts reaffirmed the notion that there were just and unjust ways to engage in armed conflict.

In 1948, the UN General Assembly passed the Universal Declaration of Human Rights (UDHR) and the Convention for the Prevention and Punishment of the Crime of Genocide. During the same time period, the International Committee of the Red Cross had been working to update regulations with respect to protection and medical care for the sick and wounded as well as shipwrecked sailors (Conventions I and II), the treatment of prisoners of war (Convention III), and the protection of civilians (Convention IV). The resulting Geneva Conventions (1949), still in force at the beginning of the twenty-first century, have been ratified by nations around the world and copied into military field books.[8] After international consultations lasting several years, two additional protocols were enacted in 1977 and signed by many countries, although not by as many as those that had signed the initial conventions. Protocol I prohibited military attacks that caused 'superfluous injury' and 'unnecessary suffering . . . which would be excessive in relation to the concrete and direct military advantage anticipated'. It also prohibited indiscriminate attacks, attacks on agricultural areas and food stock, attacks on cultural objects, as well as severe damage to the natural environment'.[9] Protocol II extended the sway of these conventions to armed conflicts within countries so long as dissidents operated 'under responsible command' within identifiable areas.[10]

From the 1960s, a number of authors and groups began to make deliberate reference to the Just War tradition, the philosophical question of justifiable war. Some, like Christian ethicist Paul Ramsey, invoked morals to prompt policymakers to think more rigorously and responsibly about the use of lethal force in a world where wars had become much more deadly. Others, like Michael Walzer, used them to dissect American military efforts in Vietnam. Still others, turned to them as a way to foster clarity and restraint in military practice. The standards and language of Just War had not been used formally either by proponents or by critics of military policies during the Second World War, even though standards regarding noncombatant immunity were clearly directly parallel to the tradition. Just War distinguished between standards to guide the uses of armed force (*in bello*) and to determine when and where the resort to armed force was called for (*ad bellum*). The former were traditionally limited to norms of noncombatant immunity and the principle of proportionality. According to the latter, the resort to armed force ought to be done for a good cause, authorized by a proper authority, pursued with the right intent and as a last resort, and undertaken with a reasonable chance of success. During the last third of the twentieth century these ideas were used more frequently to consider new problems such as nuclear deterrence and possible inter-state wars, and to review former wars and alternatives like economic sanctions.[11] By the beginning of the twenty-first century, ideas from the Just War tradition had been incorporated into the reports of several highly regarded international commissions, including the recent report of the Secretary General's High-Level Panel on Threats, Challenges, and Change.[12]

Before moving on to this analysis, it is worth observing that neither the post-war military tribunals nor the Geneva Conventions looked closely at questionable military activities by the allied powers. Neither raised questions about the bombing of civilian targets. Neither raised questions about how allied powers had used military force to establish and protect their empires. Through this immediate post-Second World War period, efforts to establish normative standards regulating and restraining the exercise of lethal force had been undertaken largely by the industrialized nations of Europe, North America, and East Asia. Preoccupied with the horrors of the wars in which they had just engaged, representatives from these countries focused especially on limiting the occasion and conduct of wars between nations.

Just uses of armed force

In the post-war years, the norms with respect to just uses of armed force were articulated for the most part in relation to the following three considerations: one, noncombatant immunity; two, efforts to outlaw or greatly restrict the use of weapons that cause excessive and often indiscriminate injury; and, three, the call to act in keeping with the norm of proportionalty. In varying degrees, these norms influenced both military conduct and the public debates about it.

Noncombatant immunity

Central to the Geneva Conventions was the assumption that unarmed persons, whether they were wounded soldiers, soldiers laying down their weapons to become prisoners, or civilians, should not be intentionally and directly targeted by armed force. To distinguish soldiers from civilians, the Geneva Conventions required that the former operate under orders, wear clothes or signs indicating they were soldiers, and carry their weapons visibly. Although traditional Just War discourse had distinguished soldiers from civilians in the language of guilt and innocence, International Humanitarian Law has more practically drawn the line between armed and unarmed.

During the Second World War, opposing forces by turns honoured and ignored these guidelines. Ground forces complied overall, although there were numerous violations. Occasionally both allied and axis powers deliberately attacked merchant ships, directly flaunting this standard. For this reason, in recognition of equivalent complicity, the post-war military tribunals did not level these particular charges against axis military leaders being tried.[13] The most serious breach of noncombatant immunity was the incarceration, torture, and deliberate murder of unarmed civilians deemed to be enemies of the state. Nazi concentration camps were the most blatant and horrible example of this violation. The standard of noncombatant immunity was also controversially violated by the practice of aerial bombing of civilian sites. Ostensibly, bombs should be aimed at military targets in so far as this is possible. So long as this standard is observed, harm caused to nearby non-military areas might be excused as collateral damage. Debate arose about the legitimacy of attacking not-strictly military sites with bombs. For example, to what extent was it legitimate to attack the transportation lines used to bring weapons, energy, manpower, and other supplies to the military front? A good case might be made for including these sites as military targets. However, during the Gulf War, when the allied forces bombed the electric grid in Iraq so that Iraqi forces could not use anti-aircraft and anti-missile weapons to attack coalition planes and missiles, they also cut off the electricity supply for millions of civilians, who depended on this power in a number of ways, including its use to pump fresh water. The subsequent injury to civilians was extensive.[14]

A more protracted debate has taken place on the legitimacy of targeting civilians both because of their tacit support for the military policies of their government and in the hopes of affecting and turning their hearts and minds against their government and its military campaign.[15] To a degree, all sides during the Second World War adopted this stance. Using this rationale, the Allies, for example, undertook area bombing, including the bombing of cities. While the Allies debated among themselves about whether this bombing should be strategic, focused mostly on military targets and associated infrastructures, or have wider, more general targets, there were still some vocal protests about these policies both during the war and later.

The Jesuit John Ford raised questions about the utility as well as the morality of obliteration bombing.[16] After the war, the US government undertook studies, led by John Galbraith, which determined that the bombing raids on Germany and Japan had had little effective impact on the economic capacity of these countries to continue their war efforts. The loss of life both for the pilots flying these bombing missions and for the civilians who suffered as a result seemed unjustified in strictly utilitarian terms.[17]

When he addressed this question in the 1970s, Michael Walzer, in his book *Just and Unjust Wars*, argued that the convention against deliberately attacking civilian targets was both morally compelling and practical. The attacks on civilian targets typically resulted in extensive damage and suffering, with little or no demonstrable military advantage. However, Walzer allowed for one exception: in the case of a supreme emergency. He cites as an example the period just before the United States entered the Second World War, during which time the British forces' resort to area bombing might well have been justified.[18]

To an extent, the debate about the morality and utility of area and strategic bombing has had some impact over time, both on military strategy and on public discussion of military practices. For example, in both the Gulf War and subsequent Iraq war, attacks by coalition forces were officially aimed either at strictly military targets or at areas that were deemed to be strategically important for the Iraqi war effort.[19] Publicly, the bombing raids of the North Atlantic Treaty Organization (NATO) in the 1999 war over Kosovo were defended in equivalent terms, even though attacks affected a number of non-military targets, such as bridges in Serbia at a great distance from Kosovo itself. In this case, the practice of waging a war exclusively by means of aerial attacks occasioned considerable criticism for putting large numbers of civilians at extreme risk for reasons that were not militarily necessary.[20] Was this an example, as the International Commission on Kosovo later argued, of an illegal but legitimate exercise of lethal force?[21]

The norm of noncombatant immunity has also affected debates over the use of economic sanctions and blockades as seemingly less violent ways of waging war. These kinds of actions have often been championed as alternative, less destructive, yet still effective ways of exerting pressure on governments – for example, when seeking to deter foreign policies that seriously violate norms of non-aggression and human rights. Many countries adopted these kinds of tactics in opposition to the apartheid regime in South Africa. However, a number of observers have raised serious questions about who is most affected by these measures. The economic sanctions against Iraq during the 1990s, for example, had significant impact on the health and well-being of the poorest strata of Iraq society, resulting in thousands of civilian deaths. While it may be possible to devise more limited and targeted sanctions – aimed, for example, to restrict arms trade – general sanctions may well violate the conventions protecting noncombatants.[22]

As the twenty-first century begins, the most serious challenge with respect to noncombatant immunity arises with respect to the increasing number of situations, as in civil wars and insurgencies, in which armed struggle takes place in the presence of ordinary citizens, most of whom remain unarmed.[23] In these settings, while those with arms operate under command, they do not always dress so that they can be identified as soldiers and do not always display their weapons openly. In many situations they have taken shelter among unarmed people with whom they share ethnic loyalties, and thereby have been able to avoid detection by opposing forces. From a strict interpretation, as they fail to wear identifying insignia and display weapons openly, these armed indigenous forces may not have qualified as soldiers when they were caught and therefore may not have qualified as prisoners able to avoid criminal punishment for their part in the hostilities. Those opposing these indigenous forces often find themselves in the uncomfortable position of either attacking their enemies broadly as they find shelter among their people and thus inevitably targeting noncombatants, or abstaining from attack to avoid civilian casualties and correspondingly yielding to the indigenous forces.

Debates about how to manage these situations continue. In the 1950s, the British successfully fought indigenous forces in Malaya by relocating large numbers of civilians to other areas. However, that option has simply not been available in most settings. Initially, the British dealt with insurgents in Northern Ireland by treating them as criminals and defining their own strikes as police action. This language, which regarded the force used against insurgent groups as policing, has been widely employed to describe armed efforts to deal with insurgents in many areas, including Vietnam, Colombia, and even Palestine. However, it is not clear that framing the issue in this way is either accurate or useful. After all, for the most part these groups have not been unorganized law-breakers. Rather, they have been part of well-organized political movements, which in varying degrees have gained legitimacy in the eyes of the people by representing their aspirations, voicing their anger, and addressing many of their social welfare needs. A number of observers have, therefore, argued that effectively opposing such insurgencies requires more than common military strategy. It calls for highly focused military tactics that must be exercised in conjunction with effective intelligence, apt political strategy, and social and economic initiatives that address the concerns of the civilian population.[24]

The ongoing debate on acts of terror intersects with ongoing efforts to find viable ways of limiting the targets of lethal force to protect noncombatants. Armed attacks become acts of terror in so far as they target civilians indiscriminately with the purported purpose of inspiring fear and terror, hoping thereby to gain support through intimidation for the attackers' political dispositions. Suicide bombings, missile attacks on civilian neighbourhoods, and hostage-taking constitute prime examples of such acts of terror. Insurgent groups frequently resort to acts of terror, it is sometimes believed, because they lack the means to attack combatants directly. However, acts of terror have been used frequently and extensively by established governments. Both the German government under Hitler and the Russian government under Stalin terrorized their own populations by means of secret police, abductions, assassinations, and torture. Area and obliteration bombing were also acts of terror. In these instances, the targets were usually indiscriminate and the aim was to frighten the attacked population into changing their de facto political wills.[25]

Without fully acknowledging the nature of acts of terror, arguments about uses of terror tactics have understandably focused primarily on effective and fitting ways to reduce the incidence of such acts. To what extent can and should those opposing acts of terror be exempted from the ordinary laws protecting civil liberties? To what extent, after ample warning had been given to those residing in areas that those committing acts of terror used for shelter, was it legitimate and effective to attack these neighbourhoods as a whole? To what degree, in violation of the general prohibition on reprisals, was it justified and effective to respond to acts of terror with even more lethal attacks on the civilian areas from which those attacks originated?[26] The debate regarding acts of terror and appropriate responses has been characteristically volatile and has often proceeded in relation to quite different agendas. Debates unfolded this way, not primarily because, as some argued, one side's terrorist was inevitably another side's freedom fighter, but more often because discussions regarding acts of terror – that is, a particular way of waging war – often became conflated with discussions of fitting responses to insurgencies – that is, armed indigenous political movements in opposition to established governments. These remain two quite different although at times interrelated issues. It is possible to summarize ongoing discussions about this matter with two modest and tentative observations. One, apart from the oppressive practices of police states, and with a few other exceptions, it is not at all clear that acts of terror have been militarily or politically effective against opposing forces over the long term, whether enacted by established governments or by indigenous insurgents.[27] Two, even these often heated debates indirectly indicate a growing and widely held public affirmation that lethal force should not be used for indiscriminate attacks upon civilian targets, except when rare and unusual circumstances might render such an attack effective as a last resort.

The norm of noncombatant immunity, whether expressed by the Geneva Conventions, the sentences of war tribunals, philosophical and political discussions about Just War, public outcries against terrorist attacks, or military handbooks, has gained broad international recognition and modest authority. Military leaders have adjusted their practices to take account of it, although typically defending these policies in pragmatic terms. Even those who question the validity of such a norm in modern warfare indirectly acknowledge its legitimacy as they identify situations – such as Walzer's reference to supreme emergencies – when it may be justified to override it.

Efforts to limit or prohibit the use of weapons that cause excessive and indiscrimate injury

Beginning in the mid-nineteenth century, those concerned to introduce restraint in armed conflicts have attempted to outlaw or severely restrict the uses of certain types of weapons that cause excessive injury. The arguments for these prohibitions have always been twofold. One, it has been argued that the damages caused by these weapons result in egregious suffering, often to noncombatants or soldiers already hit and unable to attack. Overwhelmingly, these weapons have inflicted suffering on civilian populations. Two, it was argued that the harm done was not militarily necessary. The same ends could be advanced as effectively or more effectively by the use of other weapons that inflicted less indiscriminate suffering. A number of European nations adopted the 1869 Saint Petersburg Declaration, which banned expanding projectiles, such as exploding bullets, because these weapons result in superfluous injury. Reacting to the use of gases and chemical weapons during the First World War, a number of nations later adopted the 1925 Geneva Protocol prohibiting the 'Use of Asphyxiating, Poisonous, or Other Gases, and of Bacteriological Methods of Warfare'.[28] The significant number of nations that supported this treaty did so out of humanitarian concern mixed with a considerable dose of practical self-interest. It was difficult if not impossible to restrict the harm caused by these weapons: they contaminated battle areas, rendering them impassable for the armed forces using them. For the most part, these weapons have not been subsequently employed, except by the Iraq government both against some of its own citizens and against Iranians during its war with Iran, and, more recently, by the Syrian government against rebel forces. A number of countries still have substantial stockpiles of these weapons. Thus, in spite of the 1993 international Chemical Weapons Convention banning chemical and biological weapons, there is still realistic cause for concern regarding the possible use of these kinds of weapons.

Towards the end of the century, a large number of countries endorsed the Ottawa Treaty banning the use of land mines in times of war. Again, the rationale was twofold. In disproportionate numbers, these weapons, which often remain hidden for many years after wars are concluded, result in crippling injuries and death to civilians, often children, who are not connected with war efforts. Furthermore, because forces often lack a clear map of where the land mines were laid, these areas become threatening to all sides.

Since the Second World War, most attention has focused on nuclear weapons. The five permanent members of the United Nations have all developed the capacity to produce nuclear weapons and to launch them in various ways – from planes, submarines, or missile silos – often from great distances. Both the American government and the Soviet Union developed huge stockpiles of these weapons, and India, Pakistan, Israel, and North Korea have developed the capacity to build and launch nuclear weapons as well. At the same time, scientists have discovered ways to utilize some of the same nuclear technology to generate electrical energy. Correspondingly, a number of countries, including not only those with nuclear weapons but others such as Canada, Japan, and Germany, have developed systems of nuclear energy. The sense of threat posed by the potential use of nuclear weapons has been extensive and intense, not only because of their immediate destructive capacity but also because of the danger of exposure to radioactivity for months and years after any nuclear explosion. Many have feared that these weapons might be used carelessly or that the use by one side would occasion a cycle of retaliatory attacks resulting in unimaginable damage.

Debates regarding the potential uses and limitations on the uses of nuclear weapons have proceeded in many different national and international media, councils, and conferences. Some have argued for the possibility of tactical, battlefield use of these weapons.[29] Others have argued that any use of nuclear weapons was unconscionable.[30] Although nuclear bombs were dropped by Americans planes on the Japanese cities of Hiroshima and Nagasaki, nuclear weapons have not been used subsequently. Most importantly, the nuclear powers, led by the United States and the Soviet Union, worked together with other nations to construct the 1968 Nuclear Non-Proliferation Treaty and to establish the International Atomic Energy Agency. By this Treaty, nations could develop atomic energy, subject to international inspection, and the possession of actual nuclear weapons was restricted to the five permanent members of the Security Council, augmented later by Israel, Pakistan, India, and North Korea. Step by step, the Soviet Union and later Russia, together with the United States, have taken modest steps to reduce their stockpiles of nuclear weapons. Efforts to restrict the proliferation of these weapons have continued in the twenty-first century with regard both to North Korea's actual weapons and to fear that Iran might be secretly developing this capacity.[31]

Since the Second World War, there has been much moral agonizing about the possible use of nuclear weapons. By their nature, these weapons cause extensive, indiscriminate harm. This harm seems disproportionate to the ends sought or any harm already suffered except a prior nuclear attack. Correspondingly, during this period a number of countries have publicly adopted 'No First Strike' positions. However, the major nuclear states seemed to feel that being ready to use nuclear weapons in response acted as a deterrence against the use of nuclear weapons by others. Major nuclear states overtly expressed the intention that, if they were attacked, they would strike massively not just military sights but population centres. Most people felt that such action, if actually taken, would be both immoral and self-defeating, because such an attack would probably incur more nuclear response. However, in practice, these threats have seemed to function as effective deterrents.

Many have argued that it is hopelessly idealistic to attempt to establish global restrictions with regard to the uses of particular weapons. By their nature, armed forces seek to put into use whatever weapons will help them succeed. However, nuclear weapons constitute a unique kind of danger. They cause massive and indiscriminate harm. They are very expensive and difficult to produce. It is not easy to make them, put them in places where they can be readily deployed if necessary, and protect them either from inadvertent accidents or from those who might seek to disable them by stealth. In the years since Hiroshima, thousands of near accidents have occurred with these weapons.[32] Correspondingly, many countries that might have developed nuclear weapons have chosen not to do so, thereby reinforcing the widespread belief that these weapons are by their nature morally questionable.

The norm of proportionality

The basic principle of proportionality can be stated in several ways. When engaging in armed conflict, powers should not use excessive force – thereby putting more people, buildings, and fields in harm's way – when the same ends can be achieved with less force. They should not put their own forces at excessive risk seeking ends for which they are not able to marshal appropriate means. Nor, in response to injuries suffered on account of enemy attacks, should agents cause harm and destruction greatly in excess of the injuries they have experienced. Means and ends should be proportionate to each other. The norm of proportionality has been less explicitly defined by public documents than the standards respecting noncombatant immunity and inadmissible weapons. It is not overtly articulated in any convention or treaty. Its influence is, however, pervasive, if more subtle. The language of proportionality enters again and again as these documents consider whether certain practices – such as the use of chemical weapons, refusing to give quarter to surrendering enemy soldiers, or indiscriminate bombing – genuinely work to further military and political objectives or whether they are unnecessary, egregious, and thus disproportionate.

In practice, questions of proportionality have been typically considered in pragmatic, almost cost–benefit terms. International courts have invoked the norm of proportionality since a 1928 ruling by an arbitral tribunal established by the Versailles Peace Treaty, arbitrating a Portuguese claim that, in 1914, German ships had used excessive force against their forts in Angola. The International Court of Justice has invoked this norm in a number of recent cases, such as its determination that the United States acted disproportionately when it bombed an Iranian oil platform in the Persian Gulf, killing many civilians, in response to an attack on a US warship with no casualties.[33] Often taking a pragmatic form, ideas about proportionality were widely invoked by both the critics and the defenders of the Vietnam War, as well as by those defending and opposing the arguments about nuclear deterrence.[34] For example, although he concluded that threatening to use nuclear weapons was morally wrong because it would always be wrong to use such weapons, Michael Walzer nonetheless observed that the credible nuclear threat seemed to have deterred the use of nuclear weapons by enemies and was therefore justified.[35]

In interesting and at times paradoxical ways, the norm of proportionality has functioned to intertwine high moral purpose – the wish to expose and reduce destruction occasioned by the misuse of lethal force – with instrumental preoccupation with improving the effectiveness and efficiency of military practice. In the process, as David Kennedy has observed, military planners have begun to use humanitarian rhetoric, while humanitarians have frequently sounded like military strategists.[36]

Just responses to those who violate these standards

In a variety of ways since the Second World War, normative concerns about just uses of armed force have gained wider attention, greater public prominence, and increased authority. These standards have been invoked by post-conflict tribunals and national courts. Some countries have justified their own threats to use lethal force because, they argue, other countries have egregiously violated these standards with respect, for example, to the use and threatened use of prohibited weapons. After the Second World War, tribunals in Nuremberg and Tokyo tried and convicted a number of axis leaders as criminals. Similar international tribunals heard complaints about alleged war crimes committed by particular leaders during armed conflicts in the former country of Yugoslavia and in Rwanda. In the late 1990s the International Criminal Court (ICC) was established to hear cases with respect to alleged war crimes and crimes against humanity. Thus, it has been widely accepted that, if international norms with respect to the uses of lethal force are to have any real global authority, then officials violating these standards must from time to time be brought before appropriate tribunals.

In practice these tribunals have operated selectively, hearing cases with respect to some but not all of the most blatant violations of humanitarian law. For example, the post-Second World War tribunals did not hear cases with regard to attacks on maritime commerce nor with regard to overt bombing of civilian targets, since both sides had violated these standards. In settings such as Cambodia and Rwanda, where complicity in war crimes and genocide was so widespread, efforts to try some but not others as criminals has seemed to many to show a kind of one-sided justice favouring the victors.[37]

Frequently, insurgent groups have been characterized in criminal terms because from time to time these groups have targeted noncombatants and engaged in assassination-like attacks against others. The criminal label has often been employed to justify and excuse questionable practices, including both the excessive use of force by attackers against those they regard as criminal and the unwillingness to explore political means to resolve conflicts at hand. For example, Israel's response to Hamas was viewed in these terms, as was the United Kingdom's treatment of the Irish Republican Army (IRA) for so many years, and Sri Lanka's actions towards the Tamil Tigers. In more general terms, we might well observe that, even as a number of global normative standards gain in influence and authority, we have yet to find effective, widely agreed-upon means of holding accountable those who violate these norms. Nonetheless, we have found ways of holding at least some of these violators to account, however symbolically.

The just resort to armed force

The question of the just resort to armed force has typically been used to determine whether or not there was sufficient warrant for taking up arms to attack another party and whether it was justifiable at a particular point in time to employ lethal force in battle. But the question of just resort inevitably raises at the same time a range of interrelated questions, regarding especially, one, the understanding of aggression; two, who properly should be exercising directing authority with respect to the use of armed force; three, what might and should be the fitting relationship between military and political strategy; and, four, whether armed force might be used to intervene in other states for humanitarian purposes. As we will see, the process of addressing these interrelated questions regarding the just resort has measurably affected how armed force is understood and used.

The question of aggression

From the middle of the nineteenth century until the Second World War, the question of just resort to armed force did not really arise as a matter of public discussion. It was assumed that sovereign governments possessed the authority to use armed force to protect the security of their realms. Questions about the resort to armed force were not included in the discussions that led to the Hague treaties and Geneva Conventions. To be sure, the pacifist view that any resort to armed forced was morally wrong gained enough influence in a number of countries in the years between the world wars for representatives of these countries to enact and later sign the Pact of Paris (also referred to as the Kellogg–Briand Pact) in 1928, outlawing war and aggression. This treaty remained more an expression of hope and idealism than a binding and compelling standard that countries felt they were obliged to honor no matter what. Nonetheless, in spite of its association with pacifist idealism, after the war this pact did come to serve as an authoritative point of reference both for the UN Charter and for the post-war international military tribunals. Both of these identified the resort to unprovoked aggression as a war crime. The charter allowed for the use of armed force in only two circumstances: one, when it was authorized by the Security Council to address any action that seemed to threaten the overall system of global security; and, two, by individual nations to defend themselves against aggression.

How adequate have these guidelines been? They provided a framework for the Security Council to endorse the use of armed force to defend South Korea against armed invasion of its territory in 1950 and, forty years later, to support the use of armed force against the armed invasion of Kuwait by Iraq in 1989. Having waged two world wars within a little over thirty years, the industrialized countries of Europe, North America, and East Asia largely abided by this standard in so far as they did not engage in any further wars against each other. The United States attempted to justify its war efforts in Vietnam as a defence of the South against aggression from the North, although this rationale was widely challenged.[38] These standards were not, however, invoked to defend Iran against the invasion by Iraq or Afghanistan against the invasion of the Soviet Union, because there was little political will in the Security Council with regard to these cases.

Questions about when and how to resort to armed force in the years since the Second World War have rarely fitted neatly within the normative framework established by the UN Charter. Many conflicts were intra-national, as, for example, when indigenous parties sought to establish national sovereignty in a colonial context. Consider, for example, the armed conflicts in Indonesia in the late 1940s, Vietnam in the 1950s, 1960s and 1970s, as well as Congo, Angola, Mozambique, Sudan, Liberia, and Zimbabwe at various times during the second half of the twentieth century. Consider the ongoing struggles over the partition of India and Pakistan and between Tamil and Sinhalese groups in Sri Lanka. Consider as well the battles between various peoples in the Middle East, including Syria, Israel, Palestine, and Lebanon, as well as the conflicts in Cyprus. Think about the fights for independence in Algeria, ethnic conflicts in Kenya, guerilla uprisings in Colombia, and army-led attacks on citizens in Argentina and Chile. The normative models that established guidelines with respect to armed conflict between nations provided little explicit help in thinking about and responding to these conflicts. Nor, as we shall see, did these models offer clear guidelines for situations in which governments committed atrocities against their own people or allowed these acts to be done by armed groups within their countries.

Nonetheless, in the years since the Second World War, a number of initiatives have been undertaken to extend and broaden the principles that determine when parties may justifiably resort to lethal force to defend themselves and their interests against their aggressors. Thus, Protocol II of the Geneva Conventions, enacted in 1977, allows peoples oppressed by alien or tyrannical regimes to resort to force to defend themselves and supports their will to govern themselves against such powers. In this instance, aggression can be understood not only as assault from other states but also as political systems that de facto assault the lives of peoples and their wish to govern themselves.[39]

In practice, a number of parties have also argued for the right to use lethal force pre-emptively. Is it necessary, they have asked, to wait to be attacked before one can justifiably use armed force as a defence against aggression? Given evidence that opposing forces are being mobilized and deployed in readiness to attack, is it morally acceptable to launch a pre-emptive strike? This question was raised by the Israeli attack in the Six Day War against Egyptian, Syrian, and Jordanian forces that were being readied for what seemed like an imminent attack on Israel. It was raised again when the United States sought justification for attacking Iraq before Iraq had had the opportunity to use suspected weapons of mass destruction against its enemies. Walzer subsequently defended Israel's attack as justifiably pre-emptive, not only because of the manifest intent by opposing forces to injure but also because the failure to act would have 'seriously risked their territorial integrity or political independence'.[40] Many have agreed in principle with the types of arguments Walzer used, although this example remains controversial. In general terms, the principle of pre-emption is that, faced with an imminent and well-organized threat of armed attack, a state may justifiably attack first, particularly when the failure to do so would mean losing the capacity effectively to retaliate and defend itself against further attacks. Stated in these terms, the principle broadens the basic rationale for resorting to armed force as defence against aggression, and has been widely accepted and employed. There has been, however, much less support for preventive attacks, as in the case of America's war against Iraq, which was justified not as a pre-emptive defence but rather as the means to bring about a range of political changes. Prior to the First World War, military planners in a number of European countries adopted the position that it was acceptable to initiate the use of force as a preventive measure to avoid being the unfortunate object of another country's attack. In practice, this position allowed for acts of aggression against enemy states and seemed to invite equivalent acts of aggression from these enemies. The UN Charter formally outlawed these kinds of attacks.

The many armed conflicts of nation states formed in the decades since the Second World War have taken varied forms, such as military coups, civil wars, ongoing struggles for independence, and insurgencies as dissident groups have sought either to challenge the official government or to assert their own independence. Typically, intra-state conflicts (conflicts within states) have lasted many years longer than inter-state conflicts (conflicts between states). The international community – largely working through the United Nations, sometimes through regional organizations such as NATO or the Economic Community of West African States, and sometimes just through the initiative of one other nation – has launched a number of different kinds of peacekeeping initiatives in the hope of restraining violence in these contexts. These third-party interventions have acted variously to maintain truces, quell disturbances, police borders, restore order, supervise elections, and engage in other peacekeeping operations. From a historical perspective, these interventions have represented a new kind of international action, where the interests of the larger community of nations in peace and order has led to armed interventions not primarily designed to invade and occupy enemy territories. In post-conflict situations, these peacekeeping operations have shown overwhelming benefits: these countries are markedly less likely to experience further civil conflict while their economies are likely to remain in better shape.[41] Between 1990 and 2005, there was a steady and dramatic decline in genocides, armed conflicts, and deaths that were due to armed conflicts, followed by a moderate rise in these figures since 2005.[42]

Over time, those involved with launching peacekeeping operations have learned a good deal. The initial operations often took the form of unarmed or lightly armed teams of international observers, stationed at the boundaries between antagonistic parties such as India and Pakistan in Kashmir, Israel and its neighbours, and Greek- and Turkish-speaking Cypriots. Over time, peacekeeping forces were assigned more and heavier arms. For the most part, they were initially restricted to using their weapons in self-defence. Over time, their mandate has been broadened in places to allow for the use of force to defend the populations they were called upon to protect. By 1988, there had been only thirteen such missions, and eight of these had been completed. In the 1990s the number of UN peacekeeping operations greatly increased. There were eighteen missions in 2001. In 2005, more than 103 countries were contributing a total of 65,000 troops.[43]

The disastrous aspects of several peacekeeping missions – in Bosnia, Somalia, and Rwanda – during the 1990s led to serious rethinking about the way these operations were conceived and supported. In retrospect, given that their positions in supposedly safe areas were in the midst of ongoing belligerence, the peacekeeping forces in Bosnia were too few in number and too lightly armed. When the peacekeeping mission was dramatically strengthened, they were better able to defend the populations they had been assigned to protect and provide breathing space in the conflict. This allowed for diplomatic initiatives that in turn led the Dayton Accords to succeed. The peacekeeping forces in Somalia had initially been assigned the task of providing protection to aid programmes delivering food, which were being attacked by tribal militia. The United States spearheaded the international forces' decision to attack particular militias – an unsuccessful move that resulted, in October 1993, in American forces being attacked and humiliated. American forces then felt overexposed and withdrew. This failure contributed to the reluctance of the United States as well as some European countries to get overly involved when another civil conflict began to unfold in Rwanda at the beginning of 1994. A small, lightly armed UN peacekeeping operation had been assigned to the conflict between the Hutu and the Tutsi, which had been ongoing since the very poor, densely populated country gained independence from Belgium thirty years earlier. Fearing that the Hutu-led government was planning a major assault on the Tutsi, the Canadian general leading this mission appealed for more troops and arms. His appeal was ignored. After a plane carrying the presidents of Rwanda and Burundi was shot down, the Hutu engaged in a widespread attack, killing 800,000 Tutsi people within a couple of months. The undermanned and under-equipped peacekeeping force was incapable of stopping or even limiting the genocide. As a result of these events in Bosnia, Somalia, and Rwanda, as well as the increased demand for peacekeeping missions elsewhere, it became imperative to rethink the aims and means of these operations. A special UN Commission reported in August 2000 that these operations had to project credible force, and that in some settings, in order not to become complicit in atrocities being committed by one side, peacekeepers might have to ally more closely with the other side.

As we reflect on these peacekeeping operations, it seems reasonable to arrive at several conclusions that are in general consonant with the moral traditions associated with International Humanitarian Law. To begin with: there is strong evidence that the use of armed force for peacekeeping has been beneficial in reducing the subsequent possibilities of further armed conflict in post-conflict states. However, when and how armed force is used by peacekeepers requires the thoughtful exercise of political judgement and initiatives to determine both the character of the conflicts and the relative legitimacy of contesting parties. Relevant authorities must be identified and opportunities for negotiations seized. In some settings, peacekeeping forces may be called on to preserve truces between opposing forces. However, if one side has resorted to acts of terror, peacekeepers may well need to identify relatively safe areas to protect noncombatants, whether those attacking are government or insurgent forces. Establishing diplomatic contacts is likely to be complex. In settings where one side has clearly gained greater legitimacy in the eyes of the people, peacekeepers may be called upon to limit the conflict in ways that de facto support this party at the expense of neutrality. As contemporary guidelines for fighting insurgencies insist, peacekeeping forces should assign priority to making contacts with the people and working to protect them. In all settings peacekeepers are well cautioned to think and act proportionately about their operations. Peacekeepers faced disaster in Bosnia and Rwanda because the means they employed were inadequate to the tasks they had been assigned to accomplish. In Somalia, they pursued an end for which they had neither adequate means nor a clear mandate, nor had they identified the relevant local authorities with which they might have coordinated their armed attacks.

From the review of these several different examples – from discussion of pre-emptive strikes to the responsible uses of peacekeeping, from the wording introduced in Protocol II to the imposition of no-fly zones – it is clear that concerned groups have explored ways of broadening and deepening the principle that allows people justifiably to resort to lethal force to defend themselves against aggression. In the process, this principle has become less a legalistic code that might be invoked in an international tribunal and more a set of normative points of reference for exercising responsible judgements.

The question of authority

During the period since the Second World War this question of authority has assumed many forms. For example, was there someone in charge of the forces fighting the Dutch in Indonesia? Who were they? What legitimacy did they have? To what extent did the Viet Cong possess recognizable legitimate authority among the people of Vietnam? Did the province of Katanga have a legitimate mandate to declare independence from the newly independent Congo? Which of the contending forces in Angola had greatest claims to authority? Who organized and therefore should be held accountable for the genocide in Rwanda? Who commanded the liberation forces in Algeria? Were the insurgents in Afghanistan, Pakistan, Somalia, Chechnya, Colombia, Peru, or Kosovo operating in response to responsible authorities or as disorganized lawbreakers or rebels? Fundamentally, these questions ask whether and to what degree those undertaking to exercise lethal force were doing so under the command of recognized structures of authority, which gave direction, assumed accountability, and could be engaged in negotiations. The inclination of many established governments, especially former imperial powers, has been to treat these insurgent forces as disorderly rabble, as lawbreakers or delinquents with whom one should not engage in negotiations. When captured, insurgents have often correspondingly been treated as criminals, not prisoners of war. For a long time, even after the withdrawal of their troops, America remained unwilling to recognize that the Viet Cong exercised legitimate authority in the eyes of large numbers of Vietnamese. In spite of initial reluctance, over time many established powers have come to acknowledge the legitimacy of insurgents such as the IRA, the Viet Cong, and the Sudanese Liberation Army, and the latter have in turn openly acknowledged their leaders as legitimate political authorities. Thus debates about whether the resort to armed force was justified in turn occasioned debates about whether these resorts were in fact directed by responsible authorities recognized as legitimate by the actors involved, and whether those authorities were able to exercise effective control over, and demand accountability from, those engaged in hostilities. The question of authority is inextricably connected with debates about whether the resort to force is justified, not primarily because it is necessary to gain the approval of certain bodies, like the Security Council, but because the exercise of armed force should always be directed, as the Geneva Protocol indicates, by leaders or councils who can be held accountable, can exercise restraints, and can respond to political initiatives.[44]

Questions about the relationship of military actions to political purposes

A third set of discussions has focused on the relationships between political and military action. This discussion was occasioned by a number of diverse examples. What kinds of diplomatic or nation building strategy might best accompany peacekeeping efforts in places of weak or divided governments as in Bosnia, Kosovo, Somalia, or Congo? After their initial military successes in Afghanistan and Iraq, what were the appropriate political responsibilities of NATO and coalition forces in working to establish effective and legitimate government structures? To what extent did it make sense to form new governments using ex-patriots who were well connected with the occupying forces? Were there viable alternative strategies that involved greater utilization of indigenous and possibly insurgent groups? Did the role taken by occupying forces in Germany and Japan after the Second World War provide useful or unhelpful examples? Some observers maintained that there was a need to develop a set of *post-bellum* supplementary guidelines to Just War arguments to anticipate more fully the political challenges of which these military crises were symptoms.[45] Reflecting in part on his experience mobilizing NATO forces in Bosnia, General Rupert Smith correspondingly argued that, in the wars that became typical in the second half of the twentieth century, military and political strategy needed to become far more integrated.[46] These examples underline the ancient counsel that military strategies should uphold, be closely connected with, and support equally well-thought-out political strategies. As well, these examples challenge us to rethink the Just War criteria of just intent; to question not only motives but also the underlying political purposes connected with the resort to armed force.

How parties envision the relationship between military strategies and political purposes has often impacted on how they have sought to bring armed conflicts to an end. Much of the discourse regarding the just resort to armed force has focused on decisions to initiate the use of violence. However, it is as important to think realistically both at the outset and during the struggle about how particular conflicts might end and how these ends will function to realize specific and legitimate political purposes.[47] Although belligerents often rhetorically invoke idealized purposes – 'to make the world free for democracy' or 'to destroy the enemy' – in most cases conflicts have ended as diplomats from the opposing parties have entered into negotiations with each other or with third parties. To avoid what seem like politically unacceptable compromises, sometimes parties have sought the unconditional surrender of opposing forces so that as victors they would be at liberty to impose their own political purposes. However, even in situations where parties have sought to annex or colonize the territories of their opponents, they have usually had to find groups and individuals indigenous to these areas to help govern occupied lands. Because in most cases ending armed conflicts involves the political effort to negotiate reasonable terms, it becomes important to exercise armed force in ways that allow these kinds of political communications to take place.[48]

Questions about humanitarian interventions

A fourth set of debates has addressed the question of when and on what basis it might be justified for outsiders to intervene with lethal force on a humanitarian basis. Should outsiders use armed force on behalf of peoples who appear to outsiders to be oppressed by their governments or other armed parties? The question has arisen recently in places such as Cambodia, Sierra Leone, East Timor, Congo, the Darfur region of Sudan, Zimbabwe, Chechnya, Bosnia, Kosovo, Syria, and Iraq. Interested parties have discussed this question in terms of humanitarian interventions, the politics of rescue, and what to do about rogue regimes.[49] For many it seemed morally outrageous to stand by and witness scenes of ethnic cleansing, genocide, human rights abuses, and war crimes and do nothing when it seemed that the assertion of modest amounts of armed force by outsiders might appreciably and effectively reduce the atrocities. In fact, outsiders have intervened forcibly in some of these settings –such as Somalia,

Congo, Bosnia, Kosovo, and Iraq – although not always with clear success nor without controversy. In contrast, observers point to several examples where outside interventions have been both militarily successful and widely applauded internationally. These include India's intervention on behalf of the efforts of Bangladesh (East Pakistan) to declare its independence from Pakistan; Tanzania's intervention against the military forces of Idi Amin in Uganda on behalf of Amin's opponents; Vietnam's intervention against the Khmer Rouge in Cambodia and in support of alternative political parties; the intervention of a number of countries on behalf of the people of East Timor against the efforts of the Indonesian military to occupy the country; and the British and Nigerian intervention on behalf of the government against rebel forces that had seized control in Sierra Leone. What conclusions might be drawn from reviewing not only these clear cases, but also cases where the results were more ambiguous and controversial, or still others, like the 1994 genocide in Rwanda, where the failure to intervene seemed to lead to even more extensive atrocities?

The idea of humanitarian intervention from the outside seems altruistic and globally responsible. In a number of settings, humanitarian interventions might easily be viewed as the logical extension of previous UN peacekeeping roles. Not only would these outsiders protect the delivery of aid, but they could also defend the local people against warlords who oppressed them. Not only would outsiders protect refugee camps, but they could also seek to defeat armed insurgents that threatened them. As responsible stewards, outsiders by themselves or through the United Nations could use force to bring stability and order to areas torn by civil strife. These ideas, however, received wary responses from many representatives of developing countries. Too often in the past, similar sounding rhetoric had served as a mere excuse, when occupations by colonizing and imperial forces were justified in the name of fighting the slave trade, overcoming armed struggles between local ethnic opponents, or defending their own trading or mining outposts from local attacks. Humanitarian interventions might become a means of arbitrarily taking sides in domestic struggles.

During the 1980s and 1990s, the push for humanitarian interventions proceeded to seek reasons to resort to armed force besides the defence against aggression. Some cited authors in the Just War tradition who had argued that force could be justifiably used to right wrongs or punish evildoers.[50] Restricting the justifiable use of armed force to acts of defence seemed at times to have had the de facto effect of tolerating oppression and permitting atrocities. The use of force by outsiders might have made a difference in Rwanda; it had played a constructive role in places such as Bangladesh and Sierra Leone. While debates continued regarding the causes that might occasion the just use of force, other debates revolved around the question of state sovereignty.[51] Did this principle of sovereignty, articulated in the UN Charter, in practice allow governments to oppress their own people? Were there not bases for modifying or overriding this principle? Did governments in some ways compromise or diminish their sovereignty – their actual political authority – by the way they governed?

For many people the NATO-led attack against Yugoslavia on behalf of the ethnic Kosovars – who had been subjected to ethnic-cleansing raids – exemplified the character of humanitarian interventions. Outsiders were using their force, potentially risking their lives, to come to the aid of an oppressed people. They were, however, intervening with armed force in another sovereign state. To be sure, because they were waging aerial attacks, their risks were minimal. In practice, these outside forces sided with the nationalist movement in Kosovo, a movement with considerable local legitimacy. There was much debate over whether this kind of intervention was justified, especially because, in the case of Kosovo, it initially seemed to occasion greatly increased ethnic-cleansing attacks in that area.[52]

As the debates for and against humanitarian interventions raged back and forth, a group of international actors attempted radically to reframe this discussion. In September 2000, the foreign minister of Canada, Lloyd Axworthy, arranged for the Canadian government to appoint an International Commission on Intervention and State Sovereignty. It was co-chaired by Gareth Evens, President of the International Crisis Group and former foreign minister from Australia, and Mohamed Sahnoun, a diplomat from Algeria and Special Advisor to the UN Secretary General. This commission argued that the case for humanitarian intervention ought to be recast as an expression of what the commission designated as the fundamental principle of sovereignty – namely, 'The Responsibility to Protect'. This was the core responsibility of each sovereign state. This responsibility called for governments to provide security for their people, to ensure protection of their basic rights, and to work for their well-being. In so far as governments assumed this responsibility, other states were in fact prohibited from intervening without the express consent of the home government. However, if home governments failed to meet this responsibility and allowed or contributed to atrocities being committed against their own people, then the international community – acting through the Security Council or other willing countries – was warranted to intervene to assume this responsibility to protect.[53]

These outsiders might act in a number of different ways to help prevent a crisis, to help respond to actual crises, and/or to help rebuild after crises, using in the process a wide range of possible economic, political/diplomatic, legal, military, and peacekeeping initiatives. Rather than focusing narrowly on whether and how the resort to armed force might be called for, 'Responsibility to Protect' adopted a much wider, more political way of thinking about these kinds of issues. The report argued that the international community ought to be ready to act in less intrusive ways before crises became excessively aggravated. If crises did eventually become aggravated, then, according to the report, before using armed force, those prepared to act – whether the Security Council or other nations – ought to be guided by a set of criteria that correspond roughly – with some notable differences – to those of Just War. There were references to proper purpose, last resort, proportional means, balance of consequence, and the seriousness of the real or threatened harm – that is, genocide, crimes against humanity, war crimes, ethnic cleansing, or other mass atrocities. There was no reference to aggression, understood as the use by one country of armed force to attack another country.[54]

In 2004, these basic principles were restated by a special international advisory group – the Secretary General's High-Level Panel on Threats, Challenges, and Change – charged by the United Nations with proposing possible means of reforming that organization.[55] The language of 'Responsibility to Protect' was echoed in the Outcome Document of the September 2005 World Summit attended by the heads of state from a number of countries. At the same time, a number of representatives from developing countries expressed misgivings about these ideas, worrying that they represented a new way of packaging old ideas about justifiable interventions by industrial countries. Nonetheless, overall, these principles have in modest ways gained greater public hearing and more legitimacy as credible, useful, and more balanced ways of thinking about when and if the resort to armed force might be a justifiable means of addressing mass atrocities perpetrated within state borders.

In summary, what is it possible to say about the development of global ethical standards post-Second World War with respect to the resort to armed force? No clearly articulated and widely shared standards with respect to the just resort to uses of lethal force have gained authoritative public recognition, as the Geneva Conventions have. At the same time, certain considerations and principles – regarding, for example, the importance of the role played by appropriate accountable authorities and the importance of coordinating political and military strategies – have gained in prominence and legitimacy. In part in response to the atrocities in Rwanda and Bosnia, debates regarding the use of humanitarian force have failed to develop globally acknowledged, legally binding standards. Nonetheless, they have succeeded in modestly but measurably shaping the normative discourse regarding this question. To a degree this discourse makes greater use today of the rhetoric associated with the Just War tradition. For example, as they debated whether to use armed force in the Middle East, the Balkans, and Africa, proponents and opponents argued about whether the possible resort to armed force in these cases constituted a last resort, was likely to succeed, and would result in benefits that would outweigh anticipated harm and costs.[56] Moreover, in important ways, as a result of experiences shaped by peacekeeping, the struggles of new nations, and other conflicts, thinking about the nature of aggression – and correspondingly, about fitting ways of defending oneself – has been recast not in legal terms but as a set of normative considerations. What matters most, it seems, are not rules themselves but learning from experience to find ways to negotiate with others and exercise responsible political judgement.

Armed force and the call for righteous action

Many of the contemporary debates about the proper uses of armed force reflect the Just War tradition and those who have subsequently invoked its writings. For example, while discussing contemporary events in Iraq, Palestine, and Serbia, even a secular newspaper like *The Economist* makes reference to this tradition of discourse.[57] So do legal scholars like David Kennedy. The military handbook introduced by the United States in 2006 called for troops to be nation-builders as well as warriors.[58] Just War rhetoric is found in the language of UN reports and the International Commission on Intervention and State Sovereignty. While much of the current rhetoric used to criticize and defend uses of armed force reflects this Christian tradition of moral discourse, a number of scholars have also explored ways in which other moral traditions, such as Judaism, Hinduism, and Confucianism, articulate parallel ideas, often in similar terms. One can find in these faiths, for example, support for principles such as noncombatant immunity, the priority for seeking to resolve conflicts by negotiations before resorting to armed force, and the importance of using means proportionate to desired ends.[59] Similarly, there are a number of authoritative writings in Islam that pointedly decry acts that cause excessive, militarily unnecessary harm, result in injury to children, or directly target civilians. In a parallel fashion, Muslim writings make reference to the importance of responsible authorities, just causes, right intentions, and last resort.[60]

If we review this evidence as a whole, it seems possible to perceive common features or emerging elements of global ethical consensus among established governments and religions with respect both to *jus in bello* and *jus ad bellum*. To be sure, this consensus is not shared by all of the various kinds of pacifists, on the one hand, or the diverse groups of insurgents, suicide bombers, and state organized terrorists, on the other hand. Moreover, individual countries continue to find excuses from time to time for actions that deviate from this consensus. Still, what is common among those who support it is a shared wish to find and champion ways of exercising armed force with fitting restraint.[61] Given the possibility that others will resort to lethal force either to engage in aggression or to commit atrocities, the use or threat of armed force may then become imperative in defence against these acts. These uses ought effectively to realize these objectives but to avoid in so far as possible unnecessary injury. This line of reasoning is now widely expressed in many places, including public debates, the proposed 'Draft Code of Offenses against the Peace and Security of Mankind', religious discussion about the peace process, as well as reflections by ex-generals like Rupert Smith.[62]

Nevertheless, it is important to call attention to the fact that there is another tradition or rather another set of traditions of ethical discourse about the uses of armed force that is older, yet still frequently invoked. Using the rhetoric of honour, self-sacrifice, and glory central to these traditions, political and military leaders rally people to take up arms and to face and rise above extreme risks. This rhetoric works to motivate people to do what they would ordinarily not be inclined to do: both willingly to put up with severe deprivations and to launch armed attacks on others whom they do not know. Often the rhetoric of these traditions depicts present or imminent crises in terms of polar opposites: defending civilization against barbarians, supporting the region of peace against the regions of war, advancing democracy against the axis of evil, promoting liberty against totalitarianism, and/or fostering people's liberation against demonic and sadistic colonial or postcolonial oppressors. Taking up arms is often described as a particularly virtuous act, an expression of piety, and/or a means of gaining transcendent personal objectives. Correspondingly, armed force is used, in these traditions of discourse, not just pragmatically to defend against aggression, to curtail atrocities, or to restore order; rather, it is used to destroy evil forces and to remove completely the possibility of future threats. These traditions of discourse, which often use religious imagery and highly ideological rhetoric, arise from widely different sources but share certain common themes. To contrast these patterns of thinking with the Just War traditions, we refer to these as the 'righteous war' traditions of ethical discourse.[63]

These traditions have been characterized by their sense of urgency and their zeal. Often the enemies they focus on are not just the leaders of the forces they oppose but also the peoples and cultures associated with their opponents. Enemy people are often regarded as in some way culpable or guilty if for no other reason than that they continue to allow themselves to be governed by questionable leaders. Such thinking has been used to justify both aerial bombings and crippling economic sanctions against civilian populations. Offensives are not merely viewed as a means of protecting people and their communities: frequently they are viewed as well as a means of overcoming passivity and the sense of humiliation. Characteristically, the 'righteous war' discourse seems to tolerate if not openly advocate what might seem like excessive use of armed force. However, in many situations it functions as the natural way of rallying people to engage and support the use of armed force.

We can illustrate the character of 'righteous war' by reviewing several well-known expressions. For example, in the call to arms the conflict is often depicted as a crusade or holy war. For such campaigns, people are called to make huge sacrifices in order to fight a dangerous evil, while extra virtue is typically attached to those who respond to this call. Those promoting the use of armed forces as a crusade or holy war indicate their beliefs that these campaigns transcend ordinary pragmatic calculations about benefits and costs, good and bad. Participants in these struggles are often regarded as particularly praiseworthy. Although the traditions of moral reasoning in Islam with regard to armed force in many ways parallel the Just War doctrine that has been influential in Europe, some of this 'righteous war' reasoning has been used to rally Muslims against foreign occupying forces, such as the Mongolians who invaded the Middle East in the thirteenth century. More recently, militants like Osama bin Laden justified attacks on enemy civilians both to defend the lands of faith against foreign occupying forces and as justifiable reprisals for harm suffered by Muslim civilians.[64]

Often using apocalyptic religious imagery, the language of 'righteous war' has been voiced by a number of otherwise quite different groups prepared to use acts of violence against largely unarmed persons, attacking everything from secular nationalists, to abortion clinics, to religious opponents.[65] The recently proclaimed war on terror, launched in response to these kinds of acts, was often framed by its advocates as a righteous campaign in which 'liberty and justice' were, in the words of a US policy statement, to be defended by the 'unprecedented – and unequaled – strength and influence' of the United States to fight 'a war against terrorists of global reach'. Recognizing 'that our best defense is a good offense', America would not let its 'enemies strike first'; rather, it would prevent further harm from occurring 'by identifying and destroying the threat before it reached' American borders.[66] A generation earlier, invoking the rhetoric of 'righteousness', Frantz Fanon described how acts of violence and 'violence alone' would both serve as a 'cleansing force', freeing 'native[s] from [their] inferiority complex', and allow the masses of people living in a colonized area to gain their freedom and understand basic social truths.[67]

In no way do these various expressions of 'righteous war' constitute anything like a shared global ethic with respect to armed conflict. To be sure, they function like an ethic, bestowing normative approval and disapproval on various acts, but they do so using the particularistic language of their own groups. The rhetoric of 'righteous war' cannot easily be used to deliberate about tactics and timing, about military and political strategies. Rather, it functions to inspire and motivate. In many ways, proponents of the emerging global ethic on just exercise of armed force have purposely worked at developing an alternative, more restrained perspective on armed force and to do so in terms that people can use and refer to despite their religious, political, and cultural differences. However, because of the overlapping uses of similar terms – expressions such as 'Just War', 'worthy causes', 'right intentions', and 'military necessity' – and because moral discourse is used both to deliberate (and therefore to evaluate, plan, and justify) and to motivate (and, therefore, to inspire, praise, and blame), 'righteous war' themes occasionally influence the debate about the responsible resort to and uses of armed force.

Current status of global ethics in practice with respect to the use of lethal force

During the past several generations, more governments and more people have used the set of common terms that we have reviewed in this chapter to discuss, criticize, direct, and defend the uses of armed force. We can point to both direct and indirect evidence that this loosely organized, albeit coherent set of normative ideas has gained a measure of global public authority. Both in the Balkans and in Rwanda, for example, these principles have been used to establish international military tribunals where leaders accused of war crimes and crimes against humanity are tried. The ICC has heard dozens of cases of people accused of violating these standards. Furthermore, a number of countries, such as South Africa, Chile, and Argentina, that suffered from extended periods of intra-state armed conflict, including state-sponsored cruelty, have subsequently established tribunals to enact what has been called transitional justice. These tribunals have extended amnesty both to members of the established governments and to rebel forces if otherwise illegal violent acts were committed as part of an armed struggle – that is, they were regarded not as criminal acts but as acts of war if in loose compliance with the emerging rules of just warfare. To cite another kind of evidence, in the years since the Second World War there has been a decline in the resort to inter-state war, and mortality levels in these wars has declined. Although these were widely supported in the Second World War, there has also been a decline in the use and defence of area bombings. Additionally, the ideas and standards of this global ethic are frequently cited by politicians, international civil society groups, and international commissions.[68] There are, thus, diverse kinds of evidence that this global ethic regarding armed conflict has gained a modest measure of acceptance and influence.

The contemporary challenge facing proponents is that, over the past couple of generations, the theatre for these conflicts has characteristically shifted from between states to within states, from being on battlefields separated from civilians to sites of struggle in the midst of unarmed people. Many observers have correspondingly wondered whether the ethical traditions associated with International Humanitarian Law and Just War discourse still have relevance. Were not the guidelines outmoded that called for noncombatant immunity, that sought to ban certain weapons, and that justified resort to armed force primarily in response to aggression? In any case, were not these normative ideas misguided and/or excessively idealistic?[69] These questions and critiques, raised with renewed intensity as the twenty-first century began, have been voiced regularly from the time of the initial efforts to craft rules of warfare in the mid-nineteenth century.

Two issues have especially attracted attention. The first issue concerns the use of non-lethal chemical weapons, especially in settings where insurgents place themselves and their weapons within civilian areas. While these kinds of weapons are prohibited in military conflicts, some, like tear gas and tasers, have been used by police forces to control crowds and disarm lawbreakers. Even if some civilians might also suffer temporarily in the process, using these kinds of weapons to incapacitate belligerents might inflict much less harm than trying to attack armed opponents using conventional and thereby more lethal weapons. However, the Chemical War Convention prohibits their use. We are thus confronted with a conundrum. It may well be possible over time to amend this convention. In the short run, introducing changes seems likely to put at risk the international agreement that required many years to enact. Accordingly, this issue does not really call into question the relevance of the existing standards in changing circumstances as much as it calls attention to obstacles associated with gaining widespread acceptance of high-level policy changes.[70]

A second issue revolves around the tactic of targeted killings of leaders of opposing forces. In general, the war conventions have forbidden assassinations of enemy soldiers and authorities for a number of reasons. Assassinations have been censored when they are used to target those bearing weapons because of the ways they make particular enemy soldiers especially vulnerable. Such attacks have been prohibited more generally when targeting non-military personnel because they remove the opportunity to engage in political negotiations with recognized authorities in order to bring armed conflicts to an end. Lethal force in principle ought to be used to incapacitate those using it directly or those supplying the latter with weapons. Targeting political authorities violates these basic norms. However, targeted killing of these kinds of authorities seems like an attractive way of undermining the efforts of opponents by decapitating their leadership. During the past several decades a number of parties have increased their resort to the use of targeted killings, especially as a means of fighting against insurgent groups that use terrorist attacks. The debates about targeted killings have become more intense over time as some states, like the United States, have successfully been using armed unmanned electronically guided flying machines – drones – to kill leaders of militant Muslim terrorist organizations. These attacks have also killed many civilians who were not targeted. While these attacks seem to violate a US law against the assassination of enemy leaders, they have been excused because they have successfully killed many of these leaders and have been redefined not as assassinations but as military strikes against present foes.[71]

The increased resort to targeted killings does seem to take place in violation of the normative standards associated with Humanitarian Law and the Just War tradition. Those who defend the use of this tactic have argued that the utilization of targeted killing has been successful and has resulted in less overall harm to all parties concerned than possible alternatives. Critics in turn have raised a number of concerns. Thus, when these attacks take place within countries such as Yemen or Pakistan not at war with those launching these attacks, the attacks themselves violate the sovereignty of these countries. By killing off leaders of enemy groups, the attacks greatly reduce, if they do not altogether void, the political possibilities of reaching negotiated settlements. In practice, these kinds of targeted killings – especially using drones – not only aggravate widespread opposition to the utilization of this tactic but have in some places occasioned sympathy for the attacked groups. Thus, a kind of military success, on the one hand, has aggravated social and political discontent, on the other hand. Finally, the increased use of targeted killings sets a bad example.

The normative debate about the utilization of targeted killings remains unresolved. These killings are not acts of terror, which deliberately aim to strike at noncombatants in order to foster fear. Targeted killings directly seek to incapacitate groups using lethal force. They might be described, like the bombings in Serbia during the war over Kosovo, as justified illegal acts. In any case, no compelling global consensus has yet emerged with respect to these acts.[72]

Beginning in the nineteenth century and continuing especially in the years since the Second World War, those who worked to craft and foster global ethics with respect to the exercise of lethal force have recognized that humans will continue to take up arms for varied reasons. Proponents of this ethic have taken it for granted that diverse states, parties, and groups will resort to lethal force in settings where they find themselves oppressed by alien and tyrannical regimes, when they become inspired by what they regard as righteous visions, and when they can and choose to assert their power for their own ends. Alarmed by abusive force unleashed during the Second World War, worried by how lethal modern weapons can be, and influenced by traditions of humanism and civility, proponents of this ethic have sought to develop normative frames of reference in the hope that those using armed force will exercise fitting restraint.[73]

Clearly, many of those in the contemporary world who choose to take up arms know nothing of this ethic or choose to ignore it if they do. Nonetheless, over the past several generations the set of standards associated with International Humanitarian Law and the Just War tradition have been invoked more frequently as they have gained in respect and authority. They have been referred to by courts, commissions, politicians, governments, and civil society groups considering issues such as the ongoing conflicts between Israel and Palestine, recent struggles in Sri Lanka, appropriate responses to the civil war in Syria, and successful and legitimate ways to address those who resort to acts of terror.

Many wonder about the relevance of this normative tradition in a world where armed conflicts have become asymmetrical and so many take place intra-state. However, we can observe that, over time, almost all insurgent groups using acts of terror have either failed, as a result of a combination of factors including internal conflicts, political opposition, fitting military defences, and negotiations, or transformed into civil political groups. Defeating these groups has not typically required using means that violate the ethic of Just War.[74] In any case, acts of terror have not only been employed by insurgents, armed tribes, and local mercenaries as expressions of irregular warfare.[75] In the case of atrocities in Vietnam, Bangladesh, Rwanda, and Iraq in addition to area bombings of cities during the Second World War, acts of terror have been committed by established states.[76] However, while they were once defended or at least tolerated, these kinds of acts are no longer viewed as justifiable.

It is inappropriate to regard the emerging global ethic with respect to the use of armed force as an expression of simple idealism. Rather, as they have gained greater recognition and practical authority, its standards have informed public debate and thinking about military strategy in both international and national contexts. More consideration is now given to the rights of noncombatants and to the disutility and illegitimacy of using weapons that inflict diffuse harm – such as chemical and nuclear weapons. Politicians and military strategists are more likely to reflect on whether particular uses of armed force correspond with standards of proportionality. Diverse parties are more likely to question whether and in what ways military operations appropriately advance or undermine political purposes. Furthermore, as part of ongoing conversations, various governments, international commissions, and civil society groups have been actively exploring the fitting role third parties can and should play in conflicts internal to particular countries. Considered as a whole, the emerging global ethic regarding the uses of lethal force finds itself expressed as much in ongoing public reflections, deliberations, and negotiations as in particular documents associated with International Humanitarian Law and Just War doctrine.

Notes

1. See Johnson, *Just War Tradition and the Restraint of War*; Johnson, *Can Modern War Be Just?* On the role of the International Committee of the Red Cross, see Ignatieff, *The Warrior's Honour*, pp. 109–63.
2. 'General Orders No. 100' was drafted in 1862 by Francis Lieber, a law professor and a recent immigrant from Germany. See Hartigan, *Lieber's Code and the Law of War*. For an alternative view of the purpose and role of the Lieber Code, see Nelson, 'An American War of Incarceration'.
3. See Best, *Humanity in Warfare*; Best, *War and Law since 1945*.

4. Various estimates have been made of the numbers killed. Smith estimates that of the 15 million killed in the First World War, 6.5 million were civilian and of the 56 million killed in the Second World War, 39 million were civilians. Smith, *The Utility of Force*, pp. 125, 141.

5. See Kennedy, *The Parliament of Man*; Thakur, *The United Nations, Peace, and Security*.

6. See 'Charter of the International Military Tribunal at Nuremberg', in Ratner and Abrams, *Accountability for Human Rights Atroicites in International Law*, pp. 306–8.

7. See Taylor, *Nuremberg and Vietnam*.

8. The titles for these four conventions are as follows: (1) 1949 Geneva Conventions for the Amelioration of the Condition of the Wounded and Sick in Armed Forces in the Field; (2) 1949 Geneva Convention for the Amelioration of the Condition of the Wounded, Sick, and Shipwrecked Members of the Armed Forces at Sea; (3) 1949 Geneva Conventions Relative to the Treatment of Prisoners of War; and (4) 1949 Geneva Conventions Relative to the Protection of Civilian Persons in Times of War. See Roberts and Guelff (eds), *Documents on the Law of War*, pp. 157–337.

9. 1977 Geneva Protocol I Additional to the Geneva Conventions of 12 August 1949, and Relating to the Victims of International Armed Conflicts. See Roberts and Guelff (eds), *Documents on the Law of War*, pp. 387–446, nos 35, 51, 53, 55.

10. 1977 Geneva Protocol II Additional to the Geneva Conventions of 12 August 1949, and Relating to the Protection of Victims of Non-International Armed Conflicts. See Roberts and Guelff (eds), *Documents on the Law of War*, pp. 447–63.

11. See Ramsey, *War and the Christian Conscience*; Ramsey, *The Just War*; Walzer, *Just and Unjust Wars*; Walzer, *Arguing about War*, ch. 1; Johnson, *Just War Tradition and the Restraint of War*; Johnson, *Can Modern War Be Just?*

12. United Nations High-Level Panel Report on Threats, Challenges, and Change, *A More Secure World*.

13. See Taylor, *Nuremberg and Vietnam*, ch. 1.

14. See Kennedy, *The Dark Sides of Virtue*, ch. 8.

15. See Smith, *The Utility of Force*, pp. 120–41.

16. Ford, 'The Morality of Obliteration Bombing'.

17. See Parker, *John Kenneth Galbraith*, ch. 9.

18. See Walzer, *Just and Unjust Wars*, chs 9, 16; Walzer, *Arguing about War*, ch. 3.

19. Indirectly recognizing the normative claims regarding noncombatant immunity, some Americans justified the extensive bombing of Hanoi in December 1972 as strategic.

20. See essays by Walzer, Elshtain, and Miller in Buckley (ed.), *Kosovo*, pp. 333–5, 363–5, 384–98.

21. See Goldstone and Fritz, 'Fair Assessment'.

22. See Walzer, *Just and Unjust Wars*, ch. 10.

23. See Smith, *The Utility of Force*, chs 7–9.

24. See Walzer, *Just and Unjust Wars*, ch. 11; Walzer, *Arguing about War*, ch. 10; O'Donovan, *The Just War Revisited*, ch. 2. The ambiguous character of many refugee camps well illustrates this ongoing conundrum. See Terry, *Condemned to Repeat?*

25. See Walzer, *Arguing about War*, ch. 10; Carr, *The Lessons of Terror*; Stern, *Terror in the Name of God*; Juergensmeyer, *Terror in the Mind of God*.

26. See Elshtain, *Just War against Terror*; Ignatieff, *The Lesser Evil*; Dershowitz, *Why Terrorism Works*.

27. We are directly arguing against the position taken by Alan Dershowitz, *Why Terrorism Works*, in which he appears to argue that the PLO gained power and public recognition by acts of terror, just as the Israelis had done by terrorist acts in the 1940s. In contrast, we argue that the PLO gained authority and public regard because, as an organized political movement, it represented the political will of a sizeable population who had long lived in the area of Palestine without effective political representation. This organization gained international regard in spite of its acts of terror. The acts of terror – and the courage, self-sacrifice, and willingness to defy the authorities represented by these acts – may well have helped it gain charisma among its own people. For a fuller statement of this argument, see Cronin, *How Terrorism Ends*.

28. 1925 Geneva Protocol for the Prohibition of the Use in War of Asphyxiating, Poisonous or Other Gases and of Bacteriological Methods of Warfare; see Roberts and Guelff (eds), *Documents on the Law of War*, pp. 137–45.

29. See Ramsey, 'A Political Ethics Context for Strategic Thinking'; Lieber and Press, 'The Nukes We Need'.

30. See the extensive discussion in Murnion (ed.), *Catholics and Nuclear War*.

31. For a historical review of the efforts to control the use and proliferation of nuclear weapons, see Thakur, *The United Nations, Peace, and Security*, ch. 7.

32. See Schlosser, *Command and Control*.

33. See Franck, 'Proportionality in International Law'; Nolte, 'Thin or Thick?'

34. See Kennedy, *The Dark Sides of Virtue*, ch. 8; Kennedy, *Of War and Law*, p. 89.

35. Walzer, *Just and Unjust Wars*, ch. 17. More recently, it has been

argued that governments representing the international community could be justified in launching military attacks to disable sites used to store or manufacture chemical weapons (in Syria, for example), so long as it were possible to launch these attacks in ways that neither caused excessive harm nor aggravated the ongoing civil war in that country. In practice, however, it is often difficult to meet these kinds of conditions.

36. See Walzer, *Arguing about War*, ch. 1; Kennedy, *Of War and Law*.
37. See Marchak, *No Easy Fix*.
38. See Taylor, *Nuremberg and Vietnam*, ch. 5.
39. 1977 Geneva Protocol II; see Roberts and Guelff (eds), *Documents on the Law of War*, pp. 447–63.
40. Walzer, *Just and Unjust Wars*, p. 85.
41. Collier, *Wars, Guns, and Votes*. After first calculating the typical economic costs to countries of civil wars – from actual damage to lost opportunities for production and wages – and then calculating the costs for typical peacekeeping operations, Collier estimates the economic benefits from peacekeeping operations exceed the costs of war by about four times (pp. 87–100).
42. Human Security Centre and Human Security Report Project, *Human Security Report 2005*; Human Security Centre and Human Security Report Project, *Human Security Report 2009/2010*; Carpenter, 'Fighting the Laws of War'.
43. See Thakur, *The United Nations, Peace, and Security*, ch. 1; Kennedy, *The Parliament of Man*, ch. 3.
44. See O'Donovan's discussion of authority in *The Just War Revisited*, pp. 18–32.
45. See Langan, 'Justice after War and the International Common Good'; Prins, 'Conditions for *Jus in Pace* in the Face of the Future'; Kaldor, 'From Just War to Just Peace'.
46. See Smith, *The Utility of Force*, chs 7, 8, 9, and Conclusion.
47. See Rose, *How Wars End*.
48. In many cases successful efforts to suppress insurgent groups using terrorist tactics have involved not only actions designed to capture or target leaders and to attack them directly but also actions to negotiate with them. See Cronin, *How Terrorism Ends*; Powell, *Talking to Terrorists*.
49. See Fisher 'Humanitarian Interventions'; Schulte 'Rogue Regimes, WMD, and Hyper-Terrorism'; Walzer, *Arguing about War*, ch. 5; see also essays by Skidelsky and Ignatieff, Brzezinsky, and Little, in Buckley (ed.), *Kosovo*, pp. 317–22, 336–43, 356–9.
50. See Johnson, 'Just War Thinking in Recent American Religious Debate over Military Force'; O'Donovan, *The Just War Revisited*.
51. For a well-researched survey of the philosophical, political, and legal

debates regarding humanitarian intervention, see Preda, 'Moral Justification for Unilateral Humanitarian Intervention in Order to Stop or Prevent Human Right Violations'.
52. See various essays collected in Buckley (ed.), *Kosovo*.
53. International Commission on Intervention and State Sovereignty, *The Responsibility to Protect*. See Evans, *The Responsibility to Protect*.
54. If aggression were defined more broadly as the use of armed force or violence (or the threatened use of armed force or violence) in ways that violate the humanity (and human rights) of those under attack, then all the acts associated with mass atrocities would constitute either direct assaults (acts of aggression) or instances of what was at one time referred to as 'institutional violence'. Accordingly, from the perspective of the Just War tradition, those who sought to defend themselves against these attacks would be justified either in resorting to armed force and/or seeking help from others who could help them defend themselves, so long as their acts were guided by the other Just War considerations.
55. United Nations High-Level Panel on Threats, Challenges, and Change, *A More Secure World*.
56. In different terms this point is made both by Kennedy in *The Dark Sides of Virtue* and *Of War and Law*, and by Walzer, in *Arguing about War*.
57. *The Economist*, 'Mind those Proportions'; *The Economist*, 'Gaza: The Rights and Wrongs'.
58. This handbook, FM 3-24, is discussed by Parker in 'Knowing the Enemy'.
59. See essays on Judaism, Hinduism, and Confucianism in Brekke (ed.), *The Ethics of War in Asian Civilizations*.
60. See Kelsay, *Arguing the Just War in Islam*.
61. This point is well argued by Johnson in *Just War Tradition and the Restraint of War* and *Can Modern War Be Just?*
62. See International Law Commission, *Draft Code of Offenses against the Peace and Security of Mankind*. The ILC has been working on this code since it was initially mandated by the UN General Assembly in 1947. By the mid-1990s the ILC had prepared not only a draft code but also a draft statute for an International Criminal Court to hear cases of actions that breach this code; Smith, *The Utility of Force*.
63. We have deliberately not used terms such as crusade, holy war, or jihad, because these words are associated with particular expressions of the more general phenomenon, for which we have coined the term 'righteous war' discourse.
64. See Kelsay, *Arguing the Just War in Islam*, chs 4, 5, 6.

65. See Stern, *Terror in the Name of God*; Juergensmeyer, *The New Cold War?*; Juergensmeyer, *Terror in the Mind of God*.

66. The words in quotation marks are taken from a document entitled 'The National Security Strategy of the United States of America', reprinted in Avram (ed.), *Anxious about Empire*, pp. 187–213.

67. Fanon, *The Wretched of the Earth*, pp. 73, 117.

68. See, e.g., the Human Rights Watch's report on the 2006 war between Hezbollah and Israel, *Why They Died: Casualties in Lebanon during the 2006 War*, available at <http://www.hrw.org/node/10734/section/5> (last accessed 29 January 2015.

69. Critiques like these have been expressed by O'Donovan in *The Just War Revisited* (ch. 3, 'Immoral Weapons'); see also Cornish, 'The Ethics of "Effects-Based" Warfare'; Fisher, 'Humanitarian Interventions'.

70. For a useful discussion of these issues from a slightly different perspective, see Gross, *Moral Dilemmas of Modern War*, chs 1, 4.

71. Ibid. chs 1, 5, 10; Cronin, *How Terrorism Ends*, ch. 1; Byman, 'Why Drones Work'; Cronin, 'Why Drones Fail'; Coll, 'Remote Control'.

72. See Goldstone and Fritz, 'Fair Assessment'; see also Albert Camus's discussion of the moral complexities of targeted killings in *The Rebel*; Juergensmeyer, *Terror in the Mind of God*.

73. Pinker, *The Better Angels of our Nature*.

74. Cronin, *How Terrorism Ends*.

75. Boot, 'The Evolution of Irregular War'.

76. Mishra, 'Unholy Alliances'.

7 The Practices of Global Ethics with Respect to Poverty

Introduction

In this chapter we provide a historical account of the changing ways humans have considered and responded to poverty from pre-industrial times up to the beginning of the twenty-first century. We note shifts in attitudes and actions, in particular the emergence during the second half of the twentieth century of a widely shared view of poverty as a global concern and a condition that can and should be overcome. While no clear, universally accepted normative standards exist on either the nature of poverty or how to address it, we can nonetheless observe a widely shared general consensus that poverty is a major global problem and that both public and private agencies in all countries ought to work to reduce it.

For the purpose of this chapter we define poverty as the condition of households whose access to and control over economic resources over time are so limited that they cannot provide for themselves adequate and decent living arrangements (food, shelter, clothing, healthcare, education, insurance, and the like). People living in these households correspondingly experience markedly higher levels of malnutrition, illness, and deprivation than members of non-poor households. Considered as a group, they live much shorter lives. Compared to others, they face higher risks and more uncertainties and are able to exercise less power over the conditions of their own lives.[1]

Clearly, what is required to live adequate but decent lives varies in significant ways based on the activity by which people meet their basic needs – by hunting and gathering, by raising crops and animals, by undertaking odd jobs, or by some form of employment, entrepreneurial activity, or investment – and also on the kinds of risks associated with these diverse economic activities. Employees, for example, can often access and control greater economic resources than simple peasants, as their wages and salaries increase, but they also may face greater risks associated with termination of their employment owing to accidents, economic depressions, or old age. For a large proportion of humans in the contemporary world, especially those residing in economically developing areas, the poverty threshold for households is $2.25 per person per day or the non-monetary equivalent. In industrialized societies the approximate poverty-demarcating income level is higher. If we use this standard as a rough guide, approximately one in three humans was living in an impoverished household at the beginning of the twenty-first century. While impoverished households were found in all societies, as the century began there were especially large numbers of poor people in the least developed countries, in rural areas of a number of developing countries, and in the slums of large cities in both industrialized and developing countries.[2]

Responses to poverty in pre-industrial and industrial times

For centuries, a life of poverty or near-poverty was the common fate of most humans. Compared to the world today, rates of illness, hunger, and illiteracy were much higher. On average, people lived much shorter lives. To be sure, many households managed to live decent lives in spite of their poverty. Moreover, most societies found ways of helping many of those in greatest need, through hospitality, aid, and charity. In this Malthusian world, poverty was widely experienced and typically regarded not as a dishonourable but rather as a shared fate. Because only the poorest of these households were typically viewed as those who might benefit directly from charity, many households we would today regard as impoverished did not regard themselves as poor.[3] To be sure, the actual circumstances of impoverished households varied enormously from those eking a living in difficult situations to those facing extreme conditions owing to natural disasters or political unrest. During these centuries, poverty was generally regarded as a morally neutral local matter. Governing regimes, such as imperial rulers in China, India, and Ancient Rome, sometimes stored food supplies to provide for the poor in times of famine. On a smaller scale, extended families, villages, and tribal groups often found ways to offer help to orphans, widows, handicapped people, and others who were especially vulnerable.

As overall population increased and societies were transformed by the commercial revolution and then the Industrial Revolution (1750 and later), public attitudes towards poverty began to change dramatically. In areas with expanding economic opportunities owing to increased commerce and industry, many people began to view poverty as a moral problem that could and should be overcome. Although these changes occurred in different ways in different cultures and locales, the development of the English Poor Laws illustrates some of the common characteristics of this perspective. Beginning in the fifteenth century and increasing thereafter, as urban centres grew and local markets expanded, cities attracted large numbers of people seeking shelter and work. Local parishes, which had previously organized local charities, found themselves overwhelmed. There seemed to be more poor people than they could adequately help. Moreover, many of these homeless men seemed dangerous. To a large degree, the new urban poor were simply rural poor who had migrated to the cities in response to rural poverty, a process that would continue to be repeated worldwide in the centuries to follow. In order to deal with the emerging situation, the British enacted vagrancy laws, developed workhouses, raised local taxes for relief payments, and found ways of distinguishing between what they referred to as the deserving and undeserving poor. The needy poor were offered charitable assistance. Attempts were made to force the able-bodied poor to work.[4]

During these periods, views of poverty were very mixed. Some responded with increased hospitality and charity. Others saw poverty as an indictment of the rich and as the consequence of industrialization aggravating the misery of the poor. Many were inclined to blame the poor for their patterns of consumption, for their failures to save and work harder, and for the size of their families. In many areas local institutions were established to aid poor children and to provide meals and shelter for those in dire need.

As societies industrialized, the extent and character of poverty changed markedly. Most significantly, industrialization resulted in much more productive economies, with increases in jobs, wages, and standards of living. To be sure, the processes of industrialization were initially very disruptive. Large numbers of households moved from rural to urban areas. Increasingly people worked in different locales from where they lived. Wages for new industrial jobs were often low and not secure. Working conditions were frequently deplorable. Nevertheless, over time the proportion of the households in these societies living at subsistence or less steadily declined. Over the period of several generations, industrialization expanded economic opportunities, raised income levels, and offered chances for better jobs and promotions, thereby enhancing living conditions for many households. While it aggravated the circumstances of some and exposed others to new forms of economic insecurity associated with industrial accidents, unemployment, and retirement from wage employment, industrialization over time has greatly reduced the extent of poverty.

In response to increased industrialization and to periodic economic crises during the late nineteenth century through the period of the depression of the 1930s, most industrializing countries developed national social welfare policies that have had a direct bearing on poverty. These included not only social insurance programmes, government funded public assistance, and publicly subsidized investments in particular kinds of businesses, but also increased spending on public education. Beginning in Germany in the 1880s, industrialized nations enacted legislation to establish programmes to provide workmen's compensation, old age pensions, and unemployment benefits. To a degree, industrialized countries also provided public assistance for certain categories of impoverished households, including mothers with dependent children, disabled individuals, and the indigent. Gradually, over time, many of these industrializing countries established minimum wage laws, thereby ensuring to some extent that workers might keep their households out of poverty. Significantly, governments in many of these countries began to establish and fund public schools at both the primary and secondary levels. In many regions, levels of primary education became compulsory. During and subsequent to the depression of the 1930s, in a number of industrialized countries, governments began to offer subsidies for targeted businesses, directly or in the form of tax breaks, so that these firms could hire additional workers. In the United States, tax reductions were offered for mortgage payments, and various public works were initiated to stimulate jobs in the construction industries.

By the second half of the twentieth century, social welfare programmes had greatly expanded in most industrialized countries. It is worth observing that, while many impoverished households benefited from this wide range of public programmes – social insurance, public education, subsidized work opportunities, minimum wage standards – most of the beneficiaries were middle- and upper-class households. They qualified for larger pensions and benefited in greater numbers and often over longer periods of time from subsidized public education. In many countries, they also drew greater benefits from public health insurance programmes. Nonetheless, in several ways these public social welfare programmes have created a social minimum. They have been able to reduce and manage the risks associated with the industrial labour markets and to provide social infrastructures to make these markets work better. As economic crises and depressions have increased the numbers of households suffering from poverty, governments have worked to manage and limit the damage and, correspondingly, they have reduced or limited the extent of poverty. In this way, government policies to regulate banks and manage financial markets have indirectly functioned to reduce poverty in industrialized and industrializing countries.

The growth in public spending on social welfare, broadly understood, was made possible both by increased wealth produced by industrialization and through efforts to gain legitimacy for public expenditures, as tax reforms created policies designed to tax households and firms in some measure related to their ability to pay.

As many North Atlantic countries industrialized during the eighteenth and nineteenth centuries and the first part of the twentieth century, a number of them expanded imperially, establishing colonies in, developing trade with, and extracting resources from large areas in Asia, Africa, Latin America, and islands in the Pacific Ocean. By these means they were able to establish a measure of both economic hegemony and political control in many of these developing areas. To be sure, these imperial expansions had begun as early as the sixteenth century, as a number of countries – particularly Portugal, Spain, England, France, and the Netherlands – developed commercial ties, trading posts, and colonies, and overtly conquered lands in these areas. As the North Atlantic countries industrialized, economic links with these developing areas intensified and political controls became more manifest.

While some local populations benefited by these imperial involvements through increased educational and employment opportunities, access to modern medicine, and expanding commerce, for many others the problems of poverty became more severe. Large proportions of the indigenous populations in the Americas suffered and died from diseases that the European agents and settlers unknowingly brought with them. During the last quarter of the nineteenth century in India, the British colonial regime forced local farmers to grow cotton for export to British textile firms rather than rice for local consumption. This directly worsened food crises in India, which were already aggravated by drought, and resulted in the death of millions.[5]

In his study of the origins, causes, and consequences of industrialization, Gregory Clark calls attention to the 'great divergence' thereby occasioned, as industrialized countries enjoyed much higher standards of living while economic conditions in many non-industrialized countries worsened.[6] Clark explains this divergence in part by describing how non-industrialized countries typically made much less efficient uses of modern technologies such as railways and manufacturing systems. He argues that they lacked the spirit of innovation that has been so important in the industrializing countries. However, others argue that the great divergence was occasioned in greater part by the ways colonial practices exploited non-industrialized economies. Acemoglu and Robinson, for example, call attention to the ways Europeans in pursuit of wealth and power uprooted and/or enslaved millions of people in Southeast Asia, Africa, and the Americas.[7]

We can briefly summarize our analysis thus far in the following terms. By the middle of the twentieth century, views and responses to poverty had markedly changed in the industrializing countries. No longer was poverty viewed as an inevitable and pervasive condition affecting large proportions of the population, to be responded to locally with hospitality, charity, and forbearance. In time poverty began to be viewed as a public problem, to which national and provincial governments ought to respond. Correspondingly, social welfare policies emerged, including several different kinds of public social insurance programmes, family allowances, public assistance, publicly funded primary and secondary education systems, and minimum wage laws.

It was not until the latter half of the twentieth century that poverty began to be viewed both as a global issue and as one calling for coordinated global responses. During this time period, several trends markedly affected both the conditions and perceptions of poverty worldwide. The growth in industrialization and commerce during these years helped a number of national and local economies to expand and correspondingly reduce poverty rates in affected areas. These changes were especially noteworthy initially in countries such as the Republic of Korea, Taiwan, Singapore, Malaysia, and Thailand, and later in countries such as Brazil, Chile, and Turkey. The impact of industrialization and expanding commerce was particularly impressive in China and India. During these years the numbers of impoverished individuals in these countries declined by over 350 million. One dimension of the larger processes of growth of industry and commerce, and the corresponding use in both cases of modern scientific discoveries, was the expanding uses of irrigation, fertilizer, and new seed varieties to increase agricultural productivity. This increased productivity – especially associated with the so-called Green Revolution in places such as India and Mexico – significantly added to the wealth of these areas.

As countries further industrialized, thereby expanding the total sum of domestic wealth, the volume of wealth that could be taxed for public revenues also increased. Governments were able to use these additional revenues to develop or augment social and physical infrastructures – social insurance programmes, public schools, roads and transportation facilities, strengthened police forces, and the like – thereby growing and stabilizing industrial labour markets. Overall, processes of economic growth both directly expanded economic opportunities for many otherwise impoverished households and also helped to fund public welfare policies and programmes, reducing effects of poverty in these areas.

However, the benefits of industrialization and expanded commerce have in part been offset by two other trends: namely, a sharp increase in global population and a marked growth in economic inequality, especially in the years since 1980.

Between 1950 and 2011, global population increased from about 4 billion to 7 billion. In most of the industrialized countries, increased economic productivity more than matched the growth in population, which in these areas remained stationary or increased moderately, owing in part to immigration. However, the total global population increased most in the least economically developed areas of the world. As a result, in many settings, even modest economic expansion was not able to keep pace with population growth. In spite of modest economic developments, in many areas per capita income did not improve.

Global patterns of economic development remained uneven during the post-war years. Although the extent of inequality within many industrialized countries declined between 1930 and the mid-1970s, by 1980 this trend had reversed. Rising standards of living in many areas were accompanied by increasing economic inequalities. The gap in per capita income between the wealthiest and poorest households increased in many countries, while the gap in per capita income between the inhabitants of the richest and poorest countries also increased. In many developing countries, inequality was directly embodied in the contrasting circumstances of enclaves and households growing wealthy while the masses remained economically insecure. Thus, during the second half of the twentieth century, while global rates of poverty declined in many areas owing to economic growth and more generous public social welfare policies, the total number of impoverished households increased as a result of remarkable growth in world population and uneven economic development.

During the post-war years, global responses to poverty assumed three different but complementary and at times overlapping expressions. These consisted in: one, a humanitarian focus on helping those in great need; two, a variety of efforts initiated to foster economic development in underdeveloped areas; and, three, various expressions of outrage at continuing forms of global social and economic injustice.

Global humanitarian assistance

On a number of occasions before the Second World War, groups of people had organized international movements to offer aid or to address issues related to poverty. For example, Herbert Hoover and others in the United States led initiatives offering humanitarian relief to people rendered bereft and homeless by the First World War. In the nineteenth century, diverse movements sought to end the practices of slavery in the Americas and Africa. Later in that century, continuing up to the present, national Red Cross and Red Crescent organizations cooperated internationally to offer aid to prisoners and the wounded in times of war and others in need in times of peace.[8] During the second half of the twentieth century the number, variety, and scale of these internationally coordinated humanitarian programmes greatly increased. They became more fully institutionalized and more consciously global, with respect to the sources of aid, the mandates with which they operated, and also the concerns that they addressed. This expansion of global humanitarian aid has been referred to as a revolution in moral concern and as the awakening of the global conscience.[9]

One of most representative expressions of global humanitarianism in these years has been the effort to respond to problems of refugees. The Second World War, the 1948 war between Palestinians and Israelis, and the separation of the former South Asian British colony into the modern states of India and Pakistan gave rise to millions of homeless refugees. The wars in Europe and their aftermath created almost sixteen million refugees or displaced persons. The war in the Middle East led to one million Palestinian refugees. International civil society organizations such as CARE (1945) and Oxfam (1942) were initially established to offer relief to refugees and persons displaced and suffering from hunger as a result of the wars in Europe. In response to these crises the UN General Assembly helped to establish the United Nations Relief and Rehabilitation Administration (1943–8) and the International Refugee Organization (1946–51) as temporary measures, and then in 1949 and 1950 respectively, on a permanent basis, the UN Relief and Works Agency for Palestinian Refugees and the Office of the UN High Commissioner for Refugees. In 1951, a UN Convention relating to the Status of Refugees was enacted.

Over the years, these and other agencies have established refugee camps all over the world to provide refugees with shelter, food, healthcare, and asylum. In 2010, there were more than thirty-six million refugees, displaced persons, or other populations of concern worldwide, created by wars in Southeast Asia, Rwanda, Congo,

Afghanistan, Central America, the Middle East, and many other places. Refugee agencies have operated with a set of basic principles, well articulated in the UN Covenant. They have sought to find durable solutions: succour has been offered to all persons, without discrimination, who are unable or unwilling to return to the areas from which they fled; no one has been forced to return; efforts are made to find these persons permanent residence; refugees fleeing persecution are not penalized for illegal entry or stay in the areas to which they have fled. Over time, a large proportion of refugees from past crises have indeed returned to their homelands or have been successfully settled in other communities. However, in a number of cases, such as Somali refugees in northern Kenya, Palestinian refugees in Gaza, and Burundian refugees in Tanzania, people have been living in what were initially thought of as temporary refugee camps for more than a generation.

There have been many expressions of global humanitarianism in the post-war years. The number of civil society and government-sponsored organizations originating in industrialized countries and offering aid and services in developing countries has greatly increased. There are thousands of such organizations, such as Doctors without Borders, Engineers without Borders, the Peace Corps, World Vision, and Street Kids International, offering their services. Wealthy donors and philanthropies, the Gates Foundation and the Rockefeller Foundation, for example, have joined the cause. Many such agencies have very specific purposes, like the one that flies a plane taking doctors and nurses for a week at a time to a particular location to diagnose and operate on cataracts and other illnesses affecting vision. Tens of thousands of volunteers have spent time offering humanitarian services in developing countries. In many cases, global humanitarian aid has assumed the form of donations of money, food, water, and other goods offered in direct response to a particular crisis, such as drought and famine in countries near the Horn of Africa; tsunamis in Indonesia, Japan, and Sri Lanka; the hurricane in Honduras; earthquakes in Pakistan, and floods in Bangladesh. AIDS victims have been cared for; bed nets have been offered to protect people from malaria-carrying mosquitoes; agricultural specialists have helped farmers; school programmes have been developed.

Global humanitarian assistance in its diverse forms has also received donations from governments and businesses. For example, as an expression of global humanitarian concern, in 1967 eight donor countries, including the USA, the European Community, and Canada, agreed to provide a regular yearly supply of food aid to needy countries. In 1999, this was equivalent to 5.4 million metric tons of wheat. The Food Assistance Convention (redrafted in April 2012) continues this commitment, but allows for more flexibility in the forms of assistance and in the national levels of commitment, as well as more transparency and inclusiveness in governance of this programme. To cite a different kind of example, a number of international businesses have cooperated to provide medication and services to people infected by the HIV virus.

This marked expansion in global humanitarian assistance has not been insignificant. To be sure, much of this aid has been delivered within particular contours, as diaspora communities of Jews, Greeks, Sri Lankans, Pakistanis, and others, as well as religious communities, have offered help to those with whom they are related by ethnicity, nationality, or religion. In many situations humanitarian aid has been offered by governments to countries with which they sought political alliance. Nevertheless, in many other cases, aid has been extended simply to answer a need, thereby strengthening the sense of global interconnection. Although it is worth observing that, for the most part, poverty itself has not been the need identified for relief by humanitarian aid, beneficiaries of this aid have indeed, overwhelmingly, been members of impoverished households. Correspondingly, these programmes have helped to enhance the life conditions of poor people in many ways. For example, it is estimated that food programmes saved the lives of 90,000 Somalis in the two years before December 1992.[10]

Nevertheless, these global humanitarian programmes have not been without their ambiguities. A number of problems have arisen. Aid has been offered to some in need while others equally needy for periods of time have been largely ignored – such as child soldiers in parts of Africa, many impoverished households in Congo, and the indigenous rural poor in parts of India. Food supplies destined for starving families have been looted by armed rebel groups. Some aid organizations have been notoriously inefficient. In the process, global humanitarian initiatives have attracted a number of articulate critics.[11]

Their criticisms have assumed several typical forms associated with ongoing risks and dilemmas endemic to global humanitarian aid. One such is that, for better or for worse, these programmes have at times become closely connected with political agendas, both in the countries receiving aid and in those offering it. For example, Doctors without Borders was initially formed because physicians helping during the 1960s civil war in Nigeria felt that the International Committee of the Red Cross's stance of strict neutrality was inhumane. These doctors identified with the Biafrans as victims, only to recognize much later that Biafra's political leaders were prolonging a war they had already lost and were seizing aid in order to make their situation look worse.

In many settings, aid for refugees becomes highly politicized, as settlements established to care for homeless refugees in turn become well-armed base camps from which insurgents can continue to attack their enemies. For example, camps established to care for millions of Rwandan Hutu refugees in eastern Congo and north-western Tanzania served also as staging grounds for military attacks back in Rwanda and in Congo. Refugee camps for Palestinians in Gaza, Salvadoran refugees in Honduras, Cambodian refugees in Thailand, and Afghan refugees in Pakistan have functioned similarly. In these circumstances, humanitarian workers have often felt that, in the process of offering food and medical assistance, they were also indirectly supporting and legitimizing partisan military action.

The famine in Somalia in the early 1990s confronted aid workers with what seemed like distressing alternatives. In addition to the famine, the country was suffering from civil war between tribal and sub-tribal factions. These groups looted the food supplies and attacked those delivering aid. Humanitarian groups began to pay off factions not to attack and then finally called for military aid in order to protect those distributing food, water, and medical care. In the process, aid efforts became intertwined with partisan groups and with the military intervention by US-led UN troops that also seemed aligned with particular political forces. Red Cross organizations have long argued that aid should be delivered impartially and neutrally, but in Somalia they found themselves also paying off factions and calling for military support.[12]

By the end of the 1990s there was much debate over how humanitarian aid organizations could best manage these kinds of dilemmas. Should they, as some argued, recognize the inevitable political contexts in which they operated, and forthrightly acknowledge their political role? Or should they work harder to preserve their character as charitable organizations and remain politically independent and impartial? In the process of providing aid to and through groups associated with political stances, were they legitimizing political factions? Or, by trying to remain neutral, were they ignoring blatant abuses?

A second type of criticism is related to the perceived zeal and idealism with which humanitarian organizations pursue their objectives. This has found several different expressions. For example, because aid workers were often well off, well educated, and moved by commitments to justice and well-being formed within the culture of their own liberal democratic countries, they sometimes, wittingly or unwittingly, assumed an aura of moral virtue. Many were tempted to overvalue their own intentions. They saw themselves as being involved in a civilizing mission to overcome local practices that aggravated the living circumstances of those they sought to help. Wearing ethnocentric blinders, some aid workers found it hard to understand and value local customs and politics that seemed, at first glance, to perpetuate injustices, exacerbate poverty, and serve the interests of local elites.[13] From a different perspective, especially as they sought to raise funds for their activities, humanitarian workers tended at times to oversimplify the complex situations in which their organizations worked and to romanticize and overrate the importance of their own efforts.

A third type of criticism revolved around the impacts of these programmes on those they sought to help. Many wondered whether aid programmes tended to foster dependency among beneficiary populations and organizations. Recipient groups benefited from donated food, medical care, technical supplies, as well as revenues to support national and local government budgets. In many cases, these benefits seemed to become indispensable. Other local sources of goods seemed to be inadequate, unreliable, and insufficient. Consequently, many international humanitarian groups debated strategies for how they might effectively manage this kind of dilemma. Most international humanitarian organizations have recognized as well that their programmes were not really designed to overcome the poverty of those they assisted. For example, although they typically publicize stories of members whose successful use of small business loans lifted them out of poverty, most microcredit organizations fully recognize that for the most part their programmes have served the more modest purpose of helping impoverished households live more decent lives.

A fourth form of criticism has focused on the de facto ways humanitarian programmes may legitimize or reinforce existing local and global political structures that are considered unjust and oppressive. Humanitarian efforts have frequently been coordinated in recipient countries by current political elites, who arrange to dispense services and benefits disproportionately in ways that strengthen their political leverage. In the process, humanitarian programmes de facto support patterns of authority that both legitimize these elites as good citizens and extend extra benefits to them.[14] From a complementary perspective, humanitarian programmes have been criticized because they do not directly criticize the global structures of power, variously exercised by transnational corporations, global financial institutions, and imperial national governments.

By the first decade in the twenty-first century a clearly articulated common global ethic had not yet emerged with respect to humanitarian aid and services. We have just reviewed the ways issues related to the delivery of this aid have been debated since the 1970s. Still, even as we observe the differing views regarding these issues, it is possible to discern several deeply held shared ethical assumptions regarding humanitarian responses to global poverty. For example, the distresses suffered by these households – famine, homelessness, illness, lack of education – are so severe and occasion such risk that it is widely assumed that effective and compassionate response is needed. Even though these problems may affect people at great distance, their plight cannot be ignored.[15] To be sure, billions of people do just that – ignore the plight of those in distress. Nonetheless, a growing number of internationally coordinated efforts have been established to address these problems. And, although they may disagree about various tactics and strategies for delivering humanitarian aid, a growing consensus is emerging that alternative ways of delivering assistance must be found; good intentions alone are not sufficient. Yet, issues with respect to the delivery of humanitarian assistance are neither simple nor complicated in the ways that technical problems are. They are complex and involve multiple variables that typically are all in motion at the same time. Therefore, it is important for humanitarian organizations to be on the alert for unanticipated consequences of their activities, and critically to monitor these activities, from the ways they recruit donors and volunteers and collaborate with other organizations to the ways they target and deliver aid.

Finally, while some forms of humanitarian assistance can be offered impartially and neutrally without any political associations, in many settings it is neither possible nor desirable that humanitarian aid should comply with these standards. In these situations, aid programmes often need to find ways of working with local and national political organizations, whether they are formal or informal. A number of those involved in current debates regarding humanitarian assistance have set forth strong views regarding these matters, often developed in response to situations in which programmes of humanitarian aid have aggravated problems at hand, such as delivery of aid in refugee camps that have become armed encampments. Ambiguities in these settings have been real and not easily resolved. Although many particulars are hotly debated, most would agree with the points we have made. It is important to gather and use intelligence, and to learn from situations in which things have gone awry.

Fostering economic development

A second major orientation to global poverty has focused on ways to foster economic growth in underdeveloped areas. In 1922, Sun

Yat-sen, in a book on the economic development of China, conceived of the idea of internationally coordinated support to help develop impoverished areas. This idea regarding development was then publicly incorporated by the admistration of Franklin Roosevelt as an integral part of its Good Neighbor policy enacted with Latin American countries in the late 1930s and early 1940s. As the war ended, this orientation was widely embraced as a way both of revitalizing countries ravaged by Second World War and of fostering economic development and poverty reduction more generally.[16] The World Bank, the Marshall Plan, and the Economic and Social Council of the United Nations were all established with mandates to foster economic development in areas of need. The focus on development became much more pronounced during post-war years as colonies and trust areas of the former imperial powers became independent nation states. Lebanon, Syria, Iraq, Jordan, India, Pakistan, Indonesia, the Philippines, and Cuba gained independence in the 1940s. First Ghana and then dozens of other African states became sovereign states in the 1950s and 1960s. By the 1970s, the new nations, which had all become members of the UN General Assembly, greatly outnumbered the old states that had been the founding members of the United Nations. What especially characterized almost all these new states, as well as many of the Latin American states that had once been colonies as well, was that poverty remained extensive in these areas, which were in turn all economically underdeveloped.

For many, it made sense to think about the reduction of global poverty in terms of economic development. In part, the industrialized countries felt they had greatly reduced the extent of poverty in their own societies as their economies had grown and expanded. Many in the underdeveloped countries were interested in finding ways to develop their own economies. At the same time, many investors in industrialized societies were seeking ways to mine and exploit the resources of the developing world – to locate and extract minerals and petroleum, to purchase agricultural goods that were or might be grown in these areas, and to find customers for their products. Economists from the left and the right seemed to concur that economic development provided a reliable way of expanding economic opportunities in the form of new jobs, expanding commerce, and increased national wealth. As we will see, what they have disagreed about, throughout the post-war years, have been the most effective ways of fostering genuine, sustainable, and balanced economic development.

The emerging global ethic that regarded economic development as a way of reducing global poverty assumed a number of verbal and organizational expressions. President Truman's 1949 inaugural address set forth the broad outlines of this ethic in what became known as the Point Four Program: it was going to foster development for the half of the world living in unspeakable misery. In 1951, the United Nations produced a report on the same topic. The 1955 Bandung Conference of non-aligned states echoed these themes from the perspective of developing countries.[17] By the 1970s the World Bank had come to regard poverty reduction as well as economic development as integral parts of its mandates. In 1978, it began to publish annual world development reports. The United Nations Conference on Trade and Development (UNCTAD) was established in 1964 by the General Assembly at the urging of the New Nations. UNCTAD was viewed initially as a forum for developing countries and as an alternative to the General Agreement on Tariffs and Trade (GATT), which was seen as primarily serving the interests of the industrialized countries.

In the 1970s especially, UNCTAD championed what it referred to as 'A New International Economic Order', one that provided more real opportunities for developing countries. Over the years UNCTAD has especially sought to reduce poverty by strengthening the income-generating capacity of commodity producers and finding ways to lessen or manage their economic risks. In recent years it has regularly produced reports focusing on the fifty and more least developed countries. In 2011 UNCTAD had a membership of 193 nation states. The United Nations Development Programme (UNDP), established in 1965, has especially focused on promoting a more multidimensional view of poverty and a broader, more humane view of development. Since the early 1990s it has annually gauged and published the results of its measures of human development, which takes into account not only income levels but also infant mortality rates, longevity, and literacy rates, as well as levels of educational attainment.

The commitment by a number of industrialized countries to make regular and sizeable contributions to foreign aid has become one of the most important organizational expressions of this emerging global ethic. A significant number of countries have been offering foreign aid contributions. However, the size of contributions as a percentage of national income has tended to decline over time, and aid itself has often assumed questionable forms, such as military assistance, tied aid, and aid in the form of providing commodities bought from, and, therefore, benefiting, their own domestic producers. As we will see, much debate has revolved around the character and effectiveness of state aid. Nonetheless, this aid has functioned as a major institutionalized expression of the ethic that sought to address global poverty by fostering development.

In 1986, the UN General Assembly adopted the Declaration on the Right to Development. Invoking the Universal Declaration of Human Rights (UDHR), this declaration, in idealistic and aspirational language, described development as a comprehensive multidimensional process aiming at the improvement and well-being of persons and peoples. 'Every person and all peoples are entitled to participate in, contribute to, and enjoy economic, social, cultural and political development, in which all human rights and human freedoms can be fully realized.'[18] The declaration maintains that national and international states have the duty to cooperate with each other to foster development and remove obstacles in the way of development, including colonialism, racism, and foreign domination.

From the outset, different countries and organizations adopted different strategies in the hope of fostering sustained economic development. In the 1960s and 1970s, the World Bank funded large physical infrastructure projects, such as the construction of dams, port facilities, power grids, and transportation systems. Initially, many countries like Indonesia hoped to foster development through state-owned or controlled businesses in the hope that development would benefit their countries as a whole rather than advantaging particular enterprises and their owners. However, by the late 1960s Indonesia had abandoned this model. Instead, it deliberately sought to privatize industries and attract more foreign investors. During the 1960s and 1970s many developing countries, especially in Latin America, followed an import substitution model, hoping to develop and protect their own national industries. Over time, donor countries variously placed their hopes for economic growth in developing countries in increased investment in schooling, transfers of modern technologies, technical assistance programmes, large construction projects, and efforts to foster family planning.[19]

Although the focus on development remained widespread among both donor countries and the great majority of economically underdeveloped countries throughout the latter half of the twentieth century, some countries succeeded in exemplary ways, some countries made modest progress, and many countries made no progress at all. The economies of a handful of East Asian countries – Japan, Taiwan, Hong Kong, Singapore, and Malaysia – grew remarkably from the 1960s through the 1980s. In contrast, during the 'lost decade' of the 1980s, the economies of most African states stagnated. More generally, while the economies of many developing countries expanded modestly in the 1960s and 1970s, they contracted severely during the 1980s and 1990s. While in the poorest fifth of all countries the average per capita income grew by 1.9 per cent per year from 1950 to 1975, it grew by only 0.5 per cent between 1980 and

2001; while in all other countries per capita income grew by 2.5 per cent per year between 1950 and 1975, it grew by only 0.9 per cent between 1980 and 2001.[20]

From the perspective of the developing countries, a series of economic shocks occurred in the 1970s and early 1980s that aggravated their economic possibilities. The dramatic rise in fuel prices increased the cost for energy and food, which in turn was affected by increased costs for transportation, fertilizer, and mechanized farming. At the same time, as a result of marked changes in exchange rates, the value of their currencies declined relative to that of the industrialized countries. Consequently, the debts they had already accrued became much more difficult to pay. In addition, many developing counties, such as Argentina, Chile, Bolivia, Angola, and Uganda, experienced forms of civil conflict that disrupted commerce and industry, destroyed properties, depleted state funds, and cost lives.

After several decades of concerted efforts to foster economic development, why had so many countries failed to make more progress? While some blamed the legacy of colonialism, many donor organizations and governments felt that the governments of developing countries had failed to exert appropriate discipline with respect both to their economies and to their own spending and policies. In a set of recommendations, later characterized as the Washington Consensus, these donor organizations and countries called for developing countries to reduce public spending, privatize government-owned businesses, and liberalize trade with the rest of the world. In particular, the World Bank and the International Monetary Fund (IMF) agreed to provide additional loans, which developing countries sought (to a significant degree to meet interest payments on their current loans), on the condition that they agreed to certain structural adjustments in their economic policies in keeping with the principles stated above. These policies functioned to protect the investments of the lending organizations and fostered greater fiscal accountability in developing countries' governments. These policies also resulted in reduced public spending for education, health, and infrastructure and rendered domestic agriculture and industry more vulnerable to competition from the more technologically advanced and, in the case of agriculture, more publicly subsidized firms of the industrialized countries.

During the 1980s and 1990s, structural adjustment policies attracted large numbers of defenders and critics. For the most part the economies of the countries that had been subjected to these policies grew modestly at best. The most dramatic examples of economic growth took place in countries such as China, India, Thailand, Brazil, Chile, and Turkey, which had not been the primary targets.

Economic expansion in the latter countries resulted in massive reductions in the numbers of impoverished households.

Overall, the global economy grew steadily during the second half of the twentieth century in ways that significantly reduced the overall rate of poverty. Nonetheless, at the turn of the century, approximately one in three persons remained impoverished, using the World Bank's figure of income of $2.25 or less per person per day as a rough gauge.[21] There were 100 million more persons suffering from absolute poverty (less than $1 per person per day) in 2000 than in 1990.[22] A half-century of development aid and programmes had had much less impact than expected. The continued massive levels of poverty in spite of these efforts and the overall expansion of the global economy called for serious reconsideration of what had worked and what had not, and why development policies had yielded such uneven results.

Many have pointed to the failures of the governments of low-income regions, which have often shown themselves to be weak, wasteful, autocratic, self-serving, and corrupt, misspending donor funds on lavish projects rather than basic infrastructure. While there is considerable evidence to support this line of reasoning, these arguments do not explain continuing poverty in large parts of rural China, India, and Bangladesh, nor do they account for the pervasive poverty in urban slums all over the world.[23] In contrast, many others have argued that the economies of low-income areas have failed to develop because of resource exploitation by former colonial powers and businesses from industrialized countries. These powers and interests and the local elites aligned with them continue to claim title to disproportionate shares of the most productive lands in low-income countries, for both mining and agricultural purposes.[24] International businesses stand accused of shunning developing areas and failing to invest in them,[25] using abusive transfer pricing and mispricing practices to avoid paying their fair share of taxes in these areas, and overworking, underpaying, and abusing labourers.[26] Still others have argued that the economic development of these areas has been blocked and frustrated by the bias of international trade regimes. For example, the efforts of developing countries to sell agricultural goods and by-products have been undermined by export tariffs and tax supports for domestic agriculture in industrialized countries, while dispute panels of the World Trade Organization (WTO) have decided unfavourably on their efforts to protect their infant industries.[27]

Many others have argued that the lack of economic development in certain countries and areas arises primarily on account of particular conditions, such as lack of natural resources, distance from port facilities, excessively high birth rates, and high rates of internal conflict and violence.[28] Characteristically, rates of schooling and literacy remain very low. Even when exposed to modern technologies, these areas are unable to make productive use of them. Overwhelmingly, impoverished people have to make do with incomes that are not only meagre but also very uncertain and life conditions that include exposure to health risks, unsafe housing, violence, and inadequate supplies of food and water.[29]

In response to varied critiques of international aid programmes, the Organization for Economic Cooperation and Development (OECD) invited representatives from donor and recipient countries to a high-level forum in Rome in 2003 to discuss ways to improve the effectiveness of aid programmes. Representatives from more than sixty countries met two years later in Paris to produce the Paris Declaration on Aid Effectiveness. This declaration emphasized five principles: ownership, alignment, harmonization, results, and mutual accountability. Like poverty-reduction strategy plans, these principles call for developing countries to establish their own objectives and strategies and for donor groups to work together, to align their programmes with these strategies, and to foster greater mutual accountability. More countries and more civil society representatives have been involved at subsequent high-level fora on aid effectiveness, meeting in Accra in 2008 and Busan in 2011. The outcomes of this global initiative have been mixed. Greater attention has been paid to the problems of delivering aid in fragile states. Changes have been instituted in many countries to make aid finances more transparent. Beginning in 2005, the UNDP put in place serious country-based efforts to monitor the degree to which aid programmes in developing counties were modified to operate in keeping with ten targets established in accordance with the basic principles of the Paris Declaration. However, few of these targets had been reached by 2010. Furthermore, few steps were taken to deal with the ways aid programmes sometimes get captured by national elite groups in developing countries.[30]

Often, ideologically informed debates about aid programmes have raged on in the effort both to account for the failure of so many economies and sub-economies to develop and to propose alternative policy directions. At the same time, in spite of many strongly articulated different views, a degree of normative consensus has emerged regarding the most important features of poverty and ways to foster fitting forms of development.

Thus, for example, with a few exceptions, the commitment to foster economic growth as a central strategy for reducing poverty continues to be widely supported. To be sure, there have been those who have argued that industrialized countries were pushing development on peoples who really would rather choose to remain undeveloped. However, when directly queried, most impoverished peoples seem to prefer some form of development, which they in turn associate with greater access to health services, education, clean water, and more reliable sources of income, as well as longer lives.[31] The commitment to development has been voiced by those who criticize as well as those who support aid, by people in developing as well as in industrialized countries, by the opponents and defenders of increased global trade. This shared assumption is well articulated both in recent Least Developed Countries Reports of UNCTAD and in the 2008 Growth Report of the Commission on Growth and Development. This commission was composed of twenty-one high government officials, former presidents, and Nobel Prize economists from all over the world. While acknowledging that economic growth was not an end in itself, this report observed, nonetheless, that growth has the possibility of sparing people in general from poverty and drudgery. Moreover, it creates the resources to provide more adequate healthcare service, better education, fuller and more nourishing diets, and generally more opportunities.[32]

Over time this shared commitment to growth has become more nuanced and sophisticated in several ways. In the first place, economic development itself is now widely viewed as multidimensional, variously involving the construction of physical and social infrastructures, the adoption of more effective technologies, the utilization of innovations, and the development of labour markets and local and distant commerce. A number of different, mutual supporting initiatives are required to move economies beyond the steady state typical of undeveloped – pre-industrialized – areas. In the second place, there is also a wide recognition that forms of development need to be appropriate to local conditions and possibilities. What is likely to foster economic growth in Malawi, Sierra Leone, Bangladesh, or Bolivia is likely to be dramatically different. Correspondingly, there has emerged a much wider and more overt acknowledgement that fostering development can be difficult, that there are no panaceas, and that best-designed efforts may not work as expected. Thus, it is important to learn from past experiences and experiments and to appreciate fully not only the deprivations, risks, and uncertainties facing low-income communities but also the often-overlooked assets they possess.

Thirdly, a number of observers now argue that many impoverished economies have thus far failed to develop as expected because they live in conditions appropriately described as poverty traps. This term was popularized by Jeffrey Sach's 2005 book *The End of Poverty,* and was widely used in a number of regional and global studies, including the 2002 Least Developed Countries Report of UNCTAD as well as Paul Collier's study of fifty-four least developed countries, entitled *The Bottom Billion*.[33] Used analytically, this term calls attention to a number of factors that make it especially difficult to foster sustained economic growth in these areas. Sachs referred to the absence of social, legal, and physical infrastructures. Collier analysed the ways in which ongoing poverty tended to be associated with aggravated civil conflicts, which in turn are associated with ongoing poverty. He also examined the ways in which weak and erratic governments, certain geographical factors, and what has been referred to as the 'resource curse' also tend to undermine development prospects. In his study of the billion or more people living in slums around the world, Mike Davis observed how the lack of healthy sanitation and water supplies, inadequate housing, the presence of widespread disease, aggravated levels of crime, and the absence of secure well-paying jobs condemned most of those living in slums to perpetual poverty.[34]

From our perspective, it is not necessary to determine which of these analyses seems most accurate or compelling. Rather, what these several observers have emphasized are the ways in which a number of different, not fully anticipated factors have undermined or frustrated efforts to initiate economic growth in these impoverished areas. For example, Banerjee and Dunflo note how existing microcredit schemes typically do not help impoverished households *overcome* poverty. Rather, not insignificantly, these schemes help poor households live better. For the most part, they are not really organized to lend the amounts of money necessary for fledging entrepreneurs to purchase the necessary supplies and to hire the numbers of employees they would need to be truly successful.[35] The notion of poverty traps has thus served as a sober reminder that fostering sustained economic growth in impoverished areas may be much more difficult than was expected when development programmes were originally initiated.

Fourthly, advocates of development now increasingly point to the importance of developing the capacity of low-income communities to address these problems themselves. This shift in focus is well illustrated by the change in the conditions attached to concessional lending to developing countries by the World Bank and the IMF. Beginning in 1999, recipient countries were no longer required to adhere to strict demands set by the donor agencies to privatize government-owned businesses, liberalize foreign trade, and reduce government spending. Instead they were being called upon to involve relevant stakeholders in order to produce country-specific plans to reduce poverty over the medium and long term. Several features of these Poverty Reduction Strategy (PRS) plans have been noteworthy. The stakeholders involved included various civil society organizations, government officials, and community representatives. It was also expected that PRSs would be designed in ways that would strengthen social safety nets, improve governance, and develop appropriate sectoral policies with respect to education, health, the environment, and social protection.

What has been especially distinctive about this initiative has been the requirement that recipients could and should both develop their own strategies and develop their capacities to guide the process effectively. The World Bank has since sought to support and reinforce PRS processes by encouraging national governments in recipient countries to integrate PRS reviews with government budgeting processes, for two reasons: first to foster closer conversations and collaborations between civil society organizations and politicians involved in the PRS processes with the government bureaucrats involved in budget reviews; and, second, to strengthen domestic government capacity for financial accountability.[36]

Fifthly, those concerned with fostering economic growth in poverty-stricken areas have begun to examine more seriously the real or potential impacts of internationally connected businesses: either to foster sustained economic development or to impede it. These current discussions differ from the well-publicized, broadly damning critiques of international business, like David Korten's *When Corporations Rule the World*,[37] in that they recognize that internationally connected businesses and supply chains, operating in more sustainable ways, have played and can play a constructive role in fostering economic development.[38] This line of argument has been especially set forth by C. K. Prahalad in his book *The Fortune at the Bottom of the Pyramid: Eradicating Poverty through Profits*.[39]

Nonetheless, these discussions, while retaining a commitment to economic growth, have recognized the unexpected ways by which otherwise thriving investments in developing countries have sometimes had ill effects, especially in connection with analyses of the so-called resource curse. For example, many such investments have ended up intensifying local conflicts, destabilizing and distorting government practices, and rendering the larger national economies more dysfunctional. In many areas the wealth engendered by extractive businesses has, for instance, inflated local consumer prices to the disadvantage of the poor, badly affected exchange rates thus rendering foreign debts harder to pay, and occasioned aggravated rent-seeking by politicians and government officials.[40] Correspondingly, international businesses, whether they are involved in extractive industries or not, have been widely challenged by industry associations, international banks, and others to find ways of operating so that they help foster inclusive, sustainable, and balanced rather than insular and unsustainable growth in the economies of developing countries.

We can further observe the characteristic features of this emerging global commitment to economic growth as a means of reducing poverty by looking at two current global initiatives, namely, the Millennium Development Goals (MDGs) and the Doha or Developmental Round of negotiations of the WTO. The global initiative referred to as the Millennium Development Goals was adopted by the United Nations and 193 member countries in 2000. It involves eight broad goals and twenty-one measurable targets, which these countries committed themselves to realize by 2015. In the process, these countries collectively promised to halve the proportion of people that were experiencing extreme poverty (less than $1.25 per person per day) and hunger in 1990, universally offer primary education to all school-age children, promote gender equality, reduce child mortality, improve maternal health, more successfully combat HIV/AIDS, malaria, and other diseases, and become more environmentally responsible. They also pledged to pursue these objectives through global partnerships for development that fostered links between developing and industrialized countries and between businesses, civil society, and governments.

Several features of the MDGs are noteworthy. In keeping with the UNDP, which oversees this initiative, development is defined by the MDGs in terms of a number of broad indices, most of which can be viewed as indicators of enhanced human capabilities. Development is not viewed narrowly in relation only to increased per capita income. Attacking hunger, promoting gender equality, enhancing infrastructures, and improving healthcare and education are all viewed as integral to the processes of development. Responsibility for making progress with respect to these goals is widely shared not only by the signatory governments but also by international organizations, local and international businesses, and civil society organizations in so far as they are in position to make a difference.

While this initiative might well be viewed as an exercise in global idealism, significant progress has been attained with respect to a number of these goals. Overall, the proportion of humans experiencing extreme poverty in 1990 had already been cut in half by 2010, to a significant degree because of the dramatic declines in extreme poverty in countries such as China, Vietnam, and Brazil and the not insignificant declines in places such as India, the Middle East, and Latin America. Primary school enrolment had also increased appreciably. The percentage of people without access to fresh water in 1990 was cut in half by 2010. A number of counties, like Kuwait, had made noteworthy improvements in gender equality. Infant and maternal mortality rates declined by more than 50 per cent during the same period. Considerable strides have been made with respect to the treatment of people suffering from HIV.

What has been especially impressive has been the wide variety of projects and programmes undertaken by governments, businesses, and civil society organizations initiated in order to help meet this broad set of goals. These included the Poverty Reduction Strategy plans designed by developing countries' governments in order to qualify for concessional loans, the international debt reduction schemes initiated by industrialized countries, and thousands of local government and civil society projects organized to improve education, extend credit, improve healthcare, and facilitate access to potable water. For example, a number of developing countries have instituted cash transfer programmes, such as Bolsa Familia in Brazil and Oportunidades in Mexico, that make payments to families whose children regularly attend school and keep periodic health check-up appointments. In order to inspire similar experiments, the Earth Institute at Columbia University together with the UNDP initiated the Millennium Villages projects in fourteen African locations to demonstrate the possibilities of greatly improving the life conditions of impoverished households through appropriate, locally organized, low-cost, comprehensive projects.

As an example of their commitment to the MDGs, a number of industrialized countries meeting in Mexico in 2002 pledged, according to the accompanying Monterrey Consensus, to work together to improve and coordinate financial resources for development. In 2005 the G8 leaders of the largest industrialized countries launched the Multilateral Debt Relief Initiative. In 2010 these leaders, who had by then expanded their numbers to include the heads of the twenty largest economies (the G20), further expressed their commitment by endorsing the Seoul Development Consensus, which called for balanced, sustainable, and resilient economic growth.

These diverse but complementary UN-initiated programmes have been widely criticized. It has been argued that the measures were imprecise, that accomplishments in many areas fell short of the goals, that too much attention was still being placed on overseas development assistance, and that an excessive portion of the latter has assumed the form of debt relief rather than capital investments. Still, because the MDGs were designed as aspirational rather than obligatory goals, what has been impressive has been the extensive number of coordinated efforts undertaken both locally and internationally to work towards these objectives.

However, the particular character of the MDGs global initiative as well as some of its intrinsic weakness is evident in the lack of any kind of central attention devoted to seeking to develop and strengthen the overall economies and public administrations of developing areas. The MDGs focused on enhancing human capabilities while also acting responsibly with respect to the environment. With occasional exceptions, programmes initiated by the MDGs did not directly explore ways to expand local or distant commerce, ways to attract investments, and/or ways to increase the productivity of industry or agriculture. Nor did these programmes directly work at fostering institutional development and organizational learning within the often weak public administrations of developing countries.

The 2010 Seoul Development Consensus of the G20 attempted to articulate a broader, complementary view of development. Modelled on a statement initially developed by Oxfam as an alternative to the so-called Washington Consensus, the Seoul Development Consensus called for more efforts by industrialized countries to help the economies of developing countries become strong, balanced, and resilient. Working as partners with developing countries, the G20 should, according to this manifesto, develop programmes that result in job creation, infrastructure development, enhanced trade, knowledge-sharing, and greater utilization of local resources in developing countries.[41]

By 2012, a number of international initiatives had been put in place to develop a coherent global programme to take the place of the MDGs after 2015. A UN system task team has offered its proposals for a post-2015 development agenda. These were further elaborated and expanded both by a high-level panel appointed by the UN Secretary General as well as by an open working group of thirty persons appointed by the General Assembly to represent clusters of nations. In addition, the Earth Institute organized the Sustainable Development Solutions Network to mobilize expertise to address specific concerns related to the post-2015 development agenda.

These several initiatives, which also involved other groups like Academics Stand Against Poverty, shared a number of commitments. They recognized that the approach utilized by the MDGs had been helpful and that a similar approach – identifying particular goals, further specified in relation to measurable targets that allowed each country to set its own policies and agenda – ought to be utilized for the period until 2030. However, on consideration of the post-2015 development agenda, most of these groups thought the United Nations this time ought to adopt a much broader vision that would, as the title of one report stated, seek not only to 'eradicate poverty' but also to 'transform economies through sustainable development'. However, as the proposed 'Sustainable Development Goals' have become more global – seeking to foster inclusive economic develop-ment, good governance, and greater peace – they have become more visionary and also more difficult to operationalize in relation to measurable targets.[42]

The Doha Development Agenda of the WTO represents another globally coordinated effort to help the economies of low-income countries grow by bringing about appropriate changes in the inter-nationally accepted rules governing multilateral trade. After the initial efforts post-Second World War to create an international trade organization had failed, the industrialized countries created GATT. This worked as an arena where countries could establish rules that sought generally to liberalize and regularize trading rela-tions with respect to specified manufactured goods. Over the next several decades the country membership in GATT slowly increased and the range of goods covered expanded. Few developing countries were part of GATT. However, by 1979, as more developing countries joined, it was recognized that developing countries deserved 'special and differential treatment' with respect to GATT rules. Generally, it was assumed that 'special and differential treatment' meant that developing countries would be granted longer periods of time before they had to comply with GATT rules.

Beginning in 1986, GATT members entered into a new set of nego-tiations, referred to as the Uruguay Round, regarding matters such as trade-in services, agricultural trade, and rules with respect to intellec-tual property. These negotiations led to agreements on an even wider range of goods and services. By the time GATT had been replaced by the creation of the WTO in January 1995, it included most of the developing countries as well as all the industrialized countries. Because these low-income countries had not gained as much from the Uruguay Round as they had hoped at its outset, the member nations of the WTO made a commitment to undertake a new round of development negotiations designed to address the concerns of the developing countries. At their ministerial meeting in 2001 at Doha, Qatar, WTO member countries instituted a new set of multilateral negotiations dedicated to fulfilling this mandate.

By 2014 these negotiations had been going on for more than a decade. Reaching agreements in the WTO has never been easy, because any agreement requires the support of all member countries. Because countries have quite different interests with respect to trade, mutually beneficial agreements are achieved only through hard bar-gaining, give-and-take negotiations, and compromise. Developing countries argue that current patterns of agricultural trade remain deeply unfair, because industrialized countries offer trade-distorting subsidies to their domestic growers, while agricultural products from developing countries are subject to tariffs and quotas. Invoking the provisions for 'Special and Differential Treatment', the developing countries also seek to protect their own growers, manufacturers, and service providers from forms of international trade that might threaten domestic firms. The industrialized countries have taken opposing views that better serve the interests of their own domestic firms.

Nonetheless, almost all countries recognize that fostering and appropriately liberalizing international trade will yield significant benefits for all countries and especially developing countries. Although negotiators have reached a common understanding with respect to most issues, an overall agreement has eluded them. Because these multilateral negotiations have been frustrating and exhausting, since the beginning of the twenty-first century many industrialized countries have focused instead on developing bilateral agreements with particular developing countries. In practice these agreements tend to favour the industrialized countries. Still, the commitment to helping foster economic growth in low-income countries through trade continues to find expression, not only in the willingness to pursue multilateral negotiations but also in several other initiatives. These include the European Union's 'Anything But Arms' initiative and the United States' African Growth and Opportunity Act, both of which have eliminated tariffs on a wide range of products originating in Africa. In addition, in 2007, the WTO as a whole adopted an Aid for Trade programme to help develop administrative and infrastructural capacities so that low-income countries are better able to engage in international trade.[43]

Since the Second World War, the global commitment to facilitate and enhance economic growth in developing countries as a means of reducing poverty has gained more extensive, more organized, and more sophisticated support. Development has come to be viewed as a multidimensional process, not always easily realized, that can best be pursued by locally owned and coordinated initiatives. Organizationally, the commitment to development as a means of reducing poverty has been embodied in a number of internationally coordinated efforts. These include the Poverty Reduction Strategy of the World Bank and IMF, the UN MDGs, the WTO Doha Development Agenda, as well as other efforts, such as the EU 'Anything But Arms' initiative and actions taken by a number of international businesses to make their operations more socially and environmentally responsible. In the many years since Sun Yet San wrote his book, Truman announced his Point Four programme, the Bandung conference was held, and UNCTAD and UNDP were inititiated, the global commitment to development has become more fully institutionalized. However, it remains subject to disagreement about optimal ways to proceed and risks being sidelined by other political agendas in both developing and industrialized states.

Addressing social and economic injustices

For many people, global poverty has been primarily viewed as a glaring symptom of global injustice. How was it possible, those concerned have asked, for more than two billion people to live in poverty with incomes of less than $2.25 per person per day when economies all over the world continued to expand producing great affluence for so many? Why were almost one billion people daily suffering from hunger and malnutrition when there was enough food worldwide for all? Why, since the 1980s, had the wealthiest strata of societies become wealthier while the bottom strata became mired in poverty? What made it possible for so many people living in comfort to ignore the devastating conditions of others living in poverty? These kinds of questions have been raised by many people in both industrialized and developing countries, by both individuals and organized constituencies: by labour parties and producer cooperatives, by proponents of fair trade, social activists, academic dissenters, and thoughtful liberals, to name a few characteristic examples.[44] For example, from the beginning of the twentieth century, a number of observers have argued that underdevelopment of non-industrialized areas was due in large part to industrialized nations' exploitation of resources, in the process transferring extensive wealth to their own countries.

To be sure, many of those concerned about the injustice of global poverty expressed their views as isolated individuals, local or national organizations, or particular political parties. However, there have been a number of internationally organized efforts that expressed these ideas as well. During the cold war period, an association of non-aligned states voiced its concerns about the ways dominant power alignments seemed to overlook and aggravate problems of poverty in the developing Third World. In 1993, leaders from a number of Asian countries meeting in Bangkok issued a declaration arguing that the right to development was being obstructed for millions by the international economic order that had widened the 'gap between the North and the South, the rich and the poor'.[45] In the late 1990s, civil society groups from all over the world joined a movement to protest against the debt crisis that plagued a number of developing countries and, through the internationally organized Jubilee Debt Campaign, sought to encourage changes in policies by major banks and industrial countries to ease this crisis.

Interestingly, a number of groups began raising questions about the ways projects undertaken in the name of development – from large dams to urban renewal, from highway construction to the construction of mining sites – have in fact often aggravated the poverty of residents and workers thereby displaced. Local and international civil society groups, like the International Accountability Project, have protested and lobbied for safeguards to be instituted to protect those adversely affected by these kinds of projects. More dramatically, a wide range of labour and civil society organizations from diverse countries staged a series of well-organized public anti-globalization protests, first at the ministerial meeting of the WTO in Seattle in 1999 and then at other trade negotiation meetings in places such as Genoa, Quebec City, and Washington.[46]

Partially as an outgrowth of the anti-globalization protests and partially as an outgrowth of the increasing global collaborations by civil society groups, in 2001 a World Social Forum (WSF) was convened in Porto Alegre, Brazil, under the slogan 'Another World is Possible'. This gathering, which attracted more than 10,000 participants from all over the world, provided what organizers referred to as an open space. In this space people from diverse non-government and non-partisan groups were able both to protest against the current unjust world order dominated by, they said, hegemonic and imperialistic corporations and governments and to explore ways to construct viable alternatives from the ground up. Over the next decade annual meetings of the WSF were held, sometimes at a single site and sometimes at multiple sites, attracting much larger numbers of attendees. These meetings served not as legislative or even representative councils but rather as gatherings to facilitate dialogue and exchange and thereby to express solidarity among all peoples and protest against dehumanizing and unjust practices. Without developing any particular analysis, WSF gatherings reaffirmed the normative view that global poverty continued to exist not just because it might take time for impoverished areas to catch up but also, fundamentally, because current patterns of power and wealth unfairly reinforced structures that disadvantaged the poor.

Criticism of the ways contemporary patterns of wealth and power reinforce global structural injustices that occasion and maintain poverty have been expressed in diverse and often overlapping ways. While some have attacked the current world order, others have criticized the colonial legacy; while some have pointed the finger at current practices of capitalism, others have focused more on the abuses associated with neo-liberal economic policies; and still others have argued that these patterns of injustice reflect the institutionalization of changes associated with globalization. These diverse critics shared the common assumption that global poverty has become so extensive because of the unjust distribution of life opportunities. These injustices can and should be addressed, and, correspondingly, it was assumed that the extent of global poverty could and should be reduced. Unless efforts were made to limit and overcome these injustices, continued economic development and even expanded humanitarian assistance were unlikely to make much difference. Many of these critics have pointed to the steady increase in economic inequality since the late 1970s, both globally and within many countries, as reliable evidence that underlying injustices in the ways economic and political systems were operating were not being addressed with fitting seriousness.[47]

Protests against global injustices have directed their criticism at a wide array of issues. In the paragraphs that follow, we look at five issues that have especially attracted global attention.

One, many have argued that contemporary global poverty problems are due to unjust distribution of property rights, especially in countries with higher incidences of poverty. In many countries, including especially South Africa, Brazil, Chile, Argentina, and India, as a result in part of the colonial legacies, land remains much more unequally distributed than other forms of wealth, such as income. Many indigenous peoples in these and many other countries feel that their traditional claims to land have been ignored or extended only token recognition. These issues have received greater attention over the past several generations as both governments and firms in the extractive industries have sought to benefit from the minerals and fuels located in and beneath the surfaces of these lands.

Accordingly, in many areas, what seems called for are fundamental and appropriate land and property reforms. The expected reforms would, it is assumed, distribute property titles more broadly, more equitably, and more fairly through the population as a whole. Those who were already working the land, such as homesteaders and settlers, would gain greater title. The claims of those who had traditionally been associated with lands from which they had been fairly recently expelled would gain greater credibility. Moreover, less weight would be given to the claims of absentee-landlords not involved directly in cultivating the lands to which they claimed title. To be sure, these issues are complex and often not easily resolved. Many have assumed, like the Peruvian economist Hernando De Soto, that impoverished peoples would greatly benefit from the right to make property claims on lands they were using for cultivation or grazing in rural areas or their household structures in urban shanty towns. With legal title to these properties, they could better protect them, insure them, sell them, and expand their credit by using them as collateral to borrow.[48] It was also widely assumed that once low-income households had gained legal title to their properties, they would also make much more productive use of them. There was some evidence in favour of this belief in places like China, where farmers who had previously worked on collective agricultural enterprises gained title to portions of these operations both individually and as cooperatives and then cultivated these lands much more productively. However, in practice, the results of land titling programmes have been mixed.[49] Nonetheless, the issue regarding fitting and fair allocation of land and property has gained increased attention as a factor determining the extent and character of global poverty.

Two, many observers have argued that global financial markets operate in ways that both disproportionately benefit the very wealthy and aggravate problems of global poverty. From the perspective of the poor, financial markets seem to function so that the wealthy get wealthier and the poor get poorer. In fact, low-income households have little access to these markets. Typically, for example, before the recent expansion of microcredit schemes, low-income households either could not obtain credit beyond small amounts or could obtain credit only at exorbitant rates.[50] They rarely participated in other financial markets except indirectly.

Global financial markets exacerbate global inequalities in part simply because, over the past several hundred years, and especially since the late 1970s, financial wealth has grown much more quickly than the wealth associated with industry and commerce. Over the centuries, as financial institutions have developed a wide range of new financial instruments, from lines of credit and publicly traded shares to financial derivatives, they have found ways of expanding the overall money supply both globally and within specific countries to the benefit of those well placed to take advantage of these innovations.[51] As the overall supply of money has expanded, those who are well off have disproportionately benefited. The disparity between financial markets, on the one hand, and commercial and labour markets, on the other, has been especially evident in the marked increase in trading values in equity markets since 1989. Although equity markets typically rise and fall, overall those with investments have greatly benefited from the expansion of these markets since the early 1990s. Because pension funds have purchased large amounts of equity shares, it has been argued that the growth of equity markets has more generally benefited industrial societies.[52] Certainly, many people have been able to receive pension benefits that greatly exceeded the contributions made by themselves and their employers, as a result of expanding financial markets. However, while many people have indeed benefited, the range of benefits has been skewed in favour of the wealthy.[53]

Three, during the past several generations there have been protests in countries all over the world against labour market injustices. To be sure, these protests began with industrialization. Over time, with the organization of trade unions, governments in industrial countries instituted labour laws to guarantee safe and healthy working conditions, minimum wages, job security, and diverse fringe benefits. The International Labour Organization (ILO) has developed standards with respect to these concerns in countries that are beginning the processes of industrialization or passing through intermediate stages. However, in many areas contemporary protests regarding the injustices of labour markets focus on several issues not yet resolved by current labour laws and social welfare legislation. At the top, contemporary labour markets seem to offer excessive rewards to the highest-paid executives, entertainers, sport figures, and professionals. Over the past several decades, the ratio of earnings of those with the highest pay to the pay of other workers in the same industries has grown much, much faster than the economy as a whole. Resentments against this growing inequality have also increased.[54]

At the other end of labour markets, even though the global economy seems to be working satisfactorily, increasingly large numbers of workers find themselves unemployed or underemployed. In 2013 The Economist estimated that 300 million young people globally were neither in school nor regularly employed. The unemployment rates among young people in places such as South Africa, the Middle East, North Africa, and southern Europe were exceedingly high. In addition, even larger numbers of employed people, both young and old, both in these areas and globally, were working at part-time or part-year jobs without job security or fringe benefits, and with earnings below relevant poverty lines.[55] Although groups like the Occupy movement have protested internationally in very general terms about growing inequality, and have in the process attracted considerable public attention, these movements have not found ways to focus on particular institutional arrangements that seem to have engendered these disparities in contemporary labour markets. Protests continue against these kinds of labour market injustices, but they remain diffuse, often local, sometimes popular, but usually not as effectively organized as trade unions or political parties, and thus ill equipped to institute changes in public or corporate policies.

Four, many people suffer from poverty, it has been widely argued, because of the ways women are abused, mistreated, discriminated against, and ignored. This complaint has been widely voiced over the past several generations by UN conferences, local and global women's movements, religious groups, political movements, and impartial observers. Evidence for this complaint has assumed multiple expressions, from official international reports on the millions of missing women to popular media accounts of the suffering and distress of particular girls and women.[56] In ways that greatly affect both the extent and the character of global poverty, women in many areas receive less education, lower wages, and fewer opportunities to choose how they will live. In many areas they are more likely to face discrimination at work. Millions of women, even in recent times, have suffered from sexual abuse, abduction, female genital cutting, and servitude.[57] Many otherwise well-designed anti-poverty initiatives have not succeeded because insufficient efforts were undertaken to involve relevant women in implementing these programmes. In multiple ways, injustices against women affect both the extent and the character of global poverty and undermine well-meaning efforts to address and alleviate its associated problems.

The complaint that injustice experienced by women in turn affects the incidence and pattern of global poverty is serious and compelling. Considerable attention has been directed to such complaints by global conferences hosted by the United Nations, by national and international women's groups, by microcredit groups that primarily offer loans to women, by a women's movement organized in East Africa to plant trees, and by sympathetic political parties in many countries. Progress has been made. In keeping with the MDGs, the proportion of girls receiving primary and secondary education has greatly increased both globally and in many developing countries. Nonetheless, in many areas opposition to this education has also increased. In many places, women continue to be discriminated against with respect to property rights, inheritance claims, wage levels, chances for promotion, and opportunities to move, and the economic opportunities of affected women and their households have correspondingly diminished.

Five, an overwhelming proportion of the 370 million indigenous peoples of the world today remains impoverished. Their poverty results from a number of different and complex factors, including lack of effective political power, the fact that the economies of many of these groups continue to be depressed, and their marginal relation to more productive economies. Many would argue that the poverty of indigenous people also reflects the many ways these peoples have suffered from injustices. Many of their lands have been seized. Many of them have been uprooted from places where they used to live. They have experienced considerable discrimination with respect to schools, workplaces, and the delivery of social services. In many settings, they have been over-regulated and disempowered. However, during the past several generations a number of parallel initiatives have been launched in countries all over the world to appreciate the cultures of indigenous peoples more fully, to provide them with more educational opportunities, and to collaborate more openly with respect to fitting uses of indigenous lands by the extractive industries.

Beginning in the 1980s, concerted worldwide efforts were undertaken to craft a Declaration on the Rights of Indigenous Peoples, adopted by the United Nations in 2007.[58] This declaration asserts the right of these peoples to maintain and strengthen their own institutions and culture, to pursue development on their own terms, to determine their own political arrangements, and to use and develop the lands that they own or legitimately occupy by reason of tradition. This declaration has received wide support. Nonetheless, countries such as the United States, Canada, Australia, and New Zealand, all of which contain sizeable indigenous populations, have endorsed the declaration only in principle, refusing to sign for technical legal reasons, and the fact that the broad language of the declaration seems to allow for claims to lands that passed out of indigenous peoples' control centuries ago. Although stated in terms of rights and principles, the declaration has functioned in practice as a point of reference for identifying injustices that indigenous peoples have suffered and agenda items for negotiating constructive changes.

In addition to responding to poverty as a global concern, either by supporting diverse forms of humanitarian assistance or by working to foster economic development, in the years since the Second World War millions of people and hundreds of organizations have responded to poverty as a global problem by working to identify and address injustices that, they have argued, either occasion or reinforce patterns of global poverty. Sometimes these advocates for global justice have worked in concert through organizations like the ILO or gathered together in meetings like the WSF, or partnered to create the UN Declaration on the Rights of Indigenous Peoples. Typically, while voicing parallel concerns, they have worked through countless national and local initiatives. Overall, these advocates for global social justice have succeeded in extending credit to low-income households, expanding the property claims of impoverished individuals and families, and defending the rights of low-income women. Most importantly, they have identified and protested particular unjust practices – such as abusive transfer pricing, discrimination against minorities, systems to facilitate tax avoidance, and the expansion of conditional labour markets – that have functioned to aggravate the poverty of the poor. These diverse advocates for social justice have been quite vocal. On the one hand, they have called attention to particularly vulnerable populations, such as low-income women, indigenous peoples, un- and underemployed youth, and oppressed minorities, who have suffered from unjust treatment. On the other hand, they have pointed to the particular contemporary ways financial markets, property markets, and labour markets have operated to occasion, greatly expand, intensify, and reinforce aggravated inequalities in income and wealth.

These diverse advocates of social justice have shared a common moral tone. Given the resources, knowledge, and productivity of modern societies, they have insisted that global poverty should not exist to anywhere near the extent it does. From their perspective, global poverty exists not just because of a lack of economic growth and not just because humanitarian assistance has not been enough. Rather, in important ways impoverished households suffer from poverty as they do because other people and institutions are operating in ways that are unfair. The strength of this argument has been well expressed by its advocates through their articulate and impassioned critiques and protests.

Conclusions

In the past several generations, poverty has come to be viewed as a global problem calling for a global response. This changing perspective on poverty gained support and credibility as a consequence or correlate of a number of other changes. These included the emergence, postcolonially, of widespread interest in fostering the economic growth and exploiting the resources of the developing countries, responses to the devastation caused by the world wars and subsequent conflicts and natural disasters, as well as the recognition of continuing poverty in industrialized countries. Growing concerns about global poverty gave rise to a number of international organizations and initiatives, such as the UNDP, the UN Commission on Trade and Development, Oxfam, and World Vision, as well as initiatives such as the World Bank program with regard to Poverty Reduction Strategies, diverse microcredit programs, international charters like the Declaration on the Rights of Indigenous Peoples, and the WSF. In this chapter we have reviewed the mandates and work of a number of these organizations and initiatives.

No one code, statement, or set of principles can express the shared moral convictions that have informed these diverse activities. The practices of global ethics with respect to poverty have in common the conviction that global poverty is a problem that must be addressed by concerted, internationally coordinated actions. However, these practices have actually assumed many different forms, most typically expressed through three quite different but often overlapping grand strategies. The first strategy has assumed the form of humanitarian assistance, embodied in public welfare, succour for refugees, and aid programmes as well as efforts of thousands of civil society organizations and the social responsibility initiatives of businesses. The second strategy has focused on fostering economic growth in developing areas, using a wide range of tactics organized by governments, businesses, and civil society associations. The third strategy has focused on injustices that seem to have either occasioned or reinforced the poverty of the poor. Those concerned about global poverty have often not only favoured some strategies over others but frequently expressed considerable criticism of those adopting alternative strategies or tactics. Questions about how best to address and reduce the extent of global poverty have given rise to heated exchanges, in part because many initiatives aimed at reducing poverty have been only moderately successful, and in part because those seeking to make a difference have been motivated by contrasting values and ideologies. Characteristically, the practice of global ethics with respect to poverty takes place amid multiple agendas, values, and points of view. Notwithstanding, ethical practices have created a number of international organizations and initiatives devoted to helping impoverished households and reducing global poverty. They have strengthened the view that poverty is a global problem that must be addressed. They have had sufficient impact for global citizens to make measurable progress in realizing a number of the MDGs, such as reducing the extent of extreme poverty found in 1990 by half by 2015 and significantly expanding primary education.

Notes

1. See Banerjee and Duflo, *Poor Economics*, chs 2, 6.
2. See Collier, *The Bottom Billion*; Davis, *Planet of Slums*.
3. Simmel, 'The Poor'; Clark, *A Farewell to Alms*, chs 3, 5.
4. Trattner, *From Poor Law to Welfare State*; de Schweinitz, *England's Road to Social Security*.
5. Davis, *Late Victorian Holocausts*.
6. Clark, *A Farewell to Alms*.
7. Acemoglu and Robinson, *Why Nations Fail*, chs 9, 12.
8. Keck and Sikkink, *Activists beyond Borders*.
9. Rieff, *A Bed for the Night*, p. 51.
10. Terry, *Condemned to Repeat?*, p. 41.
11. See Rieff, *A Bed for the Night*; Easterly, *The White Man's Burden*;

Terry, *Condemned to Repeat?*; Kennedy, *The Dark Sides of Virtue*; Moyo, *Dead Aid*; Orbinski, *An Imperfect Offering*.

12. Foley, *A Thin Blue Line*, pp. 55–6.
13. Criticisms along these lines have been voiced by Rieff, *A Bed for the Night*; Kennedy, *The Dark Sides of Virtue*; Rozack, *Dark Threats and White Knights*.
14. For further elaboration of this argument, see Moyo, *Dead Aid*; Collier, *The Bottom Billion*, ch. 7.
15. For typical arguments on why it is so imperative to respond, see Singer, *The Life You Can Save*; Pogge, *World Poverty and Human Rights*.
16. Helleiner, *The Forgotten Foundations of Bretton Woods*.
17. Rist, *The History of Development from Western Origins to Global Faith*, chs 4, 5.
18. United Nations General Assembly, *Declaration on the Right to Development*.
19. For a critical review of these initiatives, see Easterly, 'The Elusive Quest for Growth'.
20. Easterly, *White Man's Burden*, p. 39.
21. World Bank, *World Development Report 2000/2001*.
22. Wolfensohn, 'Foreword'.
23. Davis, *Planet of Slums*.
24. For a sustained analysis of how business interests of these industrialized countries have impoverished developing countries, see Klein, *The Shock Doctrine*.
25. The Group of Lisbon, *Limits to Competition*.
26. Baker, *Capitalism's Achilles Heel*; Schoenberger, *Levi's Children*; Klein, *No Logo*.
27. Stiglitz and Charlton, *Fair Trade for All*.
28. Collier, *The Bottom Billion*.
29. Banerjee and Duflo, *Poor Economics*, chs 2, 3, 4, 5.
30. For the Paris Declaration and other accounts of the high-level meetings for aid effectiveness, see <http://www.OECD.org> (last accessed 30 January 2015); see also Kaufmann, 'Aid Effectiveness and Governance'; United Nations Development Programme (UNDP), *Implementing the Paris Declaration on Aid Effectiveness*.
31. Sen, *Development as Freedom*, chs 1, 4.
32. United Nations Conference on Trade and Development (UNCTAD), *The Least Developed Countries Report 2006*; The Commission on Growth and Development, *Growth Report 2008*.
33. United Nations Conference on Trade and Development (UNCTAD), *The Least Developed Countries Report 2002*; Sachs, *The End of Poverty*; Collier, *The Bottom Billion*.
34. Davis, *Planet of Slums*.

35. Banerjee and Dunflo, *Poor Economics*.
36. World Bank and German Federal Ministry for Economic Cooperation and Development, *Minding the Gaps*.
37. Korten, *When Corporations Rule the World*.
38. See, e.g., Culpeper et al. (eds), *Global Development Fifty Years after Bretton Woods*; Nelson, *Business as Partners in Development*; Bird and Herman (eds), *International Businesses and the Challenge of Poverty in the Developing World*; Bird et al. (eds), *International Business and the Dilemmas of Development*; Bird and Velasquez (eds), *Just Business Practices in a Diverse and Developing World*.
39. Prahalad, *The Fortune at the Bottom of the Pyramid*.
40. Auty, *Sustaining Development in Mineral Economies*; Auty, *Resource Abundance and Economic Development*; Humphreys et al. (eds), *Escaping the Resource Curse*.
41. See briefing note by Oxfam International, *The Making of a Seoul Development Consensus*; see also the campaign by the International Council on Mining and Metals, and the Equator Principles developed by some of the largest global banks; available at <http://www.icmm.com/our-work/sustainable-development-framework/10-principles> and <http://www.equator-principles.com> (last accessed 30 January 2015).
42. See United Nations documents: UN System Task Team on the Post-2015 UN Development Agenda, *Realizing the Future We Want for All*; Open Working Group on Sustainable Development Goals, *Outcome Document*; and *A New Global Partnership ... The Report of the High-Level Panel of Eminent Persons*.
43. Our account of the Doha Round relies largely on Stiglitz and Charlton, *Fair Trade for All*.
44. For characteristic expressions of these sentiments, see Pogge, *World Poverty and Human Rights*; Singer, *The Life You Can Save*
45. Sullivan and Kymlicka (eds), 'The Bangkok Declaration', in *The Globalization of Ethics,* appendix F, article no. 8, p. 264.
46. See Barlow and Clarke, *Global Showdown*.
47. Milanovic, *Worlds Apart*.
48. See De Soto, *The Mystery of Capital*. See also Banerjee and Dunflo, *Poor Economics*, ch. 8.
49. Meinzen-Dick, 'Property Rights for Poverty Reduction'.
50. Caplovitz, *The Poor Pay More*.
51. See Ferguson, *The Ascent of Money*.
52. Drucker, *The Unseen Revolution*.
53. Piketty, *Capital in the Twenty-First Century*, offers considerable historical evidence in support of the kind of analysis we have made.
54. Frank and Cook, *The Winner Take All Society*.

55. *The Economist*, 'Generation Jobless'.
56. See Sen, *Development as Freedom*, ch. 7; Nussbaum, *Women and Human Development*; Waring, *If Women Counted*.
57. Kristof and WuDunn, *Half the Sky*.
58. United Nations General Assembly, *Declaration on the Rights of Indigenous Peoples* (2007), available at <http://www.un.org/esa/socdev/unpfii/documents/DRIPS_en.pdf> (last accessed 30 January 2015).

8   The Globalization of Business Ethics

Introduction

Since 1980, a number of developments have taken place that have markedly influenced the global role of businesses and how people regard business practices. International trade and investment have expanded greatly, along with the number of businesses engaged internationally. The largest of these have seen a marked expansion in their size and wealth. Business practices have migrated into other sectors, where business models are used to evaluate and manage the operations of governments, hospitals, schools, and universities, as well as civil society organizations. Moreover, these organizations increasingly look to businesses as sources for funding and volunteers. At the same time, there has been a slow but steady decline in the size and capacity of organized labour groups to act as a countervailing force able to hold businesses publicly accountable. In industrialized countries, governments have continued to generate new regulations with respect to business practices, especially as they impact on the environment and consumers, but businesses often find ways to manage these regulations to their own advantage. In developing countries, governments have exerted much less influence. One response to these trends has been a mounting interest in developing guidelines for ethically responsible business practices.

By 2010, more than 7,000 firms had formally adopted the ten principles of the UN Global Compact calling for businesses to proclaim and comply with human rights, to support the basic rights of labour, to promote greater environmental responsibility, and to work against corruption in all forms. By this time, in more than forty countries, local chemical manufacturers had adopted national versions of the Responsible Care guidelines that require firms to operate in ways that protect the safety and health of workers and respect the natural environments in which they work. By the end of the first decade of the twenty-first century hundreds of firms were working with the World

Business Council for Sustainable Development. And before they can obtain start-up loans, mining firms must undertake extensive social and environmental impact assessments that may be required by local governments and lending agencies. The International Organization for Standardization has not only established a code, the ISO 14001, to certify whether businesses have established appropriate management systems for responsible environmental practices; it has also developed a corresponding guidance standard, the ISO 26000, with respect to socially responsible business practices. Along with thousands of other leading corporations, since 1999 Shell has audited its businesses annually against social and environmental, as well as financial, performance targets. At the same time, ethical investment funds have sprung up to serve those interested in investing in socially responsible businesses.[1]

During the same period of time and in response to these developments, numerous efforts have been initiated locally, nationally, and internationally to render these businesses more socially responsible and more publicly accountable. For example, protests against global business practices interrupted the meetings of the World Trade Organization (WTO) in Seattle in 1999 as well as meetings in a number of other cities in subsequent years.[2]

This chapter focuses especially on a number of coordinated, transnational initiatives to foster and assure responsible practices among businesses that have been initiated since the 1980s. We examine the various ways in which norms for international business practices have been promoted and are being established: by treaties, such as the North American Free Trade Agreement (NAFTA) and the Kyoto Protocol; by the requirements of intergovernmental organizations like the World Bank; by the efforts of social and ethical investors; by industry-centred associations, such as the Forest Stewardship Council and the Responsible Care initiative among chemical producers; by a number of non-governmental organizations (NGOs), such as the Caux Round Table (CRT), the UN Global Compact, the Global Reporting Initiative (GRI), and Business for Social Responsibility, organizations established precisely to foster common international standards for responsible business; by civil society advocacy groups such as Human Rights Watch, Amnesty International, Maquila Solidarity Network, and Greenpeace. We will identify common themes evident in these different, sometimes opposing, and frequently overlapping initiatives, referring in particular to emerging normative assumptions about stakeholder engagement, the social and environmental as well as financial accountability of businesses, and sustainable business practices.

What we see emerging are the outlines of a set of identifiable normative assumptions regarding responsible business practices. These shared assumptions have taken the form of a practical ethos, an interrelated field of publicly held and discussed moral expectations, which have been variously institutionalized and are regularly invoked. This emerging ethos is not best expressed in any single document. Rather, this shared set of cultural assumptions influence and inform not only the activities of a number of national and international organizations, such as the Global Reporting Initiative, the UN Global Compact, and the UN Guiding Principles on Business and Human Rights, which forthrightly attempt to hold business more socially and environmentally accountable.

Lest we seem to be claiming too much, let us add several caveats. First, the emerging global business ethic to which we refer differs in form and substance from the kinds of international business ethics proposed by philosophers such as Thomas Donaldson and Thomas Dunfee.[3] It cannot be exclusively identified with any particular set of principles or any particular philosophy, but rather is characterized by a set of broad, culturally communicated assumptions about characteristic stances of businesses in society.

Second, although this emerging ethic is widely invoked, it has everywhere failed to gain full compliance among international businesses, even from firms such as Shell, BP, Rio Tinto, the Body Shop, and 3M, which have widely proclaimed their commitment to it. This discrepancy between profession and practice for the most part has not, we think, been blatant hypocrisy. It arises for reasons that include conflicting commitments, weakness of will, forgetfulness, organizational inertia, and the forceful resistance of others. It may also partly reflect the normal time lag that occurs as organizations institutionalize new policies and learn new ways of acting. Discrepancies also reflect the fact that businesses naturally vary in the depth of their commitment: while many embrace these normative ideas as practical ways of managing social, environmental, and economic risks, others add to this a genuine sense of moral responsibility.[4] In spite of all inconsistencies, the following developments are noteworthy. A significant and growing number of international businesses do invoke notions of stakeholder engagement and social accountability, and have invested in organizing their practices in the light of them. In addition, diverse civil society organizations, such as Amnesty International, Greenpeace, and Human Rights Watch, and diverse intergovernmental bodies, such as the United Nations Commission on Trade and Development (UNCTAD) and the World Bank, seek to hold businesses accountable to these moral expectations.

Third, nonetheless, it is important to recognize that this emerging ethic is limited in a number of important ways, to which we will direct attention near the end of this chapter. Certain moral concerns have been overlooked as the global business ethic has evolved, including the appropriate role of labour and labour organizations, and the extent to which businesses add or diminish economic value. Ideas about sustainability have been embraced, but not the larger ecological crises to which global environmental groups have especially called attention. The focus of the emerging global business ethic on concerns such as stakeholder engagement, accountability, corporate governance, and honest dealings represents an important, but not an exhaustive, range of the ethical issues associated with international business practices.

Taking into account all these considerations, we use the term 'global business ethics' to refer to a particular set of normative assumptions about business practices that are expressed and embodied in a number of contemporary initiatives that either are transnational in their organizational form or deal explicitly with the practices of transnational businesses.

Contemporary expressions of the emerging global business ethic

In response to the growing influence of transnational enterprises, there were several efforts during the 1970s to establish comprehensive binding international rules for business practices. On the one hand, the International Labour Organization (ILO) both developed new covenants with respect to the treatment of labour and campaigned for more countries to incorporate these and previous covenants into their national statutes and codes. On the other hand, in 1974 a group of seventy-seven developing countries worked through the United Nations to call for the establishment of a New International Economic Order. In that year the United Nations endorsed this idea and established the UN Centre on Transnational Corporations. In 1976, this centre called for the creation of a legally binding Code of Conduct for Transnational Enterprises. Neither of these initiatives was successful in establishing binding codes for international businesses. There was considerable resistance both by governments of industrialized countries and by various business associations. Having recently been subjected to increasing regulations related to discrimination, fiscal audits, occupational health and safety, minimum wages, as well as air and waste emissions, many businesses in the industrialized nations objected to further government regulations. The corresponding failure to establish and reinforce binding international standards for transnational enterprises has been variously interpreted.[5] In any case, at that moment it would have been very difficult to develop a rigorous code that would have had a chance of being adopted into law by a sufficient number of industrialized national governments to make it internationally effective.

As these attempts to establish binding comprehensive international codes for transnational enterprises failed during the late 1970s and early 1980s (the initiative to create a UN code for international businesses lasted until 1992), efforts to render international businesses socially responsible and publicly accountable took a number of different forms. Actions to establish binding regulations were aimed at much more specific targets, such as the Montreal Protocol regulating chemical processes that endangered the ozone layer of the atmosphere, the Kyoto Protocol on global warming, and the 1997 statute of the Organization for Economic Cooperation and Development (OECD). prohibiting the bribing of foreign officials. Other standards were embodied as particular stipulations in regional treaties such as NAFTA or the European Union (EU), especially with respect to environmental and labour practices. Beginning in the 1980s and increasing in numbers during the 1990s, a number of industry-specific codes were instituted as well. These included the Responsible Care initiative, introduced first in the late 1980s by the Canadian Chemical Producers' Association, the Forest Stewardship Council's international certification programme begun in the mid-1990s, and the Global Mining Initiative instituted by the International Council on Mining and Metals in the late 1990s.[6] In 1992, the International Organization for Standardization introduced an environmental standard, the ISO 14001. Since then, thousands of firms have worked to gain certification in keeping with this standard. Since the early 1990s, the Socially Responsible Investment movement has greatly expanded. By the end of the first decade of the twenty-first century, thousands of firms are regularly assessed by social investment funds and institutional investors with respect to their social and environmental performance, as well as their governance practices.

Beginning in the mid-1980s, a number of significant initiatives were undertaken by international civil society organizations to encourage greater social accountability among international and national businesses (see Table 8.1). We will briefly describe several of these associated with the Caux Round Table, Social Accountability International, the Global Reporting Initiative, and the UN Global Compact.[7]

The Caux Round Table (CRT) was founded in 1986 by an assortment of business executives from Mexico, the United States, Thailand, Lebanon, Japan, and Europe meeting in Caux, Switzerland. The

Table 8.1 Major global ethical standards with respect to business practices

Date of initial version	Standard
1976	OECD Guidelines for Multinational Enterprises
1986	Caux Round Table Principles
1989	IFC calls for environmental impact assessments
1992	International Organization for Standardization: ISO 14001
1992	World Business Council for Sustainable Development
1997	Social Accountability International establishes SA8000
1997	The Global Reporting Initiative established by CERES and UNEP
1999	OCED Principles of Corporate Governance
1999	UN Global Compact
2000	Voluntary Principles on Security and Human Rights
2002	Extractive Industries Transparency Initiative
2003	Equator Principles
2006	IFC Performance Standards on Environmental and Social Sustainability
2009	Global Economic Ethic – Consequences for Global Businesses
2010	International Organization for Standardization: ISO 26000
2011	UN Human Rights Council: Guiding Principles on Businesses and Human Rights

meeting had been called by Giscard d'Estaing, former vice-chair of the INSEAD business school in France, and Frederick Philips, former president of Philips Electronics in the Netherlands. The executives who gathered at Caux agreed to establish an ongoing association to encourage collaborations among businesses in various countries committed to fostering responsible business practices. The CRT initially envisioned itself in much the same terms as the InterAction Council, a group formed by former heads of state – that is, as a group of elder business statesmen working internationally to promote honest and ethical business practices. By the early 1990s, leadership of the CRT had passed to Ryuzaburo Kaku, the former chairman of Canon Inc., who especially championed a business philosophy known by the Japanese word *Kyosei*, meaning broadly 'living and working together for the common good'. As a result of meetings sponsored by the Minnesota Center for Corporate Responsibility, in 1992 the CRT developed a set of explicit guidelines for responsible business practices. The guidelines sought to embody ideas associated with the Japanese philosophy of *Kyosei*, principles concerning business found in Pope John Paul II's encyclical *Centissimus Annus*, and practical managerial counsel from the Minnesota Center.

Since 1986, the CRT has sponsored annual global dialogues, gathering in a different country each year. It has frequently collaborated with the International Chamber of Commerce, Transparency International, Rotary International, the International Organization for Standardization, the UN Global Compact, and the International Bar Association. The CRT has developed a self-assessment instrument by which businesses can evaluate their social and environmental impact in relation to forty-nine graded items, including their interactions with their stakeholders. Seven basic principles inform the evaluation, including justice, trust, respect for the environment, and a larger sense of business statesmanship.

CRT members have welcomed and fostered inter-faith discussions about responsible business practices. They have attempted to facilitate discussions and actions leading to more ethically responsible governmental practices. They have gained active members from businesses all over the world, including, in addition to those countries already mentioned, Australia, China, Russia, Germany, and Malaysia. They have overtly worked to find connections between their views of responsible business practices and traditional religious and philosophical ethics. For example, one CRT paper explored the similarities between the CRT's views and Chinese traditions associated with both Confucius and Mo Tzu, while another, based on a consultation between Christian, Muslim, and Jewish scholars, reflected on the recent global economic crisis in the light of the shared values of these faiths. In modest ways, the CRT has helped to shape the emerging global business ethic, especially through its advocacy of what it refers to as 'Moral Capitalism', and by its efforts to call for greater business attention to the problems of corruption.[8]

Social Accountability International (SAI) represents a different and in some ways more practically oriented initiative. It has sought to foster responsible business practices globally by developing an objective certification instrument for which business could qualify by successfully maintaining performances, especially with respect to labour practices that correspond to a number of basic ILO standards. These standards, referred to as the SA 8000, were initially developed in 1997 by the Council on Economic Priorities, a non-profit research group based in New York City. It was hoped they would become an ISO-like certification process with respect to labour practices. Firms gain certification by having their practices audited by registered, objective third parties. By 2012, several thousand firms from more than 65 countries, representing more than 65 different industries and more than 1.8 million workers, had sought to receive certification in keeping with these standards. These numbers have steadily increased. In the meantime SAI has sponsored extensive training programmes to promote both awareness of these standards and compliance with them. By 2012, SAI had trained more than 30,000 business people.

Whereas the CRT has sought to promote responsible business practices by hosting high-level conferences and workshops among executives from around the world, and advocates voluntary self-assessments by businesses, SAI has been working to encourage responsible labour practices by offering businesses a common objectively administered certification process.[9]

The Global Reporting Initiative (GRI) has campaigned for socially responsible businesses in ways that at first seem broadly similar to the approach of Social Accountability International. However, the GRI has aimed at a broader range of issues, including a number of social and environmental concerns not directly related to labour practices; it has also fostered auditing practices less focused on particular performance measures than on full public disclosure of relevant information. The GRI has especially worked to encourage firms to report on their activities as they relate to a number of standardized queries or indicators concerning economic impacts on stakeholders, environmental impacts, treatment of workers, impact on society, and product responsibility. The GRI has also developed a set of principles to guide how these reports should be prepared: that is, in ways that are at once transparent, balanced, complete, and relevant in terms of their content; and clear, accurate, comparable, and timely in their form.

The GRI was initially founded in 1997, a joint initiative of the Coalition for Environmentally Responsible Economies (CERES), and the United Nations Environment Programme (UNEP). CERES itself had been established a decade earlier by business leaders and concerned citizens after the sinking of the oil tanker *Exxon Valdez* in Alaskan waters. The GRI was established to provide businesses worldwide with a common framework for undertaking annual reports on their activities and impacts. By using a common framework, it was hoped that these diverse annual reports would then make statements that could be compared. GRI's basic reporting guidelines have been modified several times, recently in 2011, the product of widespread involvement from businesses, civil society organizations, trade unions, an international association of professional accountants, and academics. The GRI reporting guidelines are comparatively thorough. They ask for detailed answers to questions about the economic performance of firms and their marketing practices, their environmental practices, their labour relations, their social interactions, and their performances with respect to product responsibility. The GRI coaches firms on how to develop what those involved variously refer to as sustainability reports or triple bottom line public disclosures. There have been several different estimates of the number of firms with which GRI has been seriously involved. In 2005, it was estimated that as many as 600 firms from 34 countries were using GRI reporting guidelines. By 2011, more than 6,000 firms from 60 countries had assessed their performances using GRI guidelines. During these years, the GRI has worked closely with the UN Global Compact, thereby expanding the number of businesses using its guidelines to report on their progress in implementing the Compact's ten principles. Its board of directors includes representatives from businesses in Brazil, Germany, South Africa, the United Kingdom, and Hong Kong, as well as from labour groups, human rights groups, and the World Business Council of Sustainable Development.[10]

The GRI has developed a number of sets of standards for particular sectors, such as, for example, mining and metals, oil and gas, financial services, the media, food processing, as well as construction and real estate. The GRI spent more than two years developing each of these sectoral standards. It has a network of more than 30,000 associates in businesses, civil society organizations, universities, accounting organizations, and governments working to enhance business practices broadly in keeping with principles of sustainability, accountability, stakeholder inclusion, and transparency.

By the beginning of the second decade of this century, the UN Global Compact had become the most visible representative of these diverse international efforts to foster responsible businesses practices. The Global Compact was initiated by the United Nations in 2000 in response to a suggestion by Kofi Annan, the UN Secretary General. On the surface the UN Global Compact consists of a set of ten broadly stated principles, which businesses that join the compact agree to support and champion. Businesses should:

1. support and respect the protection of internationally proclaimed human rights within their sphere of influence;
2. ensure that their own operations are not complicit with human rights abuses;
3. uphold the freedom of association and the effective recognition of the right to collective bargaining;
4. uphold the elimination of all forms of forced and compulsory labour;
5. uphold the effective abolition of child labour;
6. eliminate discrimination in respect of employment and occupation;

7. support a precautionary approach to environmental challenges;
8. undertake initiatives to promote greater environmental responsibility;
9. encourage the development and diffusion of environmentally friendly technologies;
10. work against corruption in all its forms, including extortion and bribery.

As members of the UN Global Compact, firms are expected to embrace these principles, to work publicly to advance their realization, and regularly to report on ways they have acted to improve their own operations in keeping with these standards. These ten principles are stated as aspirational goals, much like the six standards that initially comprised the Sullivan Principles, which were adopted by a number of American firms working in South Africa during the 1970s, 1980s, and 1990s. The compact does not require member firms to undergo regular objective audits to measure their compliance with these standards. Rather, commitment is gauged by active efforts to promote the compact and to participate in learning forums and policy dialogues sponsored by it. Forty-three firms had joined the compact by 2001. The number had reached 3,000 by June 2006. Although at one point more than 7,000 firms in 145 countries had become signatories, by 2012 the figure was around 5,300 businesses, because the UN Global Compact delisted a number of firms it felt were not making concerted enough efforts to support its basic principles.

In practice, the UN Global Compact is involved with a number of other activities. Like the CRT, it has actively and widely encouraged lively discussions about socially responsible business practices. While not directly engaging in efforts to monitor member firms, it has encouraged them to utilize standardized self-assessment tools such as those developed by the GRI.

The UN Global Compact has also been very actively involved in promoting collaborations and partnerships between businesses, UN agencies, and civil society organizations. At its formation, the compact itself represented an alliance between six UN organizations committed to working with it, namely: the Office of the UN High Commission on Human Rights, the UN Environment Programme, the International Labour Organization, the UN Development Programme, the UN Industrial Development Organization, and the UN Office on Drugs and Crime. The compact has gone on to help facilitate working relations between particular private firms and UN organizations, especially those concerned with health, food supplies, trade and industry, and children.[11] The International Chamber of

Commerce has worked closely in the formation and expansion of the UN Global Compact and in the development of many of its initiatives.

From its inception, the UN Global Compact has elicited criticism from a number of civil society groups and critics of current global business practices. As the compact was initially being formed, an international group of more than seventy academics and civil society leaders argued forcefully that the United Nations should not establish this organization and should develop a 'Citizens Compact' instead. They argued that many firms, such as Rio Tinto and Shell, which had exploited workers and despoiled environments, would readily join the UN Global Compact as a way of improving their reputation without having to undergo public scrutiny of their practices through objective, external audits. They asserted that the compact endorsed the questionable assumption that free market capitalism provides an intrinsically valuable way of fostering development. They objected to the way the compact seemed to endorse greater collaboration with private enterprises at a time when these partnerships needed to be critically re-examined.[12]

In spite of these criticisms, the UN Global Compact has steadily grown in membership, expanded its involvements, and increased its influence. Supporters of the compact have responded to these criticisms in various ways. Because of political obstacles confronting any attempt at creating comprehensive international regulations for businesses, supporters have argued that the UN Global Compact contributes to fostering more responsible business practices by exerting moral pressure and by working with businesses to raise the standards of performance. The UN Global Compact has worked to form national networks of compact members in more than 100 countries as diverse as Australia, France, Syria, and India. In order to strengthen the message of the compact, Claude Fussler of the World Business Council for Sustainable Development, Aron Cramer of Business for Social Responsibility, and Sebastian van der Vegt of the ILO edited a practical booklet called *Raising the Bar*. This booklet describes tools, sets forth examples, and provides detailed information and resources to help businesses put into practice each of the ten principles.[13] Especially worth noting is that information about these tools, cases, and resources has been supplied by a number of civil society groups, businesses, labour organizations, and UN agencies from all over the world. Perhaps in order to address the concerns raised by its critics, the UN Global Compact has worked especially hard to develop increasing numbers of working relationships worldwide between businesses, civil society groups, labour groups, and UN organizations. It has also worked to describe the ten principles in terms of sets of practical steps, along which businesses can proceed from their current level of performance further to reduce human rights violations, enhance working conditions, assume a more pro-active stance towards environmental problems, and reduce levels of corruption.[14]

Beginning in 1989, the World Bank through its International Finance Corporation (IFC) began to require that its clients seeking loans for project financing undertake a thorough environmental impact assessment as a condition for receiving loan money. As a result, many firms, especially firms in the extractive industries ini-tiating projects in developing countries, began to examine both the environmental risks that their projects might occasion as well as how they might act to mitigate these risks. In the late 1990s, this requirement was broadened to include social impact assessments. In 2005, the IFC stiffened these requirements by establishing a compre-hensive set of Performance Standards on Environmental and Social Sustainability – a wide range of detailed expectations that became a condition for receiving funding. These performance standards covered environmental and social risks, working conditions, commu-nity health, land acquisitions and resettlement practices, biodiversity, and indigenous peoples.

These standards establish obligatory requirements. For example, they require that firms undertake serious assessments of their risks and impacts, develop the organizational capacity to manage these risks and impacts, not employ children in any ways that are economi-cally exploitive, and consult with and obtain the free, open, and vol-untary consent from people affected by their projects. The standards also set aspirational requirements. For example, firms are expected to reduce greenhouse gas emission, promote the sustainable use of natural resources, and protect cultural heritage from harm by project activities. Additionally, firms are called upon to exert as much influ-ence as they can so that their suppliers also act in keeping with the Performance Standards. Firms seeking IFC funding are correspond-ingly required to demonstrate how they expect to incorporate all these standards into their operations. In idealistic language, the IFC says that it seeks 'to fight poverty with passion and professionalism for lasting results, to help people help themselves and their environ-ment by providing resources, sharing knowledge, building capacity, and forging partnerships in the public and private sectors'.[15]

In 2003, a group of twelve large international banks instituted the Equator Principles as a way of demonstrating their support for IFC's Performance Standards. Essentially these principles require that firms seeking project funding from these private banks meet the same requirements spelled out by the IFC. By 2012, the number of banks supporting the Equator Principles had grown to seventy-six, representing thirty-two countries.[16]

What has eventually become the UN Human Rights Council's Guiding Principles on Business and Human Rights began life in a mid-1980s draft document on 'Norms for Transnational Corporations and Other Business Enterprises'. However, governments and businesses widely objected to this effort to establish global ethical standards. Those objecting argued that norms for business should be established by national governments, which have jurisdiction over businesses, not by an international agency with no authority to implement its rules. However, during the next two decades concern continued to increase about cases of human rights violations by international businesses. Even the first ministerial conference of the WTO in 1995 proposed that some kind of standard be developed governing business practices and human rights. In 2005, the UN Human Rights Council appointed a special representative to undertake research and consultations into the possibility of establishing such a standard. After broadly based consultations, the UN Human Rights Council issued the 'Guiding Principles on Business and Human Rights' in June 2011.

In its basic formula, the Guiding Principles identify both the state's and the corporation's duty to protect human rights, and the requirement that both provide adequate remedies to situations in which human rights are neglected or abused. Accordingly, governments are called upon to enforce existing national and international law with respect to business practices as they affect human rights, both positively and negatively. Businesses are expected to operate in keeping with the International Bill of Rights (composed of the Universal Declaration of Human Rights (UDHR) and the subsequent covenants enacted to implement the declaration) and the Fundamental Principles and Rights at Work of the ILO. Businesses are expected to announce their commitment to human rights publicly, as agents who are in position to affect in major ways both the manner and the degree to which the human rights of people are recognized and respected. In particular, businesses are called upon to exercise due diligence regarding these matters as they affect their own employees, their suppliers, and the communities in which they operate.

Many have expressed criticism of the Guiding Principles because these standards for businesses are expressed as normative counsel rather than obligatory requirements.[17] However, these principles have been crafted as universally applicable standards that could be invoked as evidence that firms are or are not exercising due diligence regarding matters that materially affected the firm and its stakeholders. Most importantly, the Guiding Principles were designed as a

consolidated expression of widely held existing laws and customary practices. Accordingly, states are correspondingly expected to
protect human rights by ensuring that businesses act in keeping with
their responsibilities.[18]

In 2009, at a meeting at the United Nations called by the UN
Global Compact, the Global Ethic Foundation presented a Global
Economic Ethic – Consequences for Global Business. This ethic
closely followed both the form and the content of the Declaration
toward a Global Ethic endorsed by the Council of the Parliament
of the World's Religions in 1993 and discussed in Chapter 3. The
ethic is a very general statement invoking basic oft-cited principles
regarding justice, tolerance, non-violence, honesty, and respect for
life and opposing obvious wrongs such as compulsory labour, corruption, unhealthy labour conditions, and unsustainable business
practices. While recognizing the legitimate role of competition and
the pursuit of self-interest, the ethic condemns 'the deliberate pursuit
of personal advantage to the detriment of one's partners'. At its
inauguration, it was endorsed by international figures such as Mary
Gordon, Desmond Tutu, Jeffrey Sachs, and Michel Camdessus. In
order to foster concerted collaborative efforts to tackle ethical issues
with respect to business practices, the drafters of the ethic assumed
that it was necessary to develop a single basic universally recognized
charter.[19] While the ethic has had little direct impact on business
practices, it has functioned as an idealistic expression of basic values
affirmed by a number of international political and business leaders.

Salient features of the emerging global business ethic

Concerns have long been voiced about the social responsibilities
of businesses. Since the beginnings of industrialization, critics have
expressed outrage at the ways some businesses have despoiled the
environment, mistreated workers, bribed public officials, and exerted
disproportionate influence on public policies. On the other hand,
business people and associations have long histories of supporting
civic projects, donating to charities, endorsing conservation projects,
and working to upgrade the conditions and quality of life at work.
The examples and commitments to socially responsible business contained in this chapter point, however, to the emergence of something
new with respect to the practice of business ethics. What is emerging
is a widely shared belief that any business that is allowed to operate
must endeavour to do so in socially responsible ways. The evidence
that this ethic is widely held comes from businesses themselves,
from the initiatives of the IFC and the Equator Principles, from the

efforts of industry associations, from the expanding role of social and ethical investing, and from positions taken by organizations such as the UN Global Compact and the International Organization for Standardization.[20] For example, in 2005, 64 per cent of the 250 largest multinational firms included accounts of their social and environmental impact as part of their annual reports. In the same year, shareholders filed 360 different shareholder resolutions calling for businesses to act in ways that were more socially or environmentally responsible.[21]

This emerging ethic is invoked under different labels, each based on a slightly different mixture of objectives and standards and arranged in different value rankings. The following terms have been used to define and characterize this ethic: corporate social responsibility, global business citizenship, corporate citizenship, sustainable business practices, socially responsive business, business ethics, and businesses that operate in terms of a triple bottom line. Some of these approaches are more oriented towards environmental issues and others towards labour practices; some towards auditing functions and others towards trade; some reflect the viewpoints of executives while others grow out of the concerns of NGOs acting as corporate watchdogs. Although a number of organizations such as the UN Global Compact, the Global Reporting Initiative, Business for Social Responsibility, and accountancies like KPMG actively collaborate with each other, other initiatives, including initiatives by industries and activist groups, remain quite independent. The diversity of these approaches makes it unlikely this emerging global business ethic will be formulated as a common code or creed in the foreseeable future. Nonetheless, the approaches have a number of features in common. In the paragraphs that follow we will comment on five interrelated themes, noting how this emerging global business ethic especially emphasizes (1) the ways businesses are socially and environmentally embedded, (2) their social accountability, (3) the importance of stakeholder engagement, (4) the value of transparency, and (5) concern for the responsible practice of corporate governance.

Businesses as socially and environmentally embedded

One of the striking features of the emerging global business ethic is the assumption that the performance of a business must be viewed in terms of its impact on the social and natural environments in which it operates. Businesses are thus viewed as social organisms that are expected to protect or add to the wealth of societies as they utilize natural and human resources to produce goods and services. They add to or deplete societal wealth in many ways, including the ways they generate wages, pay taxes, make returns on investments, help upgrade skills, deliver products and services, and make use of local suppliers.[22]

As a byproduct of this view of businesses as socially and environmentally embedded, a number of observers now argue that businesses can and should contribute towards the well-being and development of the societies in which they operate, not through non-business civic and charitable activities but through the ways they engage in their business practices. These assumptions are central to organizations like Businesses for Social Responsibility, as well as to industry initiatives such as the Forest Stewardship Council, the Global Mining Initiative, and Responsible Care. These same assumptions informed the project sponsored by the World Bank and the International Business Leaders Forum to demonstrate ways international businesses can and have worked to reduce poverty in developing countries.[23]

The language of 'sustainability' has frequently been used to discuss the ways in which businesses are interconnected with natural environments. Many of the largest mining firms have chosen to refer to their overall social and environmental responsibilities in the language of sustainability.[24] Most businesses, and especially firms in extractive industries, use the term to indicate their broad commitment to operate in ways that minimize environmental harm, use resources effectively, minimize or eliminate waste, and overall add value to the areas in which they operate. By contributing socially, many businesses hope to compensate for the ways in which they are using up non-renewable natural resources. However, a stricter view of sustainability, measured in terms of the overall finite resources of the planet, would judge that most businesses, including all businesses in the extractive industries, are operating in ways that are not sustainable because they are in fact using up finite natural resources.[25]

Social accountability

In its various expressions this emerging ethic argues that businesses should be held accountable for the diverse ways in which they affect societies. This focus on accountability has arisen in several complementary ways. In the first place, firms are now increasingly being held accountable for secondary effects of their practices, which they previously regarded as externalities for which they should not be held accountable. For a long time, businesses have treated as externalities their impact on a wide range of environmental and social phenomena, such as the ways their physical discharges affected local air and water supplies, the ways their hiring practices affected local labour markets, the ways their remuneration policies affected local retail markets, and the ways their transfer pricing practices affected local public revenues. In addition, they often treated as externalities the ways the overuse or misuse of their products (such as cigarettes, alcohol, infant formula) affected the health and safety of their customers and the ways their sourcing disadvantaged primary producers. Increasingly, firms are being called to account for these practices. They are being sued by governments, civic groups, and individuals who have been adversely affected. As they develop large projects, they are being challenged by public and private lenders – in keeping with the Equator Principles and social investment standards – to take into account the possibility that these projects may have disruptive or harmful secondary impacts. Increasingly, they are required to consider possible influences of these kinds of secondary effects in their impact assessments.

In the second place, the increased emphasis on accountability is manifested in the call for a public accountability of business practices. Businesses are being called upon to provide public reports of how well they are performing, not only with respect to financial indicators but also with respect to standards used to gauge social and environment interactions. An initial interest in social audits in the 1970s gained and then lost momentum. The demand for social and environmental audits re-emerged in the 1990s with much greater intensity and much wider support, championed by local and international civil society organizations and ethical investment funds, and reinforced in some countries by legal requirements. Furthermore, as we have indicated above, a number of international NGOs, such as the GRI, the SAI, and Verité, have been created in order to help firms perform these audits in credible ways. Even established accountancies such as KPMG and PricewaterhouseCoopers now offer services to help firms perform regular, reliable, and reputable social and environmental audits.

Stakeholder engagement

The focus on social accountability in the emerging global business ethic is interwoven with an emphasis on stakeholder engagement. What the diverse advocates of this emerging ethic hold in common is the assumption that the performance, impact, and value creation of business must be viewed in relation to all their relevant stakeholders and not just those who as shareholders or proprietors can be designated as legal owners. The stakeholder model of business has been variously articulated and interpreted by supporters and critics.[26] Many see stakeholders as outsiders who nevertheless have some interests in how businesses operate, legitimately or not so legitimately depending on their point of view. For example, Porter and Kramer criticize the stakeholder model, arguing that, 'by seeking to satisfy stakeholders . . . companies cede primary control of their CSR agendas to outsiders'.[27] In contrast, most of the supporters of the emerging global business ethics view stakeholders as integral to a firm's activity as a business. After all, they argue, how can a firm continue to do business without ongoing, and often mutually beneficial, interactions with employees, suppliers, customers, creditors, and investors? Although each of these stakeholders bears distinct kinds of risks and invests value in firms in different ways, the performance and wealth creation of firms is contingent upon how well the firm's executives and governors manage the interactions among and between all of these constituencies.

Rather than treating these constituencies simply as factors of production, the stakeholder model calls for businesses to collaborate forthrightly with them, on the grounds that greater understanding and commitment will, in turn, lead to more effective outcomes. The model also calls for firms to recognize they are accountable to stakeholders. In the process, the stakeholder model provides a fuller framework for thinking both about effective business strategy and about socially responsible business practices.[28] The social responsibilities of businesses emerge directly from their interactions with these stakeholders and from the interest of firms in finding socially acceptable ways to manage these interactions.

The increasing credibility of the stakeholder model is evident even in the way some of its critics invoke its premises within their criticisms. In an often-cited essay, Milton Friedman criticized the efforts of businesses to get involved in addressing environmental issues and unemployment. He argued that executives should not attempt to address social problems, about which they had no expertise. Moreover, he argued, as they expend the resource of their firms – funds, personnel time, organizational know-how – on these kinds of social issues, they are thereby diverting resources that might otherwise benefit employees, customers, and investors. Thus, in the process of overtly arguing that 'the Social Responsibility of Business is to Increase Its Profit',[29] Friedman also acknowledged that businesses are accountable to their customers and employees as well as investors, and that, in addition to operating legally and without fraud, companies ought to act in keeping with societal values.

Transparency

The emerging global business ethic calls for businesses to operate transparently and without engaging in corrupt practices. The impact of this ethic has been uneven. On the one hand, there has been an increased outcry against corruption, with groups like Transparency International gaining greater public attention. Governments have enacted new regulations, such as the Sarbanes–Oxley Act in the United States and the OECD rules against bribery. Corrupt governments, like that of Indonesia in the 1990s, have been censured and overthrown. Led by the UK Prime Minister, the extractive businesses adopted the Extractive Industries Transparency Initiative in 2002. However, problems persist, not just in the forms of extortion and bribery, but also with much higher cost to the public in terms of tax avoidance and lost revenues, and in forms of abusive transfer pricing schemes and mispricing. Baker estimates the total annual loss to the developing world from these practices reaches almost $500 billion.[30]

Responsible Corporate Governance

The emerging global business ethic includes considerable reference to responsible governance practices. Boards of directors are expected to exercise due diligence as they carry out their fiduciary responsibilities to govern their firms. Special commissions attended to this concern in a number of countries, including Canada, the United Kingdom, and South Africa.[31] Current discussions, especially those fostered by institutional investors, increasingly emphasize the oversight functions of boards and their duty to represent the interests of firms as a whole, including their interactions with stakeholders. At the same time, much attention has been directed to the composition and the practices of governing boards. Boards are likely to act more responsibly, it is argued, if they include a number of publicly minded outside directors and if they have well-established and effective subcommittees. For the most part, discourse about responsible practices of corporate governance have remained fairly general.[32]

Significance

The emerging global business ethic has expanded in the articulation of its expectations and gained in influence since the mid-1990s. As a result, many more firms are developing their own codes, arranging for corresponding audits, reporting on their social and environmental impacts to shareholders and others interested, and establishing corresponding managerial systems to administer these activities. Over time a growing number of business and industry associations have adopted various versions of this ethic (1) as a means of managing risks, (2) as a way of protecting their reputations, (3) out of self-interested recognition of the ways practising this ethic enhances their own business interests, (4) in response to pressure from civil society organizations and transnational institutions like the World Bank, and (5) in good conscience, out of a commitment to the values of an increasing number of business people.

For many people, this emerging global business ethic makes sense precisely because it provides a proactive way of managing the wide-ranging and often unexpected risks that firms now face as a consequence of how they manage their social and environmental interactions. After all, businesses may be sued for products they have legally marketed – such as cigarettes and children's toys – if subsequently consumers were harmed as they used these products. They may be sued for the ways their working conditions subsequently affected the health of former employees. How they act towards social and environmental issues may also affect share value and sales volumes. For example, in response to the way community groups perceived Talisman, a Canadian oil company, to be operating in Sudan, a campaign was launched to persuade investors to sell their shares. As a result, the value of these shares was markedly reduced. To cite another example, in 1995 Shell faced a large consumer boycott in Europe organized by those who objected to the corporation's plan to sink a redundant oil platform in the North Sea, even though this act had been approved by government regulators. In general, retail brands face reputational risks if the consuming public is led to regard their products as having been produced by morally questionable environmental, social, or labour practices. In order to manage such risks, a number of retailers, such as Nike, Liz Claiborne, and Levi Strauss, have worked to improve the labour conditions of their suppliers and have contracted with third-party groups to monitor these workplaces.[33]

Clearly, the appeal of this emerging global business ethic is, in part, its practical role in helping to manage an expanding range of risks faced by businesses. For example, in the United States when businesses have set forth codes of conduct with which they seriously attempt to comply, their liabilities for mishandling risks have been reduced under federal sentencing guidelines. The assumption is made that these firms have been operating with due care and due diligence. More generally, business ethics is viewed as an integral feature of risk management, both by alerting businesses to consult with their stakeholders to anticipate and to identify potential risks and by prompting quick responses when challenges do arise.[34]

For many business people, public commitment to business ethics in the form of standards of accountability, sustainability, stakeholder engagement, and responsibility is seen as a way of protecting and enhancing reputation in a world of widely published abuses, accidents, and criticisms. After accidents such as the chemical disaster at Bhophal, India, the sinking of the *Exxon Valdez*, and multiple exposés of sweatshop working conditions by suppliers in developing countries, individual firms and industry associations began to embrace these ethical standards. In this vein, the diamond industry committed itself to the Kimberley Process as a way of protecting its reputation after violent conflicts in Sierra Leone, Liberia, Angola, and the Democratic Republic of the Congo tainted the industry with the label 'blood diamonds'.

In many cases, businesses adopted various normative standards with respect to labour conditions, safety, sustainability interpreted loosely, transparency, and stakeholder engagement simply because adherence to these norms rendered their operations more productive. Consider the following examples. In the early 1990s, a large Canadian petrochemical business spent tens of millions of dollar in order to comply with the standards of the chemical industry's Responsible Care initiative. The firm worked to improve safety, to develop plans with the community for responding to emergencies, to reduce emissions, to protect ground water, and to enhance the working conditions of employees. In the process, the firm saved more than it had invested as a result of more efficient use of feedstock and more effective use of workers.

Often businesses and industry associations have committed themselves to ethical standards in response to targeted pressure by civil society groups such as Greenpeace, Mining Watch, Human Rights Watch, and Business for Social Responsibility, as well as pressure by global institutions such as the IFC, the Equator Banks, and the OECD. In many instances, business people have embraced these standards simply because they feel it is the right thing to do. Like the executives who endorsed the CRT's call for 'moral capitalism', many business people in good conscience feel that businesses ought to operate in ways that respect their employees and the communities and environments in which they work.

Thus, the commitment to the emerging global business ethic has been multidimensional. Nonetheless, for all its virtues, it is a partial ethic. It does not include within its scope a number of concerns relevant to contemporary business practices. We discuss five such concerns.

One, there are concerns related to the extensive power of the largest, usually multinational, companies. Many of these firms have budgets that far exceed the revenues of most developing countries. In both industrialized and developing countries, businesses have been accused of exerting disproportionate influence over political processes. In addition, whether this wealth was obtained by legal, questionable, or fraudulent means, thousands of businesses shelter earnings in offshore banking accounts, where they are neither taxed nor appropriately audited.[35] During the same time that businesses have grown in wealth and power, organized labour has declined in size and influence, and thus in its capacity to act as a countervailing force against the influence of business.

Big businesses may, of course, exert their power in many ways. They may, as Rio Tinto did before it began mining in Madagascar, use their connections and surplus wealth to spend more than $50 million undertaking social and environmental impact studies, initiating conservation policies, and working to develop the capabilities of local government and community groups. They may, as Shell has done since the turn of the century, devote millions to developing more responsible environmental and community development programmes. However, businesses may also, like some of the large retailers, such as Walmart, force smaller, local firms out of business. They may also use their power to override or gain exceptions to zoning laws, environmental restrictions, or labour codes. Because of their wealth, they are able to hire ample numbers of lawyers and accountants to persuade courts, trade dispute boards, and government agencies that questionable practice can also be regarded as legitimate.

Extensive power vested in large businesses may be used for good or ill. In either case, it is a relevant ethical question to consider fair and effective ways for restraining or balancing this power and for holding it accountable. This question is especially relevant as the involvement of international businesses in developing countries has grown. For the moment, we are not suggesting a strategy for addressing this question. We are merely indicating that for the most part this issue has not been addressed head on by the advocates of the emerging global business ethic.

Two, the emerging global business ethic thus far has not directly acknowledged the extent and the ways international business practices since the 1980s have tended to aggravate economic inequalities in many areas. With several noteworthy exceptions such as China and Brazil, since about 1980, there has been a steady and marked increase in inequality in income levels both within many industrialized countries and between the wealthiest and the poorest countries. These trends result from a number of factors, including shifting exchange rates, ineffective public policies with respect to development, increased cost for energy, tax laws favourable to the rich, and trade barriers against agricultural products from developing countries. These trends also reflect business practices that elevate executive salaries and at the same time engage more conditional (part-time or part-year) workers. The growth of conditional labour markets has had widespread and as yet not fully examined social consequences for those affected, who not only work fewer hours without many of the usual fringe benefits but also work at jobs without any promise of a career.[36]

Three, while many businesses have attempted to act in more environmentally responsible ways, globally some environmental issues have reached an extremely critical stage, as we have discussed in Chapter 4. For example, viewed globally, the Earth's climate has continued to heat up in ways that are speeding the melting of the polar ice caps. Viewed globally, humans are seriously reducing ocean fish stocks, the extent of arable lands, the volume and access to potable water, and the extent of lands covered by forests. Viewed globally, even while more countries seek to develop their economies, there do not appear to be enough resources, so that even half of all humans could enjoy the standard of living of the most industrialized countries. As they currently operate, businesses affect all these trends. Viewed globally, it seems that being environmentally responsible in what have become conventional ways is just not sufficient. Bolder and more concerted actions are called for. Again, we are not here proposing how businesses should be addressing these issues. We are simply calling attention to the fact that the emerging global business ethic, as it is typically expressed, has not yet seriously incorporated these concerns with the urgency they demand.[37]

Four, the emerging international standards with respect to business practices thus far have had little or no impact on global financial practices. Much concern has been expressed about the power of financial institutions, about the increasing negative role of tax havens, and about the decided advantage of those with financial wealth to be able to increase their wealth. Many expected that the financial crisis of 2007–8 would have occasioned widespread vocal calls for more robust global financial standards. However, aside from commendable efforts to foster transparency and reduce corruption, few steps have been taken to develop global standards with respect to the financial sector.[38]

Five, advocates and sponsors of the emerging global business ethic seldom directly acknowledge the fact that many businesses are already adhering to an alternative, pervasively invoked and widely assumed, global business ethic. This alternative ethic, with all its attendant norms and values, is variously expressed in neo-liberal economic terms. Often articulated as if it were not a moral model at all but a basic statement of timeless economic truths, this contemporary ethic invokes values of individual choice, maximizing self-interest, efficient market exchanges, and the use of financial measures and controls to guide business practices. As variously expressed by writers such as Friedman and Buchanan, this ethic has had a powerful hold on contemporary public debates about preferable development policies, effective business strategies, and the appropriate roles for governments with respect to business practices. Typically, proponents of this ethic argue that, as a matter of course, firms should operate to maximize returns for shareholders and view all other issues strictly in economic terms.[39]

In a speech delivered in 1990, John Williamson outlined the major features of this ethic, which he referred to both as 'the Washington Consensus' and 'the common lore of wisdom embraced by all serious economists'. These features included an emphasis on fiscal discipline, trade liberalization, privatization of public businesses, reduced government regulations, the reorientation of public expenditures, secure private property rights, and the self-interested pursuit of economic advantage. At the moment we do not wish to debate the merits of this neo-liberal economic ethic. Rather, we want to note the influential role it has played, shaping norms with respect to viable business strategies, popular economic analyses, as well as the policies of international financial institutions.[40]

In several ways, the supporters of the emerging global business ethic indirectly refer to and critique the neo-liberal alternative. But the influence of the neo-liberal economic ethic is demonstrated by how advocates of the emerging global business ethic articulate ways of modifying and humanizing rather than directly countering the neo-liberal model. Thus, for example, the emerging global business ethic argues for a stakeholder rather than a shareholder model for thinking about the basic character of business organizations. In the process, they call for a broader, more humane view of businesses. Similarly, by adopting a risk management perspective, they connect meaningfully with the commitment of neo-liberals to protect and maximize the economic value of firms. In the process they provide a larger, more responsive approach for anticipating benefits and risks that could be associated with decisions as to social and environmental practices. Additionally, to the economic focus of the neo-liberals, advocates of the emerging global business ethic add a reminder that businesses as well as economies are socially embedded. When the social dimensions of economic practices are overlooked or taken for granted, people are likely to misrepresent the ways economies work and businesses succeed. In the process, the emerging global business ethic is frequently offered as a complement and modification rather than as a substitute for the reigning neo-liberal model.[41]

Conclusion

We have argued in this chapter that a new global business ethic has been emerging in response in part to the processes of globalization. This ethic is variously expressed by a series of initiatives such as the Caux Round Table Principles. This emerging ethic incorporates several basic shared normative assumptions. Accordingly, businesses are viewed as socially embedded and socially accountable. They are viewed as being responsible to their stakeholders and not just to their shareholders. They are expected to operate in transparent ways. Business ethics, in turn, is regarded as a smart and effective way of managing large numbers of risks that businesses face. However, we have also called attention to several limitations with respect to this emerging ethic. While, on the one hand, this ethic offers an enlarged view of the social responsibilities of business, this ethic overlooks or gives insufficient attention to several important ethically charged developments, including the persistence of inequality globally since the 1980s, the crisis character of a number of environmental concerns, and the increasing power of the business world itself. At times, this emerging business ethic also seems to ignore the fact that another, extremely influential global business ethic – the neo-liberal economic ethic – already exists.

Notes

1. For a useful example of the criteria used to evaluate ethically responsible firms, see Pellizzari, *Conscious Consumption*.
2. Barlow and Clarke, *Global Showdown*.
3. Donaldson and Dunfee, *Ties that Bind*.
4. Donaldson, 'De-Compacting the Global Compact'; Zadek, *The Civil Corporation*.
5. Rowe, 'Corporate Social Responsibility as Business Strategy'; Smucker, 'Pursuing Corporate Social Responsibility in Changing Institutional Fields'.
6. Moffet et al., 'Responsible Care'; Rhone et al., 'Two Voluntary Approaches to Sustainable Forestry Practices'; Dashwood, *The Rise of Corporate Social Responsibility*.
7. Another initiative that we do not describe and analyse in this chapter is the set of standards called Principles for Global Corporate Responsibility: Bench Marks for Measuring Business Performance, developed in the late 1990s by KAIROS, the Canadian Ecumenical Justice Initiatives, the Interfaith Center on Corporate Responsibility (USA), and the Ecumenical Council for Corporate Responsibility

(UK). This was an international effort by three very active, religious-based civil society organizations, each involved in monitoring and exposing irresponsible and harmful business practices. By their organized protests and acts of public criticism, groups of this kind had an influence, however indirect, in shaping the emerging global business ethic discussed in the body of this chapter.

8. For more information on the CRT, see Cavanaugh, 'Executives' Code of Business Conduct'; Goodpaster, 'The Caux Round Table Principles'; Küng, 'A Global Ethic in an Age of Globalization'; Young, *Moral Capitalism*.

9. For more information on SAI and the SA 8000, see Leipziger, *Corporate Responsibility Code Book*; Kearney and Gearhart, 'Workplace Codes as a Tool for Workers'.

10. For more information on the GRI, see Hedberg and von Malmborg, 'The Global Reporting Initiative and Corporate Sustainability Reporting in Swedish Companies'; Enderle, 'The Ethics of Financial Reporting, the Global Reporting Initiative, and the Balanced Concept of the Firm'; Adams, 'Tools, Guidance, and Standards for Corporate Social Responsibility and Sustainability Reporting'.

11. Nelson, *Building Partnerships*.

12. Sethi, *Setting Global Standards*, ch. 7.

13. Fussler et al. (eds), *Raising the Bar*.

14. For more information on the UN Global Compact, see McIntosch et al. (eds), *Learning to Talk*; Elson, 'Human Rights and Corporate Profits'.

15. International Finance Corporation, *Policy on Environmental and Social Sustainability*, p. 2.

16. See the Equator Principles (July 2006), available at <http://www.equator-principles.com> (last accessed 20 January 2015); Thomas, 'Equator – Risk and Sustainability'.

17. Cragg, 'Ethics, Enlightened Self-Interest, and the Corporate Responsibility to Respect Human Rights'; Wettstein, 'Silence as Complicity'.

18. Muchlinski, 'Implementing the New UN Corporate Human Rights Framework'.

19. Global Ethic Foundation, 'Manifesto: Global Economic Ethic'.

20. See Waddock, 'Building the Institutional Infrastructure for Corporate Responsibility'.

21. Porter and Kramer, 'Strategy and Society'.

22. Although this is our particular formulation, this assumption has been widely articulated by others. See Zadek, *The Civil Corporation*; Blair, *Ownership and Control*; Blair, *Wealth Creation and Wealth-Sharing*; Moser, 'MNCs and Sustainable Business Practice'.

23. Nelson, *Business as Partners in Development*. See also Prahalad,

The Fortune at the Bottom of the Pyramid; Forstater et al., *Business and Poverty*. The low-income countries least linked by trade and investments to businesses in industrialized countries have had the lowest per capita income. Those that are more linked have generally had higher income levels (Legrain, *Open World*; The Group of Lisbon, *The Limits to Competition*).

24. Dashwood, *The Rise of Corporate Social Responsibility*.
25. Jackson, *Prosperity without Growth*.
26. Freeman, *Strategic Management: A Stakeholder Approach*; Freeman, 'The Stakeholder Approach Revisited'; Crook, 'The Good Company'.
27. Porter and Kramer, 'Strategy and Society', p. 82.
28. Clarkson, 'A Stakeholder Framework for Analyzing and Evaluating Corporate Social Performance'.
29. Friedman, 'The Social Responsibility of Business is to Increase its Profit'.
30. Baker, *Capitalism's Achilles Heel*, chs 3–5.
31. Charkham, *Keeping Good Company*; Bishop, 'Corporate Governance'; Hansmann, *The Ownership of Enterprise*.
32. See Cragg and Matten, 'Ethics, Corporations, and Governance'.
33. Drohan, 'Talisman in Sudan'; Klein, *No Logo*, chs 16–18.
34. Anderson, *Corporate Survival*.
35. Baker, *Capitalism's Achilles Heel*, chs 2–3.
36. Milanovic, *Worlds Apart*; Sennett, *The Corrosion of Character*.
37. Brown, *Who Will Feed China?*; Peters, *In Search of the Good Life*.
38. Palan et al., *Tax Havens*; Piketty, *Capital in the Twenty-First Century*; Helleiner, *The Status Quo Crisis*.
39. Finn, *The Moral Ecology of Markets*, chs 2–3; Fligstein, *The Transformation of Corporate Control*; Daly and Cobb, *For the Common Good*.
40. Williamson, 'What Washington Means by Policy Reform'; Rodrik, *One Economics, Many Recipes*, pp. 16–17; Stiglitz, *Globalization and its Discontents*.
41. Zadek et al., *Responsible Competitiveness*. There is considerable debate over the question of whether firms acting in keeping with responsible business practices are economically more successful. Margolis and Walsh surveyed more than 127 studies and discovered mixed results. The so-called business case for socially responsible business practices remains weak (Margolis and Walsh, 'Misery Loves Companies'). As Simon Zadek, the head of AccountAbility, observed 'There is no universal business case for being good, despite what we might wish' (Zadek, 'Paths to Corporate Responsibility', p. 6).

PART III

Religions, Religious Issues, and the Practices of Global Ethics

9 The Interfaith Movement: Local and Global Dimensions

What is the 'interfaith movement'?

In the process of globalization, the world's religions have played a key role. Throughout history, religions have been transmitters of worldview, culture, and ethics through diffusion and missionary activity, especially in the colonial period. They have been both agents and objects, creating and also receiving the impact of events. In some places, religious plurality has existed for millennia, but with increased migration in modern times religious diversity has grown everywhere, while global media make known the political and social importance of religion. As mentioned in the Introduction to this book, globalization can be understood as a double process of more interconnectedness in fact and also more consciousness of this interconnectedness, of which global ethics is an expression. As the majority of the world's people remain adherents of some religion, the immediacy of greater religious diversity has offered difficult challenges. One response of religious communities has been the interfaith movement, which since the mid-twentieth century has developed an ethics and practice of interreligious relations and has assumed a vital role within civil society.[1]

What is the 'interfaith movement'? The term 'interfaith' refers to relations between two or more religions. 'Interreligious' and sometimes 'multi-faith' are also used, while 'ecumenical' is sometimes given a broader sense than relations among Christian churches, its more usual meaning. We here employ 'interfaith' without prejudice to any other terms or entering debate about which is preferable, and also note that 'interfaith' has now come into use as a noun. We take as our criterion of interfaith any organized and ongoing activity that intentionally involves more than one religion, a broad definition that safeguards against underestimation of the scope of the movement.

Throughout the world today, there are thousands of interfaith programmes, projects, organizations, and groups.[2] No one knows just how many there are, since no systematic global study has been done, but there are almost certainly well over 10,000, maybe many more. They appear to be increasing rapidly. Most of them are local, but interfaith work is found at all levels, from neighbourhood groups through city, state, national, and regional associations to world assemblies. It is of many different types, including city interfaith councils, local interfaith centres, coalitions working on specific issues, interfaith relations offices or committees of religious bodies, official dialogues, local congregation-to-congregation partnerships, campus chaplaincies, youth groups, formal and informal groups for study and sharing, training for police, corporation employees or healthcare personnel, academic programmes, and more. While the interfaith movement is most developed in North America and Western Europe, some degree of interfaith activity seems to have emerged everywhere that civil society is found.

In what sense is interfaith work a 'movement'? We propose the characterization of a movement as an activity that can spread horizontally through its particular values, aims, and methods. It may include thousands of groups loosely related by certain common moral norms, a cluster of shared goals, and a known set of practices. These groups do not depend on authorization or material support from one or a few centres or on charismatic leaders, although such leaders may at times play a role. Our definition of a movement provides an accurate picture of the aggregate of interfaith groups in different parts of the world, which are not sponsored, coordinated, or directed by any single organization or bureaucracy. It is also consistent with the general definition of social movements given in the sociological literature, which stresses that a movement is a form of collective behaviour seeking change. Social movement theory often focuses on aspects of 'protest', redress of grievances, and empowerment, but allows for goals of attitudinal and even spiritual change as well as change that is structural and political.[3]

Illustrations may be helpful here of movements that are made up of groups loosely connected by shared values, common aims or goals, and a known practical method. Each of these enables the movement to spread. One example might be women's consciousness-raising groups in the United States in the late 1960s and early 1970s. The moral values impelling this movement can be summed up as equal human dignity and rights for women. The commonly understood aim or purpose of the groups was to get at the truth about the situation of women as a step towards organizing women's efforts to achieve greater freedom. A very specific summary of the method can be found in a leaflet distributed in 1971 by the Chicago Women's Liberation Union, which tells how to start such a group: it should be small (not more than twelve), it should meet in a member's home or a women's centre, members should speak going around a circle so that no one dominates, each woman should speak from her own experience, and the group should discuss roughly one question a week. The leaflet includes a list of suggested questions.[4] These women's groups spread very rapidly once their basic purpose and this simple but powerful method had become known. Another example of a movement fitting our definition is the Christian Base Communities in Latin America. Beginning in the late 1960s in Brazil with a special focus on the poor, these groups saw themselves as the most fundamental unit of the church. The values of this Catholic movement were peace, justice, and uplifting the poor, as taught in the Gospels. The aims of the movement were to strengthen Christian life, give mutual aid and service to the members, and, when ready, to take action for social change and against oppression. Its approach was egalitarian and person-centred. An autonomous base community was to be 'human-sized', small enough for all members to know each other, and include both men and women, families and people of all ages. It should not have any special qualifications for membership and usually had a local geographical foundation. A base community typically started with a Bible reflection group where the members gathered to talk with one another about their lives in the light of the Gospel but moved on to concrete programmes. It made use of music and the arts, often original. The role of a facilitating 'pastoral agent' could be played by a layperson, not necessarily a priest or vowed religious.[5]

Values and aims of the interfaith movement

What are the shared values, aims, and methods of the interfaith movement? Its overarching value has been peace in the fullest sense, which includes justice, eliminating poverty, and sustainability with protection of the natural world. As Hans Küng has famously said: 'No peace among the nations without peace among the religions.' One aim or purpose of interfaith work has therefore been primary: to lessen conflict and tension between religious groups and to strive for harmony between people of different faiths. Commitment to this aim took great impetus from the mass violence of the mid-twentieth century. Both the Holocaust and the reconsideration of Christian mission in the era of decolonization have been catalysts in this commitment. More recent and ongoing violence and armed conflicts in which religion has been a factor have sharpened awareness of the urgent need for interfaith engagement. Dialogue and other ways of fostering better relations between people of different religious traditions are a category within a still larger set of endeavours with the goal of peace, including conflict resolution, 'intergroup relations', reconciliation where atrocities have taken place, intercultural exchanges, and the Alliance of Civilizations initiated by the United Nations.

A second aim of interfaith work has been to bring religious communities together in joint action on issues of common concern. Multi-religious cooperation on critical issues has taken place at all levels and has included work on human rights, poverty, healthcare, and the environment. While it may well be thought that acting together is a strategy that will be more effective than acting separately, it is also true that the recognition that there are problems that face all of us and not just some of us affirms the overarching value of peace and complements the specific aim of ending conflict. Also, in addition to progress on the issues being addressed, understanding and better relations between religious communities have very often been an added outcome of collaboration.

A third aim of interfaith work has been to achieve deeper mutual understanding between people of different religious traditions by providing basic education and at times also by enquiry into the deeper theological and spiritual questions such as whether we worship the same God or seek to apprehend the same sacred reality. Efforts to achieve better understanding have included scholarship and the creation of educational materials, basic education both formal and nonformal, site visits, dialogues between scholars of religion and also between rank-and-file adherents, and the sharing of arts and observances including contemplative practices.

It is clear that these three aims of interfaith are not mutually exclusive but overlap. While individuals have gravitated to different kinds of work, in essence the goals of the interfaith movement as a whole cannot be separated. The 2002 founding declaration of Inter-Faith Action for Peace in Africa (IFAPA) encapsulates this indivisibility of goals:

> We make this commitment inspired by the teachings and/or norms of our respective religions . . . We commit ourselves to working for the protection of human life and the environment in Africa. We will work to bring about peace, and to forestall violent conflict, through genuine inter-faith dialogue and intervention in different segments of the African continent.[6]

Whatever its modalities, interfaith work has held in view the aim of building better human relationships through direct encounter and dispelling prejudice and stereotypes through sharing of personal experience and accurate information about the religions of the participants.

The practices of the interfaith movement

The generally known method or practice of the interfaith movement has involved concrete action to build good relations among people of different religions. Since this means real interpersonal relationships, face-to-face encounters have been viewed as indispensable, and it can be practised most fruitfully at the local level, where direct contact can be frequent and ongoing. While there has long been a distinction between 'dialogue' and 'cooperation', there has been some confusion concerning the use of the word 'dialogue'. The notion naturally persists that dialogue is a kind of conversation and does not include cooperation or action. Some would take 'dialogue' to indicate meeting to speak and to share experiences, and would say that this should then lead on to shared action. Others speak of 'dialogue in action' and also 'the dialogue of life'. In Christian churches, 'dialogue' has sometimes been construed as a whole outlook and way of life. In spite of this inconsistency, the word 'dialogue' has become inextricably associated with the interfaith movement because of its adoption by both the Roman Catholic Church and the World Council of Churches for theological and policy initiatives issuing in numerous programmes since the 1960s.[7]

There is a common stereotype that interfaith work consists mainly of dialogue – 'just talking' – and is therefore irrelevant to real, urgent problems. To this one must respond that in reality the majority of interfaith work is in the form of issue-oriented practical programmes. Moreover, in cases where the parties involved have never before had a conversation with one another, talking itself has been a critically important form of action. But, because of the prevailing stereotype, we prefer not to take 'dialogue' as a one-word equivalent for the method of the interfaith movement, although it is tempting to do so. 'Encounter' or 'engagement' might be better. We should emphasize that the known and shared method that has enabled the movement to spread has been active engagement with people of other faiths. Its aim has been to cultivate human relationships of respect and appreciation in place of non-relationships of ignorance, prejudice, and hostility.

As Gustav Niebuhr eloquently argues in his book *Beyond Tolerance*, this engagement means not merely coexistence or tolerating those of other faiths, but deliberately reaching out and interacting with one's neighbours with the goal of creating true community that embraces interfaith diversity.[8] Such intentional cultivation of relationships does indeed involve a good deal of conversation – or dialogue – as well as cooperation on common tasks and the non-verbal sharing of culture and spirituality. Whatever design and implementation of these three activities has been appropriate and effective in a given cultural and social setting has been pragmatically adopted. Niebuhr describes how in 1991 Rabbi Jerome Davidson of Temple Beth-El, a Reform synagogue on Long Island, New York, went with some of his congregation in search of their Muslim counterparts. The dialogue group they formed in 1992 with Dr Faroque Khan and other members of the Islamic Center of Long Island began as two dozen people meeting in someone's home. They went step by step for years with caution and sensitivity, beginning by talking of familiar, easy topics such as holidays and family rituals, then of scriptures and beliefs, working their way towards discussion of women, religious minorities, and the situation in the Middle East. When the attacks on the World Trade Center happened a decade later, they were no longer strangers, had developed a significant level of trust, and were able to work together in the aftermath of that horrific event.[9] This was also true of other long-standing interfaith groups around the United States, who had developed relationships among their members strong enough to be effective in a major crisis.

The ethics of dialogue and encounter

Detailed evidence of the values that are expressed in interfaith activities can be obtained by actual participation, talking to participants, and looking at written materials. Whatever their procedures, programmes have the aim of building positive human relationships and dispelling prejudice and stereotypes, working to achieve this through direct encounter.[10] The word 'dialogue' is not necessarily self-explanatory and often is not even used. Nonetheless, the practice of interfaith encounter, informed by certain values and aims, constitutes the known method by which the movement has spread and which has helped give it coherence. When people of different religions meet for interfaith encounter, they have done so with an initial assent, however inchoate or pragmatic, to certain moral values inherent in the process. There have been certain presuppositions about what is supposed to happen and expectations that participants will conduct themselves in certain ways, becoming more skilful with time, and that they will have, or learn, certain attitudes. The specific 'rules' of good relations may or may not have been distributed in writing, yet they do exist and are a necessary tool for actual practice. They have substantive ethical content. Implicitly or explicitly, it is agreed that this process is about bettering actually existing human relations and is founded on respect for persons or human dignity.

The ongoing cultivation of respect and appreciation for the other has been at the heart of interfaith practices.

To look further into these practices, let us turn to a few of the written documents that give a prescriptive account of dialogue and interreligious relations.[11] These have in each case been composed in order to facilitate the actual practice of dialogue by serving as a point of reference. We begin with one created by one of the oldest interfaith organizations, the National Conference for Community and Justice (NCCJ), which was founded in the United States in 1927 and known until the 1990s as the National Conference of Christians and Jews. Its purpose was originally to respond to 'the resurgence of organized hate groups in the United States after World War I'.[11] A one-page statement of guidelines, 'Rights, Risks and Responsibilities of Dialogue', is worth quoting extensively, as it is concise, born of long experience, and is in substance characteristic of such statements. It begins:

> Dialogue is a process through which people share openly and honestly their views, attitudes, beliefs and feelings about a subject. The goal of dialogue is to deepen and widen our understanding of ourselves and the other people with whom we are in dialogue.
>
> Genuine dialogue implies the possibility of being changed by the experience; therefore, dialogue is inherently risky! For true dialogue to occur, participants must have a safe environment of mutually accepted rights and responsibilities. These rights and responsibilities are rooted in two fundamental values: respect for the human person and trust in the benefits of dialogue.[12]

The document goes on to list five rights of the dialogue participant: (1) to express one's belief, ideas, and feelings, (2) to define oneself without being labelled by others, (3) to ask questions, (4) not to change or be forced to change, and (5) to have what one says held in confidence. There are also five corresponding responsibilities: (1) to listen patiently and without judgement, (2) not to make untested assumptions about others, (3) to answer questions in ways that help the other understand, (4) to grant basic human respect to others, even in times of conflict or disagreement, and (5) to evaluate one's own values and attitudes. The NCCJ guidelines close by saying: 'Dialogue is not: a sermon, a debate, accusatory, defensive, small talk, an attempt to convert.'[13] A companion document giving 'Communication Guidelines' and 'Ground Rules' urges, inter alia, 'cultural sensitivity' and 'when disagreement occurs, keep talking', as well as repeating the norms of listening, honesty, patience, risk-taking, and respect.[14]

The Inter Faith Network for the United Kingdom, founded in 1987, is a national-level network of dozens of interfaith organizations, religious communities, and educational and academic bodies. Its one-page set of guidelines, 'Building Good Relations with People of Different Faiths and Beliefs', is also extremely concise and composed with great care for practical use by its affiliated groups. It is divided into three sections. The first provides six norms for exercising good will in dealing with those of other faiths:

1. respecting others' freedom within the law to express their beliefs and convictions;
2. learning what others believe and value and letting them express this in their own terms;
3. respecting the convictions of others about food, dress, and social etiquette and not behaving in ways that cause needless offence;
4. recognizing that all of us at times fall short of the ideals of our own traditions and never comparing our own ideals with other people's practices;
5. working to prevent disagreement from leading to conflict;
6. always seeking to avoid violence in our relationships.

The guidelines continue: 'When we talk about matters of faith with one another, we need to do so with sensitivity, honesty and straightforwardness.' This means

1. recognizing that listening as well as speaking is necessary for a genuine conversation;
2. being honest about our beliefs and religious allegiances;
3. not misrepresenting or disparaging other people's beliefs and practices;
4. correcting misunderstanding or misrepresentations not only of our own but also of other faiths whenever we come across them;
5. being straightforward about our intentions;
6. accepting that at formal interfaith meetings there is a particular responsibility to ensure that the religious commitment of all those who are present will be respected.

Note that the word 'dialogue' is not used. The third section of the document calls for the observance of the same attitudes and practices when trying to persuade others to join one's own faith (an instance of a voluntary code of conduct for proselytization – see Chapter 10).[15]

The close resemblance between these two sets of guidelines is immediately apparent. The foundational value is human dignity or respect for all persons. Beyond respect, which is manifested in non-harming, we should wish to expand ourselves by learning from another, even if this is difficult. In conversation with those of other religions, the most important attitudes besides respect are a willingness to learn, sincerity, and honesty. The most important practices are listening, being truthful, and avoiding misrepresentation of either one's self or the other.

One of the best known of all guidelines on dialogue is 'The Dialogue Decalogue' by theologian Leonard Swidler, first published in 1983 and reprinted dozens of times internationally in a number of languages, including Chinese, Japanese, and Arabic.[16] The ease of global dissemination of this statement even before the Internet and its subsequent wide influence should be kept in mind as we consider how a 'movement' is formed. Each 'commandment' in the 'Decalogue' is followed by Swidler's commentary. He prescribes the fundamental attitudes of listening, openness to change, truthfulness, fairness, and respect, being 'at least minimally self-critical', and finally, 'Each participant must attempt to experience the partner's religion or ideology "from within"'. 'The Dialogue Decalogue' is a much more elaborate account than the other two just discussed, which were composed specifically for actual use in meetings.

The above examples of guides to interfaith encounter are representative of many more that could be examined. A review of these and others shows that they invariably stress the same points. The practice of interfaith encounter is morally constituted not only because its goal is harmonious human relations through face-to-face meeting and learning, but also because the practice itself both demands and gives the opportunity for the cultivation of certain virtues. These may be summed up as respect for others, sincerity and honesty, and non-violence. The moral norms embedded in the practice are viewed as applying to people of all traditions, since the very purpose of the practice is to enable communication and improve relations between persons of diverse backgrounds. The practice of dialogue or engaged encounter is the manifestation of a global ethics of 'good conversation'. The practice must, however, be carefully fitted to culturally defined norms of interaction, which may involve elaborate, specific rules of propriety and courtesy linked to age, gender, and other determinants of social level, a subject that is the domain of socio-linguistics as well as ethics. It is perhaps for this reason, among others, that the words 'equality' or 'equals' are not prominent in the guidelines (except that Swidler states that dialogue must take place between equals). 'Respect' remains central and must do the work of upholding human dignity, while coerciveness of all kinds is prohibited.[17]

The interfaith movement at the local level

As illustrations of how activities at the grass-roots level embody these values, aims, and practices of the interfaith movement, we offer here brief descriptions of a few local interfaith organizations, taking our examples from different regions.

The Interfaith Center of New York (ICNY) was founded in 1997 by the Very Revd James Parks Morton, who during twenty-five years as Dean of the Cathedral of St John the Divine had come to believe that interfaith relations 'are at the heart of urban ministry'.[18] From the start, its mission was to be a permanent urban centre and to include all the religions of an extremely diverse city, rather than form an interfaith 'council' of clergy. The plan, since realized, was to work with the city's grass roots religious communities and a range of non-religious organizations. The ICNY has focused on the cooperation model of interfaith relations in the conviction that deeper mutual understanding naturally arises when members of different communities work together on issues of common concern. With a strong commitment to social justice, the ICNY has addressed a range of issues including domestic violence, incarceration and re-entry, environmental justice, healthcare, youth, poverty, substance abuse, hate crimes, and religious freedom. The ICNY works not only to bring people of diverse religions together in partnership, but also to connect these partnerships to secular institutions, including other civil society groups, the court system, and city government. Work on hate speech, immigration issues, and police–community relations are instances of this religious–civic connection. Its educational programmes have included training in religious diversity for secondary school teachers and graduate students in social work. According to the director Revd Chloe Breyer: 'On the one hand, our work offers civics education to grass-roots religious leaders. On the other, we help religious leaders educate civic officials about the gift of religious diversity. When it comes to religions in the city, diversity is strength.'[19]

The Interfaith Encounter Association (IEA), located in Israel, was founded in 2001 by a group of long-time interfaith activists. The organization's website recounts:

> Interfaith dialogue was established in Israel in the late 1950s by a small group of visionaries (which included Martin Buber). Despite decades of commendable interfaith activities in the country, only an extremely limited circle of individuals have recognized that religious faith and commitment without dialogue threatens the stability of society.

The founders perceived an urgent need to draw larger numbers of people into interfaith encounter. The IEA's statement lists its guiding principles and goals as follows: equal representation of all faiths, equality of the genders, outreach to individuals from all faiths, age groups, walks of life, and levels of society, outreach across the religious–secular divide and political spectrums, continual recruitment through committed activists on the regional and local levels, implementation of interactive programmes that effectively change outlooks and attitudes, continual development of new interactive models for effective encounters, and ongoing evaluation of all strategies and programmes.[20] The IEA has over forty ongoing encounter groups, including Israeli–Palestinian, women's and youth groups; all these make use of a written set of eight-point encounter guidelines and focus on one theme at each meeting. The IEA has more than 8,000 individual 'affiliates' and cooperates with seven Palestinian organizations; it also maintains involvement in international interfaith bodies.

A unique example of interfaith work is in the island of Bali in Indonesia, which has the world's largest Muslim population. Background on interfaith in Indonesia here contextualizes the Balinese example. Although almost 90 per cent of the country is Muslim, Islam is not its state religion nor is Indonesia a 'secular' state. Rather its governing ideology is the Pañcasīla, or Five Principles,[21] and its national motto is 'Unity in diversity'. Responding to interreligious and interethnic violence, in 1967 the government convened an interfaith conference affirming the ideal of interreligious harmony. Zainul Fuad quotes Karel Steenbrink's comment that the meeting was 'a failure' as there was 'unhealthy debate',[22] but this initial attempt then led on to subsequent encounters with an improved atmosphere. In 1969, the Indonesian government issued a decree, renewed in 2005, mandating government leaders in provinces and districts to promote harmony among religions and requiring them to support communities in the establishment of forums known as Forum Kerukunan Umat Beragama (FKUB) or Inter-Religious Harmony Forum. These forums can today be found throughout Indonesia, and are composed of leaders from different traditions whose mission is to foster dialogue, 'accommodate aspirations of religious organizations', and bridge misunderstandings between religious communities.[23] In 1980, the government set up a formal and official governmental Forum for Interreligious Consultation of five major religious bodies.[24]

Bali is a Hindu majority area with Muslim, Christian, Confucian, and Buddhist minorities. In Denpasar, the main city in Bali, a council of religious leaders on the provincial level was established in 1975, succeeded by a FKUB forum. According to I Gusti Made Ngurah, former regional head of the Bali Province of Religious Affairs, the motives for interfaith in Denpasar are religious diversity of the population, the existence of tensions, and 'enthusiasm' for establishing harmony. The goals of the dialogue process, increasingly successful as it has matured, are philosophical insight and 'spiritual development', which enables harmony, better relations on the practical level among members of diverse groups, and the capacity to foresee and avoid conflicts. An advantage for the process is that 'the values of the Balinese local genius [*menyama braya*] are accepted to be the guideline when conducting a dialogue'.[25] This 'local genius', says Diane Butler, can be described in terms of 'the Balinese principle of Tri Hita Karana [three causes of happiness] that aims toward a harmonious human–nature–God/Source of Life relationship in accord with place–time–conditions', as well as 'the wisdom of *eka-aneka/* one–many in dialogue'. These principles not only are a resource for interfaith relations in the present but also have inspired important interreligious creativity in past centuries in Bali. The practice of dialogue to establish harmony has been an integral part of Balinese village culture for centuries, and the harmoniousness created by this process has traditionally been believed to radiate out from the hamlet level into the wider society. Based on these long-established ideas, a process of building interfaith understanding through the sharing of the traditional arts is carried forward by the organization Yayasan Dharma Samuan Tiga, founded in Bali in 2001 by I Wayan Dibia, Suprapto Suryadarmo, Diane Butler, and others.[26] Thus interfaith work in Bali represents a distinctive combination of national government initiative and deeply rooted local cultural values.

One more important example of interfaith work at the local level, but in this case 'multiple–local', is the 'Cooperation Circles' of the United Religions Initiative (URI). Founded in the United States in 2000 after several years of international consultation, the URI is the world's largest grass-roots interfaith network. Its Cooperation Circles are self-governing and self-funded groups, now well over 600 in number in all regions. The instructions for creating a Cooperation Circle require that a Cooperation Circle must have at least seven members and should include people from 'at least three different religions, spiritual expressions or indigenous traditions' (organizations may also join). Each group is asked to give itself a name, to decide what its decision-making process will be, and to choose its particular purpose. Cooperation Circles range in size from under ten to thousands of members, and work on issues as varied as urban reforestation in Delhi, social cohesion in Catalonia, and rescuing child soldiers in Uganda. As URI began only in the mid-1990s, this rapid growth is notable. Not only is this a sign of growing interest in interfaith but it also shows the effectiveness of a simple, replicable, and flexible method in the spread of a movement.[27]

Global dimensions

A number of interfaith organizations, including some of the oldest, have a global focus.[28] Among their varied programmes, these groups hold international meetings of religious leaders. After more than a century of such meetings, especially in the last decades of the twentieth century, the Millennium World Peace Summit of Religious and Spiritual Leaders was held at the United Nations and the Waldorf-Astoria Hotel in New York on 28–31 August 2000. It was an ambitious event with over 1,000 religious leaders in attendance. The meeting did not, however, lead to the establishment of a permanent interreligious council to be an advisory body to the United Nations, as some had hoped. Little over a year later, the events of 9/11 took place and changed the interfaith landscape. While some had pictured interfaith 'summits' taking place at the United Nations every ten years, so far this plan is in abeyance, although the United Nations is developing closer collaboration with the interfaith movement in other ways.

As of 2015 the world's most developed officially representative interfaith body is Religions for Peace (formerly called the World Conference on Religion and Peace), founded in 1970. Its organizational structure includes a World Council and over seventy-five Interreligious Councils at the country level. A World Assembly of the organization's high-level religious leaders and regular members meets every five years. Religions for Peace places emphasis on working with the United Nations on conflict resolution, development, and other issues. A different model is that of the International Association for Religious Freedom (IARF), the oldest international interfaith organization, founded in 1900 with a strong Unitarian and Free Christian background. Its members are religious organizations and individuals that share its traditional liberal and reform-minded values. The IARF has ninety organizational members and chapters in twenty countries and holds a global assembly every four years.[29] The URI has already been mentioned. The world's largest interfaith gathering is the Parliament of the World's Religions. In 1993, the Parliament was held in Chicago to commemorate the centenary of the first such event, also in Chicago, in 1893. This began the series of 'modern Parliaments' held in Cape Town (1999), Barcelona (2004), Melbourne, Australia (2009), and Salt Lake City, Utah (2015). The average attendance at a Parliament is about 8,000 people. In contrast to Religions for Peace, the Parliament is organized on a movement model. Religious leaders do attend, but most participants are from local groups; all come in their private and individual capacity and not as official representatives. The Parliament gathering is open to all and includes an array of programmes on critical issues, dialogues, cultural performances, religious observances, and spiritual practices. The Parliament aspires to convene the global interfaith movement as much as this is feasible, given the movement's scope.[30]

The idea that there should be an officially representative organization of all the world's religions persisted through the twentieth century. Some envisioned this as a 'United Nations of religions'. In actuality, in spite of the periodic occurrence of 'summits' and the existence of global organizations, no such body exists, nor is it likely to come into existence in the foreseeable future. The reasons are not only the severe tensions between religions. After all, the United Nations was founded and continues in spite of international conflicts. Rather, the reasons that a 'United Nations of religions' hardly seems possible at this time have to do with the non-comparability of the United Nation's member states with the world's religions. To appreciate the difficulty, we have only to ask these questions: How many 'religions' are there? What counts as 'a religion' and what are the criteria? Which of these 'religions' will be represented and by whom? And on any of these questions, who shall decide? While the United Nations has just under 200 member states, the World Council of Churches alone has almost 350 member churches, which is still only a portion of the world's Christians – to say nothing of other religions. There is a political process for existing states to decide what entities they will recognize as new states. Could any such process exist for religions, in the sense that 'a religion' might be considered a discrete entity comparable to 'a state'? Moreover, it is also possible and even probable that the word 'religion' may become increasingly problematic in the future.[31]

Questions about the exercise of power involved in making decisions about how 'religions' can be officially 'represented' are complex, intractable, and troubling. Even if some solutions to these problems may be discerned, the practical challenges of establishing an ongoing institution with the enormous budget that would be needed seem insurmountable. The United Nations is a standing body with its General Assembly every year, while the World Council of Churches Assembly is held every seven years, and, as we have seen, international interfaith bodies convene every four or five years, all with financial difficulty. How would a permanent, official council of the world's religions, with many more members than 200, be funded? Again, power issues arise. Given these obstacles, the present variety and dynamism of the international interfaith organizations seems to be a good thing, and, while the officially representative process has its merits, the movement model also has evident strengths.

Within the United Nations structure itself, there has been little place for religion as such. The General Assembly is a secular body made up of its member states (although the Holy See has Permanent Observer status). At the same time, religious communities and interfaith organizations do have a role to play at the United Nations, since civil society groups can associate to the United Nations as non-governmental organizations (NGOs). And beginning in the mid- to late 1990s, some UN officials began to see that the interfaith process could provide a useful mediating structure or 'buffer' by which the UN organization and governments could relate to religion without the problems of dealing directly with religious institutions. This has led to new initiatives, including official consultations on interreligious and intercultural dialogue, the launch in 2006 of the Tripartite Forum on Interfaith Cooperation for Peace as a partnership of governments, UN agencies, and civil society organizations, and the establishment in 2010 by the General Assembly of World Interfaith Harmony Week in the first week of February.[32] Among the interfaith and religious NGOs as well as in the United Nations more broadly, there is increasing acceptance of 'spirituality' and personal expressions of faith; recent developments include the founding of the NGO Committee on Spirituality, Values, and Global Concerns, and the Spirituality Caucus.[33]

The interfaith movement and global ethics

What is the relation between the values embodied in the actual practice of interfaith work and the principles found in formal statements of global ethics? The three paradigmatic global ethics documents, the Universal Declaration of Human Rights (UDHR), the 1993 interfaith Declaration toward a Global Ethic (DTGE), and the Earth Charter, were all intended to be statements of principles that could serve as the basis for national and international law, and in all three the universal moral norms there defined were held to be already present in the world's diverse traditions. These norms were drawn out by a broad comparative study of the world's religious, cultural, and legal traditions that preceded the drafting. In the universalist ethics then set forth, inductively known and convergent fundamental values such as human dignity, non-violence, and sustainability were assumed to trump many of the particularities of individual religions. Each of the three documents begins with a vision of a transformed world accompanied by a vehement warning concerning the global crisis. Their affirmation of peace, justice, freedom, and community has, indeed, been called forth by this crisis. These values are seen to arise from within each of the religions, and, in spite of varied expressions, they have been articulated as universally normative. In this global vision of our common future no one religion is privileged, and the central norm of human dignity, extended to the community of all life in the second two documents, takes precedence over particularities of tradition. The vision of world peace with justice and care for the Earth necessarily includes harmony among the world's religions, and specific human rights seek to ensure this harmony. Religious diversity is thus protected, but in a limited way. Religions are protected as long as they do not conflict with the common good and these core values, which in any case are held to be already affirmed by them. There are indeed areas of incompatibility; gender equality and religious freedom are two well-known examples. As a global ethics affirms universal moral norms, all the religions are relativized at the same time that they are fulfilled.

In this chapter we have tried to show that the overarching value of the interfaith movement is the fullness of peace spoken of in religious teachings and envisioned in statements of global ethics. To live out a commitment to this peace, the movement's aim or purpose is to build respectful human relationships through practices of engaged encounter that express certain moral values and cultivate certain virtues. In doing this, its practices will lessen conflict, foster partnerships on issues, and deepen mutual understanding. Does interfaith work offer a pragmatic ratification of the principles of global ethics? It does, in the sense that there is a strong continuity between the formal and explicit statements of global ethics documents and the moral values more informally and implicitly embodied. Interfaith ethics, however, adds something: there is a striking difference in the language employed. The global ethics documents often use a formal and legally oriented language addressing states and institutions as well as individuals. Guidelines for interfaith dialogue speak in the language of the virtues and seek to mould our attitudes and character, telling us what kind of persons we need to become to increase interfaith harmony. In a practice seeking to build relationships of respect, it is important to act with sincerity, propriety, and sensitivity, as well as with a sense of timing and proportionality in knowing when and how points of conflict can be raised. In interfaith encounter, we must cultivate these skills and not merely act in accordance with principle. In this sense, the practices of the interfaith movement demonstrate ways of interacting from which others involved in the practices of global ethics can learn. Both the practical ethics of the interfaith movement and the formal statements of global ethics are expressions of a universalist ethics that holds the reconciling vision of peace above all divisive differences.

Notes

1. 'Civil society' may be defined as the sector of society made up of voluntary associations formed for any purpose other than commercial and not government-sponsored.
2. For a detailed analysis that has been drawn on here, see Pedersen, 'The Interfaith Movement'; for a full-length history through the early 1990s, see Braybrooke, *Pilgrimage of Hope*.
3. Beaford et al., 'Social Movements'.
4. Chicago Women's Liberation Union, herstory project, 'A History of the Chicago Women's Liberation Union'; see also Sarachild, 'Consciousness-Raising'.
5. See Hebblethwaite, *Base Communities*, and Deelen, 'The Church on its Way to the People'.
6. Inter-Faith Action for Peace in Africa, 'Embracing the Gift of Peace'.
7. See Sheard, *Interreligious Dialogue in the Catholic Church since Vatican II*, ch. 2. The launch of the word 'dialogue', with all its rich meaning, in interfaith activity, was probably the following series of events: in August 1964 Pope Paul VI promulgated the Encyclical *Ecclesiam Suam*, which treats 'dialogue' at length and holds it up as the new model for mission or 'apostolic endeavour', emphasizing that this is to be done in love and not with force, discussing the transcendent origins of dialogue and much more. The Pope says: 'To this internal drive of charity which tends to become the external gift of charity we will give the name of dialogue, which has in these days come into common usage' (section 64; note that not all versions include this final phrase). A little more than a year later, the Second Vatican Council document *Nostra Aetate* (1965) uses the word 'dialogue' and the World Council of Churches subsequently takes it up. A generation or so later interfaith activity is everywhere associated with 'dialogue'. But what happened before *Ecclesiam Suam* so that the Pope says that 'dialogue' has 'come into common usage'? It is likely that much credit must be given to Martin Buber, who said we should live in dialogical relationship and wanted to apply this in practice to Israeli–Palestinian relations. In this historical context Buber was early as well as a great figure. His *I and Thou* was published in 1924, so there was ample time by 1964 for his ideas to become influential.
8. Niebuhr, *Beyond Tolerance*.
9. Ibid. pp. 92–5.

10. In psychology such efforts, along with other kinds of encounter, are studied in relation to the 'contact hypothesis' originated in 1954 by Gordon W. Allport, which holds that direct personal contact, even if not intentional and organized, has the effect of reducing prejudice. See his *The Nature of Prejudice*, and Davidio et al. (eds), *On the Nature of Prejudice*.

11. National Conference for Community and Justice, 'An Overview of the Evolution of the NCCJ', p. 1.

12. National Conference for Community and Justice, 'Communication Guidelines and Ground Rules for Useful Dialogue/Rights, Risks and Responsibilities of Dialogue'.

13. Ibid.

14. Ibid.

15. Inter Faith Network for the United Kingdom, *Building Good Relations with People of Different Faiths and Beliefs*.

16. Swidler, 'The Dialogue Decalogue'.

17. It should be noted that such sets of guidelines for interfaith encounter are part of a much larger body of literature on dialogue and group process that includes conflict resolution, interethnic relations, organizational development, and spiritual exploration.

18. Bell, 'With New Center, Rev Keeps the Interfaith'.

19. Personal communication. For detailed information about the ICNY and its programmes, see its website <http://interfaithcenter.org/> (last accessed 12 January 2015).

20. Interfaith Encounter Association, 'Our History, Values and Relationship'.

21. The Pañcśila are: belief in the one and only God; just and civilized humanity, the unity of Indonesia, deliberation for consensus, and social justice for all Indonesia's people.

22. Fuad, 'Religious Pluralism in Indonesia', p. 65.

23. See Nahrowi, 'Religious Pluralism in Indonesia'.

24. Fuad, 'Religious Pluralism in Indonesia', p. 69. Achmad Munji cites Interfidei, founded in 1991 and based in Yogyakarta, Java, as 'the oldest organization focusing on interfaith issues in the country' ('Building a Shared Home for Everyone', p. 109).

25. Ngurah, 'Dialogue of Inter Religious Community Members in the Multicultural Community of Denpasar City'.

26. An important interreligious event 1,000 years ago in Bali was the deliberation for reconciliation of religious communities in the village of Samuan Tiga c.989–1011. See Butler, 'Religiosity in Art Inspired by Samuan Tiga and Tejakula, Bali'.

27. See <http://www.uri.org/cooperation_circles/create_a_cooperation_circle/get_started> (last accessed 12 January 2015).

28. For an analysis, see Marshall, *Global Institutions of Religion*, ch. 4.

Histories of a number of international organizations up to 1993 can be found in Braybrooke, *Pilgrimage of Hope.*

29. Detailed information about Religions for Peace is available at its website: <http://www.religionsforpeace.org/?lang=en> (last accessed 12 January 2015). Details on the International Association for Religious Freedom are available at the website: <http://iarf.net> (last accessed 12 January 2015).

30. Detailed information about the Parliament and its convening organ-ization, the Council for a Parliament of the World's Religions, is available at its website: <http://www.parliamentofreligions.org/> (last accessed 12 January 2015).

31. Apart from critiques of the term 'religion' as indicating a Western concept, currently the term 'spirituality' is becoming more and more salient, while increasing numbers of people identify themselves as 'spiritual but not religious'. As well, those who adhere to 'non-religious' worldviews, such as atheists or humanists, in some places ask to be included in the interfaith process. Before long this may lead to meetings of 'religions, spiritualities, traditions, and convic-tions' or some other reconfigured wording.

32. See <http://www.worldinterfaithharmonyweek.com> (last accessed 12 January 2015).

33. For an overview of religion and spirituality at the United Nations, see Weiner and Karam (eds), *Religion and the United Nations.*

10 The Ethics of Proselytizing and Religious Freedom

Reasons for seeking or not seeking converts

Not long after his enlightenment, the Buddha sent out his monastic disciples to preach the Dharma. He said to these sixty monks:

> Go now and wander for the welfare and happiness of many, out of compassion for the world, for the benefit, welfare, and happiness of gods and men. Let not two of you go by one way.[1] Teach the Dharma that is good in the beginning, good in the middle, and good in the end, with the meaning and the letter. Explain a holy life that is utterly perfect and pure. There are beings with little dust in their eyes who will be lost through not hearing the Dharma.[2]

The Buddha's charge to his followers has been compared to the Great Commission at the end of the Gospel of Matthew, in which Jesus says: 'All authority in heaven and on earth has been given to me. Go therefore and make disciples of all nations, baptizing them in the name of the Father, the Son and the Holy Spirit, and teaching them to obey everything that I have commanded you' (Matthew 28:18–20).[3] Likewise at the close of Mark's Gospel, Jesus says: 'Go into all the world and proclaim the good news to the whole creation. The one who believes and is baptized will be saved and the one who does not believe will be condemned' (Mark 16:15–16). In the Qur'an, God requires believers to call or invite (da'wah) others to Islam, saying 'Invite [all] to the Way of your Lord with wisdom and beautiful preaching, and argue with them in the ways that are best and most gracious' (16:125)[4] and 'Let there arise out of you a band of people inviting to all that is good, enjoining what is right, and forbidding what is wrong' (3:104). The message of the Qur'an is to be promulgated to all: 'It is nothing less than a Message to all the worlds' (68:52); 'We have not sent you but as a universal [Messenger] to men, giving them glad tidings, and warning them [against sin]' (34:28). For Buddhism, Christianity, and Islam alike, the message to be propagated is universal in intent. In an 1873 lecture, Max Müller identified Buddhism, Christianity, and Islam as the 'missionary religions' in contra-distinction to the 'non-missionary religions' Judaism, Hinduism, and Zoroastrianism;[5] his contemporary Cornelius Tiele likewise distinguished between proselytizing and non-proselytizing religions. The distinction is part of the concept of 'universal religion' that was developed in theology and the study of religion in the late nineteenth century and remains current today.[6] In this chapter we consider the ethics of proselytization and its relation to the human right of religious freedom, a subject that is widely debated and a source of tension in interreligious and international relations.

If the aim of proselytization is to win someone to my religion, we must ask why should that be my aim in the first place? Why should I try at all to get you to convert? The passages just quoted convey two reasons. First, it is commanded. Followers of the religion are told by its highest authority – the Buddha, Jesus, and God speaking through the Prophet Muhammad – to spread the teachings of the religion. Second – and let us put this in the simplest way possible – the stated purpose of spreading the teaching is the good of others, or beneficence. This may not be the actual or only purpose in any situation. But, speaking theologically, to spread the teaching is an obligation of paramount seriousness, which no adherent of these three religions at least can easily dismiss. This then raises the further and crucial question of the nature of the good to be obtained by embracing a given religion. What is at stake in the attempt to win another to my religion? What is gained if I succeed, or lost if I fail? Here the reason to try to convert another and the end result of conversion come together in the vision of the highest and most complete good. The good to which the Buddha's Dharma leads is the lessening of suffering and ultimately its complete end with the attainment of enlightenment. When the Buddha says that those beings with 'little dust in their eyes' will be needlessly lost if they do not hear the Dharma, he means that they will continue to go through repeated births subject to the suffering inherent in unillumined existence. Scriptural narratives of the Buddha's life do not indicate other ways to the final goal than the Buddha's way. For Christians, the good news to be proclaimed is salvation from the consequences of sin, a salvation often called 'eternal life'. Just what salvation is and how it is attained are understood differently by Christians of varied theologies. Traditionally, however, it has been construed eschatologically as the saving of souls from damnation.[7] Such a view of salvation has been intrinsic to the Christian missionary enterprise through most of its history. In Islam, the motive of preaching is to bring those who hear to do good, reject evil, and believe in and worship only the one God; evildoers – be they hypocrites, idolaters, or atheists – who turn away from God though they have been 'warned' will receive the just penalty of their deeds in the hereafter.

Each of these three religions offers a way to what it defines as the highest good and points out the consequences of not accepting this way. Is this way the only way? If it is, the task of proselytization becomes far more consequential morally. If the followers of other ways are bound to be lost, conversion is then far more urgent. Yet the meaning of 'lost' is not the same for Buddhism, Christianity, and Islam. And it is also possible to answer the question 'Are followers of other religions "lost"?' by saying 'Maybe not, not necessarily, or not completely'. One who does not attain enlightenment endures more rebirths, but this is true for Buddhists as well as for non-Buddhists. In both Islam and Christianity views diverge as to whether damnation is eternal, and in Islam it could be said that judgement depends more on deeds than on belief. These are vast and contested questions in soteriology, with great implications for relations between religions.

We should also consider the so-called non-proselytizing religions. We may anticipate that the vision of ways to the highest good may be different if the obligation to proselytize is not present. Some religious traditions not only do not proselytize actively but also do not accept converts at all. The practice of certain Native American religions is not permitted by authorities within the tradition except to those who are born to it. The way to harmony with the Creator, the community of all life, and the Earth depends on bioregional context and inheritance, so that one might be advised instead to seek out one's own indigenous tradition. The Yoruba religion, on the other hand, does accept converts who are not of African descent. Wande Abimbola argues that, since all human beings have originally come from Africa, the oneness of humanity tells against any wish to exclude non-Africans, even though the religion is indigenously African.[8] The Yoruba way is open if the requirements of initiation are met, but no claim is made that this is the only way to be in relationship with God and the gods or Orishas, God's appointed powers. While Judaism accepts converts, the process involves a test of sincerity as well as prior knowledge of the life one is entering as a Jew. The particular character of God's covenant with the Jewish people allows for other covenants, such as the Noahide, and Judaism recognizes that there is a place in the world to come for righteous Gentiles.

Among the Asian traditions, Buddhism has a formal process of conversion. Although Sikhism does as well, it does not seek converts.[9] Jainism does not have a conversion process.[10] While some

Hindu authorities have devised procedures for formally becoming a Hindu, historically this change seems not to have been clearly demarcated.[11] In East Asia the question of conversion is even more amorphous, as multiple belonging is accepted. Today and in the past some have engaged in a de facto self-conversion to one or another Asian religion through adoption of the culture and practices of the tradition they wish to join. Does this happen without any proselytization? The answer is not quite clear in modern times, when many spiritual teachers from Asia have travelled beyond their home countries to share their spiritual paths. Some years ago Albert Nambiaparambil, a Catholic priest from Kerala who pioneered the interfaith movement in India, was reminded that Swami Vivekananda did not go to America and the 1893 World's Parliament of Religions in order to convert others. He replied with intensity: 'Yes, but he went to Chicago *to say who he was*!'[12] For some 'saying who you are' may be proselytization; for others it may be manifesting one's religion, sharing the good, or a form of 'witness'. Today many Christians concerned about abuses emphasize the key distinction between proselytization and 'witness'.[13] Surely Swami Vivekananda had little admiration for Christian missionaries, yet he was a superbly compelling witness for the Vedāntic universalism, which he spoke of as accepting all religions. For him and other 'non-missionaries' who bear witness, it is acknowledged that the highest good may be attained in some way other than adopting one's own religion. One can also argue, as S. Mark Heim does, that different religions may lead to different 'salvations' or kinds of spiritual fulfilment that are all real but not the same.[14] Yet in teaching about one's religion, the ethics still remains one of beneficence or doing good to others. It is when differently conceived goods are at odds that interreligious conflicts arise.

Religious freedom and its relation to proselytizing

With the hope that the religious and ethical nature of proselytization has been clarified somewhat, we turn now to the complex problem of the relation of proselytization to religious freedom. Article 18 of the Universal Declaration of Human Rights (UDHR) says: 'Everyone has the right to freedom of thought, conscience and religion; this right includes freedom to change his religion or belief, and freedom, either alone or in community with others and in public or private, to manifest his religion or belief in teaching, practice, worship, and observance.'[15] Article 18 of the 1976 International Covenant on Civil and Political Rights (ICCPR) has significantly different wording from the UDHR: 'Everyone shall have the right to freedom of thought, conscience and religion. This right shall include freedom to have or to adopt a religion or belief of his choice . . .'; the alteration from 'to change his religion or belief' was made at the request of Muslim majority countries.[16] It is nevertheless held that freedom to 'adopt' a religion includes in practice the freedom to change one's religion.[17] Article 18 goes on: 'No one shall be subject to coercion which would impair his freedom to have or to adopt a religion or belief of his choice' and further states that the limitations on religious freedom shall be only those necessary 'to protect public safety, order, health, or morals or the fundamental rights and freedoms of others'.[18] Here the moral norm of human dignity, affirmed as universal, trumps any obligation to try to bring others into a particular religion, regardless of its truth as believed in by its adherents. The tensions inherent in the right of religious freedom, as well as its potential conflict with other human rights, are obvious. Since proselytization is essential to certain religions, the right of religious freedom clearly includes the right to proselytize – but always without coercion. The formulation of the right of freedom of religion and belief is intended to protect religious diversity, nonconformity, and dissent from interference and persecution by either the state or non-state actors.

Arvind Sharma argues that the original language of the UDHR on freedom to change one's religion signals a bias in favour of Western religions, which not only proselytize but view religious belonging in an exclusivist way: one can have only one religion at a time, and in 'having or adopting' a religion one must reject all others.[19] To this one must respond, first, that this language was revised early in the evolution of the human rights regime. Moreover, the language of the documents does not favour one kind of religion over another, but rather is comprehensive, so that all, and all kinds of, religious beliefs and practices are protected. Some religions place more importance on teaching publicly than others, but they are entitled to protection as much as those that place less.

At this point, difficulties do arise in practice with regard to what counts as coercion.[20] Colonized and missionized peoples point to the collaboration of religious institutions with the power of governments in massive projects of conquest and conversion. In the past, such triumphalism intended the destruction of whole religious traditions and the cultures with which they were coextensive. Some say it still does. Missionaries may be backed by international bodies and endowed with skilful organizational and ample material resources. Let us look at the forms coercion or alleged coercion can take. First, there are incontrovertible examples such as threats of death, torture, expulsion, loss of property or employment, withholding medical treatment, the abduction of women with rape and subsequent forced marriage and conversion, and the manipulation of children, including abduction. All are undoubtedly heinous forms of coercion. There is another form of alleged coercion, however, that is the subject of ongoing controversy. This is what is called 'inducement' or 'allurement', in which conversion is said to be caused or influenced by the conferral, promise, or perceived prospect of material gain and social advantage: money, employment, healthcare, and education, and, in general, opportunities for 'a better life'.

If by changing religious affiliation one stands to gain some advantage in life, does this mean that one's conversion is 'coerced'? We may often think of the embrace of a religion other than one's tradition of origin as the result of a religious quest, a spiritual journey taking years of reflection and exploration. In considering inducements, however, we should remember that for countless people a change of religious affiliation has been exceedingly pragmatic. Some American examples: Japanese immigrants who change from Pure Land Buddhism to the United Church of Christ, Muslims from Africa who become Catholics, and Jews who become Episcopalians. These moves may seem like part of a calculated strategy of assimilation. A convert may feel that all the available religions are good and choose to adopt the one that makes it more possible to get along in life. A person may also convert in order to marry someone of another faith or to find a spouse. Such pragmatism may be condemned by some, but we cannot necessarily say that a pragmatic conversion is forced. Such a conversion may involve little or no spiritual reflection, and then again it may actually have a deep spiritual component. The Pew Forum on Religion and Public Life has reported that 28 per cent of Americans have changed their religious affiliation.[21] Who has the authority or the competence to investigate and determine how 'pure' and sincere any given conversion is? It is hard to see any way that pragmatic, self-interested, but also voluntary conversions can be regulated by law while preserving fundamental freedoms.

In spite of this, there are still serious and complex problems in the association of material benefits and conversion. These lie especially in the connection of proselytization to humanitarian aid and development work by missionaries, especially among the disadvantaged, ill, and suffering. But, although there are extensive Buddhist humanitarian aid programmes, so far we are not aware of complaints that Buddhists have linked aid to proselytization. A. Rashied Omar comments that, 'while a few Muslim groups have imitated Christian aid evangelism, by and large the Muslim use of relief for *da'wah* purposes pales into insignificance when compared with that of Christian efforts'.[22] Among Christians, there can be little question that a link between humanitarianism and proselytization does exist. The US invasion of Iraq was looked upon by some leading American evangelicals as an opportunity to make converts, and the phrase 'aid evangelism' was openly used.[23] Numerous allegations were made at the time of the 2004 Indian Ocean tsunami that evangelical Christian groups saw the disaster as an opportunity to proselytize, and that on site some groups linked aid to religious instruction and 'church planting'.[24]

Unethical practices give rise to cynicism and a failure to grasp that Christianity calls upon its followers to care for the poor – all the poor – and the sick – all the sick. It should be added that many evangelicals will make the point that the mission of caring for the poor and the sick and the mission of bringing the Gospel to the unevangelized are continuous. In a commonly used phrase, they are called to care for both the physical and the spiritual needs of those they serve, so that their theology of mission is a kind of seamless garment. While we decry 'ulterior motives' in humanitarian aid, we must remember that not only material aid but also sharing the Gospel are looked upon by many as expressions of love of neighbour. At the Millennium World Peace Summit of 2000, these issues were hotly debated. Cardinal Franz Arinze summed up as follows: All religions teach us to serve the poor. Conversion from one religion to another must always be free, voluntary, and uncoerced. One should neither be forced to convert nor prevented from converting. It is obvious that we cannot prohibit all conversion, and we shall not stop giving aid to the poor 'because they might like our religion'.[25]

Limiting conversion

In India, discussed here as an illustration, the issue of 'conversion' is highly politicized. Hindu nationalist groups campaign against all forms of missionary activity, declaring that the only purpose of Christian humanitarian work is allurement to convert. An exacerbating factor is mass conversion by members of oppressed castes,[26] who, if converting from Hinduism to Christianity or Buddhism, refer to themselves as Dalits (meaning 'oppressed' or 'crushed'). These group conversions may involve as many as several thousand people at a time.[27] One response has been formal reconversion to Hinduism, one possible use for the ritual of *śuddhi* ('purification') promoted by the Ārya Samāj, a leading Hindu reform movement founded in 1875.[28] Some of the Śaṅkarācāryas, pre-eminent leaders of orthodox Hinduism, have stated that, because God has placed each of us in the particular religious context that is best for us, none of us should leave the religious tradition into which we are born,[29] and, even if one is dissatisfied with one's own religion, one does not have a 'right' to convert to another religion.[30]

A number of Indian states have passed anti-conversion or 'Freedom of Religion' laws prohibiting the conversion by force, inducement, or fraud. Criticisms of these laws include vague language on all three of these points, making an exception of conversion to an 'indigenous' religion or the religion 'of one's forefathers', assigning disproportionate punishments, and failing to distinguish disturbance of 'public order' from minor disturbances or breaches of the law.[31] As well, critics say that the laws' focus on disadvantaged groups, women, and children is paternalistic, seeing them as susceptible and weak. Laura Dudley Jenkins points out: 'The anti-conversion laws reinforce social hierarchies by portraying certain already disadvantaged groups as innately weak and credulous.'[32] Anantanand Rambachan observes that the convert is often despised by his or her original community:

> We see the act of conversion as one of primal rejection and, because our traditions so deeply define our identities, as one of disloyalty to us and our community. Our response is accusatory. We characterize the convert as a childlike and immature individual who is incapable of exercising choice and judgment. We prefer to think that the convert does not cross religious boundaries because of any legitimate dissatisfaction with inherited tradition or anything of intrinsic worth in the other.[33]

We may add that nineteenth-century Boston Protestants spoke of being 'religiously seduced' if one of their number became a Catholic,[34] that in the 1970s, if a young person joined the Unification Church, he or she was said to be 'brainwashed', and that Catholics have been known to say about the conversion of Latin American Catholics to Pentecostalism that the Central Intelligence Agency (CIA) is behind it. It is easy to cry 'coercion' or 'allurement' when members of one's own community leave, but it is also a way to deny the agency of those persons, describing them as easily manipulated and incompetent. In this light, legal protectionism is a slippery slope down to loss of religious freedom along with other civil rights.

It is instructive to compare India with a country in the West where proselytization is prohibited by law on the national level. The Constitution of Greece, while it states that freedom of conscience is absolute and all have freedom of worship, forbids proselytization. In a well-known case that reached the European Court of Human Rights in 1993, a Jehovah's Witness, Minos Kokkinakis, was prosecuted for having visited a woman in her home to speak about his religion. The law under which he was prosecuted said:

> By 'proselytism' is meant any direct or indirect attempt to intrude on the religious beliefs of persons of a different religious persuasion, with the aim of undermining these beliefs, either by any kind of inducement or by promise of inducement or moral support or material assistance, or by fraudulent means or by taking advantage of his inexperience, trust, need, low intellect or naivety.

The European Court overturned the conviction of Mr Kokkinakis on the grounds that his right of religious freedom included his right to proselytize as defined in the European Convention on Human Rights, of which Greece was a party. The woman in question, a Mrs Kyriakaki, was the wife of the cantor in her local Orthodox church. A dissenting opinion of the European Court painted Mr Kokkinakis as a wily, campaign-hardened, smooth-talking militant who 'swooped' upon 'a naive woman' in an attempt to beguile her 'simple soul'. This was after it had been observed by a dissenting appeals judge in Greece that 'no evidence showed that Kyriakaki was particularly inexperienced in Orthodox Christian belief or was of particularly low intellect or naive'.[35]

This brings us to the question of 'coercion' through psychological pressure, which for some includes theological argument or even just the expression of religious beliefs that differ from that of the potential convert, because these expressions may disturb that person's prior belief, as indeed they are intended to do.[36] Such communications could include those that seek to arouse anxiety about what will happen after death or that demonize another religion, and could be deemed pressuring or 'coercive', even if such views are sincerely held by those who express them. When one rides the subway of New York, someone is preaching (perhaps with a threat of hellfire), and one cannot leave because the train is in motion, is this coercion? This happens often, but one will never see such a preacher ejected from the train or shouted down. Is it 'coercion' if Jehovah's Witnesses come right up to one's door and knock, as they do regularly in some places? In the United States, they have won the right to do so through a series of Supreme Court cases that find that canvassing door to door is a customary and accepted form of sharing one's views in American society.[37] On some US university campuses, there are policies that one cannot discuss religious matters with a student unless he or she gives permission to do so, but one may make the initial approach.[38] In those cases when a person is protected from undue pressure by the proselytizer, the relevant rules do not forbid teaching about religion specifically. Rather they protect my privacy and I am kept safe from harassment, whether the approach to me is about religion or something else. At the same time, the freedom of religion and freedom of expression of the person approaching me are also protected. In a public setting in an open society, one is supposed to ignore or dismiss the expression of views with which one disagrees, even if they are troubling or offensive. Yet the 'thick skin' Americans are expected to have when proselytized is not and cannot be assumed everywhere.

Concluding observations

Where does this leave us? It is our hope to have shown that all this brings us to an impasse with regard to the question of regulation of proselytization by law. There does not seem to be a way to restrict it legally without dangerous risks to religious freedom. One may be sympathetic to some motives for restricting proselytization, but it is very hard to see how to formulate in legal terms what has been called 'a right to be let alone'. Some exceptional arguments might be made in the case of a small, isolated, and culturally homogenous territory such as a Native American reservation or the country of Bhutan, or in cases of large-scale infusions of money or personnel from outside a locality, but even then protectionist policies must be scrutinized. In a religiously diverse setting, legal restriction seems highly problematic if it is more extensive than the general prohibition of coercion already found in human rights documents.

In conclusion, we propose instead several kinds of constructive action as we engage in the ethical problems arising from proselytization. The first is the robust claiming of human rights. It is never enough for human rights to be inscribed in documents. Citizens must be vigilant, well informed, and dynamic in ensuring that they are able to exercise their rights. Second, religious adherents must build commitment within their own communities. Members who worry that their heritage will be damaged or lost, or just that they will lose members, must attend to religious education including precautionary teaching, foster regular observance, and be self-critical about any factors that promote voluntary departure, such as social injustice, sterile worship, shallow formation, and merely nominal belonging. Third, the development and adherence to voluntary codes of ethical conversion, especially by religious bodies, must be supported. At the July 2004 Parliament of the World's Religions in Barcelona, Seshagiri Rao presented an 'Interreligious Code of Conduct', which he had drafted. Subsequently, the World Council of Churches (which has almost 350 member churches), the Pontifical Council for Interreligious Dialogue (PCID) of the Roman Catholic Church, and the World Evangelical Alliance entered a five-year consultation process. These three bodies represent almost 90 per cent of the world's two billion Christians. In June 2011, they jointly issued the document 'Christian Witness in a Multi-Religious World: Recommendations for Conduct'.[39] This is a historic step in the right direction. In the absence of any simple legal remedies for wrongful proselytization, such voluntary ethical codes can play a very important role. Fourth, in such codes and elsewhere, the distinction between proselytization and 'witness', to use Christian language, must be spelled out and promoted. Fifth and finally, it might be helpful if actual conversion in any religious context were always a somewhat exacting process, as it is in Judaism, to ensure its voluntary nature. Jewish tradition advises that converts should be treated according to the rabbinical maxim 'Bring them close with the right hand and keep them distant with the left'.[40] This test of sincerity and commitment is admirable, but it cannot be implemented without equal sincerity by clergy or the other religionists who conduct the conversion.

We may wonder whether controversy over proselytization may fade even without these constructive measures. Throughout this chapter we have referred to religions as if they are discrete entities with clear boundaries between them, speaking as if religious belonging is exclusive, as some think it should be. This is not a true picture of religious life as really lived by much of humanity. Arvind Sharma stresses that in Asia it is well understood that one may belong to more than one religion at a time, and that proselytization aiming at 'change of religion' and exclusive adherence to a new religion are Western concepts. In Asian cultures, and indeed in some others,[41] proselytization aimed at religious exclusivism may in the past have been either meaningless or a drastic religio-cultural imposition. But now it is not only in Asia that we recognize 'double belonging', 'multiple participation', and 'practising across boundaries'. This is a well-recognized trend and can be a kind of pragmatic pluralism or an 'integral spirituality'.[42] Last but hardly least, soteriologies are shifting. A 2008 study by the Pew Forum on Religion and Public Life reported that 70 per cent of Americans and even 57 per cent of US evangelicals say that one can be 'saved' in a religion other than one's own.[43] Belief in damnation is also under challenge.[44] These heartening changes are one result of positive responses to the encounter of religions now taking place throughout the world, even though the fact of religious plurality is still unwelcome to many.

The questions and issues connected to religious freedom and conversion are especially challenging to global ethics. From an interreligious perspective and in a constructive mode, we may wish to affirm that the elements of a global ethic are already present in the world's religions, but here the right of freedom of religion can be highly problematic. Some believers may hold that it is far more important to adhere to the true religion than to be permitted to choose one's religion. In such cases, the value of religious freedom is contradicted by the very religious convictions that one is free to hold. To this some may respond that a coerced conversion or belief is actually not a valid one, and, even if there is true and false religion, still, 'Let there be no compulsion in religion' (Qur'an 2:256). For still others, the obligation to defend and remain in one's own culture and tradition may override all other duties. Yet there seems to be a measure of common ground between at least some of those who oppose proselytization and those who want to allow it. In discussions of 'ethical conversion', many have come to agree that violence and coercion are unacceptable and that both sides can affirm the norms of respect and human dignity. In spite of disagreement on belief and practice, some basic moral values shine forth as universally intelligible. The fact that we can engage at all in these discussions shows that some aspects of a global ethic are mutually understood as we try to find ways to live together as neighbours.[45]

Notes

1. See *The Book of the Discipline* (*Vinaya Pitaka*), trans. I. B. Horner, p. 28.
2. Mahavagga of the Vinaya, 1.11.1., as cited in Ñāṇamoli, *The Life of the Buddha According to the Pali Canon*, p. 52.
3. Biblical citations are from the New Revised Standard Version.
4. Qur'anic citations are from *The Qur'an*, trans. Abdullah Yusuf Ali.
5. Müller, *Chips from a German Workshop*, p. 253, as quoted in Sharma, *Problematizing Religious Freedom*, p. 175.
6. See Adcock, *The Limits of Tolerance*, ch. 3; she states that her account follows Masuzawa, *The Invention of World Religions*.
7. It should be mentioned that, in a comparative perspective, damnation and hell are not the same, since in Asian religions one does not reside in hell eternally, but only for as long as one's evil karma determines.
8. Workshop on Ifa divination, New York Open Center, 2003.
9. Tarunjit Singh Butalia, personal communication.
10. Naresh Jain, personal communication.
11. See Sharma, *Problematizing Religious Freedom*, ch. VIII.
12. Personal communication to Kusumita P. Pedersen.
13. See Acts 1:8: 'you will receive power when the Holy Spirit has come upon you; and you will be my witnesses in Jerusalem, in all Judea and Samaria, and to the ends of the earth.'

14. Heim develops this position in *Salvations*.
15. The declaration and the two covenants are widely available. We cite United Nations, *International Bill of Human Rights*.
16. Lerner, 'Proselytism, Change of Religion, and International Human Rights', pp. 511–12. The wording had already been contested during the drafting of the UDHR; see pp. 500–3.
17. As stated, for example, in the 1993 General Comment on Freedom of Religion or Belief of the Human Rights Committee. See Ibid. pp. 516–18.
18. We should also note that the 1981 Declaration on the Elimination of All Forms of Intolerance and Discrimination Based on Religion or Belief reiterates the ICCPR's language, while it also stresses respect, calls on states to take steps to eliminate intolerance, explains the nature of 'discrimination', and includes in its list of specific freedoms 'to write and issue and disseminate publications' and 'to teach a religion or belief in places suitable for these purposes' (Article 6).
19. Sharma, *Problematizing Religious Freedom*, ch. X; see also Sharma, 'Measuring the Reach of a Universal Right'.
20. For a detailed and nuanced account of objections to proselytization, see Kao, 'The Logic of Anti-Proselytization, Revisited'.
21. Pew Forum on Religion and Public Life, *US Religious Landscape Survey*, report 1, 'Religious Affiliation', ch. 2.
22. A. Rashied Omar, personal communication.
23. See Omar, 'The Right to Religious Conversion', and Kao, 'The Logic of Anti-Proselytization, Revisited', pp. 92–3.
24. See Burke, 'Religious Aid Groups Try to Convert Victims'; see Kao, 'The Logic of Anti-Proselytization, Revisited', pp. 80–1.
25. Pedersen, 'Religious Freedom, the Right to Proselytize, and the "Right to be Let Alone"'.
26. We follow the practice of Sachi G. Dastidar in using this term for those also called 'Untouchables', who, if they have not converted from Hinduism, prefer to be called by the proper name of their particular social group.
27. See Miglani and Miglani, 'Right to Religious Freedom versus Religious Conversion'; see also Croucher, 'Indian Police Obstruct Mass Conversions of Untouchables to Buddhism and Christianity', and BBC News, 'Mass Dalit Conversions in Mumbai'.
28. For a detailed history and analysis of *śuddhi*, see Adcock, *The Limits of Tolerance* and 'Debating Conversion, Silencing Caste'.
29. Bharati, *Golden Words*, p. 33.
30. Sri Jayendra Saraswati, interviewed by Saisuresh Sivaswami, *India Abroad*.
31. See South Asia Human Rights Documentation Center, 'Anti-Conversion Laws'.

32. Jenkins, 'Legal Limits on Religious Conversion in India', p. 113.

33. Rambachan, 'Hindus and Christians', p. 13.

34. Cox, 'Deep Structures in the Study of New Religions'. Cox discusses four themes or 'myths' in mainstream attacks on 'marginal' religions; among them the myth of 'the evil eye', which sees the acceptance of a new religion not as voluntary but as the result of magic, charisma, or some other kind of bewitchment.

35. See European Court of Human Rights, 'Kokkinakis vs Greece'.

36. Indian anti-conversion laws include 'threat of divine displeasure' as a form of coercion; see South Asia Human Rights Documentation Center, 'Anti-Conversion Laws', p. 64.

37. See How and Brumley, 'Human Rights, Evangelism and Proselytism'.

38. See Sharma, 'Measuring the Reach of a Universal Right'.

39. See World Council of Churches, Pontifical Council on Interreligious Dialogue, and World Evangelical Alliance, 'Christian Witness in a Multi-Religious World'.

40. See Lamm, *Becoming a Jew*, p. 88.

41. In some Native American and indigenous communities, a nominal acceptance of a new religion could be a kind of courtesy. One could also 'convert' to explore and enquire into an unfamiliar tradition. Historically such crossing of boundaries may have been much more common than is often noted.

42. Pedersen, 'Spirituality beyond the Boundaries of Religion'.

43. Pew Forum on Religion and Public Life, *US Religious Landscape Survey*, report 2.

44. See Niebuhr, 'Hell is Getting a Makeover from Catholics'; Sheler, 'Hell Hath No Fury'; and Griffiths et al., 'What to Say About Hell'.

45. We would like to thank Chad Bauman, John Berthrong, David B. Burrell, Tarunjit Singh Butalia, Naresh Jain, Ramdas Lamb, David Little, Elias Mallon, Lucinda Mosher, A. Rashied Omar, Arvind Sharma, Hans Ucko, and Matt Weiner for their helpful comments.

11 Towards a Global Ethic for Education about Religions and Beliefs in State/Public Schools

Introduction

As we observed in the Introduction to this book, the various practices of global ethics have developed in response to problem areas that have emerged or become more apparent because of globalization. Among the most significant of these is an educational one – namely, how are we to learn to live with our deepest religious, philosophical, moral, and cultural differences rather than being torn apart by them? It is in this context that the topic of religious education in public schools figures ever more prominently on the world stage.* Even before the events of 9/11, there was growing recognition that knowledge about diverse religious and secular worldviews was indispensable for basic historical and cultural literacy, as well as for the exercise of responsible citizenship in this era of an increasing experience of religious diversity. Since 9/11, discussions of religious education in public schools have taken on a greater sense of urgency and begun to attract the attention not only of scholars, educators, and interfaith activists but also of governmental and intergovernmental organizations and policymakers. It has been further heightened by subsequent

---

* Although the distinction between 'public' and 'private' schools varies from country to country, in the present discussion 'public schools' are those 'whose organization, financing and management are primarily the responsibility of, or under the primary oversight of, a public body (state, regional, municipal, etc.). A "private school" is a school in which, irrespective of whether it may receive degrees of support (including financial support) from public sources, matters of organization, financing, and management are primarily the responsibility of the school itself, or of a non-public sponsoring body' (OSCE, *Toledo Guiding Principles*, p. 20). Major sections of this chapter are drawn from Grelle, 'Promoting Civic and Religious Literacy in Public Schools'; 'The First Amendment Consensus Approach to Teaching about Religion in US Public Schools'; and 'Neutrality in Public School Religion Education'.

events, ranging from persistent Islamophobia in the West to ongoing persecution of religious minorities throughout the world.

This chapter traces the development of what appears to be an emerging international framework for thinking about the rationale and guidelines for a non-devotional, academic, and pluralistic approach to teaching about religions and beliefs in public schools. This framework rests on several assumptions and arguments about the relationship between religious education and human rights, a relationship that sets the ethical, legal, and pedagogical context for thinking about religious education in public school settings. While it may be premature to describe this emerging framework as a truly 'global' ethic, it is gaining influence in Europe, North America, and beyond.

Religious education and human rights: An emerging international framework

The emerging international guidelines for religious education represent an important by-product of the human rights tradition discussed in Chapter 1 of this book. The Charter of the United Nations and the Universal Declaration of Human Rights (UDHR), along with numerous subsequent UN covenants, conventions, and declarations, make reference to 'the right to freedom of thought, conscience and religion' (Article 18 of the UDHR) and to the role of education in promoting respect for this right (Article 26.2 of the UDHR).[1] International public concern regarding religious education began to receive serious attention in the 1990s and much more organized attention with the beginning of the new century.

In 2000 the United Nations Educational, Scientific, and Cultural Organization (UNESCO) published its 'Dakar Framework for Action – Education for All: Meeting our Collective Commitments', which emphasized the role of schools in promoting understanding among religious groups and the need for governmental institutions to develop partnerships with religious groups in educational contexts. UNESCO's Interreligious Dialogue Programme has correspondingly aimed to promote understanding between religions or beliefs and publishes pedagogical material supporting education in the field of interreligious dialogue.

The topic of religious education was the focus of the International Consultative Conference on School Education in relation to Freedom of Religion and Belief, Tolerance, and Non-Discrimination, which took place in Madrid in November 2001. This conference was organized by the UN High Commissioner for Human Rights on the occasion of the twentieth anniversary of the General Assembly's 1981 Declaration on the Elimination of All Forms of Intolerance and of Discrimination Based on Religion or Belief. The 'Final Document' of the Madrid Conference underlined 'the urgent need to promote, through education, the protection and the respect for freedom of religion or belief in order to strengthen peace, understanding and tolerance among individuals, groups and nations, and with a view to developing a respect for pluralism'.[2] It asserted that each state 'should promote and respect educational policies aimed at strengthening the promotion and protection of human rights, eradicating prejudices and conceptions incompatible with freedom of religion or belief, and ensuring respect for and acceptance of pluralism and diversity in the field of religion or belief as well as the right not to receive religious instruction inconsistent with his or her conviction'.[3] It understood that 'freedom of religion or belief includes theistic, non-theistic and atheistic beliefs, as well as the right not to profess any religion or belief'.[4]

In 2005, the United Nations launched the Alliance of Civilizations initiative. The alliance was designed to counter the narrative of a 'clash of civilizations' and the widespread influence that this idea has had on public attitudes and discourse in international policy. One of the projects of this initiative was the development of an online Education about Religions and Beliefs (ERB) clearing house. Working through a network of partner organizations including universities, civil society organizations, and other UN and intergovernmental organizations, the clearing house has aimed to provide an international forum for discussions of religious education as well as such practical resources as teaching tools and syllabi, curricula, evaluations of curricular outcomes, and consensus guidelines that have been drawn up at various national and international levels.[5]

The Council of Europe (CoE) has long been engaged with the topic of intercultural education and dialogue. Although the values of freedom of religion or belief and education for tolerance are embedded in CoE documents, it was only post 9/11 that the CoE became directly involved in discussions about the place of religion in public education.[6] Since 2002, the CoE has organized a working group and a series of conferences to consider the 'religious dimension' of intercultural education. It has sponsored the production of a reference book for educators, administrators, and policymakers to help deal with the issue of religious diversity in schools, and it has cooperated with the government of Norway in the establishment of the interdisciplinary European Wergeland Centre on education for intercultural understanding, human rights, and democratic citizenship, which includes attention to the religious dimension of such education.[7] In 2008, the CoE Committee of Ministers adopted a recommendation to member states on the dimension of religions and non-religious convictions within intercultural education, which aims to ensure that governments take into account the religious dimension of intercultural education at the level of educational policies, institutions, and professional development of teaching staff.[8]

Meanwhile, in 2007 the Office for Democratic Institutions and Human Rights (ODIHR) of the Organization for Security and Cooperation in Europe (OSCE) prepared the *Toledo Guiding Principles on Teaching about Religions and Beliefs in Public Schools*. The OSCE includes among its fifty-seven members most European states as well as Canada and the United States. The *Toledo Guiding Principles* aimed to contribute to 'an improved understanding of the world's increasing religious diversity and the growing presence of religion in the public sphere'.[9] The *Toledo Guiding Principles* were grounded on two basic assumptions: 'First, that there is positive value in teaching that emphasizes respect for *everyone's* right to freedom of religion and belief, and second, that teaching *about* religions and beliefs can reduce harmful misunderstandings and stereotypes.'[10] In addition to providing the context and rationale for teaching about religion in public schools, the *Toledo Guiding Principles* addressed the relationship between religion, education, law, and human rights; curricula and pedagogy; teacher education; and policies for the implementation of religious education programmes in ways that respect the rights of students and parents and are consistent with the human rights framework. There are many ways in which the *Toledo Guiding Principles* exemplify efforts to develop guidelines for a neutral academic approach to religious education in public schools. We will make frequent reference to them in what follows.

One noteworthy example of how a human rights-based academic approach to religious education has been translated into a specific curriculum is the mandatory course on Ethics and Religious Culture (ERC) developed for the primary and secondary schools in Quebec. The implementation of the ERC programme in 2008 was part of Quebec's shift away from a long history of confessional public schools to a non-denominational school system now identified linguistically as either French or English. Previously, students chose a course in either Catholic or Protestant moral and religious education or a course in secular moral education.[11] Social and intellectual changes associated with globalization and increasing pluralism were among the justifications offered in support of replacing this denominationally based system of religious education with a common ERC programme.

The two main objectives of the ERC programme are 'recognition of others' and 'pursuit of the common good'.[12] The programme aims to help students grasp the multiple dimensions of religion – historical, doctrinal, moral, ritual, artistic, and so on. The historical and cultural importance of Catholicism and Protestantism to Quebec's religious heritage are highlighted, but attention is also given to the influence of Judaism and Native spirituality, to other religions that are today a part of Quebec's culture, and to secular expressions and representations of the world and of human beings.[13] 'Respecting the fundamental right to the freedom of conscience and religion is the basis of all ethics and religious education.'[14]

In 2010, the American Academy of Religion (AAR), a US-based international association of religion scholars, produced one of the most comprehensive statements regarding the fitting role of education about religion in public schools. The AAR *Guidelines for Teaching about Religion in K-12 Public Schools in the United States* were based on three premises: (1) illiteracy regarding religion is widespread; (2) it fuels prejudice and antagonism; and (3) it can be diminished by teaching about religions in public schools using a non-devotional, academic perspective called 'religious studies'.[15]

The AAR *Guidelines* were formulated against the backdrop of developments reaching back to the 1980s, when a movement towards greater inclusion of religion in the curriculum of US public schools began to emerge. During this time, both the National Council for the Social Studies (1984) and the Association for Supervision and Curriculum Development (1988) issued statements calling for more attention to be given to religion.[16] Subsequently, a series of consensus guidelines based on First Amendment principles and emphasizing the distinction between *academic* and *devotional* approaches were developed, and several of these were distributed to every public school in the nation by the US Department of Education.[17] (See Table 11.1).

When it comes to the representation of religions and beliefs in teaching and curricula, all these various documents and initiatives share a number of things in common. They recognize that there are a range of different pedagogical theories and practices that have been developed within the overall context of an academic or religious studies approach to religious education. Yet they all seek to cultivate an 'empathetic' attitude among learners and, in the words of the *Toledo Guiding Principles*, 'to genuinely understand what another person is feeling and . . . to respectfully communicate another person's experience'.[18] They all require a school ethos where there is respect for difference and where human rights principles are upheld, and they all require a high degree of professionalism on the part of teachers.

Whatever pedagogical approach is taken, emphasis is placed on fairness, accuracy, and sound scholarship. For example, the *Toledo*

Guiding Principles stipulate that 'teaching about religions and beliefs should be sensitive, balanced, inclusive, non-doctrinal, impartial, and based on human rights principles relating to freedom of religion or belief'.[19] Moreover, there is the expectation that curricula will adhere to recognized professional standards. 'This implies that, among other things, the information contained in curricula is based on reason, is accurate, bias-free, up to date, and does not over-simplify complex issues. It also implies that curricula are age appropriate . . .'[20]

Beyond this stress on accuracy, scholarship, and professionalism, there is widespread consensus on a number of points having to do with what students should learn about religions in public schools. These include what the AAR *Guidelines* identify as the 'basic premises of religious studies', namely that (1) religions are internally diverse, (2) religions are dynamic and change over time, and (3) religions are embedded in culture.[21]

Besides the question of how religions and beliefs are to be

Table 11.1 Statements and initiatives regarding religious freedom and religious education

Date	Statement/initiative
1981	UN General Assembly: 'Declaration on the Elimination of All Forms of Intolerance and Discrimination Based on Religion or Belief'
1988	USA 'Religion in the Public School Curriculum: Questions and Answers'
1995, 2000, 2003	US Department of Education Guidelines on Religion and Public Education
2000	UNESCO 'Dakar Framework for Action – Education for All: Meeting our Collective Commitments'
2001	International Consultative Conference on School Education in Relation to Freedom of Religion or Belief, Tolerance, and Non-Discrimination (Madrid)
2002	CoE launches working group on the Religious Dimension of Intercultural Education
2005	UN Alliance of Civilizations launches the Education about Religions and Beliefs (ERB) clearing house
2007	OSCE: *Toledo Guiding Principles on Teaching about Religion and Beliefs in Public Schools*
2008	Quebec initiates its ERC programme
2008	CoE Recommendation CM/Rec (2008) 12 on the Dimension of Religions and Non-Religious Convictions within Intercultural Education
2010	The AAR: *Guidelines for Teaching about Religion in K-12 Public Schools in the United States*

represented, there is also the question of which ones to include in the curriculum. It is widely agreed that curricula 'should be sensitive to different local manifestations of religious and secular plurality found in schools and the communities they serve'.[22] However, this does not mean that all views need to be given 'equal time'. Rather, there are several educational criteria for including or excluding particular religions or beliefs in national or local curricula. These include:

- historical importance of religions and beliefs in a certain nation or region or globally;
- presence of particular religions or beliefs in a nation or the local community;
- media attention devoted to a particular religion or belief;
- existing misconceptions of a particular religion or belief;
- present or future likelihood of contact with adherents of a particular religion or belief.[23]

It is recognized that there are multiple ways in which education about religion might be related to the overall curriculum of public schools. So, for example, teaching about religions and beliefs might be offered as a *subject-specific course* in primary and secondary education (as it is in several European countries and now in Quebec). Or it might be *integrated* into other subjects in the school curriculum such as history, geography, literature, art, music, philosophy, civics or multi-or intercultural education (as is typical in the USA). Or it might be the focus of *cross-curricular* lessons, activities, and projects involving collaboration of teachers from various subject areas, each of whom approaches teaching about religions and beliefs from a distinct background, expertise, and perspective.[24] Whichever of these approaches is taken, 'the importance of a sensitive, fair, inclusive, unbiased and impartial curriculum cannot be overstated'.[25]

The emerging international framework also addresses the education and qualifications of religious education teachers. One issue has to do with the use of confessional or other non-professional criteria to determine who is qualified to teach about religions and beliefs. In contrast to what is current practice in many countries, there appears to be growing acceptance that an

individual's personal religious (or non-religious) beliefs cannot be sufficient reason to exclude that person from teaching about religions and beliefs. The most important considerations in this regard relate to professional expertise, as well as to basic attitudes towards or commitment to human rights in general and freedom of religion or belief in particular, rather than religious affiliation or conviction.[26]

It is often alleged that adequate preparation of teachers is especially important when it comes to religious education because of unique issues and challenges that arise in connection with this particular subject matter. The potential for controversy, conflict, exclusion, and discrimination seems particularly acute in this area. Yet research shows that many teachers do not feel prepared to deal with the topic of religion in the curriculum or with the diversity of religion, belief, and culture they encounter in their classrooms. 'Too many new teachers report that they have never taken a course that addresses such issues, and have never had direct exposure to other cultures, belief systems, or human rights principles in their apprenticeships.'[27] Teachers must learn to guard against intentional or unintentional biases and to distinguish between their individual beliefs and their professional responsibilities. Matters are complicated further by the fact that in many schools, especially in urban areas, the cultural and religious backgrounds of teachers and students do not correspond. While student populations of schools in many parts of the world are becoming increasingly diverse, members of the teaching profession are predominantly drawn from majority cultures, and their beliefs reflect majority viewpoints. This has prompted many calls for more aggressive recruitment of individuals from underrepresented communities into the teaching profession and teacher training faculty.[28]

While teacher training programmes must consider the distinctive requirements of national educational systems, there is growing recognition that commitment to freedom of religion or belief, human rights, and mutual respect should be a prerequisite for all religious education teachers. Continuing education programmes are necessary to provide the training and support required in order to keep up with new developments in the field and to adapt responsibly to the shifting social and political contexts in which teaching about religions and beliefs takes place.[29]

In sum, the human rights-based academic approach to religious education is proposed as a means of preparing students to become more responsible citizens in a world where multiple religious and non-religious worldviews exist side by side. It is understood as a

tool to transmit knowledge and values pertaining to all religious trends, in an inclusive way, so that individuals realize their being part of the same community and learn to create their own identity in harmony with identities different from their own. As such, religion education is distinguished from catechism or theology, defined as the formal study of the nature of God and of the foundations of religious belief, and contributes to the wider framework of education as defined in international standards.[30]

This approach is rooted in the conviction that more knowledge about the world's religions and beliefs will help to *promote* respect for human rights, mutual understanding, tolerance, and social cohesion and to *prevent* intercultural conflict and social instability. While granting that 'a better knowledge of religions and beliefs will not automatically foster tolerance and respect', there is nonetheless a widespread conviction that such knowledge 'has the potential to have a positive effect upon the perceptions of other's religions and beliefs and their adherents'.[31] As the UN Alliance of Civilizations states: 'People who know the facts about other religions and think critically about belief are less likely to accept ignorant stereotypes or fall prey to inflammatory actions/words.'[32]

Alongside this primarily *civic* rationale for including religious education in public schools, there is also a more purely *educational* rationale – namely, the obvious contribution that such learning makes to historical and cultural literacy. It is not possible to achieve an adequate understanding of human history and culture (literature, art, music, philosophy, law, ethics, politics) without knowing the role that religious and secular beliefs, practices, and communities have played and continue to play in human life. In the words of the *Toledo Guiding Principles*: 'Learning about religions and beliefs forms part of one's own stock of education, broadens one's horizon and deepens one's insight into the complexities of both past and present.'[33] The AAR *Guidelines* define 'religious literacy' as 'the ability to discern and analyse the intersections of religion with social, political, and cultural life'.[34]

In addition to these civic and educational justifications, a third and somewhat more controversial reason that is often given in support of religious education in public schools is its potential contribution to deeper self-knowledge and personal development.

> Learning about religions and beliefs contributes to forming and developing self-understanding, including a deeper appreciation of one's own religion or belief. Studying about religions and beliefs opens students' minds to questions of meaning and purpose and exposes students to critical ethical issues addressed by humankind throughout history.[35]

In an age when many students are not aware of their own backgrounds and traditions, let alone those of others, attention to issues of identity and heritage and to existential questions of meaning and purpose are given special emphasis by many proponents of religious education in public schools.

Against the backdrop of this threefold rationale – the contribution of religious education to civic education and respect for human rights; to historical and cultural literacy; and to self-knowledge and personal development – a number of questions about the wisdom and viability of implementing an academic human rights-based approach to teaching about religion in public schools have been raised by parents, religionists, anti-religionists, policymakers, and members of the general public. In what follows we restrict our attention to several issues raised by scholars and practitioners who generally accept the need for an academic approach to religion but who question various aspects of the framework we have been describing. These include questions about the relative weight that should be given to the civic, educational, and existential aims of religious education; about the principle of neutrality in school curricula and policies; and about whether the academic approach is too secular or not secular enough.

The aims of public school religious education: Civic? scientific? existential?

Some critics have charged that recent discussions of religious education in public schools place too much emphasis on its contributions to a civic or problem-solving agenda and not enough on its 'scientific' or more purely educational aims. They point out that the educational systems of modern secular states rest on the assumption that schools should transmit knowledge of the natural and social worlds that is grounded in scientific enquiry. Consequently, the relevance of religious education to addressing civic challenges and debates regarding multiculturalism, terrorism, human rights, tolerance, and dialogue is secondary to its value and usefulness for expanding knowledge and analytical skills in general. By focusing too narrowly on contemporary issues and challenges, education about religion may quickly become outdated or inapplicable to new circumstances and unforeseen challenges that arise. Moreover, it risks overemphasizing the role of religion and obscuring the role of economic or political factors.[36]

Granted that it will take much more than teaching about religion to address the world's problems, we still believe that the civic and educational rationales should be regarded as complementary rather than contradictory to one another. Indeed, this complementarity between civic education and the promotion of historical and cultural literacy is stressed by the *Toledo Guiding Principles*, the AAR *Guidelines*, and Quebec's ERC curriculum.

The question of what role religious education should play in the exploration and development of students' own personal identities is more complicated. While few would deny the importance of helping young people address existential issues of meaning and purpose in their lives, there remain serious debates about whether courses on religion in *public* schools are the most appropriate venues for such explorations.

In the USA, the conventional understanding of the dichotomy between devotional and academic approaches is that teaching about religion in public schools must not be based on students' and teachers' own personal religious narratives and experiences. While there is considerable latitude for student religious expression in the school environment, the American law allows much less latitude for religious expression on the part of teachers, and, in the context of the school curriculum, both students and teachers are to approach religion in a neutral 'academic' fashion.[37] Yet striving for an objective approach that sets aside one's own existential questions risks undermining students' engagement with the subject matter.

One way of thinking about the relevance of religious education to the lives of American students has been to reframe the issue in terms of the development of their identity as citizens rather than in terms of their religious or spiritual identities *per se*.[38] This approach has been taken by the California and Utah 3 Rs Projects, which are comprised of educators, scholars, and citizens and built on the conviction that the religion clauses of the First Amendment to the US Constitution provide the guiding principles for citizenship in America's pluralistic democracy. Foremost among these principles are the '3 Rs' of religious liberty – rights, responsibility, and respect.

- *Rights*: Religious liberty, or freedom of conscience, is a basic and inalienable right founded on the inviolable dignity of each person.
- *Responsibility*: Freedom of conscience is not only a universal right, but it depends upon a universal responsibility to respect that right for others.
- *Respect*: Debate and disagreement are natural elements of democracy. Yet, if we are to live with our differences, not only what we debate but how we debate is critical. A strong democracy and strong schools rest on a commitment by people of differing convictions to treat one another with civility.[39]

Reliance on the language of rights by itself can encourage and perpetuate a kind of individualism that is already rampant in US society – an individualism that often pits individuals and groups against one another and encourages a conception of citizen-as-consumer.[40] However, when linked with the principles of responsibility and respect, the fundamental importance of individual rights is acknowledged, but is combined with a notion of civic virtue – a recognition that citizens must be capable of balancing their own self-interest with the interests of the wider community if their own rights are to be preserved and if the nation's democratic experiment is to survive. Not only does the individual citizen possess rights (freedoms, liberties), but he or she also has duties or obligations to both self and other. Through the use of historical and contemporary case studies that illustrate the costs to individuals and communities when rights are violated or when responsibilities are neglected, students come to understand what is at stake in discussions of diverse religions and beliefs. In this way, the subject matter comes alive for students, not so much in the context of developing their own religious or spiritual identities, but in the context of developing their sense of self-as-citizen. The academic study of religion becomes a form of civic engagement that increases student understanding of real-world problems and solutions and fosters students' sense of themselves as effective agents in building and sustaining communities.[41]

The academic study of religion does not allow for exploration of *all* the existential and 'inner-life' questions that are relevant to the development of a student's worldview and identity. However, when viewed in terms of its civic as well as its more purely educational aims, it can allow for and encourage students to address the question that is at the heart of every search for meaning and purpose – 'How can I connect with something larger than my own ego?'[42]

The principle of neutrality or impartiality in teaching about religions and beliefs

We have seen that the emerging international standards with regard to religious education rest on the assumption that there is a difference between devotional or faith-based *religious instruction*, on the one hand, and a neutral, academic approach to *education about* religion, on the other hand. The starting point for this approach has been the understanding that instruction about religions and beliefs should not be devotionally and denominationally oriented.

> It strives for student awareness of religions and beliefs, but does not press for student acceptance of any of them; it sponsors study about religions and beliefs, not their practice; it may expose students to a diversity of religious and non-religious views, but does not impose any particular view; it educates about religions and beliefs without promoting or denigrating any of them; it informs students about various

religions and beliefs, it does not seek to conform or convert students to any particular religion or belief. Study about religions and beliefs should be based on sound scholarship, which is an essential precondition for giving students both a fair and deeper understanding of the various faith traditions.[43]

Neutrality or impartiality – neither privileging nor rejecting the perspective of any particular religious or non-religious worldview – is not only a methodological principle in scholarship and teaching; it also has ethical and legal dimensions. A key feature of the international human rights framework is the idea that, in the exercise of their responsibilities in the field of education, states have 'a duty to act in a neutral and impartial fashion where matters of religion and belief are concerned . . . and thus should not take a stand on the truth or falsity of any form of religion or belief'.[44]

The human rights framework makes it clear that public school instruction in subjects such as the general history of religions and ethics does not violate the freedom of religion or belief so long as such instruction is given in a 'neutral and objective way'.[45] Neither does public school involvement in religious instruction violate this freedom so long as 'provision is made for non-discriminatory exemptions or alternatives that would accommodate the wishes of parents and guardians'.[46]

As is the case with discussions of 'global ethics' in other spheres, we are wrestling here with a tension between the local and the universal, or, in this instance, between the national and transnational. Human rights-based religious education accepts that the particular historical, political, religious, and social factors that bear upon educational systems in different national settings preclude the emergence of a standardized approach. What is being proposed is not a uniform approach but rather a general framework within which educational authorities have broad discretion in designing, selecting, and implementing curriculum decisions in their countries.

> This does not, however, authorize breach of the fundamental right to freedom of religion or belief or other fundamental rights. While international norms do not rule out various forms of co-operation with religions and belief systems, they do require 'neutrality and impartiality' in the sense of protecting freedom of religion or belief for all individuals and groups on an equal basis.[47]

Thus, while states have considerable latitude with regard to providing religious education, international standards prohibit them from seeking to indoctrinate pupils in a particular worldview against the wishes of their parents. Public schools must respect and protect the freedom of religion or belief by maintaining a requisite degree of neutrality between worldviews in the curriculum.

To satisfy this obligation of neutrality, schools must either grant opt-out rights on the grounds of conscientious objection or design a curriculum that is sufficiently impartial and balanced. The *Toledo Guiding Principles* identify different settings in which temporary or long-term opt-out rights may need to be granted, and they explore alternative ways of structuring opt-out arrangements so as to insulate those seeking exemptions from stigma and discrimination. The *Toledo Guiding Principles* also encourage school officials to be sensitive to legitimate claims based on freedom of religion or belief, and they stress that, 'every time school personnel accommodate or reject a sincere conscientious claim, they send a signal that may build or undermine the culture of tolerance and mutual respect in the school environment'.[48]

Some observers have argued that there is no such thing as a neutral standpoint from which to approach religion or any other topic. A salient feature of our postmodern age is the recognition that all ways of thinking and teaching are influenced by personal, social, cultural, intellectual, and historical factors, and that we inevitably bring certain values to bear upon our subject matter. The academic study of religion is *different* from devotional or sectarian approaches to religion, but it is one value-laden standpoint among others. The reason why a religious studies approach to teaching about religion in public schools is justifiable is not because it is neutral, but because it is the approach that best promotes the values of a pluralistic democracy governed by secular laws.[49]

Acceptance of this point about the value-laden character of our perspectives does not necessarily mean, however, that we have to abandon the idea of neutrality in teaching about religion. On the contrary, to do so would be a mistake, because the idea of teaching about religion in a neutral fashion remains basic to both the civic and the legal framework that has been developed since the 1980s. Abandoning or blurring the distinction between neutral and non-neutral approaches to the study of religion risks undermining this hard-won civic consensus, running afoul of current law, and setting back what progress has been made towards incorporating religion into the curriculum of public schools.

Of course we must grant that a neutral academic approach to the study of religion is rooted in and committed to certain values – for example, *intellectual values* such as free and open enquiry, respect for multiple perspectives, and evidence-based argumentation. It is also committed to *ethical–political* values such as respect for freedom of religion or belief and promotion of tolerance. However, if 'neutrality' is understood as an approach in curricula, teaching, and school policies that (1) neither promotes nor denigrates particular religions nor religion in general; (2) seeks to protect religious liberty or freedom of conscience for people of all faiths or none; and (3) seeks to remain impartial between religious and non-religious worldviews and beliefs, then this remains an accurate and useful way of describing the non-devotional, academic approach to education about religion.

Too secular or not secular enough?

Some scholars and educators claim that public school neutrality towards religion actually amounts to a form of secular indoctrination. These critics typically argue that all knowledge claims are situated within one or another comprehensive worldview, a religious or non-religious framework of ultimate beliefs and values through which the rest of knowledge is interpreted. As there is no vantage point that is not rooted in one worldview or another, it is impossible to be neutral between them. On this view, attempts to study or teach about religion from a neutral perspective will end up privileging a secular or humanist worldview, and, as such, will be unfair to the religious.[50]

This line of reasoning is prominent among some Christian evangelical and Muslim parents who have accused public education of promoting a secular worldview and ethic that is at odds with a biblical or Quranic outlook and traditional moral values. Something like this line of reasoning also appears to undergird objections to the *Toledo Guiding Principles* by the Vatican, the only one of the OSCE's member states to reject the document. According to the Holy See's representative to the OSCE, the *Toledo Guiding Principles* contain 'a reductive view of religion and a conception of the secular nature of States and their neutrality that obfuscates the positive role of religion, its specific nature and contribution to society'.[51] According to a 2009 news story, the Holy See's main areas of concern were

> the danger that teaching about religions may replace the teaching of religions in some countries; the risk that religions are portrayed negatively; the non-differentiated treatment of historical religions with regard to small religious and belief groups by the OSCE/ODIHR in general; and parental rights in the religious education of their children.[52]

These concerns appear rooted in the view that a neutral approach to religious education promotes a modern Western and secular moral ideology of human rights that is intended to supplant the moral per-spectives of diverse cultural, religious, and philosophical traditions. This view has been expressed by some governments of non-Western nations and by some representatives and scholars of various religious and cultural traditions. But, as we have argued in this volume, this view is based on a misunderstanding of the historical origins and nature of the modern human rights movement.

Contrary to the perception that human rights are simply an out-growth and entailment of modern secular assumptions about human nature and moral rationality, the UDHR, for example, was in fact the product of pragmatic negotiation between representatives of dif-ferent nations and cultural and religious traditions.

> The development of the UDHR was a year and a half long process involving delegates from no fewer that fifty-six countries representing quite diverse cultural, moral, political, philosophical, and religious tra-ditions, ranging across such systems and traditions as, for example, forms of Western liberalism (from Europe and America), socialism (from Soviet Russia and the Eastern bloc), Christianity (Catholic, Protestant, Orthodox), Hinduism, Buddhism, Islam (conservative and progressive forms), and Confucianism, among others . . . the delegations could and did reach pragmatic agreement on a set of essential human rights norms, it was also recognized that, given the diversity of the world's cultural and philosophical systems and traditions, no deeper theoretical agreement would be possible, and so the delegates self-consciously chose to eschew the use of contestable metaphysical language and appeals . . . Pragmatic agreement on practical norms protective of human dignity and welfare was deemed sufficient.[53]

This pragmatic approach has continued to characterize the drafting and adoption of subsequent human rights covenants, conventions, and treaties. While diverse religious and non-religious traditions may use different idioms to describe human rights values, while they may have arrived at these values by different routes, and while they will invoke different justifications in their support, there is considerable overlap between worldviews when it comes to the values that under-gird support for basic human rights.[54]

Yet, while some argue that a neutral approach to teaching about religion is unfair to religion, others have charged that the *Toledo Guiding Principles*, the ERC programme, and the First Amendment consensus documents actually exhibit a 'pro-religious' bias rather than a genuinely 'neutral' attitude towards the subject matter. The concern of these critics is that, in the pursuit of its civic agenda, this approach too often errs in the direction of shielding religion from critical scrutiny and privileging the perspectives of religious insiders.

It is true that the *Toledo Guiding Principles* do tend to view religion as a subject matter that presents special legal and pedagogical challenges requiring it to be treated differently from regular subjects in the curriculum. For example, religion is described as a subject that 'touches upon human nature in a profound way' and that presents 'specific challenges' that must be handled with a great deal of respect, showing sensitivity 'to different local manifestations of religious and secular plurality found in schools and the communities they serve. Such sensitivities will help address the concerns of students, parents and other stakeholders in education.'[55] The *Toledo Guiding Principles* also encourage teaching that highlights 'sources from the religions that support peace, tolerance and human rights' and curricula that make reference 'to sources drawn from various religious and belief traditions that reinforce the significance of tolerance, respect and caring for others'.[56]

Consistent with the human rights framework, the *Toledo Guiding Principles* stress that the interests and rights of several parties must be acknowledged in the educational sphere of contemporary social life. In addition to students and their parents or guardians, stakeholders include not only school teachers, administrators, and subject-matter specialists but also representatives of various religion and belief communities, parent–teacher organizations and other NGOs interested in the educational process, government officials, members of the general public, and so on. Because religious education bears directly on the fundamental right to freedom of religion or belief, 'wise officials will not only respect the applicable constitutional and human rights limitations, but will be open to input from relevant stakeholders'.[57] In addition to providing regular opportunities for public input and feedback, the *Toledo Guiding Principles* encourage the establishment of national, regional, and local 'advisory bodies' that can express the 'convictions, interests, and sensitivities' of all who have a stake in how religious education is designed and implemented.[58]

Critics have charged that curricular emphasis on religions as sources for peace and tolerance rather than conflict and misunderstanding amounts to an uncritical and overly deferential attitude towards religion rather than a neutral academic one. Critics also argue that such 'stakeholders' as religious leaders and communities should play no role in determining curricula. These decisions should be made by educational professionals, as is done in the case of other 'normal' school subjects.[59]

With regard to the role of stakeholders, the *Toledo Guiding Principles* are clear that, in the advisory process, care must be given to striking an appropriate balance between the various perspectives and interests involved. Representatives of religious communities should be given the opportunity to provide input and advice, but they should not be given so much decision-making power that the state abdicates its responsibility for oversight of the content and delivery of public education. The European Court of Human Rights has made it clear that excessive involvement of religious authorities from one community in decisions that affect the rights of those belonging to another community may itself amount to a violation of the right to freedom of religion or belief. On the other hand, courts have recognized that mere involvement of religious representatives in bodies formulating public educational policies does not constitute excessive entanglement of religious authorities in public decision-making.[60] The *Toledo Guiding Principles* and the First Amendment consensus approach in the USA both counsel that good faith efforts to understand the concerns of affected parties – including representatives of non-religious belief groups and smaller, non-traditional religious groups – can go a long way toward alleviating concerns about balance and avoiding or minimizing problems.[61]

With regard to teaching and curricula, it must be acknowledged that in actual classroom practice the approach that we have been describing can be overly superficial and uncritical in its representation of religions. There is often a tendency to overstate similarities between religions, to downplay the diversity that exists *within* religions, and to avoid controversial topics. Little attention is paid to the relation between religion and power in society nor to the ways that race, class, gender, and other factors influence how some religious beliefs and expressions become culturally and politically prominent, while others become culturally and politically marginalized.[62] Of course, education about religion is not the only public school subject that has been charged with superficiality and lack of critical perspective. Self-reflective and critical enquiry regarding history, society, and politics (not to mention health and sex education) is often viewed as being fraught with controversy and perhaps more appropriately left to families or postponed until university-level education.

However, these are not deficiencies that are inherent to a neutral academic approach to religious education as such. Rather, we are dealing here with practical problems of preparation and implementation, the sorts of problems that can be remedied by better teacher education and curricular reform and innovation.

Conclusion

Has the promotion of civic and religious literacy through religious education actually contributed to tolerance of diverse religions and beliefs and respect for human rights? This is among the questions addressed by Religion in Education: A Contribution to Dialogue or a Factor of Conflict in Transforming Societies of European Countries (REDCo) – a massive three-year research project funded by a major grant from the European Commission. From 2006 to 2009 the REDCo project deployed an international team of scholars representing a range of disciplinary specializations in education, the humanities, and the social sciences. Focusing mainly on religion in the lives and schools of students in the 14–16 year age group with some attention to teacher training and classroom practices, this team carried out qualitative and quantitative research in eight countries: England, Estonia, France, Germany, the Netherlands, Norway, Russia, and Spain.

The REDCo project provides a detailed picture of young peoples' perceptions of religion and religious diversity in their own personal lives, in their societies, and in their schools. The empirical studies generated by REDCo 'can be characterized more as close shots of a specific contextual setting than as national surveys'.[63] Although the national samples are not statistically representative, they do reveal tendencies in the ways that students from different personal and religious backgrounds in different countries think about religion as a potential factor in dialogue and conflict.

Among the project's central findings is that students are conscious of increasing religious diversity in society, and in general they are of the opinion that it is important to respect the religions of others.[64] With regard to the role of religion in school life (for example, wearing discrete or more visible religious symbols, absences for religious holidays, excusal from some classes for religious reasons), the studies document a range of different attitudes that appear to be determined largely by the students' own religious backgrounds (or lack thereof), by the role religion plays in (the history of) their respective countries, and by whether religion is more or less private and withdrawn from public life and discussion. While notions of freedom and tolerance are important, students also attach great importance to 'equal treatment' and are reluctant to change too much in school policy and curriculum for the sake of a particular group of students.[65] While some students exhibit prejudices against the religions of others, especially with regard to Islam, they appear open to dialogue and hopeful that religious education can contribute to the goal of peaceful coexistence.[66]

As for religion in the curriculum, it appears that these European students generally favour an approach that provides objective information about different religions and their teachings rather than an approach that guides pupils towards religious beliefs. The majority of those surveyed appear to agree that school is a good place to learn about different religions and worldviews, and they generally regard religious education as more relevant to cultivating respect for people of different religions and learning to live together than it is for learning about themselves and developing their own decisions about right and wrong.[67]

The only large-scale empirical study of education about religion in US public schools also provides evidence of its efficacy. The study focused on Modesto, California, the first public school district in the USA to require all secondary school students to take a course on world religions. Surveys and interviews of students showed statistically significant increases not only in students' knowledge about other religions but also in their levels of passive tolerance (willingness to refrain from discrimination) and active tolerance (willingness to act to counter discrimination). Among the study's other findings were that Modesto's course had a positive impact on students' respect for religious liberty; students left the course with an increased appreciation for the similarities between major religions; and, contrary to some expectations, the course did not stir up any notable controversy in the community.[68]

Perhaps more than any other institution in modern societies, public schools are places where people from all backgrounds and beliefs interact with one another on a regular and sustained basis. Whether pluralistic societies succeed or fail in promoting tolerance and respect for human rights and freedom of conscience will depend to a great extent on the ability of schools to cultivate the skills and knowledge that will enable people to live together with their deepest differences. This chapter has focused on discussions of religious education that are taking place under the auspices of the United Nations and in the contexts of Europe and North America, but there are also robust discussions of the theory and practice of public education about religions taking place in many other parts of the world, including Australia, Japan, South Korea, Indonesia, Turkey, and South Africa.[69] These provide one more instance of global ethics in practice.

Notes

1. See also the ICCPR (Article 18); the ICESCAR (Article 13); the Convention on the Rights of the Child (Articles 14 and 28); and the 1981 Declaration on the Elimination of All Forms of Intolerance and of Discrimination Based on Religion and Belief – all readily available online.
2. Cited in OSCE, *Toledo Guiding Principles*, p. 112; the Madrid 'Final Document' is included as appendix IV in this document, pp. 109–16. An outcome of the Madrid Conference was the organization of the Teaching for Tolerance project of the Oslo Coalition on Freedom of Religion or Belief, an international network of representatives from religious and other life-stance communities, NGOs, international organizations, and research institutes, available at <https://www.jus.uio.no/smr/english/about/programmes/oslocoali tion/tolerance/index.html> (last accessed 23 January 2015).
3. OSCE, *Toledo Guiding Principles*, p. 113.
4. Ibid. p. 110.
5. See UN Alliance of Civilizations, Education about Religions and Beliefs (ERB), available at <http://aocerb.org/index.php> (last accessed 23 January 2015).
6. Jackson, 'Teaching about Religions in the Public Sphere', p. 156.
7. Ibid. pp. 157–62.
8. Recommendation CM/Rec (2008) 12 is included as appendix 1 in Jackson, *Signposts*, pp. 115–22.
9. OSCE, *Toledo Guiding Principles*, p. 11.
10. Ibid. pp. 11–12.
11. Morris, 'Cultivating Reflection and Understanding', pp. 188–211; Boudreau, 'From Confessional to Cultural', pp. 212–23.
12. Ministère de l'Éducation, du Loisir et du Sport, *Quebec Education Program*, p. 296. These objectives are presented as interdependent and common to both the ethics and the religious culture components of the programme. In this context, 'ethics' is understood as critical reflection on the meaning of conduct and on the values and norms that the members of a given society or group adopt in order to guide or regulate their conduct. Instruction in 'religious culture' promotes an understanding of religions that is 'built on the exploration of the sociocultural contexts in which they take root and continue to develop' (p. 295).
13. Ibid. p. 296.
14. Ministère de l'Éducation, du Loisir et du Sport, *Establishment of an Ethics and Religious Culture Program*, p. 6.
15. AAR Religion in the Schools Task Force, *Guidelines for Teaching about Religion in K-12 Public School in the United States*, p. i.

16. National Council for the Social Studies (NCSS), *Including the Study about Religion in the Social Studies Curriculum*. Association for Supervision and Curriculum Development (ASCD), *Religion in the Curriculum*.

17. See Haynes, 'Common Ground Documents' and 'US Department of Education Guidelines on Religion and Public Education'. Many of the First Amendment consensus documents can be found in Haynes and Thomas, *Finding Common Ground*, 9–11, 39–56, 77–88, 95–100, 121–34.

18. OSCE, *Toledo Guiding Principles*, p. 46.

19. Ibid. p. 40.

20. Ibid. p. 41.

21. AAR, *Guidelines for Teaching about Religion in K-12 Public Schools in the United States*, pp. 12–15.

22. OSCE, *Toledo Guiding Principles*, p. 41

23. Ibid. p. 42.

24. Ibid. pp. 43–5.

25. Ibid. p. 45.

26. Ibid. p. 59; see also AAR, *Guidelines for Teaching about Religion in K-12 Public Schools in the United States*, p. 19.

27. OSCE, *Toledo Guiding Principles*, p. 55.

28. Ibid. pp. 57–8.

29. Ibid. pp. 57–8.

30. Ibid. p. 24, citing 'The Role of Religious Education in the Pursuit of Tolerance and Non-Discrimination', a study prepared for the 2001 Madrid Conference under the guidance of Abdelfattah Amor, UN Special Rapporteur on Freedom of Religion or Belief.

31. OSCE, *Toledo Guiding Principles*, p. 18.

32. UN Alliance of Civilizations Clearinghouse about Religions and Beliefs (ERB) brochure, n.d., p. 2, section III. Rationale. More information about the ERB is available at <http://www.unaoc.org/what-we-do/online-platforms/erb> (last accessed 26 January 2015).

33. OSCE, *Toledo Guiding Principles*, p. 19.

34. AAR, *Guidelines for Teaching about Religion in K-12 Public Schools in the United States*, p. 4.

35. OSCE, *Toledo Guiding Principles*, p. 19.

36. Jensen, 'RS Based RE in Public Schools', p. 156.

37. On the requirement for 'neutrality', 'fairness', and 'balance' in teaching about religion and guidelines for religious expression of students in public schools, see Haynes and Thomas, *Finding Common Ground*, pp. 41–7, 232–44.

38. Grelle, 'Defining and Promoting the Study of Religion in British and American Schools', pp. 29–30, 34–5.

39. See California 3 Rs Project, available at <http://ca3rsproject.org/

pages/principle.html> (last accessed 23 January 2015); see also Grelle, 'Promoting Civic and Religious Literacy in Public Schools'.

40. See Sandel, 'Liberalism, Consumerism, and Citizenship'.
41. We owe this idea to our California State University colleagues, Kate McCarthy and Micki Lennon.
42. Palmer, *Healing the Heart of Democracy*, p. 125.
43. OSCE, *Toledo Guiding Principles*, p. 21. See also AAR, *Guidelines for Teaching about Religion in K-12 Public Schools in the United States*, p. i, for almost identical wording.
44. OSCE, *Toledo Guiding Principles*, p. 33. General principles governing religious education in public schools have been set forth by any number of intergovernmental, regional, and international human rights agreements. These include, among others, Principle VII of the Helsinki Final Act and the 1989 Vienna Concluding Document, which apply to OSCE participating states; Article 9 of the European Convention on Human Rights; and Article 18 of the ICCPR. See OSCE, *Toledo Guiding Principles*, pp. 28–9.
45. Ibid. p. 33.
46. Ibid., citing UN Human Rights Committee General Comment No. 22.
47. Ibid. p. 34
48. Ibid. p. 74. Charges of failure to grant adequate opt-out provisions to compulsory religious education curricula in Norway and Turkey have been the subject of cases brought to the UN Human Rights Committee and the European Court of Human Rights (ibid. pp. 91–108). Quebec's ERC curriculum has also been challenged in Canadian courts for failing to provide opportunities to opt out. For discussion of opt-out provisions in the USA, see Haynes and Thomas, *Finding Common Ground*, pp. 186–7, 232–3.
49. Moore, *Overcoming Religious Illiteracy*, pp. 55–6.
50. Norman, 'Worldviews, Humanism and the (Im)possibility of Neutrality', pp. 516–17.
51. Statement by Monsignor Michael W. Banach, Permanent Representative of the Holy See, at the 685th Meeting of the OSCE Permanent Council 1 November 2007, available at <http:www.osce.org/pc/28557> (last accessed 23 January 2015).
52. Fautré, 'Why Did the Vatican Veto the OSCE's Guidelines on Teaching Religion?'
53. Twiss, 'History, Human Rights, and Globalization', p. 57.
54. Norman, 'Worldviews Humanism and the (Im)possibility of Neutrality', pp. 518–19; Grelle, 'Culture and Moral Pluralism', pp. 133–5.
55. Jensen, 'RS Based RE in Public Schools', p. 132, citing the *Toledo Guiding Principles*, pp. 61, 53, 17 respectively. Similarly, the AAR,

Guidelines for Teaching about Religion in K-12 Public Schools in the United States, state: 'Teaching about religion in public schools brings with it particular challenges that teachers seldom face when addressing other subject areas' (p. 11).

56. OSCE, *Toledo Guiding Principles*, p. 41.
57. Ibid. p. 63. The First Amendment consensus approach also encourages the involvement of stakeholders in discussions about the place of religion in public schools; see Haynes and Thomas, *Finding Common Ground*, pp. 6–9, 12, 15–25.
58. OSCE, *Toledo Guiding Principles*, p. 64.
59. Jensen, 'RS Based RE in Public Schools', pp. 133–4; Moore, *Overcoming Religious Illiteracy*, p. 66.
60. OSCE, *Toledo Guiding Principles*, p. 65.
61. Ibid. pp. 63-75; Haynes and Thomas, *Finding Common Ground*, pp. 18–21.
62. AAR, *Guidelines for Teaching about Religion in K-12 Public Schools in the United States*, p. 10; Moore, *Overcoming Religious Illiteracy*, pp. 78–85.
63. Knauth et al. (eds), *Encountering Religious Pluralism in School and Society*, p. 18.
64. Ibid. p. 17.
65. Valk et al. (eds), *Teenagers' Perspectives on the Role of Religion in their Lives, Schools and Societies*, pp. 419–20.
66. Knauth et al., *Encountering Religious Pluralism in School and Society*, p. 17.
67. Valk et al., *Teenagers' Perspectives on the Role of Religion in their Lives, Schools and Societies*, p. 420.
68. Lester and Roberts, *Learning about World Religions in Public Schools*; Lester and Roberts, 'How Teaching about World Religions Brought a Truce to the Culture Wars in Modesto, California'.
69. In addition to articles in the *British Journal of Religious Education* and papers presented at the annual meetings of the AAR's group on 'Religion in Public Schools: International Perspectives', see de Souza et al. (eds), *International Handbook of the Religious, Moral and Spiritual Dimensions of Education*.

Conclusion: The Practices of Global Ethics, History, and Hope

Opportunites and challenges

We now live in a globalized world that faces huge opportunities and challenges. It is a world in which the examples of the practices of global ethics reviewed in this book have played and will continue to play an important role. We will conclude by attempting to put these practices into historical perspective.

When we look at ethics in general and at global ethics in particular as a social practice, we observe people working towards valued objectives through a wide range of activities and organizations, guided by normative standards and goals. Seen in this light, codes, covenants, and charters represent articulate expressions of a larger ethos of activities and institutions that both help to bring these normative statements into being and work to realize their valued purposes. As we have argued, these activities and institutions often play a much more influential role than the normative statements by themselves. For example, documents such as the Earth Charter, the UN Declaration on the Rights of Indigenous Peoples, and the declaration on the Responsibility to Protect put in writing ideas that had gained increased authority because of activities and commitments of many people and organizations.

We have argued that two features especially characterize those who practise global ethics. The first is their individual sense of fiduciary responsibility to respond to particular transboundary global crises and in the process to care for the Earth and its inhabitants, to honour the basic rights of all peoples, and to find humane ways of addressing conflict. The second is their commitment to work towards these ends collaboratively with others from differing cultures, faiths, and political persuasions. The practice of global ethics can thus be characterized as a cosmopolitan, Earth-centred, rights-based way of practising ethics. It is genuinely *cosmo-politan* in the traditional Stoic sense – not only an ethics deliberately engaging all peoples but also a way of practising politically related ethics with respect to the Earth, its biosphere, and all its inhabitants viewed as a single cosmos.

Global consciousness

Basic to practising global ethics is a globally informed consciousness: that is, a way of thinking and feeling about oneself, one's people, and humanity generally in relation to the Earth and its inhabitants as a whole. What is emerging, albeit more emphatically in some areas than others, is a new social imaginary in which we think about our lives, the life chances of our children, the prospects for diverse peoples, and the future well-being of our natural environments in global terms. On the one hand, we hear of terribly destructive storms, read about the depletion of particular sources of energy, or learn of the economic plight of countries unable to grow out of the most recent financial crisis, and we wonder about the extent to which these events signal underlying trends leading to even more ominous global developments. On the other hand, more and more people have become committed to addressing the kinds of border-spanning crises we have discussed in this book. Even while some become even more ardent nationalists or adherents of particular faiths, at the same time, humans are becoming aware that their present and future possibilities are affected by what happens to humans generally and to the one planet whose resources we both count upon and gravely affect. All the diverse ways of practising global ethics are informed by this sense that humans now live in a common global space.

The global challenges we face today are likely to be with us for some time. As of 2015 there were over seven billion people living on Earth, a number that demographers predict will grow to at least nine billion before it levels off. As humans proliferate, we have also been using up non-renewable resources, especially rare metals and fossil fuels; pushing up the prices of these and other limited resources beyond the means of the poorest segments of humanity; putting huge strains on many renewable resources such as fish stocks, arable lands, and aquifers; and dumping huge amounts of gases into the atmosphere in ways that have acutely affected global climate. To be sure, scientific discoveries have helped us make more productive use of land, water, fuels, and minerals, and no doubt this trend will continue. However, the challenge here remains.

Moreover, while the overall processes of industrialization have reduced the extent of absolute poverty ($1.25 per person per day or equivalent) over the past several decades, we still live in a world where nearly one-third of humans live in relative poverty ($2.25 per person per day or equivalent), where inequality between the wealthiest and poorest has steadily increased, and where tens of millions go hungry every day. At a time of their lives when they might be starting families and launching careers, approximately 300 million young people worldwide remain unemployed, underemployed, or not in some kind of full-time training or educational programme.[1] Thus, while modern economies have raised the standard of living for billions, they also leave us with unresolved and troubling conditions. In spite of years of concerted public and private efforts, poverty in many of the least developed countries remains extensive, and the population of urban slums globally has now grown to more than a billion.

As a percentage of all those living, over the past couple of generations fewer people have died violent deaths than in previous periods of history.[2] Since the Second World War, deaths caused by wars between countries and empires have declined, as have deaths resulting from civil wars and conflicts, although this trend is now rising in certain countries, including Nigeria, Somalia, Pakistan, Mali, Thailand, Syria, Iraq, and Myanmar. At the same time, the dignity and well-being of tens of millions of people continue to be violated by non-existent or inadequate health services, lack of food, and unavailable or substandard educational opportunities. In part in response to these circumstances, and to the lack of employment opportunities, the number of people deciding to join insurgent groups prepared to use terrorist tactics has grown since the turn of the century, in spite of concerted efforts to 'fight' terrorism.[3]

We might refer to a number of other challenges facing our world today, such as the threat of pandemic disease or the prospect that particular insurgents, a rogue state, or a political leader in righteous anger might decide to launch a nuclear attack. Beyond these very real threats, many would argue that a compelling challenge is to find more ways of recognizing and protecting the human dignity of women, in the light of the oppression and discrimination they face in so many places. In addition, many would call attention to our failures to respect the cultures and ways of life of indigenous peoples and to grant them full citizenship within and among the international community of nations. Finally, because our world has become globalized, we face the challenge of finding fitting ways to make responsible decisions affecting how we care and govern the Earth, its inhabitants, nations, and communities.

As we look around, we can see that people have been responding to these global challenges in a number of different ways. Some of the wealthiest and most powerful countries have attempted to extend their influence and control so that they are well positioned to manage circumstances in ways that protect and advance their interests. In sharp contrast, some communities and groups have responded to the perception of crisis with a renewed emphasis on the central value of living as much as possible as local social and economic associations and/or as distinct faith communities. To be sure, millions experience these larger crises and challenges through the distress and hardship they themselves are suffering. Living day to day with their hardships and their dreams, many are either unwilling or unprepared to take much notice of the larger ecological, economic, and political context. A not insignificant number of others have seen in these crises opportunities they can exploit to sell their products, pursue political advantage, and/or gain additional followers. Still others have responded by voicing their complaints against the injustices being perpetrated, the wrongs being done, the horrors with which the Earth and its climate are being assaulted. These are all understandable responses, and all have their champions. Most readers will be familiar with local examples of these varied ways of apprehending, interpreting, and developing strategies to global threats.

We make reference to these diverse ways of responding to the constellation of global crises in order more fully to appreciate the historical and ethical significance of what we have described in this book as the practices of global ethics. Global ethics in practice have assumed many expressions, as we have noted throughout this book, from international treaties ratified by nations to declarations affirmed by meetings of worldwide religious leaders; from charters embraced at global conferences to widely invoked conventions. The practices of global ethics have been embodied as well in diverse institutional arrangements through bodies such as the Intergovernmental Panel on Climate Change (IPCC), the International Committee of the Red Cross, the International Criminal Court, the Council for a Parliament of the World's Religions, the International Union for the Conservation of Nature, and the Equator Principles of leading world banks.

In Chapter 4, we called attention to three typical stances that those concerned have adopted with respect to environmental crises. Some have expressed alarm and outrage at the threats posed to the Earth and its inhabitants, a response described as a crisis ethic. In contrast, others have adopted a duty to care ethic, working to ameliorate particular problems through efforts to protect endangered species, recycle wastes, revivify lakes, and promote renewable energy. Still others have adopted a governance ethic, focusing on ways to develop more responsive and more effective systems for managing environmental issues on both a local and a global scale. It is possible to find illustrations of all three perspectives in the global ethics in practice focused on poverty, armed conflicts, health, human rights, and business practices. However, in a deeper, more fundamental sense all three are embodied in all expressions of the practices of global ethics, although one or another perspective may receive more prominence in a particular practice. In effect, practising global ethics characteristically evolves from a sense of global crisis, to a commitment to act responsibly and carefully to address this crisis, to a determination to do so collaboratively with others from other countries, cultures, faiths, organizations, and locales.

Global ethics in practice have made measurable and significant differences in the world over the past several generations. The adoption of the Universal Declaration of Human Rights (UDHR) has led to the adoption of similar charters by many national governments, the creation of hundreds of national and international organizations committed to advancing the respect and protection of human rights, as well as corresponding efforts to protect minority rights, civil liberties, and social rights. The Geneva Conventions have gained in authority, and concerted efforts have been undertaken by national military forces to protect unarmed civilians from direct assault. Local and international businesses have begun to exert more effort to act in ways that are socially responsible. Although they will fall short of realizing all of their objectives, the Millennium Development Goals (MDGs) occasioned significant constructive changes in a number of developing countries with respect to childhood education, health services, and rates of absolute poverty. In many places, faith communities, which had often remained ignorant or deeply prejudiced with regard to other faith communities, have entered into conversations with each other and discovered multiple ways of cooperating around particular projects. Likewise, environmental groups have found many different ways to work with each other in the hope of protecting endangered species and threatened ecosystems. If these diverse expressions of the practices of global ethics had not been undertaken during the past several generations, our world would be a very different and more threatening place.

Practising global ethics as a work in progress

Still, practising global ethics is inherently a work in progress. Those engaged are working to bring about a valued future in which humans have reasonably managed the global crises facing the Earth and its inhabitants, have made progress protecting basic human rights, and have found humane ways of resolving inevitable conflicts. This work is, of course, fragile: it may be undermined by new crises, by the intransigence of certain parties unwilling to collaborate, and by the passivity and despair of those who lack hope.

Practising global ethics is a work in progress because by its nature it encourages debates among interested parties. In previous chapters, we have noted several such debates: over climate change between experts from the IPCC and environmental experts from India; over the fitting exercise of humanitarian interventions; about the utility and justice of targeted assassinations; about how to foster valued forms of economic development. We have reviewed as well ongoing debates regarding particular declarations of global ethics, fitting standards for international businesses, and continuing social and economic injustices with respect to property, financial, and labour markets. Because of the commitment to open-ended, reciprocating dialogue, the practices of global ethics have become institutionalized as settings and occasions where people and organizations from diverse backgrounds and with dissimilar commitments can discuss, negotiate, and criticize each other while working to craft responses to global crises that can be both effective and widely supported. Accordingly, these ongoing debates represent an essential aspect of the larger practice of global ethics. As a result, individuals and groups with views as divergent as the naturalist and critic of economic globalization Wendell Berry and the gradually more environmentally concerned World Mining Association can disagree and yet both continue to work in their own ways to protect the Earth and its inhabitants.

Because it is a work in progress, there are discrepancies between the normative standards championed by the practices of global ethics and the actual responses of countries, organizations, businesses, and communities to the crises they address. Compliance with global ethical standards is uneven and significantly less than perfect. Compliance is quite high where standards have been embodied in international treaties, and especially when corresponding behaviours are regularly monitored by agencies established for this purpose. We can cite a number of examples, such as Performance Standards developed by the World Bank (as well as equivalent Equator Principles developed by leading international banks), and the Geneva Conventions monitored by the International Committee of the Red Cross as well as a wide range of civil society groups. Compliance with the UN covenants on civil and political rights, as well as those on economic, social, and cultural rights, is monitored by diverse human rights groups, UN agencies, and national governments. However, actions on the ground correspond less closely with a wide variety of declarations, charters, and international commission reports, such as declarations and charters reviewed in Chapters 2 and 3, as well as statements of groups such as the G20 and the 1992 United Nations Conference on the Environment and Development. Nonetheless, these kinds of expressions of global normative standards have had considerable impact. They have shaped public expectations, led to changes in both private and public policies, and been actively supported by political parties and civil society groups.

Expressions of global ethics face the additional challenge of gaining cooperation and compliance from people, governments, businesses, and communities accustomed to various traditions of ethical discourse. By their nature, the standards and institutions of global ethics do not reflect one particular approach to ethics, such as utilitarianism or deontology, liberalism or conservatism, Hinduism or Islam. They do not attempt to rise above or transcend the characteristic divisions into which humans have organized themselves as citizens of nations, adherents of religions, or followers of particular political and economic philosophies. Rather, whether we are referring to the UDHR, the Geneva Conventions, the MDGs, or the Convention on International Trade in Endangered Species, these standards and corresponding institutions are the products of negotiated normative agreements. In the process, these diverse global standards do seek to cultivate a new global identity, but not one that replaces particular identities. Rather, while reminding everyone that together humans share a fiduciary responsibility to care for the Earth and its inhabitants, global ethics in practice takes for granted that we will exercise these responsibilities while remaining members of various political, religious, and ideological constituencies.

Authority and hope

Even when they are defended with rational arguments, expressions of global ethics are products of history. They have come into being since the late nineteenth century but mostly in the years since the Second World War. Although representatives of ancient ethical traditions have articulated their support for particular expressions of contemporary global ethics, especially defending human rights, Just War ethics, and environmental concerns, and have even sought to identify the roots of global ethics in their own traditions, from a historical perspective practising global ethics represents an ethical innovation. Because expressions of global ethics represent historically constructed normative standards and institutions, we are faced with an important question. Should these expressions of global ethics be characterized as having only relative validity and authority? We think not, for the following reasons.

As we observed in the Introduction, specific expressions of global ethics have gained more or less authority worldwide related especially to how they were initially instituted, how widely they are invoked, and how institutional arrangements have been established to support them. Thus the arguments developed in the following paragraphs will apply more to some expressions of global ethics than to others. While discrete expressions of global ethics, such as reports of international commissions or guidelines of groups like the World Health Organization (WHO), gain credibility from their own particular mandates, all the diverse practices of global ethics have gained authority as a result of several shared features.

In the first place, all these expressions of global ethics in practice have come into being as a result of negotiations between people and organizations from different parts of the world having diverse value commitments. As such, these normative standards and institutions represent something like global social contracts. Over time, they have gained greater authority in breadth and depth to the extent that more nations, organizations, social groups, and/or faith communities acknowledge their authority. What is especially significant is not just widespread deference to these standards, but the fact that this deference comes from people of quite different cultural, political, and philosophical backgrounds. Indeed, sometimes the support for these global standards is hedged. Countries ratify international laws related, for example, to human rights but add reservations in the national versions of these laws. Faith communities have developed their own, slightly different versions of human rights conventions.[4] Nonetheless, while expressing hesitations, in the process these groups acknowledge the central importance of these global standards, even if to some degree they seek to adhere to them on their own terms. What is especially noteworthy is that over time, as our world has indeed become more globally interconnected, we have managed to engage people from diverse backgrounds to discuss, negotiate, craft, establish, and sustain a number of global ethical practices that have gained compelling authority in the process. In many instances, as these ethical practices have gained in authority, debates regarding their meaning and application have continued in parallel, representing another important aspect of the way people engage in global ethics in practice.

The practices of global ethics have especially gained in moral authority as those engaged have increasingly invoked a common set of core values, both as the ends and the presuppositions for their activities. Beyond their pragmatic purposes of addressing particular problems – such as reducing the threat of nuclear attacks, decreasing child mortality rates, or protecting endangered species –

the varied practices of global ethics repeatedly invoke several basic values, which have come increasingly to be regarded as fundamental and inviolable. They include: (1) the dignity – some would say the sacredness – of each person; (2) respect for the diversity of human communities and their opportunities or rights within appropriate limits to determine their own life course; (3) the responsibility of all humans to care for the Earth and its inhabitants in fitting ways; and (4) a commitment to initiate and maintain forthright, reciprocating, conversations with other human communities to attend to and take responsibility for global ethical issues.[5] Although they are expressed in a wide variety of terms, these values have come to be regarded as intrinsic goods. Because they are now so widely presumed, many actions long assumed to be acceptable, such as slavery, the violent subjugation of other peoples, and the deliberate slaughter of species like the buffalo, are now regarded as unthinkable evils. Interestingly, without overtly making reference to it, practising global ethics from this perspective involves using the kind of logic associated with the natural law tradition. That is, certain basic normative principles are defended as basic guides for behaviour because they work to protect and enhance corresponding intrinsic goods. In the natural law tradition, these 'goods' include life itself, human life, family life, social order, and justice. Today, global ethics in practice is typically defended by invoking 'goods', including the dignity of persons, the value of the Earth and its well-being, respect for diverse cultures, respect for science, and commitment in so far as possible to work to address global crises through dialogue and collaboration. Although these standards have assumed a wide variety of forms, those engaged in the practices of global ethics often defend their actions by indicating that they are protecting these kinds of intrinsic values.

Global ethics in practice has also gained in authority for pragmatic reasons. While this is a weaker and less compelling factor than the first two, it is not without influence. Global ethics in practice had attracted respect and deference because it has been invoked effectively and repeatedly to address a great many different concerns over the past several generations. It has been invoked to resolve conflicts, to solicit humanitarian aid in response to crises, to call a halt to particular abuses, to support the aspirations of disadvantaged communities, and to address many other concerns. With moderate success, global ethical standards have been invoked to restrain the spread of nuclear weapons, to manage threatened epidemics, to foster the education of girls in impoverished countries, to indict politicians who have allegedly committed crimes against humanity, and to reduce levels of atmospheric pollution. These standards have been invoked not only to address these concerns, but also to call attention to those who violate these global norms. To be sure, many people would point to the obvious fact that in many settings governments, businesses, and community groups act without regard to these standards. However, what is significant is the fact that they are being invoked as points of reference. In the process, we can observe that the language and rhetoric associated with these global ethical practices are now more widely invoked as taken-for-granted normative standards.

The many thousands of organizations and individuals who have engaged in the practices of global ethics during the past several decades have done so out of a wish to make a difference. Hope is vital to the practice of ethics. Without hope it is difficult to accept the risks involved in making commitments and caring about others and the Earth itself. Given the scope and complexity of the global challenges we face, without hope people are inclined simply to live as well as they can, protecting themselves from present threats and seeking their immediate advantages. However, what has characterized all those involved in the practices of global ethics is that they have acted with some measure of hope.

Hope is not confidence based on the assumption that things will inevitably get better, that progress is inherent in the modern world, or that science, which has discovered so many novel ways of solving problems in the past, will help us to address the current crises and challenges. Rather, the hopes that have invigorated the diverse practices of global ethics have been held by people fully aware that these efforts may not succeed in avoiding possible tragedies – environmental disasters, new acts of genocide, new wars, or aggravated poverty. The practitioners of global ethics take for granted that they and other humans are fallible, that human goodness is fragile, and that the best of intentions often are misleading. Hope in the current context manifests itself as willingness to trust and remain committed to act in spite of difficulties, risks, and possible setbacks.

What then are the grounds upon which practitioners of global ethics base their hope? Hope for many springs from a sense of vocation. They feel called to protect endangered species, to negotiate treaties, to monitor activities in conflict zones, and to foster interfaith dialogues. Responding to these calls assumes a hope that their efforts will make a difference. From this perspective, grounds for hope seem immanent in the vocations to which these people commit themselves. For many, hope seems to arise from a larger sense of history. When viewed over the long haul, the present moment seems to offer increasing possibilities for global cooperation that crosses boundaries of all kinds. For many, hope makes ethical actions seem rational. More than two centuries ago, Kant recognized this relationship between ethical conduct and hope. He observed that people did not think it was reasonable to act in keeping with ethical standards if as a result things would get much worse for them. He argued that the problem was not solved either by sentimental confidence that expected favourable outcomes or by deliberate efforts to modify ethical standards so that one could guarantee favourable outcomes. Commitment to ethical principles presupposed that it was reasonable to hope even if one could not provide a rational basis for that hope.[6] While Kant found grounds for hope in the belief in a transcendent deity, many today do not have recourse to such beliefs. Nonetheless, without hope, their commitments to the practice of global ethics might seem idealistic, even foolhardy. Instead, their commitments lead them to hope, because hope makes their commitments seem reasonable. Like living with despair but with the opposite effect, living with hope functions in a circular fashion to occasion more hope, not because we are able to realize all our objectives but because in an imperfect world we often find ways of addressing the inevitable challenges and setbacks that come our way. In addition, many of those involved in the practices of global ethics still find grounds for hope in the faith traditions in which they were raised. As Christians or Buddhists, Hindus or Jews, Muslims or Confucians, humanists or devoted scientists, they are already predisposed to act with hope.

Practising global ethics in a world structured by the exercise of power

Diverse practices of global ethics have emerged and gained strength in the years since the Second World War. Many would argue that during this same period the relations between many nations and peoples of the world have been shaped and regulated by what has been described as a liberal world order, led and dominated by the hegemonic role played by the United States. This liberal world order has been associated – so the argument runs – with increased global trade; modest global governance exercised by a number of multilateral organizations such as the United Nations, the World Bank, and the WHO; the increasingly important influence exercised by international civil society organizations, such as the International Union for the Conservation of Nature (IUCN), international labour groups, and diverse global charities; and efforts to regulate global interactions by reference to international law and agreements. This has been an international political and economic order. As new nations came into being, many have come to acknowledge it as a dominant frame of reference. With the end of the cold war, this liberal world order momentarily seemed to have gained in authority and influence.[7] However, it was never without challenges, both from the Soviet Union in the past and currently from countries such as China and perhaps Iran, as well as by movements like militant Islam that seek to advance other ways of establishing a world order. The liberal world order also seems to be facing serious challenges in the form of an ongoing global economic recession, the declining capacity of the United States to structure the world order as it would like, and the potentially looming crises with respect to climate, food supplies, pandemic diseases, and ongoing civil conflicts in Eastern Europe, the Middle East, and areas in Africa.[8]

While many specific practices of global ethics are embodied in institutions that have become integral to the so-called liberal world order, as a whole these practices are broader, deeper, sometimes older, and frequently independent of this international political and economic order. For example, initiatives to champion human rights, to foster the economic growth of the developing world, to protect endangered environments, to protect civilians and prisoners during war, and to encourage interfaith dialogues all began in the nineteenth or early twentieth century. Many aspects of global ethics in practice, including important features of the interfaith initiatives, human rights groups, environmental groups, and humanitarian assistance, have been championed by civil society groups that remain largely independent of the political structures of what is called the liberal world order. Although efforts have been made by proponents of particular practices of global ethics to gain governmental support and endorsement for their programmes and policies, much of the work undertaken has been carried out by non-government groups, international organizations, humanitarians, and dedicated scientists institutionally distinct from the formal worlds of politics. In decisive ways, those practising global ethics have sought to be inclusive and have deliberately sought supporters from opposing power blocks and diverse faiths, from industrialized as well as developing nations, thereby seeking not to be too closely tied to partisan positions. Furthermore, while moved by hope, many of those deeply involved with practising global ethics retain a sense of tragic realism, quite different from the political realism invoked by political philosophers. Fully aware of how structures of power shape possibilities for action and how global crises threaten human and global well-being, they are moved as well by a sense that we must imaginatively pursue possibilities and not be deterred even by inevitable disappointments.

Global ethics in practice draws from a wider range of interests than the so-called liberal world order. While particular individuals and groups associated with the practices of global ethics have at times assumed dominant roles, overall those engaged in the practices of global ethics do not represent a system of political and economic dominance. In fact, it is no advantage for practitioners to be too closely associated with an ideology like liberalism at a time when this worldview is under challenge from states like China, movements like militant Islam, and others who seek alternative and perhaps more pluralistic forms of world order. In a larger sense, those engaged in the practices of global ethics practise a kind of global politics because they are interested in developing responsible public policies with respect to global issues. Likewise, some of the organizations involved in global ethics as social practices, like the specialized UN agencies, work both to support the liberal world order and at the same time to advance global ethics agendas.

No doubt many observers regard the practice of ethics generally and the practices of global ethics in particular as hopelessly idealistic, especially in a world that seems to be threatened by unending crises and shaped by diverse financial and economic interests, political agendas, sectarian visions, and ethnic hostilities. Those with power seem to hold sway, whether their power comes from the use or threatened use of coercion, their command over economic resources, their ability to shape public opinion, and/or their control of political processes. Often those expressing high-minded ethical views seem to be involved with modest projects that may render the exercise of power somewhat less objectionable, but that fail to bring about fundamental changes.

However, as the previous chapters have attempted to illustrate, many of those practising global ethics have acted in considered ways to engage with and affect how the powerful exercise their power. In several ways the practices of global ethics – and the institutions, organizations, and people associated with these practices – have operated, not to overcome power, but to create frameworks that place limits on its just use.

To understand how the contemporary practices of global ethics have affected the exercise of power, it is useful to refer to a conceptual model developed by Douglass North and his associates, who compare how power operates in most modern industrial societies compared to almost all other societies. In modern industrial societies, various organized groups compete to exercise economic and political power in keeping with institutionalized rules and expectations. What North and associates describe as 'open access social orders' produce much more wealth than pre-industrialized societies. In most societies, elites with power organize advancing their interests and defending themselves against other elites by the exercise of violence, threat of violence, and economic influence. They are organized to exploit given sources of wealth and power to their own advantage. North and his colleagues refer to this as the natural order. It is unstable and conflict-filled, but it has been and remains the typical social order in most societies. In contrast, in many modern industrialized societies, a variety of institutional arrangements modify and to a degree limit how those with power can exercise their power. In these societies, to be sure, as a result of technological and organizational developments, the intensity and force associated with the exercise of power have increased, whether we are thinking of modern military, business, or government operations. However, how this power is deployed has also been constrained by institutional arrangements directly connected with modern law, both national and international, as well as organizational developments, modern markets, political movements, and civil society. What especially characterizes modern industrial societies is the tremendous increase in the number of organized associations, whether these are businesses, labour unions, civil society organizations, or governmental bodies. In both modest and more significant ways, these organizations act as both loci of power and means of holding accountable other loci of power.[9]

We can also employ this model in very general terms to describe similar sorts of changes by which the international practices of global ethics have in four modest but significant ways affected how power is exercised globally.

First, the practices of global ethics have functioned to legitimate and strengthen the current and evolving globalized system of states and international agencies. This is a complex multi-centred system in which nations as well as intergovernmental bodies such as the World Bank, the WTO, the WHO, the European Community, and the United Nations exercise authority and influence – sometimes to be sure with particular agendas – and at the same time act to hold accountable other states, corporate organizations, and international agencies. In complex ways, each centre of power functions to exercise countervailing force with respect to other sources of power. As a whole, this complex system of states and international agencies has functioned to establish loose but not insignificant limits that must be taken into account by those seeking to exercise power. All these intergovernmental organizations are governed by charters that spell out both norms and values for how they operate. The normative values of these charters echo and are informed by the same range of standards expressed in the common credos and institutionalized practices of global ethics that we have analysed in the previous chapters of this book.

Since the beginning of the twentieth century, a similarly complex system of international civil society organizations has grown in numbers and influence to complement this web of national and international governmental bodies. We have in mind organizations, many of which we have discussed in previous chapters, such as the Council for a Parliament of the World's Religions, Transparency International, the International Crisis Group, and the International Committee of the Red Cross. In smaller but not insignificant ways, they, too, both exercise authoritative influence and also help to hold accountable businesses and governments seeking to exercise power.[10] As a result of these several developments, we do not now live in the kind of boundaryless world championed by some international business leaders, but rather in a complex, multidimensional, diversely organized world. This is the kind of globalized world in which the practices of global ethics reviewed in this book variously function to legitimate, to manage, and to humanize the exercise of power.

Second, the practices of global ethics have helped to create and strengthen the evolving system of international law. This system is embodied in statutes such as human rights covenants and codes, International Humanitarian Law, regulations governing international trade, stipulations of the WHO, as well as in international tribunals such as the World Court, the International Criminal Court (ICC), the dispute resolution bodies of the WTO, and hearings of the UN Council on Human Rights. We have reviewed the interrelationship between the practices of global ethics and international law in a number of places in this book, especially Chapters 1, 4, and 6. Some of this 'law' is well established and well integrated into national legal systems. Much of it is emergent, but as such still compels considerable authority.[11] Overall, this evolving system of international law functions in modest but decisive ways to limit how states and enterprises are able to exercise power.

Third, in a number of ways, those engaged in the practices of global ethics have developed and encouraged others to develop means for monitoring the practices of governments, business enterprises, and civil society organizations. When we also take into account the role played by public and social media, since the beginning of the twentieth century we have witnessed growth in the extent to which various groups and agencies report on and evaluate the practices of the powerful. Hundreds of human rights groups keep track of how well governments, businesses, and non-state actors comply with or violate human rights standards. Others gauge political groups according to their particular agendas, evaluate businesses in terms of their environmental practices, judge both governments and enterprises with regard to their economic performance and their impact on global poverty. As we observed in Chapter 8, an increasing number of international businesses have instituted regular means to gauge their performances with respect to a range of normative standards. Viewed as a whole, these diverse monitoring practices serve to augment the accountability of those who exercise power. To be sure, these monitoring practices are less developed in traditional societies and in autocratic states with weak civil societies. Still, monitoring by these diverse groups does make those exercising authority and power at least modestly more accountable.

Fourth, as global ethics in practice have developed in the years since the Second World War, they have significantly altered the way people think and talk about the issues facing our world. Compared with a century ago, governments and enterprises are much more likely to be evaluated in terms of their impact on human rights, their environmental footprint, their deference to the rule of law, and their compliance with Geneva Conventions. Whereas, a century ago, multiple states openly aspired to act as imperial powers governing subjected peoples, these governments are now likely to be judged on their capacity to foster economic growth, global commerce, and educational achievements among school age children. The character of public discourse has changed in ways that do not so much limit the exercise of power but rather shape how governments and enterprises exercise power and justify their uses of power.

There are, to be sure, numerous groups that work to protect and advance their own objectives with little concern for the Earth and its well-being and little appreciation for efforts and ways of life of other communities and polities. Variously referred to as 'populists', 'fundamentalists', 'chauvinists', or local 'insurgents', these diverse groups often purposefully pursue goals that are counter to the Earth-centred, cosmopolitan, and rights-based visions associated with the practices of global ethics. They seek the good of their particular groups as they understand this end. Typically, they deeply distrust the larger social order, which seems to neglect or undermine what they hold valuable. Ironically, in their zealous defence of their own ends, these groups often aggravate divisions and feelings of distrust in the societies in which they exist. A number of these militant groups have turned quite aggressively against community members who differ in their views or oppose them.[12] Accordingly, they pose a direct challenge to global ethics in practice in a number of ways. They reject and oppose the pluralist cosmopolitan character of these practices. They tend to dismiss concerns about the larger environmental, social, health, economic, and political crises we have discussed in this book, preferring to concentrate in moralistic terms on the threats associated with those who oppose their own campaigns.

A constant challenge faced by those practising global ethics is how best to respond to those who directly oppose their vision with their own moral messages. This challenge becomes more intense when groups like these are able to command military force, whether from a formal state power, such as North Korea or Zimbabwe, or from well-organized insurgents, as in eastern Congo, Central African Republic, Syria, Iraq, or north-western Pakistan. Whether they are comparatively non-violent populists in industrialized countries or well-armed militia in the Middle East, these groups typically find ways of turning both verbal and armed attacks to their advantage by appealing to new followers. As we have discussed in Chapters 5 and 6, there are no simple strategies for addressing insurgents that resort to force. Still, there is an emerging consensus about how to create a multifaceted approach, including, for example, finding constructive ways to provide economic opportunities for those who might turn to these kinds of militant groups out of their own sense of disillusionment with existing political processes and despair about their own economic prospects.

As we have argued throughout this book, the overall practice of global ethics is a fragile enterprise. These practices have faced countless challenges, not only from those who wield power and directly oppose them, and not only from the evolving crises to which they have responded, but also from the indifference of those who attend to their own private lives and attempt to ignore the crises we have discussed. However, in many ways, the practitioners of global ethics in their diverse forms – from human rights advocates to the MDGs, from the interfaith movements to the Equator Principles, from Geneva Conventions to the Earth Charter, from the work of the IPCC to the work of the International Crisis Group – have by their actions allowed many people, groups, and states to feel hopeful. This is a hope that emanates from respect for the deeply rooted convictions, the compassionate diligence, and the willingness to listen and collaborate with strangers that have continuously marked the practices of global ethics. We still live in a troubled and turbulent world. However, practising global ethics offers constructive and promising ways of addressing this world responsibly and realistically.

Notes

1. *The Economist*, 'Generation Jobless'.
2. Pinker, *The Better Angels of our Nature*.
3. *The Economist*, 'How to Stop Fighting, Sometimes'.
4. See *The Economist*, 'Mightier than the Words'. See also Universal Islamic Declaration of Human Rights, Cairo Declaration on Human Rights in Islam, and Asian Human Rights Charter, all

found in Sullivan and Kymlicka (eds), *The Globalization of Ethics*, pp. 247–82.

5. See Joas, *The Sacredness of the Person*.
6. Kant, *Critique of Practical Reason*.
7. For several different views of this liberal world order, see Bull, *The Anarchical Society*; Ikenberry, 'The Illusions of Geopolitics'; Arrighi and Silver, *Chaos and Governance in the Modern World System*.
8. Mead, 'The Return of Geopolitics; Arrighi, *Adam Smith in Beijing*.
9. North et al., *Violence and Social Order*.
10. See Chandler, *Constructing Global Civil Society*.
11. On the status and authority of emergent law, see especially Weber, 'Emergence and Creation of Legal Norms'.
12. See Bennoune, *Your Fatwa does not Apply Here*.

Bibliography

AAR (American Academy of Religion). Religion in the Schools Task Force, *Guidelines for Teaching about Religion in K-12 Public Schools in the United States* (Atlanta, GA: American Academy of Religion, 2010) <https://www.aarweb.org/sites/default/files/pdfs/Publications/epublications/AARK-12CurriculumGuidelines.pdf> (last accessed 23 January 2015).

Abramsky, Kolya (ed.), *Sparking a Worldwide Energy Revolution: Social Struggles in the Transition to a Post-Petrol World* (Oakland, CA: AK Press, 2010).

Acemoglu, Daron, and James Robinson, *Why Nations Fail: The Origins of Power, Prosperity, and Poverty* (New York: Crown Publishers, 2012), chs 9, 12.

Adams, Roger, 'Tools, Guidance, and Standards for Corporate Social Responsibility and Sustainability Reporting', in *Disclosure of the Impact of Corporations on Society: Current Trends and Issues*, United Nations Conference on Trade and Development (New York and Geneva: United Nations, 2004), pp. 89–93.

Adcock, C. S., 'Debating Conversion, Silencing Caste: The Limited Scope of Religious Freedom', *Journal of Law and Religion*, 29/3 (October 2014), pp. 363–77.

Adcock, C. S., *The Limits of Tolerance: Indian Secularism and the Politics of Religious Freedom* (New York: Oxford University Press, 2014).

Agarwal, Anil, and Sunita Narain, *Global Warming in an Unequal World: A Case of Environmental Colonialism* (New Delhi: Centre for Science and Environment, 1991).

Allport, Gordon, *The Nature of Prejudice*, 25th Anniversary Edition (New York: Basic Books, 1979).

Alvarez, José, *International Organizations as Law-Makers* (Oxford: Oxford University Press, 2005).

Amadiume, Ifi, and Abdullahi An-Na'im (eds), *The Politics of Memory: Truth, Healing and Social Justice* (London and New York: Zed Books, 2000).

Anderson, Dan R., *Corporate Survival: The Critical Importance of Sustainability Risk Management* (New York: iUniverse, 2005).

Arrighi, Giovanni, *Adam Smith in Beijing: Lineages of the Twenty-First Century* (New York: Verso, 2007).

Arrighi, Giovanni, and Beverly J. Silver, *Chaos and Governance in the Modern World System* (Minneapolis, MN: University of Minnesota Press, 1999).

Association for Supervision and Curriculum Development (ASCD), *Religion in the Curriculum* (Alexandria, VA: ASCD, 1984).

AtKisson, Alan, Dominic Stucker and Leah Wener, *EC-Assess: The Earth Charter Ethics-Based Assessment Tool* (San José, Costa Rica: Earth Charter International Secretariat, 2008).

Audi, Robert, *Moral Knowledge and Ethical Character* (New York: Oxford University Press, 1997).

Auty, R. M. (ed.), *Resource Abundance and Economic Development* (Oxford: Oxford University Press, 2001).

Auty, R. M., *Sustaining Development in Mineral Economies: The Resource Curse Thesis* (New York: Oxford University Press, 1993).

Avram, Wes (ed.), *Anxious about Empire: Theological Essays on the New Global Realities* (Grand Rapids, MI: Brazos Press, 2004).

Baker, Raymond W., *Capitalism's Achilles Heel: Dirty Money and How to Renew the Free Market System* (Hoboken, NJ: John Wiley & Sons, 2005).

Bakkan, Peter W., Joan Gibb Engel, and J. Ronald Engel, *Ecology, Justice and Christian Faith: A Critical Guide to the Literature* (Westport, CT: Greenwood Press, 1995).

Bandura, Albert, 'Moral Disengagement', in Israel W. Charny (ed.), *Encyclopedia of Genocide* (Santa Barbara, CA: ABC-CLIO, 1999), pp. 414–18.

Banerjee, Abhijit, and Esther Duflo, *Poor Economics: A Radical Rethinking of the Way to Fight Global Poverty* (New York: Public Affairs, 2011).

Barlow, Maude, and Tony Clarke, *Global Showdown: How the New Activists Are Fighting Global Corporate Rule* (Toronto: Stoddart, 2001).

Barnett, Michael, and Raymond Duvall (eds), *Power in Global Governance* (Cambridge: Cambridge University Press, 2005).

Barnett, Victoria J., *Bystanders: Conscience and Complicity during the Holocaust* (Westport, CT: Greenwood Press, 1999).

Barrett, Scott, 'The Incredible Economics of Geoengineering', *Environmental and Resource Economics*, 39/1 (2008), pp. 45–54.

Bassiouni, M. Cherif, and Daniel Rothenberg (eds), *The Chicago Principles on Post-Conflict Justice* (Chicago: International Human Rights Law Institute, 2007).

Baumeister, Roy, *Evil: Inside Human Violence and Cruelty,* Revised edition (New York: W. H. Freeman, 1999)

Bazilli, Susan, 'Reflections of a Global Women's Activist', *Human Rights Dialogue*, 2/3 (Summer 2000), pp. 12–13.

BBC News, 'Mass Dalit Conversions in Mumbai', 27 May 2007 <http://news.bbc.co.uk/2/hi/south_asia/6695695.stm> (last accessed 12 January 2015).

Beaford, Robert D., Timothy B. Gongaware, and Danny L. Valadez, 'Social Movements', in Edgar F. Borgatta and Rhonda J. V. Montgomery (eds), *Encyclopedia of Sociology*, 2nd edn, vol. 4 (New York: Macmillan Reference USA, 2000), pp. 2717–27.

Beck, Silke, Maud Borie, Jason Chilvers, Alejandro Esguerra, Katja Heubach, Mike Hulme, Rolf Lidskog, Eva Lövbrand, Elisabeth Marquard, Clark Miller, Tahani Nadim, Carsten Neßhöver, Josef Settele, Esther Turnhout, Eleftheria Vasileiadou, and Christoph Görg, 'Towards a Reflexive Turn in the Governance of Global Environmental Expertise: The Cases of the IPCC and the IPBES', *GAIA-Ecological Perspectives for Science and Society*, 23/2 (May 2014), pp. 80–7.

Bell, Charles W., 'With New Center, Rev Keeps the Interfaith', *New York Daily News*, 5 February 2000 <http://www.nydailynews.com/archives/news/new-center-rev-interfaith-article-1.859250> (last accessed 12 January 2015).

Bellamy, Alex J., 'The Responsibility to Protect – Five Years On', *Ethics & International Affairs*, 24/2 (Summer 2010), pp. 143–69.

Bennoune, Karima, *Your Fatwa does not Apply Here: Untold Stories from the Fight against Muslim Fundamentalism* (New York: W. W. Norton, 2013).

Bergen, Doris L., 'Between God and Hitler: German Military Chaplains and the Crimes of the Third Reich', in Omer Bartov and Phyllis Mack (eds), *In God's Name: Genocide and Religion in the Twentieth Century* (New York and Oxford: Berghahn Books, 2001), pp. 123–38.

Berman, Eli, *Radical, Religious, and Violent: The New Economics of Terrorism* (Cambridge, MA: MIT Press, 2009).

Best, Geoffrey, *Humanity in Warfare: The Modern History of the International Law of Armed Conflicts* (London: Weidenfeld and Nicolson, 1980).

Best, Geoffrey, *War and Law since 1945* (Oxford: Clarendon Press, 1994).

Bharati, Sri Chandra Sekhara, *Golden Words* (Bombay: Tattvāloka, 1992).

Bird, Frederick, *The Muted Conscience: Moral Silence and the Practice of Ethics in Business* (Westport, CT: Quorum Books, 1996).

Bird, Frederick, and Stewart Herman (eds), *International Businesses and the Challenge of Poverty in the Developing World* (Basingstoke: Palgrave Macmillan, 2004).

Bird, Frederick, and Manuel Velasquez (eds), *Just Business Practices in a Diverse and Developing World* (Basingstoke: Palgrave Macmillan, 2006).

Bird, Frederick, Emmanuel Raufflet, and Joseph Smucker (eds), *International Business and the Dilemmas of Development: Case Studies in South Africa, Madagascar, Pakistan, South Korea, Mexico and Colombia* (Basingstoke: Palgrave Macmillan, 2004).

Bishop, Matthew, 'Corporate Governance', *The Economist*, 29 January 1994, pp. 1–18.

Blair, Margaret M., *Ownership and Control: Rethinking Corporate Governance for the Twenty-First Century* (Washington: Brookings Institution, 1995).

Blair, Margaret M., *Wealth Creation and Wealth-Sharing: A Colloquium on Corporate Governance and Investments in Human Capital* (Washington: Brookings Institution, 1996).

The Book of the Discipline (Vinaya Pitaka), vol. IV (Mahavagga), trans. I. B. Horner (London: Luzac [1951] 1971).

Boot, Max, 'The Evolution of Irregular War: Insurgents and Guerillas from Akkadia to Afghanistan', *Foreign Affairs* (March/April 2013), pp. 100–14.

Bosselman, Klaus, and Prue Taylor, 'The Significance of the Earth Charter in International Law', in Peter Blaze Corcoran, Mirian Vilela and Alide Roerink (eds), *The Earth Charter in Action: Toward a Sustainable World* (Amsterdam: KIT Publishers, 2005), pp. 171–3.

Boudreau, Spencer, 'From Confessional to Cultural: Religious Education in the Schools of Quebec', *Religion & Education*, 38/3 (September 2011), pp. 212–23.

Braybrooke, Marcus, *Pilgrimage of Hope: One Hundred Years of Global Interfaith Dialogue* (New York: Crossroad, 1992).

Brecher, Jeremy, Tim Costello, and Brendon Smith, *Globalization from Below: The Power of Solidarity* (Cambridge, MA: South End Press, 2000).

Brekke, Torkel (ed.), *The Ethics of War in Asian Civilizations: A Comparative Perspective* (London and New York: Routledge, 2006).

Brenes, Abelardo, 'The Earth Charter Principles: Source of Ethics of Universal Responsibility', in Peter Miller and Laura Westra (eds), *Just Ecological Integrity: The Ethics of Maintaining Planetary Life* (Lanham, MD: Rowman & Littlefield Publishers, 2002), pp. 26–36.

Brenes, Abelardo, 'Universal and Differentiated Responsibility', in Peter Blaze Corcoran, Mirian Vilela, and Alide Roerink (eds), *The Earth Charter in Action: Toward a Sustainable World* (Amsterdam: KIT Publishers, 2005), pp. 35–7.

Brown, Donald A. (ed.), *The Ethical Dimensions of the United Nations Program on Environment and Development, Agenda 21, Conference Proceedings of Interdisciplinary Conference Held at the United Nations January 12–14, 1994* (Camp Hill, PA: Earth Ethics Research Group, 1994).

Brown, Lester R., *Who Will Feed China? Wake-up Call for a Small Planet* (New York: W.W. Norton, 1995).

Brown, Noel J., and Pierre Quiblier (eds), *Ethics and Agenda 21: Moral Implications of a Global Consensus* (New York: United Nations Environment Programme, 1994).

Brown, Peter G., *Ethics, Economics and International Relations* (Edinburgh: Edinburgh University Press, 2000).

Browning, Christopher R., *Ordinary Men: Reserve Police Battalion 101 and the Final Solution in Poland*, rev. edn (New York: HarperCollins, 1998).

Brownlie, Ian, and Guy S. Goodwin-Gill (eds), *Basic Documents on Human Rights*, 5th edn (Oxford: Oxford University Press, 2006).

Brudholm, Thomas, and Thomas Cushman (eds), *The Religious in Reponses to Mass Atrocity: Interdisciplinary Perspectives* (New York: Cambridge University Press, 2009).

Buckley, William Joseph (ed.), *Kosovo: Contending Voices on Balkan Interventions* (Grand Rapids, MI: Eerdmans Publishing, 2000).

Bull, Hedley, *The Anarchical Society: A Study for Understanding World Politics*, 2nd edn (Basingstoke: Palgrave Macmillan, [1977] 1995).

Burke, Jason, 'Religious Aid Groups Try to Convert Victims', *Guardian*, 16 January 2005 <http://www.theguardian.com/world/2005/jan/16/tsunami2004.internationalaidanddevelopment1> (last accessed 12 January 2015).

Butler, Diane Carol, 'Religiosity in Art Inspired by Samuan Tiga and Tejakula, Bali: Unity in Diversity', PhD dissertation, Udayana University, 2011.

Butler, Diane Carol, I Wayan Ardika, Edi Sedyawati, and I Gde Parimartha, 'Religiosity in Art Inspired by Samuan Tiga and Tejakula, Bali: Unity in Diversity', *Udayana University E-Journal of Cultural Studies*, 5/2 (July 2011) <http://ojs.unud.ac.id/index.php/ecs/article/view/3643> (last accessed 16 January 2015).

Byman, Daniel, 'Why Drones Work: The Case for Washington's Weapon of Choice', *Foreign Affairs*, 92/4 (July/August 2013), pp. 32–43.

Caine, Mark, Jason Lloyd, Max Luke, Lisa Margonelli, Todd Moss, Ted Nordhaus, Roger Pielke Jr, Mikael Román, Joyashree Roy, Daniel Sarewitz, Michael Shellenberger, Kartikeya Singh, and Alex Trembath, *Our High-Energy Planet* (San Francisco: Breakthrough Institute, 2014).

Caldwell, Lynton Keith, *International Environmental Policy: Emergence and Dimensions*, 2nd edn (Durham, NC: Duke University Press, 1990).

Caldwell, Lynton Keith, *International Environmental Policy: From the Twentieth to the Twenty First Century*, 3rd edn (Durham, NC: Duke University Press, 1996).

Callicott, J. Baird, 'Non-Anthropocentric Value Theory and Environmental Ethics', *American Philosophical Quarterly*, 21/4 (October 1984), pp. 299–309.

Callicott, J. Baird, 'Toward a Global Environmental Ethic', in Noel J. Brown and Pierre Quiblier (eds), *Ethics and Agenda 21: Moral Implications of a Global Consensus* (New York: United Nations Environment Programme, 1994), pp. 9–12.

Camus, Albert, *The Rebel: An Essay on Man in Revolt*, trans. Anthony Bower (New York: Vintage Books, 1956).

Cançado Trindade, A. A., 'Environmental Protection and the Absence of Restrictions on Human Rights', in Kathleen E. Mahoney and Paul Mahoney (eds), *Human Rights in the Twenty-First Century: A Global Challenge* (Dordrecht, The Netherlands: Kluwer Academic Publishers, 1993), pp. 561–93.

Caplovitz, David, *The Poor Pay More: Consumer Practices of Low Income Families* (New York: Free Press of Glencoe, 1963).

Carpenter, Charli, 'Fighting the Laws of War: Protecting Civilians in Asymmetric Conflict', *Foreign Affairs* (March/April 2011), pp. 146–52.

Carr, Caleb, *The Lessons of Terror: A History of Warfare against Civilians*, rev. and updated (New York: Random House, 2003).

Carson, Rachel, *Silent Spring* (Boston: Houghton Mifflin, 1962).

Cavanaugh, Gerald F., 'Executives' Code of Business Conduct: Prospects for the Caux Principles', in Oliver F. Williams (ed.), *Global Codes of Conduct: An Idea Whose Time Has Come* (Notre Dame, IN: University of Notre Dame Press), ch. 10.

Chandler, David, *Constructing Global Civil Society: Morality and Power in International Relations* (New York and Basingstoke: Palgrave Macmillan, 2004).

Charkham, Jonathan P., *Keeping Good Company: A Study of Corporate Governance in Five Countries* (Oxford: Clarendon Press, 1994).

Chayes, Abram, and Antonia Handler Chayes, *The New Sovereignty: Compliance with International Regulatory Agreements* (Cambridge, MA: Harvard University Press, 1998).

Chicago Women's Liberation Union (CWLU), herstory project, 'A History of the Chicago Women's Liberation Union' (1971) <http://www.cwluher story.org/how-to-start-your-own-consciousness-raising-group.html> (last accessed 12 January 2015).

Cisneros, Ariane, and Shanta Premawardhana (eds), *Sharing Values: A Hermeneutic for Global Ethics* (Geneva: Globethic, 2011).

Clark, Gregory, *A Farewell to Alms: A Brief Economic History of the World* (Princeton: Princeton University Press, 2008), chs 3, 5.

Clark, William C., 'Managing Planet Earth', *Scientific American*, 261/3 (September 1989), pp. 47–54.

Clarkson, Max B. E., 'A Stakeholder Framework for Analyzing and Evaluating Corporate Social Performance', *Academy of Management Review*, 20/1 (January 1995), pp. 92–117.

Coates, Ken, *A Global History of Indigenous Peoples* (Basingstoke: Palgrave Macmillan, 2004).

Cohen, Stanley, *States of Denial: Knowing about Atrocities and Suffering* (Cambridge: Polity Press, 2001).

Coll, Steve, 'Remote Control: Our Drone Delusion', *New Yorker*, 6 May 2013, pp. 76–9.

Collier, Paul, *The Bottom Billion: Why the Poorest Countries are Failing and what Can Be Done about It?* (New York: Oxford University Press, 2007).

Collier, Paul, *Wars, Guns, and Votes: Democracy in Dangerous Places* (New York: HarperCollins, 2009).

Commission on Global Governance, *Our Global Neighbourhood* (Oxford: Oxford University Press, 1995).

Commission on Growth and Development, *Growth Report: Strategies for Sustained Growth and Development* (Washington: International Bank for Reconstruction and Development/World Bank, 2008).

Commoner, Barry, *Science and Survival* (New York: Viking Press, 1966).

Coney, Simon, *Justice beyond Borders: A Global Political Theory* (Oxford: Oxford University Press, 2005).

Connolly, Barbara, 'Increments for the Earth: The Politics of Environmental Aid', in Robert O. Keohane and Marc A. Levy (eds), *Institutions for Environmental Aid: Pitfalls and Promise* (Cambridge, MA: MIT Press, 1996), pp. 281–323.

Connolly, Barbara, and Robert O. Keohane, 'Institutions for Environmental Aid: Politics, Lessons and Opportunities', *Environment: Science and Policy for Sustainable Development*, 38/5 (June 1996), pp. 12–42.

Coonan, Terry S., 'Human Rights in the Sunshine State: A Proposed Florida Law on Human Trafficking', *Florida State University Law Review*, 31/2 (Winter 2004), pp. 289–301.

Corcoran, Peter Blaze, Mirian Vilela, and Alide Roerink (eds), *The Earth Charter in Action: Toward a Sustainable World* (Amsterdam: KIT Publishers, 2005).

Cornish, Paul, 'The Ethics of "Effects-Based" Warfare: The Crowding out of *Jus in Bello?*', in Charles Reed and David Ryall (eds), *The Price of Peace: Just War in the Twenty-First Century* (Cambridge: Cambridge University Press, 2007), ch. 10.

Council for a Parliament of the World's Religions, *Declaration toward a Global Ethic* (Chicago: Council for a Parliament of the World's Religions, 1993).

Cox, Harvey, 'Deep Structures in the Study of New Religions', in Jacob Needleman and George Baker (eds), *Understanding the New Religions* (New York: Seabury Press, 1978).

Cragg, Wesley, 'Ethics, Enlightened Self-Interest, and the Corporate Responsibility to Respect Human Rights: A Critical Look at the Justificatory Foundations of the UN Framework', *Business Ethics Quarterly*, 22/1 (January 2012), pp. 9–37

Cragg, Wesley, and Dirk Matten, 'Ethics, Corporations, and Governance', *Journal of Business Ethics*, 102/1 (March 2011), pp. 1–4.

Cronin, Audrey Kurth, 'Why Drones Fail: When Tactics Drive Strategy', *Foreign Affairs*, 92/4 (July/August 2013), pp. 44–54.

Cronin, Audrey Kurth, *How Terrorism Ends: Understanding the Decline and Demise of Terrorist Campaigns* (Princeton: Princeton University Press, 2009).

Cronon, William, 'A Place for Stories: Nature, History, and Narrative', *Journal of American History*, 78/4 (March 1992), pp. 1347–76.

Crook, Clive, 'The Good Company: A Survey of Corporate Responsibility', *The Economist*, 22 January 2005, pp. 1–22.

Croucher, Rowland, et al., 'Indian Police Obstruct Mass Conversions of Untouchables to Buddhism and Christianity', *John Mark Ministries*, 5 January 2003 <http://jmm.aaa.net.au/articles/10470.htm> (last accessed 12 January 2015).

Crutzen, Paul J., 'Albedo Enhancement by Stratospheric Sulfur Injections: A Contribution to Resolve a Policy Dilemma?', *Climatic Change*, 77/3 (August 2006), pp. 211–20.

Crutzen, Paul J., 'Estimates of Possible Future Ozone Reductions from

Continued Use of Fluoro-Chloro-Methanes (CF_2Cl_2, $CFCl_3$)', *Geophysical Research Letters*, 1/5 (September 1974), pp. 205–8.

Crutzen, Paul J., 'Estimates of Possible Variations in Total Ozone due to Natural Causes and Human Activities', *Ambio*, 3/6 (1974), pp. 201–10.

Culpeper, Roy, Albert Berry, and Frances Stewart (eds), *Global Development Fifty Years after Bretton Woods: Essays in Honour of Gerald K. Helleiner* (New York: Saint Martin's Press, 1997).

Daly, Herman E., and John B. Cobb, Jr, *For the Common Good: Redirecting the Economy toward Community, the Environment, and a Sustainable Future* (Boston: Beacon Press, 1989).

Dashwood, Hevina S., *The Rise of Corporate Social Responsibility: Mining and the Spread of Global Norms* (Cambridge: Cambridge University Press, 2012).

Davidio, John F., Peter Glick, and Laurie A. Rudman (eds), *On the Nature of Prejudice: Fifty Years after Allport* (Meriden, MA: Blackwell Publishing, 2005).

Davis, Mike, *Late Victorian Holocausts: El Niño Famines and the Making of the Third World* (London and New York: Verso, 2001).

Davis, Mike, *Planet of Slums* (New York: Verso, 2006).

de Schweinitz, Karl, *England's Road to Social Security: From the Statute of Laborers in 1349 to the Beveridge Report of 1942* (Philadelphia, PA: University of Pennsylvania Press, 1943).

De Soto, Hernando, *The Mystery of Capital* (New York: Basic Books, 2000).

de Souza, Marian, Kathleen Engebretson, Gloria Durka, Robert Jackson, and Andrew McGrady (eds), *International Handbook of the Religious, Moral and Spiritual Dimensions of Education*, vols I and II (Dordrecht, The Netherlands: Springer Academic Publishers, 2006).

Deelen, Gottfried, 'The Church on its Way to the People: Basic Christian Communities in Brazil', *CrossCurrents*, 30/4 (Winter 1980–1), pp. 385–408.

Dennis, Michael Aaron, 'Reconstructing Sociotechnical Order: Vannevar Bush and US Science Policy', in Sheila Jasanoff (ed.), *States of Knowledge: The Co-Production of Science and the Social Order* (London: Routledge, 2004), pp. 225–53.

Dershowitz, Alan M., *Why Terrorism Works: Understanding the Threat, Responding to the Challenge* (New Haven, CT: Yale University Press, 2003).

Donaldson, Thomas, 'De-Compacting the Global Compact', in Malcolm McIntosh, Sandra Waddock and George Kell (eds), *Learning to Talk: Corporate Citizenship and the Development of the UN Global Compact* (Sheffield: Greenleaf Publishing, 2004).

Donaldson, Thomas, and Thomas W. Dunfee, *Ties that Bind: A Social Contracts Approach to Business Ethics* (Boston: Harvard Business School Press, 1999).

Dower, Nigel, *An Introduction to Global Citizenship* (Edinburgh: Edinburgh University Press, 2003).

Dower, Nigel, *World Ethics: The New Agenda* (Edinburgh: Edinburgh University Press, 1998).

Drohan, Madelaine, 'Talisman in Sudan', in *Making a Killing: How and Why Corporations Use Armed Force to Do Business* (Toronto: Random House Canada, 2003), ch. 9, pp. 243–89.

Drucker, Peter, *The Unseen Revolution: How Pension Fund Socialism Came to America* (New York: Harper and Row, 1976).

Dryzek, John S., 'Green Reason: Communicative Ethics for the Biosphere', *Environmental Ethics*, 12/3 (Fall 1990), pp. 195–210.

Earth Charter Commission, *The Earth Charter* (Earth Charter Commission, 2000). Widely reprinted and available at <http://www.earthcharterinaction.org/content/pages/Read-the-Charter.html> (last accessed 15 January 2015).

Earth Charter Commission, 'The Earth Charter, Benchmark Draft I', *Earth Ethics*, 8/2–3 (Winter/Spring 1997), pp. 1, 3.

Earth Charter Steering Committee and International Secretariat, 'The Earth Charter at the Johannesburg Summit: A Report'. Unpublished typescript (2002).

Earth Ethics, 'Common Critiques of the Earth Charter', *Earth Ethics*, 8/2–3 (Winter/Spring 1997), p. 11.

Earth Ethics, 'History of the Earth Charter', *Earth Ethics* (Winter 2002), pp. 16–20.

Easterly, William, *The Elusive Quest for Growth: Economists', Adventures and Misadventures in the Tropics* (Cambridge, MA: MIT Press, 2001).

Easterly, William, *The White Man's Burden: Why the West's Efforts to Aid the Rest Have Done So Much Ill and So Little Good* (New York: Penguin Press, 2007).

The Economist, 'Gaza: The Rights and Wrongs', *The Economist*, 3 January 2009, p. 7.

The Economist, 'Generation Jobless: Youth Unemployment', *The Economist*, 27 April 2013, pp. 58–60.

The Economist, 'How to Stop Fighting, Sometimes', *The Economist*, 9 November 2013, pp. 25–9.

The Economist, 'Mightier than the Words', *The Economist*, 23 November 2013, p. 62.

The Economist, 'Mind Those Proportions: The Ethics of War', *The Economist*, 27 July 2006, pp. 43–4.

The Economist, 'The Unquenchable Fire: The State of al-Qaeda', *The Economist*, 28 September 2013, pp. 21–3.

Edwards, Paul N., *A Vast Machine: Computer Models, Climate Data, and the Politics of Global Warming* (Cambridge, MA: MIT Press, 2010).

Elshtain, Jean Bethke, *Just War against Terror: The Burden of American Power in a Violent World* (New York: Basic Books, 2003).

Elson, Diane, 'Human Rights and Corporate Profits: The UN Global Compact – Part of the Solution or Part of the Problem?', in Lourdes Beneria and Savitri Bisnath (eds), *Global Tensions: Challenges and Opportunities in the World Economy* (New York and London: Routledge, 2004), ch. 3.

Enderle, Georges, 'Ethics and Personhood: Rediscovering the Golden Rule for a Globalizing World', in Tze-wan Kwan (ed.), *Responsibility and Commitment: Eighteen Essays in Honor of Gerhold K. Becker* (Waldkirch: Gorz, 2008), pp. 1–16.

Enderle, Georges, 'The Ethics of Financial Reporting, the Global Reporting Initiative, and the Balanced Concept of the Firm', in George G. Brenkert (ed.), *Corporate Integrity and Accountability* (Thousand Oaks, CA: Sage Publications, 2004), ch. 8.

Engel, J. Ronald, 'The Earth Charter as a New Covenant for Democracy', in Peter Miller and Laura Westra (eds), *Just Ecological Integrity: The Ethics of Maintaining Planetary Life* (New York: Rowman & Littlefield Publishers, 2002), pp. 37–52.

Erickson, Paul, 'Mathematical Models, Rational Choice, and the Search for Cold War Culture', *Isis*, 101/2 (June 2010), pp. 386–92.

Erickson, Robert P., 'Genocide, Religion, and Gerhard Kittle: Protestant Theologians Face the Third Reich', in Omer Bartov and Phyllis Mack (eds), *In God's Name: Genocide and Religion in the Twentieth Century* (New York and Oxford: Berghahn Books, 2001), pp. 62–78.

Esquibel, Monica, 'Human Trafficking: A Violation of Human Rights, a Universal Issue', BA Honors Thesis, Florida State University, College of Social Sciences, 2005.

European Court of Human Rights, 'Kokkinakis vs Greece', in Henry J. Steiner and Philip Alston (eds), *International Human Rights in Context: Law, Politics, Morals*, 2nd edn (New York: Oxford University Press, 2000), pp. 476–83.

Evans, Gareth, *The Responsibility to Protect: Ending Mass Atrocity Crimes Once and for All* (Washington: Brooking Institution Press, 2008).

Ewen, Alexander (ed.), *Voice of Indigenous Peoples: Native People Address the United Nations* (Santa Fe, NM: Clear Light Publishers, 1994).

Falk, Richard, 'The Challenge of Genocide and Genocidal Politics in an Era of Globalisation', in Tim Dunne and Nicholas J. Wheeler (eds), *Human Rights in Global Politics* (New York: Cambridge University Press, 1999).

Falk, Richard, 'The Global Promise of Social Movements: Explorations at the Edge of Time', *Alternatives*, 12/2 (April 1987), pp. 173–96.

Falk, Richard, 'The Making of Global Citizenship', in Jeremy Brecher, John Brown Childs and Jill Cutler (eds), *Global Visions: Beyond the New World Order* (Boston: South End Press, 1993), 39–49.

Fanon, Frantz, *The Wretched of the Earth*, trans. Constance Farrington (New York: Grove Press/Presence Africaine, [1961] 1963).

Fautré, Willy, 'Why Did the Vatican Veto the OSCE's Guidelines on Teaching Religion?', *New Europe Online*, 25 July 2009 <http://www.neurope.eu/article/why-did-vatican-veto-osce's-guidelines-teaching-religion> (last accessed 22 January 2015).

Fein, Helen, 'More Murder in the Middle: Life-Integrity Violations and

Democracy in the World, 1987', *Human Rights Quarterly*, 17/1 (February 1995), pp. 170–91.

Ferguson, Niall, *The Ascent of Money: A Financial History of the World* (New York: Penguin Press, 2008).

Ferguson, Niall, *Empire: How Britain Made the Modern World* (London: Penguin Books, 2003).

Finn, Daniel K., *The Moral Ecology of Markets: Assessing Claims about Markets and Justice* (Cambridge: University of Cambridge Press, 2006).

Fisher, David, 'Humanitarian Interventions', in Charles Reed and David Ryall (eds), *The Price of Peace: Just War in the Twenty-First Century* (Cambridge: Cambridge University Press, 2007), ch. 6.

Fletcher, Laurel E., and Harvey M. Weinstein, 'Violence and Social Repair: Rethinking the Contribution of Justice to Reconciliation', *Human Rights Quarterly*, 24/3 (August 2002), pp. 573–639.

Fligstein, Neil, *The Transformation of Corporate Control* (Cambridge, MA: Harvard University Press, 1990).

Foley, Conor, *A Thin Blue Line: How Humanitarianism Went to War* (London: Verso, 2008).

Ford, John C., 'The Morality of Obliteration Bombing' [1944], in Richard B. Miller (ed.), *War in the Twentieth Century: Sources in Theological Ethics* (Louisville, KY: Westminster/John Knox Press, 1992), ch. 10, pp. 138–77.

Forstater, Maya, Jacqui MacDonald, and Peter Raynard, *Business and Poverty: Bridging the Gap* (London: Prince of Wales International Business Leaders Forum, 2002).

Franck, Thomas M., 'Proportionality in International Law', *Law and Ethics of Human Rights*, 4/2 (September 2010), pp. 230–42.

Frank, Robert H., and Philip J. Cook, *The Winner Take All Society* (New York and London: Penguin Books, 1996).

Freeman, Jack, and Soon-Young Yoon, 'How Important is an "Earth Charter"? Issue Dominates Rio + 5 Forum', *Earth Times*, 1–15 April 1997, pp. 1, 7.

Freeman, R. Edward, 'The Stakeholder Approach Revisited', *Zeitschrift für Wirtschafts- und Unternehmensethik*, 5/3 (2004), pp. 228–41.

Freeman, R. Edward, *Strategic Management: A Stakeholder Approach* (Boston: Pitman, 1984).

Friedman, Milton, 'The Social Responsibility of Business is to Increase its Profit', *New York Times Magazine*, 13 September 1970.

Friedman, Thomas, *The Lexus and the Olive Tree: Understanding Globalization* (New York: Random House, 2000).

Friedman, Thomas, *The World is Flat: A Brief History of the Twenty-First Century* (New York: Farrar, Straus and Giroux, 2005).

Frost, Mervyn, *Global Ethics: Anarchy, Freedom, and International Relations* (Oxford: Routledge, 2009).

Fuad, Zainul, 'Religious Pluralism in Indonesia: Muslim Christian-Discourse', PhD Dissertation, University of Hamburg, 2007.

Fussler, Claude, Aron Cramer, and Sebastian van der Vegt (eds), *Raising the*

Bar: Creating Value with the United Nations Global Compact (Sheffield: Greenleaf Publishing, 2004).

Gewirth, Alan, *Human Rights: Essays on Justification and Applications* (Chicago: University of Chicago Press, 1982).

Glendon, Mary Ann, *A World Made New: Eleanor Roosevelt and the Universal Declaration of Human Rights* (New York: Random House, 2001).

Global Ethic Foundation, 'Manifesto: Global Economic Ethic – Consequences for Global Businesses', in Hans Küng, Klaus M. Leisinger and Josef Wieland, *Manifesto Global Economic Ethic: Consequences and Challenges for Global Businesses* (Munich: Deutscher Taschenbuch Verlag, 2010), pp. 153–66.

Glover, Jonathan, *Humanity: A Moral History of the Twentieth Century* (New Haven, CT: Yale University Press, 2000).

Goldstone, Richard J., and Nicole Fritz, 'Fair Assessment: The Independent International Commission on Kosovo', in Ramesh Thakur, Andrew F. Cooper and John English (eds), *International Commissions and the Power of Ideas* (Tokyo: United Nations University Press, 2005), ch. 8, pp. 167–79.

Goodpaster, Kenneth E., 'The Caux Round Table Principles: Corporate Moral Reflection in a Global Business Environment', in Oliver Williams (ed.), *Global Codes of Conduct: An Idea whose Time Has Come* (Notre Dame, IN: University of Notre Dame Press, 2000), ch. 11.

Graffy, Elisabeth, and Steven Kihm, 'Does Disruptive Competition Mean a Death Spiral for Electric Utilities?', *Energy Law Journal*, 35/1 (May 2014), pp. 1–44.

Green, Ronald M., 'Religions and the Ethics of International Business', in Sumner B. Twiss and Bruce Grelle (eds), *Explorations in Global Ethics: Comparative Religious Ethics and Interreligious Dialogue* (Boulder, CO: Westview Press, 2000), pp. 237–51.

Grelle, Bruce, 'Culture and Moral Pluralism', in William Schweiker (ed.), *The Blackwell Companion to Religious Ethics* (Malden, MA: Blackwell Publishing, 2005), pp. 129–37.

Grelle, Bruce, 'Defining and Promoting the Study of Religion in British and American Schools', *Religion & Education*, 32/1 (Spring 2005), pp. 23–41.

Grelle, Bruce, 'The First Amendment Consensus Approach to Teaching about Religion in US Public Schools: Applications and Assessment', in Vincent F. Biondo III and Andrew Fiala (eds), *Civility, Religious Pluralism, and Education* (New York: Routledge, 2014), 127–46.

Grelle, Bruce, 'Neutrality in Public School Religion Education: Theory and Politics', in Lori G. Beaman and Leo Van Arragon (eds), *Issues in Religion and Education: Whose Religion?* (Leiden, The Netherlands: Brill, 2015).

Grelle, Bruce, 'Promoting Civic and Religious Literacy in Public Schools: The California 3 Rs Project', in Michael D. Waggoner (ed.), *Religion in the Public Schools: Negotiating the New Commons* (Lanham, MD: Rowman & Littlefield Education, 2013), pp. 91–110.

Griech-Polelle, Beth, 'A Pure Conscience is Good Enough: Bishop von Galen and Resistance to Nazism', in Omer Bartov and Phyllis Mack (eds), *In God's Name: Genocide and Religion in the Twentieth Century* (New York and Oxford: Berghahn Books, 2001), pp. 106–22.

Griffiths, Paul J., Vitor Westhelle, Alyssa Pitstick, Martin E. Marty, Carol Zaleski, John Franke, Amy Laura Hall, and Jerry Walls, 'What to Say about Hell: A Symposium', *Christian Century*, 125/11 (June 2008), pp. 22–7.

Gross, Michael L., *Moral Dilemmas of Modern War: Torture, Assassination, and Blackmail in an Age of Asymmetric Conflict* (New York: Cambridge University Press, 2010).

The Group of Lisbon, *Limits to Competition* (Cambridge, MA: MIT Press, 1995).

Gurr, Ted Robert, 'Early Warning Systems: From Surveillance to Assessment in Action', in Kevin Cahill (ed.), *Preventive Diplomacy: Stopping Wars before they Start*, rev. edn (Abingdon and New York: Routledge, 2000), pp. 243–62.

Gutman, Amy, 'Introduction', in Michael Ignatieff, *Human Rights as Politics and Idolatry* (Princeton: Princeton University Press, 2001), pp. vii–xxviii.

Hammond, Allen L., Eric Rodenburg, and William R. Moomaw, 'Calculating National Accountability for Climate Change', *Environment: Science and Policy for Sustainable Development*, 33/1 (January 1991), pp. 11–20.

Hansmann, Henry, *The Ownership of Enterprise* (Cambridge, MA: Harvard University Press, 1996).

Hardin, Garrett, 'Commentary: Living on a Lifeboat', *BioScience*, 24/10 (October 1974), pp. 561–8.

Hartigan, Richard Shelly, *Lieber's Code and the Law of War* (Chicago: Precedent Publishing, 1983).

Hassan, Parvez, 'Earth Charter: An Ethical Lodestar and Moral Force', in Peter Blaze Corcoran, Mirian Vilela and Alide Roerink (eds), *The Earth Charter in Action: Toward a Sustainable World* (Amsterdam: KIT Publishers, 2005), pp. 29–31.

Haynes, Charles C., 'Common Ground Documents', in James C. Carper and Thomas C. Hunt (eds), *The Praeger Handbook of Religion and Education in the United States*, vol. I (Westport, CT: Praeger, 2009), pp. 154–9.

Haynes, Charles C., 'US Department of Education Guidelines on Religion and Public Education', in James C. Carper and Thomas C. Hunt (eds.), *The Praeger Handbook of Religion and Education in the United States*, vol. II (Westport, CT: Praeger, 2009), pp. 449–51.

Haynes, Charles C., and Oliver Thomas, *Finding Common Ground: A First Amendment Guide to Religion and Public Schools* (Nashville, TN: First Amendment Center, 2007).

Hebblethwaite, Margaret, *Base Communities: An Introduction* (Mahwah, NJ: Paulist Press, 1994).

Hedberg, Carl-Johan, and Frederik von Malmborg, 'The Global Reporting Initiative and Corporate Sustainability Reporting in Swedish Companies',

Corporate Social Responsibility and Environmental Management, 10/3 (September 2003), pp. 153–64.

Heim, S. Mark, *Salvations: Truth and Difference in Religion* (Maryknoll, NY: Orbis Books, 1995).

Helleiner, Eric, *The Forgotten Foundations of Bretton Woods: International Development and the Making of the Postwar Order* (Ithaca, NY: Cornell University Press, 2014).

Helleiner, Eric, *The Status Quo Crisis: Global Financial Governance after the 2008 Meltdown* (Oxford: Oxford University Press, 2014).

Heschel, Susannah, *The Aryan Jesus: Christian Theologians and the Bible in Nazi Germany* (Princeton: Princeton University Press, 2008).

Houghton, John, *Global Warming: The Complete Briefing* (Cambridge: Cambridge University Press, 2004).

How, W. Glen, and Philip Brumley, 'Human Rights, Evangelism and Proselytism: A Perspective of Jehovah's Witnesses', in John Witte Jr and Richard C. Martin (eds), *Sharing the Book: Religious Perspectives on the Rights and Wrongs of Proselytism* (Maryknoll, NY: Orbis Books, 1999), pp. 276–304.

Howard-Hassmann, Rhoda E., 'The Second Great Transformation: Human Rights Leapfrogging in the Era of Globalization', *Human Rights Quarterly*, 27/1 (February 2005), pp. 1–40.

Human Rights Watch, *Why They Died: Casualties in Lebanon during the 2006 War* (2006) <http://www.hrw.org/node/10734/section/5> (last accessed 29 January 2015).

Human Security Centre and Human Security Report Project, *Human Security Report 2005: War and Peace in the 21st Century* (New York: Oxford University Press, 2005).

Human Security Report Project, Human Security Centre, *Human Security Report 2009/2010: The Causes of Peace and the Shrinking Costs of War* (New York: Oxford University Press, 2011).

Human Trafficking Project, *Florida Responds to Human Trafficking* (Tallahassee, FL: Florida State University Center for the Advancement of Human Rights, 2003).

Humphreys, Macmartan, Jeffrey Sachs, and Joseph P. Stiglitz (eds), *Escaping the Resource Curse* (New York: Columbia University Press, 2007).

Hutchinson, G. Evelyn, 'The Biosphere', *Scientific American*, 223/3 (September 1970), pp. 44–53.

Ignatieff, Michael, *Human Rights as Politics and Idolatry* (Princeton: Princeton University Press, 2001).

Ignatieff, Michael, *The Lesser Evil: Political Ethics in an Age of Terror* (Princeton: Princeton University Press, 2005).

Ignatieff, Michael, *The Warrior's Honour: Ethnic War and the Modern Conscience* (Toronto: Penguin Books, 1998).

Ikenberry, G. John, 'The Illusions of Geopolitics: The Enduring Power of the Liberal Order', *Foreign Affairs* (May/June 2014), pp. 80–90.

Inter Faith Network for the United Kingdom, *Building Good Relations with*

People of Different Faiths and Beliefs (London: Inter Faith Network for the United Kingdom, 2000).

Inter-Faith Action for Peace in Africa (IFAPA), 'Embracing the Gift of Peace', *The Johannesburg Inter-Faith Peace Declaration*, 17 October 2002 <http://www.lutheranworld.info/What_We_Do/OIahr/Issues_Eve nts/IFAPA-declaration.pdf> (last accessed 12 January 2015).

Interfaith Encounter Association, 'Our History, Values and Relationship' <http://interfaithencounter.wordpress.com/about/our-history/> (last accessed 12 January 2015).

International Commission on Intervention and State Sovereignty, *The Responsibility to Protect* (Ottawa, ON: International Development Research Centre, 2001).

International Finance Corporation, *Policy on Environmental and Social Sustainability* (Washington: International Finance Corporation, 2012).

International Law Commission, *Draft Code of Offenses against the Peace and Security of Mankind* (International Law Commission, 1954) <http://legal.un.org/ilc/texts/instruments/english/draft%20articles/7_3_1954.pdf> (last accessed 28 January 2015).

Jackson, Robert, 'Teaching about Religions in the Public Sphere: European Policy Initiatives and the Interpretive Approach', *Numen*, 55/2–3 (April 2008), pp. 151–82.

Jackson, Robert, *Signposts – Policy and Practice for Teaching about Religions and Non-Religious Worldviews in Intercultural Education* (Strasbourg: Council of Europe, 2014).

Jackson, Tim, *Prosperity without Growth: Economics for a Finite Planet* (London: Earthscan, 2009).

Jacobs, Jane, *Dark Age Ahead* (Toronto: Random House Canada, 2004).

Jasanoff, Sheila, *The Fifth Branch: Science Advisers as Policymakers* (Cambridge, MA: Harvard University Press, 1990).

Jasanoff, Sheila, 'Harmonization – The Politics of Reasoning Together', in Roland Bal and William Halffman (eds), *The Politics of Chemical Risk: Scenarios for a Regulatory Future* (Dordrecht: Springer, 1998), pp. 173–94.

Jasanoff, Sheila, 'Image and Imagination: The Formation of Global Environmental Consciousness', in Clark Miller and Paul Edwards (eds), *Changing the Atmosphere: Expert Knowledge and Environmental Governance* (Cambridge, MA: MIT Press, 2001), pp. 309–37.

Jasanoff, Sheila (ed.), *States of Knowledge: The Co-Production of Science and the Social Order* (London: Routledge, 2004).

Jenkins, Laura Dudley, 'Legal Limits on Religious Conversion in India', *Law and Contemporary Problems*, 71/2 (Spring 2008), pp. 109–28.

Jensen, Tim, 'RS Based RE in Public Schools: A Must for a Secular State', *Numen*, 55/2–3 (April 2008), pp. 123–50.

Joas, Hans, *The Sacredness of the Person: A New Genealogy of Human Rights* (Washington: Georgetown University Press, 2013).

Johnson, Chalmers, *The Sorrows of Empire* (New York: Henry Holt, 2004).

Johnson, James Turner, *Can Modern War Be Just?* (New Haven, CT: Yale University Press, 1984).

Johnson, James Turner, 'Just War Thinking in Recent American Religious Debate over Military Force', in Charles Reed and David Ryall (eds), *The Price of Peace: Just War in the Twenty-First Century* (Cambridge: Cambridge University Press, 2007), ch. 5.

Johnson, James Turner, *Just War Tradition and the Restraint of War: A Moral and Historical Inquiry* (Princeton: Princeton University Press, 1981).

Jones, Peter, 'Human Rights, Group Rights, and Peoples' Rights', *Human Rights Quarterly*, 21/1 (February 1999), pp. 80–107.

Juergensmeyer, Mark, *The New Cold War? Religious Nationalism Confronts the Secular State* (Berkeley and Los Angeles: University of California Press, 1993).

Juergensmeyer, Mark, *Terror in the Mind of God: The Global Rise of Religious Violence* (Berkeley and Los Angeles: University of California Press, 2000).

Kaldor, Mary, 'From Just War to Just Peace', in Charles Reed and David Ryall (eds), *The Price of Peace: Just War in the Twenty-First Century* (Cambridge: Cambridge University Press, 2007), chs 12–14.

Kant, Immanuel, *Critique of Practical Reason*, trans. Lewis White Beck (Indianapolis, IN: Bobbs-Merrill Educational Publishing, 1956).

Kao, Grace Y., *Grounding Human Rights in a Pluralist World* (Washington: Georgetown University Press, 2011).

Kao, Grace Y., 'The Logic of Anti-Proselytization, Revisited', in Rosalind I. J. Hackett (ed.), *Proselytization Revisited: Rights Talk, Free Markets and Culture Wars* (London: Equinox, 2008), pp. 77–107.

Kaufmann, Daniel, *Aid Effectiveness and Governance: The Good, the Bad, and the Ugly* (Washington: Brookings Institution, 2009).

Kearney, Neil, and Judy Gearhart, 'Workplace Codes as Tools for Workers', *Development in Practice*, 14/1–2 (February 2004), pp. 216–23.

Keck, Margaret E., and Kathryn Sikkink, *Activists beyond Borders: Advocacy Networks in International Politics* (Ithaca, NY, and London: Cornell University Press, 1998).

Keith, David W., 'Geoengineering the Climate: History and Prospect', *Annual Review of Energy and the Environment*, 25/1 (November 2000), pp. 245–84.

Kelsay, John, *Arguing the Just War in Islam* (Cambridge, MA: Harvard University Press, 2007).

Kennedy, David, *Of War and Law* (Princeton: Princeton University Press, 2006).

Kennedy, David, *The Dark Sides of Virtue: Reassessing International Humanitarianism* (Princeton: Princeton University Press, 2005).

Kennedy, Paul, *The Parliament of Man: The Past, Present and Future of the United Nations* (New York: Random House, 2006).

Keohane, Robert O., and David G. Victor, 'The Regime Complex for Climate Change', *Perspectives on Politics*, 9/1 (March 2011), pp.7–23.

King, Sallie B., 'What is of Value? A Buddhist Response to the Earth Charter', in Amy Morgante (ed.), *Buddhist Perspectives on the Earth Charter* (Cambridge, MA: Boston Research Center for the Twenty-First Century, 1997), pp. 77–86.

Kingsbury, Benedict, 'Reconciling Five Competing Conceptual Structures of Indigenous Peoples' Claims in International and Comparative Law', in Philip Alston (ed.), *Peoples' Rights* (Oxford: Oxford University Press, 2001), pp. 69–110.

Klein, Naomi, *No Logo* (London: Harper Collins, 1999).

Klein, Naomi, *The Shock Doctrine: The Rise of Disaster Capitalism* (Toronto: Alfred A, Knopf, 2007).

Knauth, Thorsten, Dan-Paul Jozsa, Gerdien Bertram-Troost, and Julia Ipgrave (eds), *Encountering Religious Pluralism in School and Society: A Qualitative Study of Teenage Perspectives in Europe* (Münster: Waxmann Verlag, 2008).

Korey, William, 'Human Rights NGOs: The Power of Persuasion', *Ethics & International Affairs*, 13/1 (March 1999), pp. 151–74.

Korten, David C., *When Corporations Rule the World* (Hartford, CT: Kumarian Press, 1995).

Kristof, Nicholas D., and Sheryl WuDunn, *Half the Sky: Turning Oppression into Opportunity for Women Worldwide* (New York: Alfred A. Knopf, 2009).

Küng, Hans, 'A Global Ethic in an Age of Globalization', *Business Ethics Quarterly*, 7/3 (July 1997), pp. 17–31.

Küng, Hans, *A Global Ethic for Global Politics and Economics* (New York: Oxford University Press, 1998).

Kurasawa, Fukukiu, *The Work of Global Justice: Human Rights as Practices* (Cambridge: Cambridge University Press, 2007).

Kwa, Chunglin, 'Local Ecologies and Global Science Discourses and Strategies of the International Geosphere–Biosphere Programme', *Social Studies of Science*, 35/6 (December 2005), pp. 923–50.

Kwa, Chunglin, 'Representations of Nature Mediating between Ecology and Science Policy: The Case of the International Biological Programme', *Social Studies of Science*, 17/3 (August 1987), pp. 413–42.

Lamm, Maurice, *Becoming a Jew* (Middle Village, NY: Jonathan David Publishers, 1991).

Langan, John, 'Justice after War and the International Common Good', in Charles Reed and David Ryall (eds), *The Price of Peace: Just War in the Twenty-First Century* (Cambridge: Cambridge University Press, 2007), ch. 12.

Legrain, Philippe, *Open World: The Truth about Globalization* (London: Abacus, 2002).

Leipziger, Deborah, *Corporate Responsibility Code Book* (Sheffield: Greenleaf Publishing, 2003).

Lemkin, Raphael, *Axis Rule in Occupied Europe: Laws of Occupation, Analysis of Government, Proposals for Redress* (Washington: Carnegie Endowment for International Peace, 1944).

Lepard, Brian D., *Rethinking Humanitarian Intervention: A Fresh Legal Approach Based on Fundamental Ethical Principles in International Law and World Religions* (University Park, PA: Pennsylvania State University Press, 2002).

Lerner, Natan, 'Proselytism, Change of Religion, and International Human Rights', *Emory International Law Review*, 12/1 (Winter 1998), pp. 477–562.

Lester, Emile, and Patrick S. Roberts, 'How Teaching about World Religions Brought a Truce to the Culture Wars in Modesto, California', *British Journal of Religious Education*, 31/2 (September 2009), pp. 187–99.

Lester, Emile, and Patrick S. Roberts, *Learning about World Religions in Public Schools: The Impact on Student Attitudes and Community Acceptance in Modesto, Calif.* (Nashville, TN: First Amendment Center, 2006).

Lieber, Keir A., and Daryl G. Press, 'The Nukes We Need: Preserving the American Deterrent', *Foreign Affairs*, 88/6 (November/December 2009), pp. 39–51.

Little, David, 'The Nature and Basis of Human Rights', in Gene Outka and John P. Reeder Jr (eds), *Prospects for a Common Morality* (Princeton: Princeton University Press, 1993), pp. 73–92.

Lo, Ping-cheung, 'The *Art of War* Corpus and Chinese Just War Ethics Past and Present', *Journal of Religious Ethics*, 40/3 (September 2012), pp. 404–46.

Longman, Timothy, 'Christian Churches and Genocide in Rwanda', in Omer Bartov and Phyllis Mack (eds), *In God's Name: Genocide and Religion in the Twentieth Century* (New York and Oxford: Berghahn Books, 2001), pp. 139–60.

Longman, Timothy, *Christianity and Genocide in Rwanda* (New York: Cambridge University Press, 2010).

Loreau, Michel, Alfred Oteng-Yeboah, Mary T. K. Arroyo, Didier Babin, Robert Barbault, Michael J. Donoghue, Madhav Gadgil, Christopher Häuser, Carlo Heip, Anne Larigauderie, Kai-Kuang Ma, and Georgina M. Mace, 'Diversity without Representation', *Nature*, 442/7100 (July 2006), pp. 245–46.

McGoldrick, Dominic, Peter Rowe, and Eric Donnelly (eds), *The Permanent International Criminal Court: Legal and Policy Issues* (Oxford: Hart Publishing, 2004).

McIntosh, Malcolm, Sandra Waddock, and George Kell (eds), *Learning to Talk: Corporate Citizenship and the Development of the UN Global Compact* (Sheffield: Greenleaf Publishing, 2004).

MacIntyre, Alasdair, *After Virtue* (Notre Dame, IN: University of Notre Dame Press, 1981).

MacNeill, Jim, Pieter Winsemius, and Taizo Yukushiji, *Beyond Interdependence: The Meshing of the World's Economy and the Earth's Ecology* (New York: Oxford University Press, 1991).

Mann, Jonathan M., Michael A. Grodin, Sofia Gruskin, and George J.

Annas (eds), *Health and Human Rights: A Reader* (New York: Routledge, 1999).

Marchak, Patricia, *No Easy Fix: Global Responses to Internal Wars and Crimes against Humanity* (Montreal: McGill-Queens University Press, 2008).

Margolis, Joshua D., and James P. Walsh, 'Misery Loves Companies: Rethinking Social Initiatives by Business', *Administrative Science Quarterly*, 48/2 (June 2003), pp. 268–305.

Maritain, Jacques, 'Introduction', in UNESCO (ed.), *Human Rights: Comments and Interpretations* (Paris: UNESCO, 1948), pp. i–ix. Subsequently published by Columbia University Press in 1949 and reprinted by Greenwood Press in 1973.

Marshall, Katherine, *Global Institutions of Religion: Ancient Movers, Modern Shakers*, Global Institutions Series (New York: Routledge, 2013).

Martin, Daniel, 'An Intervention on the Earth Charter', document distributed at the fourth session of the United Nations Conference on Environment and Development Preparatory Committee (New York: UNCED PrepCom IV), 4 March 1992.

Marx, Karl, *Karl Marx: Selected Writings*, ed. David McLellan (Oxford: Oxford University Press, 1977).

Masuzawa, Tomoko, *The Invention of World Religions* (Chicago: University of Chicago Press, 2005).

Mead, Walter Russell, 'The Return of Geopolitics: The Revenge of the Revisionist Powers', *Foreign Affairs* (May/June 2014), pp. 69–79.

Meadows, Donella H., Dennis L. Meadows , Jørgen Randers, and William W. Behrens III, *The Limits to Growth: A Report for the Club of Rome Project on the Predicament of Mankind* (New York: Universe Books, 1972).

Meinzen-Dick, Ruth, 'Property Rights for Poverty Reduction', in Jomo Kwame Sundaram and Anis Chowdhury (eds), *Poor Poverty: The Impoverishment of Analysis, Measurement, and Policies* (London: Bloomsbury Academic, 2011), pp. 185–96.

Méndez, Juan E., 'Latin American Experiences of Accountability', in Ifi Amadiume and Abdullahi An-Na'im (eds), *The Politics of Memory: Truth, Healing and Social Justice* (London and New York: Zed Books, 2000), pp.127–41.

Mertis, Julie, 'Truth in a Box: The Limits of Justice through Judicial Mechanisms', in Ifi Amadiume and Abdullahi An-Na'im (eds), *The Politics of Memory: Truth, Healing and Social Justice* (London and New York: Zed Books, 2000), pp. 142–61.

Metzl, Jamie, 'Information Technology and Human Rights', *Human Rights Quarterly*, 18/4 (November 1996), pp. 705–46.

Miglani, Deepak, and Dinesh Miglani, 'Right to Religious Freedom versus Religious Conversion', *Legal Service India*, c.2006, n.d. <http://www.legalserviceindia.com/articles/rel_rel.htm> (last accessed 12 January 2015).

Milanovic, Branko, *Worlds Apart: Measuring International and Global Inequality* (Princeton: Princeton University Press, 2005).

Milgram, Stanley, *Obedience to Authority: An Experimental View* (New York: Harper & Row, 1974).

Millennium Ecosystem Assessment, *Living beyond our Means: Natural Assets and Human Well-being* (Washington: Island Press, 2005).

Miller, Clark A, 'Climate Science and the Making of a Global Political Order', in Sheila Jasanoff (ed.), *States of Knowledge: The Coproduction of Science and Social Order* (London: Routledge, 2004), pp. 46–66.

Miller, Clark A., 'Democratization, International Knowledge Institutions, and Global Governance', *Governance: An International Journal of Policy, Administration, and Institutions*, 20/2 (April 2007), pp. 325–57.

Miller, Clark A., 'The Dynamics of Framing Environmental Values and Policy: Four Models of Societal Processes', *Environmental Values*, 9/2 (May 2000), pp. 211–33.

Miller, Clark A., 'An Effective Instrument of Peace: Scientific Cooperation as an Instrument of US Foreign Policy, 1938–1950', *Osiris*, 21/1 (January 2006), pp. 133–60.

Miller, Clark A., 'Epistemic Constitutionalism in International Governance: The Case of Climate Change', in Michael Heazle, Martin Griffiths and Tom Conley (eds), *Foreign Policy Challenges in the 21st Century* (Cheltenham: Edward Elgar, 2009), pp. 141–63.

Miller, Clark A., 'The Ethics of Energy Transitions', *Proceedings of the IEEE Symposium on Ethics in Engineering, Science, and Technology* (May 2004), pp. 1–5.

Miller, Clark A., 'The Globalization of Human Affairs: A Reconsideration of Science, Political Economy, and World Order', in Mary Ann Tétreault, Robert A. Denemark, Kenneth P. Thomas and Kurt Burch (eds), *Rethinking Global Political Economy: Emerging Issues, Enfolding Odysseys* (London: Routledge, 2003), pp. 211–26.

Miller, Clark A., 'Globalizing Security: Science and the Transformation of Contemporary Political Imagination', in Sheila Jasanoff and Sang-Hyun Kim (eds), *Dreamscapes of Modernity: Sociotechnical Imaginaries and the Fabrication of Power* (Chicago: University of Chicago Press, 2015).

Miller, Clark A., 'Hybrid Management: Boundary Organizations, Science Policy, and Environmental Governance in the Climate Regime', *Science, Technology & Human Values*, 26/4 (Autumn 2001), pp. 478–500.

Miller, Clark A., 'Scientific Internationalism in American Foreign Policy: The Case of Meteorology, 1947–1958', in Clark A. Miller and Paul N. Edwards (eds), *Changing the Atmosphere: Expert Knowledge and Environmental Governance* (Cambridge, MA: MIT Press, 2001), pp. 167–217.

Miller, Clark A., and Paul Erickson, 'The Politics of Bridging Scales and Epistemologies: Science and Democracy in Global Environmental Governance', in Walter Reid, Thomas Wilbanks, Doris Capistrano and Fikret Berkes (eds), *Bridging Scales and Knowledge Systems: Concepts and Applications in Ecosystem Assessments* (Washington: Island Press, 2006), ch. 16.

Miller, Clark A., Jennifer Richter, and Jason O'Leary, 'Socio-Energy Systems Design: A Policy Framework for Energy Transitions', *Energy Research & Social Science*, 6 (March 2015), pp. 29–40.

Ministère de l'Éducation, du Loisir et du Sport, *Establishment of an Ethics and Religious Culture Program: Providing Future Direction for all Quebec Youth* (Gouvernement du Québec, 2005).

Ministère de l'Éducation, du Loisir et du Sport, *Quebec Education Program: Secondary School Education Cycle One* (Gouvernement du Québec, 2006).

Mishra, Pankaj, 'Unholy Alliances: Nixon, Kissinger, and the Bangladesh Genocide', *New Yorker*, 23 September 2013, pp. 109–14.

Mitcham, Carl, and Jessica Smith Rolston, 'Energy Constraints', *Science and Engineering Ethics*, 19/2 (June 2013), pp. 313–19.

Moffet, John, François Bregha, and Mary Jane Middelkoop, 'Responsible Care: A Case Study of a Voluntary Environmental Initiative', in Kernaghan Webb (ed.), *Voluntary Codes: Private Governance, the Public Interest, and Innovation* (Ottawa, ON: Carleton University Research Unit for Innovation, Science and Environment, 2004).

Monshipouri, Mahmood, and Claude E. Welch, 'The Search for International Human Rights and Justice: Coming to Terms with the New Global Realities', *Human Rights Quarterly*, 23/2 (May 2001), pp. 370–401.

Moore, Diane L., *Overcoming Religious Illiteracy: A Cultural Studies Approach to the Study of Religion in Secondary Education* (New York: Palgrave Macmillan, 2007).

Morris, Ronald, 'Cultivating Reflection and Understanding: Foundations and Orientations of Quebec's Ethics and Religious Culture Program', *Religion & Education*, 38/3 (September 2011), pp. 188–211.

Morsink, Johannes, *The Universal Declaration of Human Rights: Origins, Drafting, and Intent* (Philadelphia: University of Pennsylvania Press, 1999).

Moser, Titus, 'MNCs and Sustainable Business Practice: The Case of the Colombian and Peruvian Petroleum Industries', *World Development*, 29/2 (February 2001), pp. 291–309.

Moyo, Dambisa, *Dead Aid: Why Aid is not Working and How There is a Better Way for Africa* (New York: Farrar, Straus and Giroux, 2009).

Muchlinski, Peter, 'Implementing the New UN Corporate Human Rights Framework: Implications for Corporate Law, Governance, and Regulation', *Business Ethics Quarterly*, 22/1 (January 2012), pp. 145–77.

Munji, Achmad, 'Building a Shared Home for Everyone – Interreligious Dialogue at the Grass Roots in Indonesia', in Rebecca Kratz Mays (ed.), *Interfaith Dialogue at the Grass Roots* (Philadelphia: Ecumenical Press, 2008).

Murnion, Philip J. (ed.), *Catholics and Nuclear War: A Commentary on 'The Challenge of Peace', the US Catholic Bishops' Pastoral Letter on War and Peace* (New York: Cross Roads, 1983).

Murphy, John F., *The United States and the Rule of Law in International Affairs* (Cambridge: Cambridge University Press, 2004).

Naess, Arne, 'The Shallow and the Deep, Long-Range Ecology Movement: A Summary', *Inquiry*, 16/1–4 (1978), pp. 95–100.

Nahrowi, Agus Hadi, 'Religious Pluralism in Indonesia: Helpful and Hindering Aspects' (Cambridge, MA: The Pluralism Project at Harvard University, 2006) <http://pluralism.org/research/reports/nahrowi/Pluralism_Indonesia.pdf> (last accessed 12 January 2015).

Ñāṇamoli, Bhikkhu, *The Life of the Buddha According to the Pali Canon* (Seattle: Buddhist Publication Society, [1971] 1992).

Nardin, Terry, 'The Moral Basis of Humanitarian Intervention', *Ethics & International Affairs*, 16/1 (Spring 2002), pp. 57–70.

Nash, Roderick Frazier, *The Rights of Nature: A History of Environmental Ethics* (Madison, WI: University of Wisconsin Press, 1989).

National Conference for Community and Justice (NCCJ), 'An Overview of the Evolution of the NCCJ'. Internal document (n.d.).

National Conference for Community and Justice (NCCJ), 'Communication Guidelines and Ground Rules for Useful Dialogue/Rights, Risks and Responsibilities of Dialogue'. Internal document (2000).

National Council for the Social Studies (NCSS), *Including the Study about Religion in the Social Studies Curriculum: A Position Statement and Guidelines* (NCSS, 1984).

Nelson, Jane, *Building Partnerships: Cooperation between the United Nations System and the Private Sector* (New York: United Nations Department of Public Information, 2002).

Nelson, Jane, *Business as Partners in Development: Creating Wealth for Countries, Companies and Communities* (London: Prince of Wales International Business Leaders Forum, 1996).

Nelson, Scott Reynolds, 'An American War of Incarceration: Guerilla Warfare, Occupation, and Imprisonment in the American South, 1863–65', in Stephen J. Rockel and Rick Halpern (eds), *Inventing Collateral Damage: Civilian Casualties, War, and Empire* (Toronto: Between the Lines, 2009).

Ngurah, I Gusti Made, 'Dialogue of Inter Religious Community Members in the Multicultural Community of Denpasar City', *Udayana University e-Journal of Cultural Studies*, 5/1 (January 2011) <http://ojs.unud.ac.id/index.php/ecs/article/view/3628/2657> (last accessed 12 January 2015).

Niebuhr, Gustav, *Beyond Tolerance: How People Across America Are Building Bridges between Faiths* (New York: Penguin Books, 2008).

Niebuhr, Gustav, 'Hell is Getting a Makeover from Catholics: Jesuits Call it a Painful State but not a Sulfurous Place', *New York Times*, 18 September 1999, pp. B-9, B-11.

Nielsen, Kai, *Globalization and Justice* (New York: Humanity Books, 2003).

Nolte, Georg, 'Thin or Thick? The Principle of Proportionality and International Humanitarian Law', *Law and Ethics of Human Rights*, 4/2 (September 2010), pp. 244–55.

Norman, Richard, 'Worldviews, Humanism and the (Im)possibility of

Neutrality', *Oxford Review of Education*, 38/5 (October 2012), pp. 515–25.

North, Douglass C., John Joseph Wallis, and Barry R. Weingast, *Violence and Social Order: A Conceptual Framework for Interpreting Recorded Human History* (Cambridge: Cambridge University Press, 2009).

Nussbaum, Martha C., 'Capabilities and Human Rights', *Fordham Law Review*, 66/2 (November 1997), pp. 273–300.

Nussbaum, Martha C., *Creating Capabilities: The Human Development Approach* (Cambridge, MA: Harvard University Press, 2011).

Nussbaum, Martha C., 'Religion and Women's Human Rights', in Paul J. Weithman (ed.), *Religion and Contemporary Liberalism* (Notre Dame, IN: University of Notre Dame Press, 1997), pp. 93–137.

Nussbaum, Martha C., *Women and Human Development: The Capabilities Approach* (Cambridge: Cambridge University Press, 2000).

O'Donovan, Oliver, *The Just War Revisited* (Cambridge: Cambridge University Press, 2003).

Oberthür, Sebastian, and Claire Roche Kelly, 'EU Leadership in International Climate Policy: Achievements and Challenges', *International Spectator*, 43/3 (September 2008), pp. 35–50.

Omar, A. Rashied, 'The Right to Religious Conversion: Between Apostasy and Proselytization', Kroc Institute Occasional Paper No. 27, Joan B. Kroc Institute for International Peace Studies, University of Notre Dame, 2006.

Orbinski, James, *An Imperfect Offering: Humanitarian Action in the Twenty-First Century* (Toronto: Anchor Canada, 2009).

Organization for Economic Cooperation and Development (OECD), 'The Paris Declaration on Aid Effectiveness' <http://www.oecd.org/dac/effec tiveness/34428351.pdf> (last accessed 22 January 2015).

OSCE (Organization for Security and Cooperation in Europe), *Toledo Guiding Principles on Teaching about Religions and Beliefs in Public Schools* (Warsaw: OSCE Office for Democratic Institutions and Human Rights, 2007).

Ostrom, Elinor, 'Beyond Markets and States: Polycentric Governance of Complex Economic Systems', *American Economic Review*, 100/3 (June 2010), pp. 641–72.

Outka, Gene, and John P. Reeder Jr (eds), *Prospects for a Common Morality* (Princeton: Princeton University Press, 1993).

Oxfam International, *The Making of a Seoul Development Consensus: The Essential Development Agenda for the G20* (2010) <http://www.oxfam. org/en/research/making-seoul-development-consensus> (last accessed 25 January 2015).

Palan, Ronen, Richard Murphy, and Christian Chavagneux, *Tax Havens: How Globalization Really Works* (Ithaca, NY, and London: Cornell University Press, 2010).

Palmer, Parker J., *Healing the Heart of Democracy: The Courage to Create a Politics Worthy of the Human Spirit* (San Francisco: Jossey-Bass, 2011).

Parekh, Bhikhu, 'Principles of Global Ethics', in John Eade and Darren

O'Byrne (eds), *Global Ethics and Civil Society* (Burlington, VT: Ashgate, 2005), ch. 2.

Parker, George, 'Knowing the Enemy', *New Yorker*, 18 December 2006, pp. 59–69.

Parker, Richard, *John Kenneth Galbraith: His Life, his Politics, his Economics* (Toronto: HarperCollins, 2005).

Parry, Martin L., Timothy R. Carter, and Michael Hulme, 'What is a Dangerous Climate Change?', *Global Environmental Change*, 6/1 (April 1996), 1–6.

Paul VI, 'Ecclesiam Suam (Paths of the Church) Encyclical Letter of His Holiness Promulgated on 6 August1964' <http://www.ewtn.com/library/ENCYC/P6ECCLES.htm> (last accessed 12 January 2015).

Pedersen, Kusumita P., 'Environmental Ethics in Interreligious Perspective', in Sumner B. Twiss and Bruce Grelle (eds), *Explorations in Global Ethics: Comparative Religious Ethics and Interreligious Dialogue* (Boulder: Westview Press, 1998), pp. 253–90.

Pedersen, Kusumita P., 'Inclusion and Exclusion: Reflections on Moral Community and Salvation', in Dieter Hessel and Larry Rasmussen (eds), *Earth Habitat: Eco-Injustice and the Churches' Response* (Minneapolis, MN: Fortress Press, 2001), pp. 33–52.

Pedersen, Kusumita P., 'The Interfaith Movement: An Incomplete Assessment', *Journal of Ecumenical Studies*, 41/1 (Winter 2004), pp. 74–94.

Pedersen, Kusumita P., 'Religious Freedom, the Right to Proselytize, and the "Right to be Let Alone"', in Arvind Sharma (ed.), *The World's Religions after September 11, Vol. 2: Religion and Human Rights* (Westport, CT: Praeger, 2009), pp. 175–183.

Pedersen, Kusumita P., 'Spirituality beyond the Boundaries of Religion', *Current Dialogue*, 47 (June 2006), pp. 29–33.

Pellizzari, Paul, *Conscious Consumption: Corporate Social Responsibility and Canada's Grocery Giants* (Toronto: EthicScan Canada, 2002).

Perry, Michael J., 'Are Human Rights Universal? The Relativist Challenge and Related Matters', *Human Rights Quarterly*, 19/3 (August 1997), pp. 461–509.

Perry, Michael, *The Idea of Human Rights: Four Inquiries* (New York: Oxford University Press, 1998).

Peters, Rebecca Todd, *In Search of the Good Life: The Ethics of Globalization* (New York: Continuum, 2004).

Pew Forum on Religion and Public Life, *US Religious Landscape Survey* <http://religions.pewforum.org/reports> (last accessed 12 January 2015).

Piketty, Thomas, *Capital in the Twenty-First Century*, trans. Arthur Goldhammer (Cambridge, MA: Harvard University Press, 2014).

Pinker, Steven, *The Better Angels of our Nature: Why Violence Has Declined* (New York: Viking, 2011).

Pogge, Thomas, *World Poverty and Human Rights*, 2nd edn (Cambridge: Polity Press, 2008).

Porter, Michael E., and Mark R. Kramer, 'Strategy and Society: The Link between Competitive Advantage and Corporate Social Responsibility', *Harvard Business Review* (December 2006), pp. 78–92.

Powell, Jonathan, *Talking to Terrorists: How to End Armed Conflicts* (London: Bodley Head, 2014).

Power, Jonathan, *Like Water on a Stone: The Story of Amnesty International* (New York: Penguin Books, 2001).

Power, Michael, *The Audit Society: Rituals of Verification* (Oxford: Oxford University Press, 1999).

Power, Samantha, *'A Problem from Hell': America and the Age of Genocide* (New York: Basic Books, 2002).

Prahalad, C. K., *The Fortune at the Bottom of the Pyramid: Eradicating Poverty through Profits* (Upper Saddle River, NJ: Wharton School Publishing, 2005).

Preda, Adina, 'Moral Justification for Unilateral Humanitarian Intervention in Order to Stop or Prevent Human Right Violations', Ph.D. Thesis in Political Theory, University of Manchester, 2006.

Prins, Gwyn, 'Conditions for *Jus in Pace* in the Face of the Future', in Charles Reed and David Ryall (eds), *The Price of Peace: Just War in the Twenty-First Century* (Cambridge: Cambridge University Press, 2007), ch. 13.

The Qur'an, trans. Abdullah Yusuf Ali, 4th edn (Elmhurst, NY: Tahrike Tarsile Qur'an, 1999).

Rambachan, Anantanand, 'Hindus and Christians: Celebrating Friendship and Facing Challenges with Hope', Lambeth Interfaith Lecture, *Interreligious Insight*, 6/3 (July 2008), pp. 8–20.

Ramsey, Paul, *The Just War: Force and Political Responsibility* (New York: Charles Scribner's Sons, 1968).

Ramsey, Paul, 'A Political Ethics Context for Strategic Thinking' [1988], in Richard B. Miller (ed.), *War in the Twentieth Century: Sources in Theological Ethics* (Louisville, KY: Westminster/John Knox Press, 1992), pp. 290–310.

Ramsey, Paul, *War and the Christian Conscience: How Shall Modern War Be Conducted Justly* (Durham, NC: Duke University Press, 1961).

Rasmussen, Larry L., *Earth Community, Earth Ethics* (Maryknoll, NY: Orbis Books, 1996).

Rasmussen, Larry L., *Earth-Honoring Faith: Religious Ethics in a New Key* (New York: Oxford University Press, 2013).

Ratner, Steven R., and Jason S. Abrams, *Accountability for Human Rights Atrocities in International Law: Beyond the Nuremberg Legacy* (Oxford: Clarendon Press, 1977).

Reeder, John P., Jr, 'Foundations without Foundationalism', in Gene Outka and John P. Reeder Jr (eds), *Prospects for a Common Morality* (Princeton: Princeton University Press, 1993), pp. 191–214.

Revelle, Roger, and Hans E. Suess, 'Carbon Dioxide Exchange between Atmosphere and Ocean and the Question of an Increase of Atmospheric CO_2 during the Past Decades', *Tellus*, 9/1 (February 1957), pp. 18–27.

Rhone, Gregory T., David Clarke, and Kernaghan Webb, 'Two Voluntary

Approaches to Sustainable Forestry Practices', in Kernaghan Webb (ed.), *Voluntary Codes: Private Governance, the Public Interest and Innovation* (Ottawa, ON: Carleton University Research Unit for Innovation, Science and Environment, 2004), ch. 9.

Rieff, David, *A Bed for the Night: Humanitarianism in Crisis* (New York: Simon and Schuster, 2003).

Rist, Gilbert, *The History of Development from Western Origins to Global Faith* (London: Zed Books, 2008).

Roberts, Adam, and Richard Guelff (eds), *Documents on the Laws of War* (Oxford: Clarendon Press, 1982).

Rockefeller, Steven C., 'Global Ethics, International Law, and the Earth Charter', *Earth Ethics*, 7/3–4 (Spring/Summer 1996), pp. 11–17.

Rockefeller, Steven C., *Principles of Environmental Conservation and Sustainable Development: Summary and Survey: A Study in the Field of Environmental Law and Related International Reports*, rev. (San José, Costa Rica: Earth Council, 1996).

Rockefeller, Steven C., *Teilhard's Vision and the Earth Charter*, Teilhard Studies Number 52 (Lewisburg, PA: American Teilhard Association, 2006).

Rockefeller, Steven C., 'The Transition to Sustainability', in Peter Blaze Corcoran, Mirian Vilela and Alide Roerink (eds), *The Earth Charter in Action: Toward a Sustainable World* (Amsterdam: KIT Publishers, 2005), pp. 165–70.

Rockefeller, Steven C., and Johannah Bernstein, *Earth Charter Commentary: Part I, Respect and Care for the Community of Life*. Unpublished typescript (2002).

Rodrik, Dani, *One Economics, Many Recipes: Globalization, Institutions, and Economic Growth* (Princeton: Princeton University Press, 2007).

Rorty, Richard, 'Human Rights, Rationality, and Sentimentality', in Stephen Shute and Susan Hurley (eds), *On Human Rights: The Oxford Amnesty Lectures 1993* (New York: Basic Books, 1993), pp. 111–34.

Rose, Gideon, *How Wars End: Why We Always Fight the Last Battle: A History of American Intervention from World War I to Afghanistan* (New York: Simon and Schuster, 2010).

Ross, Jeffrey Ian, 'Beyond the Conceptualization of Terrorism: A Psychological-Structural Model of the Causes of the Activity', in Craig Summers and Eric Markusen (eds), *Collective Violence: Harmful Behavior in Groups and Governments* (Lanham, MD: Rowman & Littlefield, 1999), pp. 169–92.

Rowe, James K. (2005) 'Corporate Social Responsibility as Business Strategy', in Ronnie D. Lipschutz and James K. Rowe, *Globalization, Governmentality and Global Politics: Regulation for the Rest of Us?* (London and New York: Routledge, 2005), ch. 6.

Rozack, Sherene H., *Dark Threats and White Knights: The Somalia Affair, Peacekeeping, and the New Imperialism* (Toronto: University of Toronto Press, 2004).

Rubenstein, Richard L., *After Auschwitz: History, Theology, and*

Contemporary Judaism, 2nd edn (Baltimore, MD: Johns Hopkins University Press, 1992).

Rubin, Jeff, *The End of Growth* (Toronto: Random House Canada, 2012).

Ruggie, John Gerard, 'Reconstituting the Global Public Domain – Issues, Actors, and Practices', *European Journal of International Relations*, 10/4 (December 2004), pp. 499–530.

Rummel, R. J., *Power Kills: Democracy as a Method of Nonviolence* (New Brunswick, NJ: Transaction Press, 1997).

Sachs, Aaron, *Eco-Justice: Linking Human Rights and the Environment*, Worldwatch Paper 127 (Washington: Worldwatch Insititute, 1995).

Sachs, Jeffrey D., *The End of Poverty: Economic Possibilities for our Time* (New York: Penguin Press, 2005).

Sandel, Michael J., 'Liberalism, Consumerism, and Citizenship', in Dwight D. Allman and Michael D. Beaty (eds), *Cultivating Citizens: Soulcraft and Citizenship in Contemporary America* (Lanham, MD: Lexington Books, 2002).

Sands, Philippe (ed.), *From Nuremberg to The Hague: The Future of International Criminal Justice* (Cambridge: Cambridge University Press, 2003).

Santoro, Michael A., *Profits and Principles: Global Capitalism and Human Rights in China* (Ithaca, NY: Cornell University Press, 2000).

Sarachild, Kathie, 'Consciousness-Raising: A Radical Weapon', in *Feminist Revolution* (New York: Random House, 1978), pp. 144–50.

Saraswati, Jayendra, interviewed by Saisuresh Sivaswami, *India Abroad*, 25 July 2003, p. A26.

Saul, John Ralston, *The Collapse of Globalism: And the Reinvention of the World* (Toronto: Viking Canada, 2005).

Schecter, Michael G. (ed.), *United Nations-Sponsored World Conferences: Focus on Impact and Follow-up* (Tokyo: United Nations University Press, 2001).

Schlosser, Eric, *Command and Control: Nuclear Weapons, the Damascus Accident, and the Illusion of Safety* (New York: Penguin Press, 2013).

Schneider, Stephen H., *Laboratory Earth: The Planetary Gamble We Can't Afford to Lose* (New York: Basic Books, 1998).

Schneider, Stephen H., 'What is "Dangerous" Climate Change?', *Nature*, 411/ 6833 (May 2001), pp. 17–19.

Schoenberger, Karl, *Levi's Children: Coming to Terms with Human Rights in the Global Market Place* (New York: Grove Press, 2001).

Schulte, Paul, 'Rogue Regimes, WMD, and Hyper-Terrorism: Augustine and Aquinas meet Chemical Ali', in Charles Reed and David Ryall (eds), *The Price of Peace: Just War in the Twenty-First Century* (Cambridge: Cambridge University Press, 2007), ch. 8.

Sells, Michael A., *The Bridge Betrayed: Religion and Genocide in Bosnia* (Berkeley and Los Angeles: University of California Press, 1996).

Sells, Michael A., 'Kosovo Mythology and the Bosnian Genocide', in Omer Bartov and Phyllis Mack (eds), *In God's Name: Genocide and Religion in the Twentieth Century* (New York and Oxford: Berghahn Books, 2001), pp. 180–204.

Semelin, Jacques, *Purify and Destroy: The Political Uses of Massacre and Genocide*, trans. Cynthia Schoch (New York: Columbia University Press, 2007).

Sen, Amartya, *Development as Freedom* (New York: Anchor Books, 1999).

Sennett, Richard, *The Corrosion of Character: The Personal Consequences of Work in the New Capitalism* (New York: W.W. Norton, 1997).

Sethi, S. Prakash, *Setting Global Standards: Guidelines for Creating Codes of Conduct in Multinational Corporations* (New York: John Wiley & Sons, 2003).

Sharma, Arvind, 'Measuring the Reach of a Universal Right', *Harvard Divinity Bulletin*, 8/4 (Winter 2000–1), pp. 10–12.

Sharma, Arvind, *Problematizing Religious Freedom* (New York: Springer-Verlag, 2012).

Sheard, Robert B., *Interreligious Dialogue in the Catholic Church since Vatican II: An Historical and Theological Study*, Toronto Studies in Theology, vol. 31 (Lewiston, NY: Edwin Mellen Press, 1987).

Sheler, Jeffery L., 'Hell Hath No Fury', *US News and World Report*, 31 January 2000, pp. 45–50.

Shelton, Dinah, 'Environmental Rights', in Philip Alston (ed.), *Peoples' Rights* (Oxford: Oxford University Press, 2001), pp. 185–258.

Sides, Patti M., 'Ethics and the Earth Charter: A Conversation with Steven Rockefeller', *Newsletter of the Boston Research Center for the 21st Century*, 18 (Fall 2001/Winter 2002), pp. 6–10.

Simmel, Georg, 'The Poor' [1908], trans. Claire Jacobson, *Social Problems*, 13/2 (Autumn 1965), pp. 118–40.

Singer, Peter, *The Life You Can Save: Acting Now to End World Poverty* (New York: Random House, 2009).

Singer, Peter, *One World: The Ethics of Globalization* (New Haven, CT: Yale University Press, 2001).

Smith, Rupert, *The Utility of Force: The Art of War in the Modern World* (London: Penguin Group, 2005).

Smucker, Joseph, 'Pursuing Corporate Social Responsibility in Changing Institutional Fields', in Frederick Bird and Manuel Velasquez (eds), *Just Business Practices in a Diverse and Developing World* (Basingstoke: Palgrave Macmillan, 2006), ch. 3.

South Asia Human Rights Documentation Center, 'Anti-Conversion Laws: Challenges to Secularism and Fundamental Rights', *Economic and Political Weekly*, 43/2, 12 January 2008, pp. 63–73.

Staub, Ervin, *The Roots of Evil: The Origins of Genocide and Other Group Violence* (New York: Cambridge University Press, 1989).

Stern, Jessica, *Terror in the Name of God: Why Religious Militants Kill* (New York: HarperCollins, 2003).

Stiglitz, Joseph E., *Globalization and its Discontents* (New York: W. W. Norton, 2002).

Stiglitz, Joseph, and Andrew Charlton, *Fair Trade for All: How Trade Can Promote Development* (Oxford: Oxford University Press, 2007).

Sullivan, William M., and Will Kymlicka (eds), *The Globalization of Ethics: Religious and Secular Perspectives* (Cambridge: Cambridge University Press, 2007).

Swidler, Leonard, 'The Dialogue Decalogue: Ground Rules for Interreligious Dialogue', *Journal of Ecumenical Studies*, 20/1 (1983), pp. 1–4. Widely reprinted and available *inter alia* at <http://globalethic.org/Center/decalog.htm> (last accessed 12 January 2015).

Takacs, David, *The Idea of Biodiversity: Philosophies of Paradise* (Baltimore, MD: Johns Hopkins University Press, 1996).

Tannenbaum Center for Interreligious Understanding, *Peacemakers in Action: Profiles of Religion in Conflict Resolution*, ed. David Little (New York: Cambridge University Press, 2007).

Taylor, Charles, *Modern Social Imaginaries* (Durham, NC: Duke University Press, 2004).

Taylor, Charles, 'A World Consensus on Human Rights?', *Dissent* (Summer 1996), pp. 15–21.

Taylor, Telford, *Nuremberg and Vietnam: An American Tragedy* (Chicago: Quadrangle Books, 1970).

Terry, Fiona, *Condemned to Repeat? The Paradox of Humanitarian Action* (Ithaca, NY: Cornell University Press, 2002).

Thakur, Ramesh, *The United Nations, Peace and Security: From Collective Security to the Responsibility to Protect* (Cambridge: Cambridge University Press, 2006).

Thakur, Ramesh, Andrew F. Cooper, and John English (eds), *International Commissions and the Power of Ideas* (Tokyo, New York, and Paris: United Nations University Press, 2005).

Thomas, William L., 'Equator – Risk and Sustainability', *Project Finance Yearbook 2004* (London: Thomson Reuters, 2004), pp. 10–16.

Thomson, Judith Jarvis, *The Realm of Rights* (Cambridge, MA: Harvard University Press, 1990).

Trattner, Walter I., *From Poor Law to Welfare State: A History of Social Welfare in America* (New York: Free Press, 1974).

Twiss, Sumner B., 'Comparative Ethics and Intercultural Human Rights Dialogues: A Programmatic Inquiry', in Lisa Sowle Cahill and James F. Childress (eds), *Christian Ethics: Problems and Prospects* (Cleveland, OH: Pilgrim Press, 1996), pp. 357–78.

Twiss, Sumner B., 'Global Ethics and Human Rights: A Reflection', *Journal of Religious Ethics*, 39/2 (June 2011), pp. 204–22.

Twiss, Sumner B., 'History, Human Rights, and Globalization', *Journal of Religious Ethics*, 32/1 (March 2004), pp. 39–70.

Twiss, Sumner B., 'Moral Grounds and Plural Cultures: Interpreting Human Rights in the International Community', *Journal of Religious Ethics*, 26/2 (Fall 1998), pp. 271–82.

Twiss, Sumner B., and Jonathan Chan, 'Classical Confucianism, Punitive

Expeditions, and Humanitarian Intervention', *Journal of Military Ethics*, 11/2 (August 2012), 81–96.

United Nations, *Convention on the Prevention and Punishment of the Crime of Genocide* (Paris: United Nations, 1948; in force, 1951).

United Nations, *International Bill of Human Rights* (New York: United Nations, 1993). Also available *inter alia* at <http://www.ohchr.org/EN/ProfessionalInterest/Pages/CoreInstruments.aspx> (last accessed 12 January 2015).

United Nations, *Nairobi Declaration* (1982) <http://www.un-documents.net/nair-dec.htm> (last accessed 15 January 2015).

United Nations, *A New Global Partnership: Eradicate Poverty and Transform Economies through Sustainable Development. The Report of the High-Level Panel of Eminent Persons on the Post-2015 Development Agenda* (New York: United Nations, 2013).

United Nations, *Rome Statute of the International Criminal Court* (Rome: United Nations, 1998; in force, 2002).

United Nations, UN System Task Team on the Post-2015 UN Development Agenda, *Realizing the Future We Want for All: Report to the Secretary General* (New York: United Nations, 2012).

United Nations, *Universal Declaration of Human Rights* (1948). Widely reprinted and available at <http://www.un.org/en/documents/udhr/> (last accessed 15 January 2015).

United Nations Conference on Trade and Development (UNCTAD), *The Least Developed Countries Report 2002: Escaping the Poverty Trap* (Geneva: United Nations, 2002).

United Nations Conference on Trade and Development (UNCTAD), *The Least Developed Countries Report 2006: Developing Productive Capacity* (Geneva: United Nations, 2006).

United Nations Department of Publication Information (UNDPI), *Agenda 21: Programme of Action for Sustainable Development, Rio Declaration on Environment and Development, and Statement of Forest Principles* (New York: United Nations Department of Public Information, 1994).

United Nations Development Programme (UNDP), *Implementing the Paris Declaration on Aid Effectiveness* (2011) <http://www.undp.org/content/undp/en/home/librarypage/capacity-building/implementing-the-paris-declaration-on-aid-effectiveness.html> (last accessed 21 January 2015).

United Nations Environment Programme (UNEP), *Declaration of the United Nations Conference on the Human Environment* (1972), *Stockholm* <http://www.unep.org/Documents.Multilingual/Default.asp?documentid=97&articleid=1503> (last accessed 15 December 2015).

United Nations General Assembly, *Declaration on the Rights of Indigenous Peoples* (2007), <http://www.un.org/esa/socdev/unpfii/documents/DRIPS_en.pdf> (last accessed 30 January 2015).

United Nations General Assembly, *Declaration on the Right to Development*, Resolution 41/128, adopted 4 December 1986 <http://www.un.org/documents/ga/res/41/a41r128.htm> (last accessed 21 January 2015.)

United Nations General Assembly, *Declaration on the Elimination of All*

Forms of Intolerance and Discrimination Based on Religion or Belief, Resolution 36/55, adopted 25 November 1981 <http://www.un.org/doc uments/ga/res/36/a36r055.htm> (last accessed 12 January 2015).

United Nations General Assembly, *World Charter for Nature*, Resolution 37/7, adopted 28 October 1982 <http://www.un.org/documents/ga/ res/37/a37r007.htm> (last accessed 15 January 2015).

United Nations High-Level Panel on Threats, Challenges, and Change, *A More Secure World: Our Shared Responsibility* (New York: United Nations, 2004).

United Nations Open Working Group on Sustainable Development Goals, *Outcome Document* (New York: United Nations, 2013) <https://sustain abledevelopment.un.org/content/documents/1579SDGs%20Proposal. pdf> (last accessed 30 January 2015).

United Nations World Summit on Sustainable Development (2002), *Johannesburg Declaration on Sustainable Development* <http://www.un-documents.net/jburgdec.htm> (last accessed 15 January 2015).

US National Research Council, *Warming World: Impacts by Degree* (Washington: National Acadmies Press, 2011) <http://dels.nas.edu/ resources/static-assets/materials-based-on-reports/booklets/warming_ world_final.pdf> (last accessed 8 January 2015).

US National Research Council, *Climate Stabilization Targets: Emissions, Concentrations, and Impacts over Decades to Millennia* (Washington: National Academies Press, 2011).

Valentine, Mark, *An Introductory Guide to the Earth Summit: June 1–12, 1992, Rio de Janeiro, Brazil* (San Francisco: US Citizens Network on the United Nations Conference on Environment and Development, 1991).

Valk, Pille, Gerdien Bertram-Troost, Markus Friederici, and Céline Béraud (eds), *Teenagers' Perspectives on the Role of Religion in their Lives, Schools and Societies: A European Quantitative Study* (Münster: Waxman Verlag, 2009).

Verlinden, An, 'Global Ethics as Dialogism', in M. S. Ronald Commers, Wim Vandekerckhove and An Verlinden (eds), *Ethics in an Era of Globalization* (Aldershot and Burlington, VT: Ashgate, 2008), ch. 11.

Victor, David G., M. Granger Morgan, Jay Apt, John Steinbruner, and Katharine Ricke, 'The Geoengineering Option: A Last Resort against Global Warming?', *Foreign Affairs*, 88/2 (March/April 2009), pp. 64–76.

Vilela, Mirian, and Peter Blaze Corcoran, 'Building Consensus on Shared Values', in Peter Blaze Corcoran, Mirian Vilela and Alide Roerink (eds), *The Earth Charter in Action toward a Sustainable World* (Amsterdam: KIT Publishers, 2005), pp. 17–22.

Vold, George B., Thomas J. Bernard, and Jeffrey B. Snipes, *Theoretical Criminology*, 4th edn (New York: Oxford University Press, 1998).

Vondung, Klaus, 'National Socialism as a Political Religion: Potentials and Limits of an Analytical Concept', *Totalitarian Movements and Political Religions*, 6/1 (June 2005), pp. 87–95.

Waddock, Sandra, 'Building the Institutional Infrastructure for Corporate Responsibility', International Workshop: Advancing Theory in CSR: An

Intercontinental Dialogue, Université du Québec à Montréal, Montréal, QC, 12–15 October 2006.

Walzer, Michael, *Arguing about War* (New Haven, CT: Yale University Press, 2004).

Walzer, Michael, *Ethics Thick and Thin: Moral Argument at Home and Abroad* (Notre Dame, IN: University of Notre Dame Press, 1994).

Walzer, Michael, *Just and Unjust Wars: A Moral Argument with Historical Illustrations*, rev, edn (New York: Harper Collins, 1992).

Ward, Barbara, and René Dubos, *Only One Earth: The Care and Maintenance of a Small Planet* (Harmondsworth: Penguin Books, 1972).

Waring, Marilyn, *If Women Counted: A New Feminist Economics* (San Francisco: Harper and Row, 1988).

Weber, Bret A., Julia Geigle, and Carenlee Barkdull, 'Rural North Dakota's Oil Boom and its Impact on Social Services', *Social Work*, 59/1 (January 2014), pp. 62–72.

Weber, Max, 'Emergence and Creation of Legal Norms', in Guenther Roth and Claus Wittich (eds), *Economy and Society* (Berkeley and Los Angeles: University of California Press, 1978), pt two, ch. VIII, sect. iii, pp. 753–84.

Weber, Max, 'Politics as Vocation', in *From Max Weber: Essays in Sociology* (1919), ed. and trans. H. H. Gerth and C. Wright Mills (Oxford: Oxford University Press, 1946), pp. 77–128.

Weiner, Matthew, and Azza Karam (eds), *Religion and the United Nations*, special issue of *CrossCurrents*, 60/3 (September 2010).

Westra, Laura, and Mirian Vilela (eds), *The Earth Charter, Ecological Integrity and Social Movements* (New York: Routledge, 2014).

Wettstein, Florian, 'Silence as Complicity: Elements of a Corporate Duty to Speak out against the Violations of Human Rights', *Business Ethics Quarterly*, 22/1 (January 2012), pp. 37–62.

Wigley, Tom M., 'A Combined Mitigation/Geoengineering Approach to Climate Stabilization', *Science*, 314/5798 (October 2006), pp. 452–4.

Williamson, John, 'What Washington Means by Policy Reform', in John Williamson (ed.), *Latin American Adjustment: How Much Has Happened?* (Washington: Institute for International Economics, 1989).

Wilson, Edward O. (ed.), *Biodiversity* (Washington: National Academy Press, 1988).

Wilson, Edward. O., *The Diversity of Life* (New York: W. W. Norton, 1999).

Wolfensohn, James D., 'Foreword', in Vinod Thomas, Mansoor Dailami, Ashok Dhareshwar, Daniel Kaufmann, Nalin Kishor, Ramón López and Yan Wong (eds), *The Quality of Growth* (New York: Oxford University Press, 2000), pp. xiii–xv.

World Bank, *World Development Report 2000/2001: Attacking Poverty: Opportunity, Empowerment, and Security* (Washington: World Bank, 2000).

World Bank and German Federal Ministry for Economic Cooperation and Development, *Minding the Gaps: Integrating Poverty Reduction*

Strategies and Budgets for Domestic Accountability (Washington: World Bank 2007).

World Commission on Environment and Development (WCED), *Our Common Future* (New York: Oxford University Press, 1987).

World Council of Churches, Pontifical Council on Interreligious Dialogue, and World Evangelical Alliance, 'Christian Witness in a Multi-Religious World', document released 28 June 2011 <http://www.oikoumene.org/en/resources/documents/wcc-programmes/interreligious-dialogue-and-cooperation/christian-identity-in-pluralistic-societies/christian-witness-in-a-multi-religious-world> (last accessed 12 January 2015).

Worldwide Fund for Nature (WWF), *The Assisi Declarations: Messages on Man and Nature from Buddhism, Christianity, Hinduism, Islam, and Judaism* (Gland: Worldwide Fund for Nature International, 1986).

Worster, Donald (ed.), *Nature's Economy: A History of Ecological Ideas* (Cambridge: Cambridge University Press, 1994).

Yearley, Steven, *Sociology, Environmentalism, Globalization: Reinventing the Globe* (New York: Sage Publications, 1996).

Young, Stephen, *Moral Capitalism: Reconciling Private Interest with the Public Good* (San Francisco: Berrett Koehler, 2003).

Zadek, Simon, *The Civil Corporation* (London: Earthscan Publications, 2001).

Zadek, Simon, 'Paths to Corporate Responsibility', *Harvard Business Review* (December 2004).

Zadek, Simon, Peter Raynard, and Cristiano Oliveira, *Responsible Competitiveness: Reshaping Global Markets through Responsible Business Practices* (London: AccountAbility in association with Fundação Dom Cabral, Brazil, 2005).

Zipkin, Amy, 'Getting Religion on Corporate Ethics: A Scourge of Scandals Leaves Its Mark', *New York Times*, 18 October 2000. C1 ff.

Index

Note: *t* indicates a table